SURREALISM AND THE ART OF CRIME

Surrealism and the Art of Crime

JONATHAN P. EBURNE

CORNELL UNIVERSITY PRESS

ITHACA AND LONDON

Copyright © 2008 by Cornell University

First published 2008 by Cornell University Press

Printed in the United States of America

Library of Congress Cataloging-in-Publication Data

Eburne, Jonathan P. (Jonathan Paul)
  Surrealism and the art of crime / Jonathan P. Eburne.
    p. cm.
  Includes bibliographical references and index.
  ISBN 978-0-8014-4674-0 (cloth : alk. paper)
   1. Surrealism (Literature)   2. Literature, Modern—20th century—History and criticism.   3. Crime in literature.   4. Violence in literature.   5. Surrealism—Political aspects—History—20th century.
6. Crime—Political aspects—History—20th century.   7. Authors—20th century—Political and social views.   I. Title.

  PN56.S87E28 2008
  809'.933556—dc22   2008002899

Cornell University Press strives to use environmentally responsible suppliers and materials to the fullest extent possible in the publishing of its books. Such materials include vegetable-based, low-VOC inks and acid-free papers that are recycled, totally chlorine-free, or partly composed of nonwood fibers. For further information, visit our website at www.cornellpress.cornell.edu.

Cloth printing   10 9 8 7 6 5 4 3 2 1

CONTENTS

List of Illustrations   vii

Acknowledgments   ix

Introduction: Surrealism and the Art of Crime   1

1 Locked Room, Bloody Chamber   18

2 On Murder, Considered as One of the Surrealist Arts   49

3 Germaine Berton and the Ethics of Assassination   74

4 Dime Novel Politics   96

5 X Marks the Spot   139

6 Surrealism Noir   173

7 Persecution Mania   215

8 The Transatlantic Mysteries of Paris: Surrealism
   and the Série Noire   244

   Conclusion: Antihumanism and Terror   266

   Notes   277

   Bibliography   303

   Index   317

ILLUSTRATIONS

1.1   Man Ray, *Waking Dream Séance* (1924)   19

1.2   Anonymous, illustration for Pierre MacOrlan's "Photographie: Eléments de Fantastique Social" (1929)   33

1.3   Crime scene photograph using the Bertillon method (ca. 1914–18)   37

1.4   Yves Tanguy, *Fantômas* (1925)   39

1.5   René Magritte, *The Threatened Murderer* (*L'Assassin ménacé*) (1926)   40

1.6   Collection of fifteen surrealist *papillons* (1924–25)   45

2.1   Man Ray, *The Enigma of Isodore Ducasse* (1920, remade 1972)   51

3.1   Surrealist group portrait surrounding Germaine Berton (1924)   77

3.2   "Pour Sauver Germaine Berton!" (1923)   82

3.3   Anonymous press photograph of Germaine Berton after her acquittal (1923)   83

3.4   Jean-Louis Forain, "Le Prochain pour 1924" (1923)   85

3.5   Robert Desnos, manuscript of *Le Cimitière de la "Semillante"* (1923)   92

4.1   Cover of *Nick Carter Detective Library* (1891)   107

4.2   Joan Miró, Man Ray, Yves Tanguy, and Max Morise, *Exquisite Corpse* (1927)   123

4.3   Anonymous, "Jack the Ripper at Age Nineteen (Drawing Executed in 1888 by His Mistress)" (1928)   134

4.4   Georges Malkine, *Portrait of Robert Desnos* (1927)   137

5.1   Frontispiece from *X Marks the Spot: Chicago Gang Wars in Pictures* (1930)   140

5.2   Page from *Documents* 4 depicting *L'Œil de la police* and Salvador Dalí's *Honey Is Sweeter Than Blood* (1929)   152

5.3   Alberto Giacometti, *Woman with Her Throat Cut* (*Femme égorgée*) (1932, cast 1940)   155

5.4   Page from surrealist pamphlet in response to the *Âge d'or* affair showing damage to the theater and to Dalí's painting (1931)   159

6.1   "Before/After" photographs of Christine and Léa Papin (1933)   177

6.2   René Magritte and Paul Nougé, "Homage to the Papin Sisters" (1934)   196

6.3   Man Ray, cover photograph for *Violette Nozières* (1933)   201

6.4   Jean Arp, untitled drawing for *Violette Nozières* (1933)   210

6.5   René Magritte, cover design ("Le Viol") for André Breton, *Qu'est-ce que le surréalisme?* (1934)   212

6.6   Salvador Dalí, "Paranoiac Portrait of Violette Naziere (Noziere)/(Nazi, Dinazos, naziere)/(Nose)" (1933)   213

7.1 Daniel Paul Schreber, map of Dr. Fleischig's Nerve Clinic (1903) 226

7.2 Leonora Carrington, map of Santander (1944) 227

7.3 Victor Brauner, *L'Étrange cas de Monsieur K.* (1933) 230

7.4 Victor Brauner, *Force de concentration de Monsieur K.* (1934) 230

7.5 Anonymous, untitled photograph reprinted in Salvador Dalí, "Analyse non-euclidienne d'une photographie" (1935) 234

7.6 Hans Bellmer, "The Doll" (1935) 236

ACKNOWLEDGMENTS

This book is about the collective nature of intellectual practice, and thus it is fitting that there should be so many people to thank for their contributions to it. I thank first of all the French Cultural Service, the Harry Ransom Center, and the Center for Humanistic Inquiry at Emory University for supporting the research and writing of this book. I also extend my thanks to the Weiss family and to the College of Liberal Arts at Penn State for their commitment to junior faculty research.

To those who shaped and guided the project from its very inception, I am immeasurably grateful: Jean-Michel Rabaté, Rita Barnard, and Michèle Richman. To my brilliant friends and colleagues who have influenced my work as well as my life: Martha Schoolman, Caitlin Wood, Jamie Taylor, Kevin Bell, Amy Elias, Gabriella Zoller, Damien Keane, Matt Hart, Chris Looby, Sven-Erik Rose, Jim Kearney, Gregg Flaxman, Donald Pease, Kris Jacobson, Michael Barsanti, Emily Zinn, Elizabeth Scanlon, Schuyler Henderson, Claire Goldstein, Alex Novak, Katie Novak, Patrick North, Billie Jo North, Patrick Alexander, Ben Lee, Lisi Schoenbach, Susan Wood, Patricia Gherovici, Liliane Weissberg, Darren Ranco, Scott Herring, Rachel Teukolsky, Walter Adamson, Ernie Freeberg, and Keith Anthony.

I am reminded each day of my excellent colleagues at Penn State, who, in their intelligence and curiosity, have fostered an intellectual community about which I might hitherto only have dreamed. Carey Eckhardt, Robert Caserio, and Robin Schulze deserve special thanks for their leadership and guidance. I am grateful to Kit Hume and Mark Morrison for providing publishing advice, and to Eric Hayot, who stepped up late in the game to offer valuable feedback. I wish to thank the many other colleagues and friends at Penn State who have buoyed me throughout the completion of this book, particularly Janet Lyon, Jim West, Michael Berubé, Brian Lennon, Charlotte Eubanks, Julia Kasdorf, Aldon Nielsen, Chris Castiglia, Djelal Kadir, Juana Djelal, Sophia McClennen, Jeff Nealon, Susan Squier, Allan Stoekl, Tom Beebee, Gonzalo Rubio, Tawny Holm, Donald Kunze, Monique Yaari, Sandra Stelts, Kathy Force, Amy Barone, Kim Keller, Lynn Selzer, Bonnie Rossman, Irene Grassi, Mona Muzzio, Sharon Laskowsky, and Cindy Bierly.

I am especially grateful to the growing number of surrealist colleagues who have become friends and intellectual sounding boards along the way. Adam Jolles and Kate Conley read chapters and vetted ideas at every stage of the project and helped make it exciting to work on surrealism in the first place. Likewise, Laurie Monahan, Elza Adamowicz, Michael Taylor, and Ian Farr have been magnificent interlocutors and friends. This project would not exist without the guidance and intellectual generosity of Jacqueline

Chénieux-Gendron, who sponsored my initial research in Paris. Mary Ann Caws deserves my undying praise, both for her excitement and generosity as a scholar, collaborator, and friend, as well as for her enthusiastic reading of this book in its manuscript form.

In addition, my work has benefited enormously from conversations with scholars I have met through the Surrealism Centre in the United Kingdom, including Dawn Ades, David Lomas, Sharon-Michi Kusunoki, Gavin Parkinson, David Sorfa, Charlie Miller, Ian Walker, Adina Kamien-Kazhdan, and Neil Matheson. I am grateful to have had the opportunity to participate in this international community of scholars.

I want to single out Sarah Maza, Christine Coffman, Elizabeth Ezra, and Randall Cherry for their expertise and camaraderie in discussing mutual interests, and especially in offering perceptive readings of individual chapters of this book.

Jeremy Braddock deserves special mention for his collaboration and friendship throughout.

Michael Richardson, having agreed to read the entire manuscript, provided unusually generous and thoughtful feedback, and I am grateful for his keen insights. I am also indebted to the anonymous first reader, whose enthusiasm for the project was matched by an invaluable rigor.

I wish to thank Ferdanda Meza at the Artists Rights Society in New York for her help with copyrights over the years, as well as Timothy Baum and Alessandra Carnielli, who generously offered their assistance in tracking down images. Thanks also to the staff at the Bibliothèque Littéraire Jacques Doucet, the Bibliothèque des Littératures Policières, the Harry Ransom Center, and the Penn State University libraries.

John Ackerman has expressed his enthusiasm for this project from the very beginning and has made the process of completing the book for publication both stimulating and anxiety-free. I cannot imagine a more pleasant publishing experience. My thanks also to Ange Romeo-Hall, Senior Manuscript Editor at Cornell University Press, and to Amanda Heller, the book's copyeditor, for their invaluable assistance in shepherding this project from manuscript to book. Kay Banning prepared the index with skill and grace.

Most of all, I want to thank my family for their belief in me, and for their continued, if motivated, interest in surrealism. To my mother and father, sister and brother, and to Gabriella, I give my warmest gratitude and love; to Carl J., Maureen, and Jonah, my love and fondest thanks as well. To my grandmother, Lady Eburne—Leonora Carrington's exact peer—I reserve a special note of thanks and love.

And to my beautiful daughter, Adelaide, who won't yet be able to read these pages, I promise that the next book I read to you will be about bunnies and trains.

And to Hester Blum, my best friend and partner in all things: this book is for you.

Early versions of portions of this book have previously appeared in print. Part of chapter 1 was published in *Surrealism: Borders/Crossings*, ed. Elza Adamowicz (Oxford: Peter Lang, 2006); a section from chapter 4 appeared in *Robert Desnos: Surrealism in the Twenty-first*

Century, ed. Marie-Claire Barnet, Eric Robertson, and Nigel Saint (Oxford: Peter Lang, 2006). Parts of chapter 6 appeared, in early form, in *Surrealism, Politics, and Culture*, ed. Raymond Spiteri and Donald LaCoss (Burlington: Ashgate, 2001), and in *Pleine Marge* 40 (December 2004). A version of chapter 8 appeared in PMLA 120.3 (May 2005); and a version of the concluding chapter appeared in *Yale French Studies* 109 (2006).

SURREALISM AND THE ART OF CRIME

INTRODUCTION

SURREALISM AND THE ART OF CRIME

The path of surrealism through the twentieth century is littered with corpses. In a century beset by war, terror, atrocity, and revolutionary bloodshed, the surrealists lived through, died from, and bore witness to these events. Yet they were far from passive historical bystanders. Participants in an international avant-garde movement that remained active for over fifty years, the writers and artists of the surrealist movement dedicated themselves to experimental intellectual practices that responded directly to the violence of twentieth-century history. And while this violence erupted most conspicuously during the mass upheavals of war and revolution, it could be confronted most explicitly, according to the surrealists, in the immediate and vulgar realm of everyday crime.

In this book I examine the role of violent crime in the writing, art, and political thought of the surrealist movement. Approaching the surrealists as politically committed interpreters of culture as well as poets and artists, I show how the group's interest in crime was fundamental to its responses to pressing political and intellectual events of the twentieth century. Though the movement was in many ways a product of the First World War, its critical imagination was hardly limited to the singular trauma of the European battlefield. For the surrealists, the social phenomenon of crime offered revealing insights into the historical forces and institutions of knowledge that shaped twentieth-century life. Rather than viewing violent crime merely as source material for artistic inspiration, the surrealists scrutinized the newspaper reports, scientific studies, and fictional accounts that both represented crime publicly and speculated about its historical consequences. This scrutiny formed the basis of the movement's own theories of representation and historical consequence.

Recognizing the popular and clinical impact of crime to be an admixture of fiction and fact, the surrealists viewed crime as a phenomenon of the marvelous, an event characterized by the discrepancies and excesses it brought to light. Louis Aragon, in a series of aphorisms published in 1925, refers to this phenomenal quality as "the contradiction that reveals itself within the real."[1] Aragon would later uphold this phenomenon as a mechanism for political change, arguing that the marvelous provides a means for diagnosing crises within existing political and cultural orders, as well as for attacking, in turn, the ideological forces that sustain them as reality. The cultural apparatuses for measuring and representing violent crime similarly rendered concrete the contradictions at work in the popular imagination, the medical-legal system, and the social order alike. The surrealist fascination with crime is fundamental, I propose, to the movement's collective project, a radical synthesis of diverse fields of knowledge that sought to transform the ordering systems through which we understand and experience modern life.

As early as 1919 the surrealist group began to follow contemporary murder cases with a growing attention to the ways in which such crimes challenged accepted categories of public order, motive, and criminal taxonomy. Throughout the movement's history, items from the back pages of popular newspapers played a critical role in shaping the group's strategy for assessing how and why certain forms of violence tended to elude public scrutiny. The surrealists also unearthed a then-overlooked corpus of European literature and thought; they recognized in the works of figures such as the marquis de Sade, the comte de Lautréamont, Arthur Rimbaud, Alphonse Allais, Anne Radcliffe, Eugène Sue, Sigmund Freud, and the German Romantics an intellectual genealogy that presented crime as an event through which systems of law, science, morality, and speculative thought suddenly came into relief.

The surrealists' interest in crime encompassed both the specificity of individual criminal cases and the broader register of political violence in modern life. Their discussions about crime and criminality extended from the fictional realm of gothic literature to the most urgent political crises of the twentieth century. In response to these crises, the group issued a steady stream of political tracts and pamphlets that sought to expose the forms of violence, both explicit and latent, exercised in the name of the state, the family, the middle class, and even the values of Western humanism. Their writing, immersed in literary and political history alike, responded to epistemological questions about the frontiers of poetic language as well as to ethical questions about how to intervene within the contemporary geopolitical order—whether in the ongoing struggles between colonialism and anticolonial resistance in Africa and the Caribbean, against the rise of fascism in Europe, in reaction to the Moscow trials and the Stalinist purges of the late 1930s, or in the Algerian and Indo-Chinese wars of the 1950s. In particular, surrealist writings and interventions debated the legitimacy of using violent force in such political crises. Especially significant to the movement's early history was the group's reaction to Abd el-Krim's anticolonial uprising in the Rif sector of Morocco in 1924, an insurrection quickly suppressed by French military intervention, with heavy casualties to Moroccan civilians. The surrealists' denunciation of this imperialist intervention as criminal accelerated the group's commitment to leftist politics; yet this engagement with orthodox communism was itself punctuated by questions about the legitimacy of violent action, as well as with broader ethical concerns about the problems of politicizing an avant-garde movement.

Surrealism's fraught relations with communism in the 1920s and early 1930s dramatically affected the group's literary practices; the demands of political militancy altered the group's sense of what it meant to write and publish experimental poetry and prose. What remained largely consistent throughout the group's debates about political writing was the prominence of an ever-expanding body of symbolist, gothic, and pulp fiction films and texts to which the surrealists appealed. Although this literary genealogy extended toward the mass media—comprising the political sphere of crime reportage, editorial speculation, and sensational journalism, whose ideological tendencies the surrealists analyzed—its function in surrealist thought and debate was primarily conceptual. That is, the intellectual genealogy the surrealists constructed for their movement served not only to constitute the imaginative basis of its textual and artistic production but also to form the historical framework through which the surrealists developed their own ethical and political positions.

Another of the movement's genealogies pertained more explicitly to the reality of social violence. Beginning with Germaine Berton, the young anarchist assassin who, in 1923, stormed the offices of the right-wing newspaper L'Action Française and killed its publishing secretary, the group championed the causes of a number of female murderers and assassins. Long before they fully accounted for the women who actually participated in surrealist activities, the surrealists understood the acts of Berton and others to be forms of historical agency in their own right, and not simply degenerate acts of perversity or evil. A decade later certain famous paranoia cases of the 1930s—Jacques Lacan's patient "Aimée" and the murderous Papin sisters—became the objects of further study for the surrealists and were read as harbingers of a darker period in Europe's future. In August 1933 the eighteen-year-old Violette Nozières fatally poisoned her father, inciting the moral outrage of many journalists when she "soiled" her father's memory by claiming that he had been sexually abusing her since she was twelve. For the public, who discounted Violette's terrible accusation, the case became a scandalous example of disgraced and degenerate youth. For the surrealists, who published a book of poems that took Violette's charge at face value, the parricide became instead a form of autobiographical revision whose desperation laid bare the structures of patriarchal power and privilege at work in the family, in the state, and in the medical-legal system as well.

I examine such criminal cases within the context of the many classifications and prognoses that the surrealist writers and artists threw into doubt. In contesting the clinical notion that criminal behavior, like insanity, or even gender, was a natural or fixed constitutional propensity, the surrealists understood such tendencies as complex patterns of behavior governed by warring forces of determination: not only by psychiatric and legal judgments but also by an individual's own conscious and unconscious drives. Without going so far as to equate criminal behavior with revolutionary activity, the surrealists viewed criminal violence as an essential part of their collective reevaluation of psychological and political motives, a project whose demands on the modern imagination, and whose contribution to the politics of liberation, promised to be nothing short of revolutionary.

This book offers a new assessment of the intellectual and political relationship of surrealism to the European public sphere. While discussing key individual works by both better-known surrealist writers and artists (such as André Breton, Louis Aragon, Max Ernst, Aimé Césaire, Jacques Lacan, Georges Bataille, Paul Éluard, and Salvador Dalí) and somewhat lesser-known figures (such as Simone Breton, Benjamin Péret, René Crevel, Philippe Soupault, Leonora Carrington, Claude Cahun, Jules Monnerot, Marcel Duhamel, Nora Mitrani, and Gérard Legrand), I take as my primary focus the movement's collective engagement with contemporary political and intellectual debates. The place of the surrealist movement in modern intellectual history has, in recent years, been increasingly well documented: as pioneers of the French reception of Hegel and Freud after the First World War, the surrealists were instrumental to later developments in Western psychoanalysis, philosophy, and aesthetics. As major public intellectuals in France between and after the wars, they were both an influence on and a target for later experimental groups, including the existential philosophers who contributed to Jean-Paul Sartre and Simone de Beauvoir's *Temps Modernes;* the lettrist and situationist movements; and the poststructuralist theorists of *Tel Quel.* And as a poetic movement mobilized against the ravages of colonialism, surrealism has been a site of engagement for anticolonial poets and thinkers as well, from the *négritude* movement of Césaire and Léopold Senghor, to avant-garde political and artistic movements in Latin America and the Caribbean, to the later theories of Frantz Fanon and Wole Soyinka.[2]

Such intersections affirm the surrealist movement's profound immersion in the intellectual life of the twentieth century yet reveal little about the urgency and specificity with which such exchanges—whether sympathetic or polemical—took place. For surrealism was itself already a synthesis, drawing from avant-garde poetics and aesthetics as well as from popular literature, from psychoanalysis and criminology, and from journalism and political philosophy. This book's focus on the surrealists' attention to criminal violence aims to understand more concretely the nature of the movement's intellectual practices, revealing the exigency of surrealist thought itself. To the extent that revolution—political, poetic, and epistemological—became the banner under which the surrealists strove to unify these fields of knowledge, understanding the group's interest in crime will offer new ways of addressing how the surrealists theorized and enacted their revolutionary project.

This book thus demands a reevaluation of the surrealist movement's contribution to modernism and twentieth-century theory. Too often, in the eyes of its critics and advocates alike, surrealism has tended to designate a quaint set of formal practices that yielded the movement's unusual, and seemingly obfuscatory, visual and verbal works as well as its broader "utopian" program of dream and revolution. Even now, in an era longing to resist the mounting pressures of orthodoxy and fundamentalism, many scholars continue to brand surrealism as an orthodoxy unto itself, albeit an orthodoxy of the bizarre. This book redresses such presuppositions, stressing the movement's fierce resistance to orthodoxy; indeed the very notion of surrealism itself demanded, in the words of André Breton, a perpetual crisis in consciousness whose methods changed as the movement's participants changed.[3] It is this insistence on change—even on crisis and internal debate—that has challenged scholars and critics with the task of defining such a tangle of writers and artists, practices and ideas. Major recent studies of surrealism have broadened the field of surrealist scholarship by focusing on the participatory and even dialectical nature of the movement, as well as by featuring writers and artists whose contributions had previously been overlooked.[4] Moving beyond the axiomatic work of defining and introducing the movement, I argue that the rifts, disagreements, and exclusions through which surrealism consistently reinvented itself reflect the volatility of a group of public intellectuals bent on challenging the existing epistemological and political order, the silent pacts that guarantee reality as an a priori set of givens.

As a collective undertaking, surrealism drew from the varied and conflicting styles of thought, areas of expertise, and individual interests of its numerous participants and dissidents. Although it was André Breton who wrote the manifestoes and stood as the movement's most visible representative, the cohesiveness and longevity of surrealism derived from the group's commitment to absorbing these conflicts and contradictions in a way that both superseded individual experience and, as Jacqueline Chénieux-Gendron has written, demanded an essentially participatory way of thinking.[5] Volatile by design, the movement's intellectual practices embodied what Maurice Blanchot later called "the demand of discontinuity" within knowledge. To the extent that surrealism "call[ed] forth the unknown through chance and play," Blanchot writes, it invited "a relation that is foreign to the ideology of continuity."[6] Georges Bataille expressed this notion of discontinuity more forcefully: the surrealist project—the invention by degrees of new forms of materialist thought that could account for political economy and unconscious desire alike—exerted a resounding impact on the fields of knowledge in which it participated. For Bataille, this impact on modern thought could best be measured in terms of ballistics. As he wrote in a 1945 review article, his understanding of surrealism could be compared to "the ballistic study of a gunshot. The stand taken by André Breton was the shot itself."[7]

Bataille, who called himself "surrealism's old enemy from within," wrote numerous reviews and reappraisals of the movement after the Second World War. As he explains in "On the Subject of Slumbers" (1946), the notion of surrealism as a literary and artistic movement whose value resides in "works" was to be avoided at all costs. Instead, Bataille, like Blanchot, privileged the movement's peculiar combination of intellectual volatility and ethical commitment as the engine of a fundamental upheaval in human consciousness: "In terms of mankind's interrogation of itself, there is surrealism and nothing."[8] Bataille's understanding of the impact of surrealism on twentieth-century thought as a gunshot is, however, more than a simple metaphor. A reference to one of Breton's most notorious pronouncements, Bataille's assessment characterizes Breton's ethical and intellectual "stand" in terms that recall the very reasons why many contemporary intellectuals dismissed Bretonian surrealism altogether. In his polemical Second Manifesto of Surrealism (1929), Breton had described the "simplest surrealist act" as an act of random assassination: firing a pistol into a crowd. Bataille recognized, of course, that Breton's statement about the "simplest surrealist act" had very little that was simple about it. Written at the height of the movement's most contentious disagreements about the nature of political commitment, Breton's claim reveals more about the Second Manifesto's relationship to its immediate audience than about the internal principles of "surrealism" as a formal concept. All the same, can Breton's words about firing a pistol into a crowd be reduced to a rhetorical gesture, or do they really denote an act of infinite cruelty? To what extent, in other words, is the surrealist movement actually measurable in terms of ballistics—or, for that matter, in terms of crime?

Breton's own words only complicate what such an act—simple or otherwise—might say about the relation of surrealism to the concepts and forms of experience it sought to synthesize. He writes: "The simplest Surrealist act consists of dashing down into the street, pistol in hand, and firing blindly, as fast as you can pull the trigger, into the crowd. Anyone who, at least once in his life, has not dreamed of thus putting an end to the petty system of debasement and cretinization in effect has a well-defined place in that crowd, with his belly at barrel level."[9] Interpretations of these lines from the Second Manifesto have fueled attacks against surrealism in general, most notably Jean-Paul Sartre's charge that the movement, like Breton's statement, represented a feeble attempt to organize "revolution" around the inner dictates of the individual—a vulgar and politically bankrupt fusion of Leninist and Freudian rhetoric.[10] Yet Breton is not invoking the "inner dictates of the individual," nor is he simply mobilizing this act of terror as a rhetorical flourish. He means it literally, but stresses that "my intention is not to recommend it above every other because it is simple, and to try and pick a quarrel with me on this point is tantamount to asking, in bourgeois fashion, any nonconformist why he doesn't commit suicide, or any revolutionary why he doesn't pack up and go live in the USSR."[11] Surrealism's struggle lay in reconciling its radical break from "the ideology of continuity" with its awareness that even radicalism tends toward the continuous and the familiar whenever it expresses itself in forms, such as gunshots, that are merely extensions of preexisting violence. The movement's approach to this ethical and epistemological issue was to face the problem of criminality itself: to seek out what could be learned from even the most appalling acts of terror, while recognizing, too, that simplicity of means did not render such acts any less difficult to comprehend. If there was anything even close to a simple surrealist act, it was the group's identification of the real act of murder itself as an object of study—the crime most difficult to understand, most difficult to resolve, and most difficult to write about.

My claim in this book is that the composite body of knowledge fashioned by surrealist writers and artists in response to the problem of criminal violence can account for even the most complex of surrealist acts: the movement's large and ever-shifting corpus of rifts and affiliations, and, more broadly, its revolutionary attempts to fuse philosophy, psychoanalysis, ethnography, and art with a commitment to political action and a transformation of lived experience. The group's analyses and debates about the status of violence in the modern world extended to the very question of using revolutionary violence as a political strategy. To what extent could political violence ever be distinguished from crime? How did anticolonial violence differ from terrorism, from ethnic cleansing, or from colonial wars of invasion? Such questions, central to the activities of the surrealist group throughout the movement's history, show the surrealists' dedication to a public intellectualism that confronted the most fundamental principles of revolution and avant-gardism.

From Criminology to Criminography

> "I fail to understand your attitude, young man. You appear to be
> hypnotized, fascinated. You speak of Fantômas as if he were something
> alluring. It is out of place, to put it mildly. . . . [T]hat is the result of a
> modern education and the state of mind produced in the younger
> generation by the newspapers and even literature. Criminals are given
> halos and proclaimed from the housetops. . . ."
>   "But it is life, sir; it is history, it is the real thing!"
>   Marcel Allain and Pierre Souvestre, *Fantômas* (1911)

Crime itself is hardly a modern phenomenon. What is modern, though, are the institutions of police detection and legal psychiatry invented to diagnose it, as well as the public eye of the media that frames it as a spectacle. This spectacle presents a disorienting array of cultural extremes: private suffering and public sensation, destruction and production, reason and unreason. Even the most horrific murder sets in motion the reactionary cultural forces that strive to account for, measure, and exploit the causes that lie behind it. Each crime scene, illuminated by flashbulbs and searchlights, becomes a site of contested meanings; each corpse sets in motion waves of public sentiment, popular imagery, and civic action that oscillate between fascination and outrage, between sensationalism and the social process of restoring order.

What I call the art of crime denotes the aggregate forms of cultural production that include the detective mysteries, crime films, sensationalist journalism, and documents of clinical opinion which, for the surrealists, offered a telling reflection of modern experience. Far from being fanciful representations of the world, these forms comprised the forensic use of photography, the socio-biological analysis of criminal types, and the medicalization of the criminal mind through the institutionalization of psychiatry. Thus the insight of the young Charles Rambert in the *Fantômas* novels by Marcel Allain and Pierre Souvestre: a mythical figure like Fantômas, the elusive criminal genius who miraculously engineers his own escape at the end of each installment of the serial, could be both "history" and "the real thing" precisely for the reasons his interlocutor cynically dismisses— that is, because of the villain's production as a spectacle by modern education, newspapers, and literature. Though aficionados of the *Fantômas* novels and films, the surrealists were not satisfied with merely replicating Rambert's enchantment. They recognized instead that understanding criminal violence required them to examine the way it was represented, studied, and consumed. In turn, the surrealist interest in crime as a cultural phenomenon made it possible to examine the broader historical forces that otherwise resisted representation—from the causes of violence and social transformation to the very problem of understanding the vicissitudes of lived reality itself.

Most prosaically, this notion of an art of crime refers to the widespread cultural forms that manufacture and reproduce the status of crime as an extraordinary event. Crime is, above all, interesting: it not only solicits attention, even fascination, but also implicates this attention, recasting even the most objective or disinterested witnesses, experts, and newspaper readers as participants. Yet paradoxically the forms of representation through which crime is measured and witnessed also suspend this interest. As a result these forms become the mere mimetic traces of the criminal event, autonomous and yet, as Theodor Adorno suggested, subject to the forms of social labor that produce it, whether legal and medical professionalism, political ideology, or the literary marketplace. Criminal discourse is at once separate from and opposed to the arbitrariness of what simply exists; as a product of social labor, though, it is nevertheless in communication with the empirical existence it rejects and from which it draws its content.[12]

As lenses for viewing the impact of modernity within everyday life in the twentieth century, cultural forms such as crime fiction and film were popular long before the surrealists arrived on the scene. The discourses on criminality that filled the early cinemas and swelled the pages of the penny press furnished a mythologized vision of modernity, providing a subversive *imaginaire du crime* through which people could come to terms with the social arrangements of the modern world. Though in commerce with the professional tactics of forensic measurement and analysis that lent such criminal representations their authority, these imaginative forms might more readily be described as what I call criminography rather than as extensions of the social science of criminology. It is criminography—the notion of crime as an art, as a form of inscription—that provides the epistemological basis for the surrealist analysis of historical transformation. In its composite nature and paradoxical relationship to science and the empirical world, criminography, like surrealism itself, tends toward the discontinuous, at once demanding and producing analysis.

In his study of Parisian popular culture during the first decades of the twentieth century, Robin Walz identifies the presence of a "pulp surrealism" that possessed certain "surrealist" tendencies *avant la lettre*—namely, an interest in "the shadowy side of mass culture" which displayed "a flagrant disregard for cultural conventions and social proprieties."[13] At the same time, however, this mythology was often subject to the heady celebration of capitalism and bourgeois morality that fueled its production and popularity. Early in the century the precipitous rise in popularity of *faits-divers* (back page news items), and the continued proliferation of cheap paperback serial novels during the belle époque and again after the First World War, certainly exploited the experience of witnessing corpses as a sensational and even erotic form of modern experience.[14] As Dominique Kalifa has argued in his historical study of French crime journalism in the late nineteenth century, popular forms of crime discourse tended to adhere to an archaic mode of thinking which, in spite of its alleged counter-modernity, never failed to adapt to the changing tastes of historical transformation, and thus to express profound ideological and social mutations.[15]

The compound nature of criminographic discourse suggests that it could never reflect a single, coherent image of modernity. As Philippe Soupault argues in "The Shadow's Shadow," an essay published in the inaugural issue of *La Révolution Surréaliste* in 1924, the newspaper reports generally considered to be "faithful mirrors" of modernity actually offer a much more heterogeneous body of information: *faits-divers* and back page announcements in popular newspapers provide both a lens into and an impossible distortion of modern social and imaginative conditions.[16] Among the surrealists there was little faith in the ability to represent modernity either empirically, through the systematic evaluation of verifiable facts, or figuratively, through the tropes and images of naturalism. Crime discourse was thus valuable because it offered both a mimetic trace and a refraction of the modern social and intellectual conditions from which it emerged. Far from a "faithful mirror" for empirical observation, the heterogeneous body of crime discourse was both an object and an instrument of surrealist analysis.

My discussion in this book thus stresses that we displace the notion of "art" from the work of the surrealists themselves—for whom aesthetics was hardly the movement's overarching concern—to the objects and texts they studied, appropriated, and circulated.

This is not to deny, of course, that the surrealist artists and writers created paintings and poems worthy of aesthetic consideration. As part of the movement's broader practices of experiment and play, however, these creative practices tended to nominate other, non-surrealist objects—flea market finds, trinkets, newspaper articles, artifacts, totems, or so-called primitive art objects—for consideration as art.[17] I argue that the surrealists studied crime in precisely this manner: without ignoring the cruelty of criminal violence itself, they understood that at the moment it becomes subject to representation, the historical event of crime begins to obey the characteristics of art as a proliferation of objects and artifacts that bear the paradoxical relation of art to the empirical world.

Rhetoric Become Matter

In recent years scholars have grown increasingly alert to the themes of criminality and violence that arose throughout the history of surrealism, particularly when the movement's relationship to historical and political reality was most at stake.[18] Traditionally, though, scholars interested in the movement's formal achievements in poetics and art have tended to focus on how surrealist techniques of collage and automatic writing invoke crime and violence in their dismemberment of existing forms, for which human bodies serve as the master signifiers. The crimes thematized or depicted in many surrealist works are thus metaphorical: dismembered corpses and tortured, violated forms serve as the "revolutionary" language used to theorize the formal techniques of reorganization and syntactic disfiguration found in surrealist practices of collage and automatic writing.[19] Such readings share with the larger field of studies in the aesthetic treatment of violent crime a tendency to reduce criminality either to a principle of pure form or to an artist's sociological raw material. The formalist embrace of criminal violence as a signifier for surrealism's experimental practices has led to a corresponding suspicion of the movement's fascination for the subject in more historicist and politically oriented scholarship. A body of critical literature from the 1980s and 1990s approaches the group's interest in crime—and the avant-garde's interest in crime more broadly—as a fundamental yet telling weakness in the movement's historical consciousness, a near-pathological means for mitigating, rather than for confronting, the political and sexual anxieties it faced.[20] Such pathological readings draw, too, from certain feminist criticisms of the surrealist movement that stress the degree to which metaphorical assaults on the body—almost always a female body—perpetuate the dehumanizing and objectifying forms of representation against which the surrealists otherwise claimed to revolt.[21] That is, such criticism maintains that surrealist works perpetuate real and epistemological violence precisely in their tendency to reduce human bodies to metaphorical ones.

Scholars interested in historicizing surrealist politics, and, in particular, in historicizing its development of new forms of ideological critique, have taken a different approach to these themes of criminality and violence. They emphasize the rhetoric and imagery of crime as responses to specific political events or systems of power; the group's rehabilitation of criminal figures only further expressed the surrealist ethos of antiauthoritarian and antihumanist struggle.[22] And although a number of surrealists did seem to champion certain criminals for their resistance to authority, the ethical consequences of such rehabilitations were very much at the forefront of surrealist discussion and debate, as we will see in chapters 2 and 3. Indeed, to overestimate the movement's interest in crime as the transgression of taboos would risk reducing crime—even real, historical crime—to an allegorical stand-in for the movement's struggle against the ideological or psychological forces it identified as repressive. Such a reduction would be misleading, not only for its oversimplification of the criminal discourse to which the surrealists responded and contributed, but also for its implicit supposition that surrealism itself might be comprehended within a static concept—transgression, shock, or the uncanny—representable by or as crime.

At the same time, some of the most important work on surrealism has taken advantage of the critical language used by the movement's contemporaries in order to articulate how surrealism developed its conceptual framework. Drawing from the work of Georges Bataille, Jacques Lacan, and Walter Benjamin, this scholarship accounts for the movement's unique and influential fusion of Marxian and Freudian models of unconscious forces of determination, albeit in ways that allegedly exceed the movement's self-understanding.[23] The early writings of Bataille, whose ardent disagreements with surrealism's understanding of Marxism and revolt in 1929–30 spawned a "dissident" surrealism around his journal Documents, have prompted recent critics to expand their study of the movement to accommodate not only the work of these dissidents but also the questions of revolt, revolution, and political violence around which their disagreements turned. In particular, the art historians and literary critics affiliated with the journal October, such as Rosalind Krauss, Hal Foster, and Denis Hollier, as well as intellectual historians like Carolyn Dean, have been instrumental in encouraging this dialectical reading of surrealism through the lens of Bataille's critique.[24] Bataille's extensive writings about the powers of horror and sacrifice have tended, however, to absorb the more divergent surrealist positions toward criminality within Bataille's own theoretical framework. In particular, by privileging conceptual intransigence and moral subversion over the so-called idealism of overt political action, Bataillian scholarship tends to dismiss (at best) or to scorn (at worst) surrealism's political militancy as idealistic, hypocritical, and naïve. A number of such critical studies, retaining the language of Bataille's attacks on surrealism from the early 1930s—and often ignoring Bataille's later postwar positions—reduce the movement's commitment to leftist politics, as well as its interrogation of criminal violence, to formal extensions of its aesthetic priorities or its rhetoric of putative revolution.

By contrast, Walter Benjamin's curiosity about surrealism dislodges the movement from any such charges of idealism or lack of intellectual discipline. Benjamin's approach to surrealism is useful for its admiration of the movement's interpretation of Marxism as a conceptual apparatus. Yet this admiration, like Bataille's skepticism, can be as distorting as it is illuminating. Benjamin understood that the surrealist writings of the late 1920s developed a critique of ideology that was both similar and influential to his own, a recognition that bourgeois values, prejudices, and privilege could be found in the most surprising places. That is, the surrealists articulated how political power found its expression in the most seemingly banal forms, such as city streets, interior spaces, and even the plots of detective novels. Scholars approaching surrealism from Benjamin's perspective have thus offered valuable studies of surrealist insights into ideological forms that neither glorify surrealist "liberation and love" nor underestimate the critical value of their interest in crime and criminality.[25] In particular, their interest in the role of surrealism in the development of a "gothic Marxism"—a form of Marxian thought that could account for the unconscious forces of individual and socioeconomic determination alike—stresses the importance of surrealism's links to historical forms that articulate similarly irrational forces: the barren streets of Eugène Atget's Paris photographs (which "have been likened to those of a crime scene"); the stormy pages of British gothic fiction, from Matthew Lewis to Anne Radcliffe; and the uncanny dolls, mannequins, and automata described by Edgar Allan Poe, E. T. A. Hoffmann, and Sigmund Freud.[26]

Yet the surrealists also dedicated themselves to confronting institutions of power and domination that were fully evident. Organizing themselves consciously to engage in political struggles against colonialism, fascism, and Stalinism, the surrealist intellectual project had as much to do with militancy as with Benjaminian gothic Marxism.[27] What unites these facets of surrealist praxis is the dynamic and heterogeneous nature of the movement itself. In examining surrealist thought within the conceptual framework of crime, I aim to resist assigning surrealism a consistent set of aesthetic, epistemological, or methodological principles. In place of any such attempt to standardize a fixed definition of "surrealism" or "the surreal"—a practice that leads inevitably to all kinds of distortions and reductions—I examine how the group itself struggled throughout its history not only to reconcile but also to draw wisdom from its own most irreconcilable ends, its fiercest debates, and its manifold intellectual commitments as an avant-garde collective.

In their efforts to reconcile political militancy with the poetic analysis of unconscious forces of determination, the surrealists resisted the temptation to posit either language or "the beyond" as safe havens for liberatory experience. As Benjamin noted in 1929, surrealist language was more dangerous than that, taking precedence "not only before meaning. Also before the self."[28] More ethical than utopian, surrealist writing and art are at once endlessly playful—dismembered, self-reflexive, allusive—and deadly serious. Dislodged from its rationalist claim to define and describe existing appearances, surrealist verbal and visual language constitutes a new form of materialism that enters instead into the more contested realm of thinking. That is, as language described by Maurice Blanchot as "rhetoric become matter," it does not so much state as refract, rearrange, delve, and surpass its own claims.[29] Thus the "participatory" form of thinking described by Chénieux-Gendron indicates an unsettling erasure of the division between animate and inanimate forms: the collective practices and polemics of the surrealist group, and the interpretive efforts its works demand, are further amplified by the material elements of surrealist activity itself—its tropes, images, and syntax, as well as its folded papers, its disseminated tracts, and its journal publications. Words do not just "make love," as Breton wrote in a 1922 essay, but in their volatile proliferation and distortion of meanings, they also undertake the work of thinking.

What is at stake in studying the surrealist movement's interest in criminality and criminography is the value and meaning of surrealism itself as the revolutionary movement in thought, and in life, that it claimed to be. Is the recourse to crime symptomatic of its own true violence, of its perpetuation of relations of gender and power, or of its other ethical, political, or methodological shortcomings? On the contrary: the rifts, disagreements, and exclusions through which surrealism consistently reinvented itself reflect the volatility of a movement bent on challenging the silent pacts that guarantee reality as a verifiable set of givens. At the same time, the outbursts of crime and terror animating surrealist work draw attention to the ways in which violent historical phenomena likewise throw into relief the conflicting systems of representation and understanding used to make sense of them. As a lens for political analysis, the varied public and institutional responses to crime—from the measurement systems of Bertillon cards to the splashy sensationalism of the penny press—could certainly be used to problematize the limits and excesses of the immediate cultural order. More profoundly, though, the discourses of crime could be read dialectically as forms of expression in themselves, as a kind of modern poetry that subverted the ideological determination of its own purposive framework. Approached in this way, crime discourse could do more than reflect contemporary social and political systems; it could form the very language through which the historical forces governing these systems might be rendered concrete.

Le Rouge et le Noir

No one was more sensitive to the changes sustained by surrealist concepts, and the surrealist group, than Breton himself. In a 1934 speech titled "What Is Surrealism?" he identifies two stages in the movement's evolution—an evolution which, he maintains, "shows that our unceasing wish, growing more and more urgent from day to day, has been at all costs to avoid considering a system of thought as a refuge; to pursue our investigations with eyes wide open to the external consequences; and to assure ourselves that the results of these investigations would be capable of facing the breath of the street."[30] Breton identifies the first stage of this surrealist evolution as the purely intuitive epoch (1919–1925), which "can be characterized by the belief, expressed during this time, in the omnipotence of thought, considered capable of freeing itself by means of its own resources."[31] What Breton called the movement's intuitive epoch, and which Walter Benjamin considered its heroic period, was characterized by a fascination for images of violence, social disruption, and murder, as well as by a belief in the subversive conceptual power of such images.

Although, as Breton claims, no coherent political or social attitude made its appearance until 1925—"that is to say . . . till the outbreak of the Moroccan war"—Carole Paligot, in her history of the political development of surrealism, argues that the subsequent passage into a period of committed, if vexed, allegiance to communism was in fact an extension of its earlier ethics of pure revolt. Breton refers to the activities of this second period as surrealism's reasoning phase, because the movement, "faced with a brutal, revolting, unthinkable fact, was forced to ask itself what were its proper resources and to determine their limits." That is, surrealism had to cease being content with the self-sufficiency of its artistic activities and experiments and instead consider "these first results as being simply so much material, starting from which the problem of knowledge inevitably arose again under quite a new form."[32] At stake in this shift was the gravity of understanding the real—not only the material conditions that perpetuate inequality and provoke violence but also the indescribable experience of violence and suffering.

This transformation in surrealist epistemology and politics did not take place without conflict. Indeed, this "red" period of communist involvement reached its climax after the publication in late 1931 of Louis Aragon's incendiary poem "Red Front," which sparked debates over whether its straightforward advocacy of assassination in the name of political change should be considered a purely metaphorical speech act, a work of communist propaganda, or an incitement to murder. Surrealism's tempestuous "red" period thus comprises the movement's attempts to explore the possibilities for revolutionary violence without either succumbing to the fascist glorification of murder or merely miming the individualist rebelliousness of anarchism.

Yet what Breton was increasingly aware of when he wrote "What Is Surrealism?" was that surrealism was in the midst of further changes in the wake not only of the "Aragon affair" but of Hitler's alarming rise to power as well. The change in surrealism's intellectual and political development inaugurated by these crises introduced what I call the movement's "noir" phase. Striving less, for the time being, to "change life" or to "change the world" than to understand the nature of causality itself, the surrealists attempted to comprehend the rapidly deteriorating political universe of the 1930s using the metaphorics of gothic literature (le roman noir) as an epistemological device. Increasingly suspicious of the dangers of stylizing terrorist violence, the surrealists made style itself the terrain for better understanding the latent forces of terror and social dissolution at work in psychic and political reality.

This book is divided, like Breton's own conception of the movement, into three sections, each of which examines the development of surrealism's analytical approach to crime. The first section consists of three chapters that discuss the epistemological and ethical preoccupations that lay within surrealist aesthetics during the movement's early years. The second section comprises two chapters documenting the movement's turn toward leftist politics, examining how members of the group confronted the distinction between revolutionary violence and murderous crime. The role of aesthetics as a form of judgment remained central to this development; under scrutiny was the function and responsibility of political agency in producing historical change. The book's third section examines surrealism's political migration from its "red" period of communist activism into its "noir" period. Characterized by what the poet Paul Éluard called an "exasperated" return to earlier, pre-communist surrealist practices, noir surrealism returned also to the most brutal imagery of violence and crime, which now became useful for understanding the latent or sublimated political drives at work in the historical emergency in which the surrealists were engrossed.[33] This section consists of three chapters, the first discussing surrealist practices in the early 1930s and the second and third discussing surrealist practices during and after the Second World War. The conclusion discusses the forms of surrealist thought that emerged during the mid-1950s, even as the movement's critical force seemed to be dissipating.

Chapter 1, "Locked Room, Bloody Chamber," studies the early and often ambivalent surrealist interest in the mechanics of the locked room mystery story. Such stories, I argue, were instrumental to the movement's developing epistemology, most significantly in giving form to the surrealists' repudiation of literary naturalism and philosophical positivism.

Chapter 2, "On Murder, Considered as One of the Surrealist Arts," focuses on surrealist treatments of more literal acts of violence. Drawing on Thomas De Quincey's famous trilogy of essays "On Murder, Considered as One of the Fine Arts," this chapter examines how surrealists such as Benjamin Péret, René Crevel, and Louis Aragon treated murder "aesthetically," as a collection of formal traits and imaginary relations. Ironically, the perverse idea of the beautiful that emerges from the often violent and unsettling texts published during the movement's early years prefigures surrealism's rejection of taste in favor of an analytical rather than an evaluative aesthetic system. By historicizing the changing surrealist responses to murder, this chapter shows how the spectacle of violent crime became a site of conflict within the movement itself.

Chapter 3, "Germaine Berton and the Ethics of Assassination," focuses on one of the most significant public figures in the group's early years, the anarchist assassin Germaine Berton. By degrees scorned and scrutinized by the press, Berton's position as a media object gave expression not only to the fractured state of French intellectual life in the interwar era but also to a conflicting body of moral, political, and even erotic desires. This chapter documents how the surrealists, in celebrating Berton, did not so much espouse her anarchist politics as view her violent act as a call to thought, a provocation to find their own means for intervening within the postwar political and intellectual sphere.

The second section of the book begins with chapter 4, "Dime Novel Politics," which focuses on the surrealist movement's entry into the French Communist Party during the Rif War of 1925. It describes the efforts of the group to define its ideas about political agency, collective discipline, and revolution in the context of the recent anticolonial uprisings in Morocco. Under particular scrutiny were the group's literary and artistic practices, especially its ties to leading intellectual periodicals. In this chapter I examine the forms of popular writing and collective activity through which the group negotiated its leftist turn. Of particular interest are the crime stories of Philippe Soupault and Robert Desnos, written at the moment of their ruptures with the surrealist movement, in 1926 and 1928, respectively. By placing these stories at the forefront of my examination of surrealist politics, I argue for the centrality of dime novel villains within the political thinking of the group, especially with regard to its ideas about revolutionary agency.

Chapter 5, "X Marks the Spot," examines the role played by the marquis de Sade's pornographic theories of revolt, liberation, and cruelty in the wake of surrealism's engagement with leftist politics. It discusses how Sade's critique of morality lay behind the series of debates around which the surrealist movement reorganized itself between 1929 and 1932, from André Breton's and Georges Bataille's disagreements about what might be called a Sadean materialism to the debates about Stalinist propaganda which led to Aragon's rupture with the group in 1932. The polemics that characterized this period in surrealist thinking revolved around the rhetoric of murderous violence through which the group tended to express its revolutionary demands. At issue was less the moral problem of appealing to murder than the ideological problem of the movement's divergent understandings of what constituted a revolutionary demand.

The surrealists' break with communism, precipitated by the "Aragon affair" of 1932, forms the basis of the book's third and final section, which contains three chapters that trace the movement's intellectual history from the 1930s through the 1950s. Chapter 6, "Surrealism Noir," consists of two parts. The first examines the murders committed by Christine and Léa Papin in early 1933, a case whose extremity, and whose intensive media coverage, tested theories of paranoia developed almost simultaneously by Salvador Dalí, René Crevel, and Jacques Lacan. The second part of this chapter discusses the parricide committed by the eighteen-year-old Violette Nozière later that same year, examining how the surrealists assessed the press coverage and legal judgment of the crime as symptoms of an encroaching political conspiracy between bourgeois "family values" and totalitarian power.

Chapter 7, "Persecution Mania," examines how surrealist theories of paranoia continued to play a role in organizing the movement's actions in the immediate prewar years, and especially during the Second World War. This chapter focuses on Leonora Carrington's autobiographical novella *Down Below* (1943–44), first published in the American surrealist magazine *VVV*, as a self-consciously paranoiac reaction to the atrocities of the Second World War.

Chapter 8, "The Transatlantic Mysteries of Paris: Surrealism and the Série Noire," continues to explore the noir cultural stance of the preceding chapter by examining the dissemination of surrealist practices throughout the public sphere in the years following the Second World War. This chapter traces the continuities between the surrealist notion of black humor; the resurgence of the gothic *roman noir*, or "black" novel, in surrealist writing in the immediate prewar years; and, after the war, the formation of the hard-boiled detective series, the Série Noire, at Gallimard. In particular, the chapter discusses the original publication of *La Reine des pommes*, the first crime novel by the African American writer Chester Himes, as part of the Série Noire. Himes's novel, I argue, not only represents a "vernacular" version of a surrealist *humour noir* but extended the surrealist question of violence and revolt into the political and racial experience of the United States as well.

The book concludes with a discussion of surrealism's continued place in recent debates about the role of the avant-garde in twentieth-century politics and about the function of leftist theory in the contemporary world. I approach these debates by assessing postwar surrealist strategies for thinking about the singularity of violent historical events. Surrealism offers a useful platform for addressing the contemporary problem of violence, I conclude, because the surrealist critical project during the 1920s, 1930s, and 1940s itself confronted the stakes of incorporating violence as a political strategy. This conclusion looks to the glossy surrealist periodical of the late 1950s, *Le Surréalisme, Même*, examining the group's published responses to the works of postwar intellectuals such as Albert Camus, Jean-Paul Sartre, and Aimé Césaire. These responses, both polemical and celebratory, reasserted surrealism's currency as an intellectual movement; more significantly, they articulated the evolving anticolonial and anti-Stalinist politics of the group in light of its condemnation of France's military actions in Algeria. Even beyond its active period as an avant-garde movement, surrealism continues to offer new ways to think about politics, history, and ideology, as well as a forum for debating the political responsibility of intellectuals.

CHAPTER ONE

LOCKED ROOM, BLOODY CHAMBER

The invention of photography dealt a mortal blow to old means of expression.

André Breton, "Max Ernst" (1921)

It is seductive to think that surrealism might somehow have been born, as if conceived and delivered in a single, originary act. Man Ray's photograph of the surrealist group crowding around a gesticulating Robert Desnos (figure 1.1) illustrates one such possible moment. The photograph, published on the front cover of the inaugural issue of *La Révolution Surréaliste* in 1924, shows a "sleeping" Desnos enacting one of the mediumistic verbal performances first described by André Breton in his 1922 essay "The Mediums Enter." The image dramatizes the singular fascination with which the group regarded Desnos's trancelike improvisations, by far the most celebrated of the group's experiments with mediumistic activities during its "période des sommeils" in 1922 and 1923. These collective activities, and Desnos's utterances in particular, formed what might be considered the experimental core of the nascent surrealist movement as it strove to differentiate itself from Parisian Dada.

As documentary evidence of these activities, Man Ray's photograph dramatizes its own historicity, its composition of gathered witnesses featuring, at its center, Simone Breton's transcription of the séances. In addition, the faces of Paul Éluard and Francis Picabia peering out from the back of the group call attention to the documentary presence of Ray's camera at the scene. Yet what is particularly striking about the photograph is how it depicts this formative moment as taking place within the confines of a single room. The intimation seems clear: the movement's collective emergence in the early 1920s as a "rendezvous of friends"—the title of Max Ernst's well-known 1922 portrait of the group—was as much a function of spatial convergence as it was of friendship or historical simultaneity.

André Breton reinforces the spatial intimacy of such congregations in the *Manifesto of Surrealism*, as well as in a number of other texts from 1924, including his tract "Introduction to the Discourse on the Paucity of Reality" and the experimental text *Poisson soluble*.

Fig. 1.1. Man Ray, *Waking Dream Séance* (1924). Surrealist group with Max Morise, Roger Vitrac, Jacques Boiffard, André Breton, Paul Eluard, Pierre Naville, Giorgio de Chirico, Philippe Soupault; (in front) Simone Collinet-Breton, Robert Desnos, and Jacques Baron, 1924. Image © 2008 ARS/Telimage. © 2008 Man Ray Trust/Artists Rights Society (ARS), New York/ADAGP, Paris.

Rhetorically gathering together his colleagues inside the ruins of an imaginary chateau, Breton describes surrealist poetics in a conceptual language similarly formulated in terms of enclosed spaces. Surrealism's experimental poetics are made possible, he claims, by the "rarefied atmosphere" the movement provided, as if the château metaphor described a scientifically controlled system for establishing conditions of collectivity and collaboration. This chateau myth, as the situationist writer Raoul Vaneigem later called it, might be said to encompass the philosophical as well as spatial ambitions of the surrealist movement as a whole: it reflected a fantasy of a unitary society "where the individual trajectory of even the humblest of men was inextricably bound up with the cosmic in a mass of fictional realities and real fictions, an atmosphere in which every event was a sign and every word or gesture magically sparked off mysterious currents of mental energy."[1] The intense exchange of gazes in Man Ray's photograph certainly evokes the mysterious currents Vaneigem describes, dramatizing the atmosphere of expectancy in the crowded room where Desnos spoke. Vaneigem was himself sharply critical of this breathlessness, which, he claimed, was organized around a nostalgic myth rather than an awakening epistemological self-consciousness. For Vaneigem, surrealism's notions of atmosphere and influence were never fully detached from the mysticism of séances and romantic rebellions.

In this chapter I argue, to the contrary, that the surrealist movement developed its field of inquiry through careful attention to the physical and fictional sites at which its activities took place. Far from succumbing to nostalgic myths about its origins, the group rigorously evaluated its relationship to intellectual history, albeit a history rendered both fragmentary and suspect by the recent world war. The rooms and châteaux Breton used to indicate the movement's collective nature were instrumental in establishing surrealism's relations with earlier forms of thought: its ties to gothic romance and literary naturalism, to experimental and forensic photography, to clinical psychiatry and psychoanalysis, and in particular to the fictional devices of locked room detective mysteries.

Surrealist activities did, of course, tend to take place on common ground. Other sites of "currents of mental energy," such as the Surrealist Research Bureau at 27, rue de Grenelle, as well as Breton's own studio at 42, rue Fontaine, have taken on a nearly mythical status in surrealist scholarship. So too have the shared residences at the rue du Château (in which Yves Tanguy, Marcel Duhamel, Jacques and Pierre Prevert, and later André Thirion and Georges Sadoul each lived) and the rue Blomet (Joan Miró, André Masson, Robert Desnos) been similarly remembered as "alembics" of surrealist activity.[2] Already, though, this multiplication of addresses contradicts the possibility of any singular origin, emphasizing instead the movement's heterogeneity. More significantly, these offices, apartments, and atmospheres are complemented in surrealist thinking by a second set of fictional spaces by means of which surrealist writers and artists articulated the emerging movement's conceptual stakes. Rather than functioning metaphorically as the sites of a "unitary society," or for that matter as the chambers of conception or birth, these latter rooms function instead as crime scenes. Such fictional spaces are no longer crowded with friends and fellow travelers but are lifeless, abandoned, and spattered with blood. It was in such locked rooms and bloody chambers that early surrealist thinking explicitly charted out its epistemological terrain, forging many of its critical concepts in an ambivalent relation to the mechanics and metaphorics of crime writing.

In the early 1920s André Breton and Philippe Soupault each attacked what they considered to be the false empiricism of crime stories they nonetheless admired, criticizing works such as Fyodor Dostoyevsky's *Crime and Punishment*, Edgar Allan Poe's Dupin tales, and Gaston Leroux's *Mystery of the Yellow Room*. Breton's and Soupault's writings emphasize how the formal structure of such "locked room" mystery stories render physical the epistemological closed circuit of literary, philosophical, and scientific positivism. What rehabilitates such tales, though, is precisely their phoniness; the mechanical rationalism of their detective story plots functions ironically, as a self-critique of the very rationalism they seem to epitomize. These locked room crime scenes thus become a means for effecting what Breton calls a "mortal blow dealt to old modes of expression," a negation not just of old forms of art but of old modes of thought and science as well.[3]

The surrealists likened this epistemological break to the impact of two nineteenth-century inventions, photography and psychoanalysis, which likewise preempted the esoteric aims of scientific positivism in the form of a mechanical procedure available to anyone. Each, the surrealists claimed, made possible the mechanical production of evidence; like the false positivism of detective fiction, this manufactured evidence could provide a means for dislodging surrealist thinking from the ideological closed circuit of contemporary thought in the aftermath of the Great War, with its emphasis on continuity, patriotism, and domesticity. This "mortal blow" thus sets the scene instead for both a surrealist aesthetic practice and, more significantly, a surrealist thinking, based on exteriority, wandering, and dérive (drift); this development finds its epitome in the hysterical wanderings of Soupault's urban fiction of the early 1920s.

The Yellow Room

In his discussion of surrealism's literary relations early in the 1924 Manifesto of Surrealism, Breton takes issue with a scene from Dostoyevsky's Crime and Punishment. The scene, he argues, is an example of "the purely informative style" that "is virtually the rule rather than the exception in the novel form." Breton qualifies his indictment of Dostoyevsky's style, though, by acknowledging that its limitations are based less in its technical faculties than on the scope of experience it chooses to represent: "in all fairness," he writes, "the author's ambition is severely circumscribed."[4] For Breton, the representation and its object are mutually implicated, since the stylistic apparatus of naturalist realism is a symptom of this kind of circumscription. His critique of Dostoyevsky hinges on the technical facility with which realist prose preserves and multiplies empty moments of experience. In the passage he cites from Crime and Punishment, the "postcards" and "clichés" (that is, photographic negatives) of description depict an especially banal yellow room from which emanates a palpable sense of domestic confinement. Here is the passage as Breton cites it:

> The small room into which the young man was shown was covered with yellow wallpaper: there were geraniums in the windows, which were covered with muslin curtains; the setting sun cast a harsh light over the entire setting. . . . There was nothing special about the room. The furniture, of yellow wood, was all very old. A sofa with a tall back turned

down, an oval table opposite the sofa, a dressing table and a mirror set against the pier-glass, some chairs along the walls, two or three etchings of no value portraying some German girls with birds in their hands—such were the furnishings.[5]

In his discussion of the passage Breton treats Dostoyevsky's room as if it were constructed directly from the logic of naturalism itself: a collage of the standard images and stylistic tropes of the "realistic attitude," the room seems to be "nothing but so many superimposed images taken from some stock catalogue, which the author utilizes more and more whenever he chooses."[6]

Breton's contempt for Dostoyevsky is surprising here, for he was an important enough figure to the proto-surrealist group for his likeness to be included in Ernst's 1922 painting *Au Rendezvous des amis*, and he continued to garner attention from other writers in the surrealist group.[7] But Breton's attack on Dostoyevsky is far from an automatic dismissal. It is instead a deliberate gesture of sacrifice through which, for Breton, *Crime and Punishment* comes to represent the exhaustion of naturalism's claim to represent the real. The photographic language of Breton's critique (which cites negatives [*clichés*] and postcards) only further supports his claim that the ability of the realist narrative to capture empirical detail had reached a dead end, exhausted by its infinite capacity for reuse. Just as photography had become domesticated by its commercial use in stock catalogues and picture postcards, naturalism was similarly circumscribed by its scrutiny of the interior life of the commonplace, whether this meant the furnishings of a petit-bourgeois domestic household, the observations of an individual consciousness, or for that matter the reliance of naturalism on a logic of social determinism. Breton's critique of Dostoyevsky's prose, in other words, targets the extent to which naturalism extends, rather than merely represents, the ideological continuities that the Parisian avant-garde had implicated throughout the war years as part of the machinery of warfare.

Louis Aragon makes a similar claim that same year in his own surrealist manifesto, "A Wave of Dreams." Aragon's text extends Breton's polemic by denouncing not just naturalist fiction but both positivism and neo-Kantian idealism alike as but slightly more sophisticated forms of epistemological confinement. Whereas Breton stresses the threat Dostoyevsky's room poses as a conceptual space, Aragon focuses on the paucity of the stock images relied on by realists in general. As if revising Breton's critique of clichés and postcards, Aragon decries the idolatry of the "shameful realist, as today's men of goodwill tend to be, who live on a compromise between Kant and Comte, [and] who think they have taken a big step in rejecting the vulgar idea of reality in favor of a reality-in-itself, the noumenon, that shabby, unmasked plaster figurine."[8] There is no such thing as categorically absolute evidence, Aragon claims. His appeal to kitsch suggests, indeed, that any such "shameful" attempt to throw off appearances in order to reach the noumenon replaces one set of stock imagery with another: the positivist's implicit adhesion to a deterministic natural law is replaced by a transcendental kernel of reality—the noumenon—which can be conceived and represented only through a priori structures of knowledge.

"Nothing," Aragon continues, "will make such people understand the true nature of the real: that it is but a relation like any other, that the essence of things is in no way tied to their reality, that there are relations other than the real that the mind can grasp, and that are also primary, like chance, illusion, the fantastic, the dream."[9] Aragon's critique privileges the phenomenal, suggesting that the concept of the real is a product, at once vernacular—a relation like any other—and derivative. For Aragon, the mind's capacity for grasping phenomena renders the realist's interest in the noumenon both shameful and banal: an ideological product, a false belief. For Breton, however, the idolatry of Aragon's "shameful realist" is more sinister; his dispute with Dostoyevsky moves beyond the critique of postcards and clichés to attack the power of their haphazard composition to seduce readers into accepting their banality as real. Whereas Aragon's critique of positivism is largely epistemological, Breton's attack on naturalism is explicitly ideological, expressing concern for the ways in which this banality reproduces itself as a determining condition of human experience. This is why Breton takes such pains to distinguish surrealism from Dostoyevsky's naturalism.

Ironically, Breton articulates this distinction in language reminiscent of the surrealist movement's own aesthetics. Breton describes surrealist poetics in terms of a pastiche of preexisting images, much as he describes Dostoyevsky's yellow room: Max Ernst's collages and overpaintings, in particular, are composed literally from the images in catalogues and educational primers, "so many superimposed images taken from some stock catalogue." What this suggests is that Breton's polemic against Dostoyevskian realism is invested less in the technical materials of naturalist realism and positivism (empirical detail, description, cliché) than in the ideological stakes of their composition and arrangement.

Unsurprisingly, then, Breton's rejection of this "realist attitude" takes the form of a refusal "to go into [Dostoyevsky's] room." As if agreeing with the narrator's assertion that there is "nothing special" about it, Breton continues:

Others' laziness or fatigue does not interest me. I have too unstable a notion of the continuity of life to equate or compare my moments of depression or weakness with my best moments. When one ceases to feel, I am of the opinion that one should keep quiet. And I would like it understood that I am not accusing or condemning lack of originality *as such*. I am only saying that I do not take particular note of the empty moments of my life, that it may be unworthy for any man to crystallize those which seem to him to be so. I shall, with your permission, *ignore* the description of that room, and many more like it.[10]

As a "crystallization" of empty moments, the room troubles Breton for its manifestation of an ideology of emptiness—laziness, fatigue, and an unreflective belief in the continuity of life. And thus, as his rather elaborate act of refusal shows, Breton has not ignored the room at all. It is more than emptiness that allows him so deftly to transform the meaninglessness described in the passage into a referendum on the "empty" ideology of its literary mode of expression. Breton is, above all, harboring a murderer.

For Raskolnikov, Dostoyevsky's protagonist, is not a passive observer of the room. The scene cited in the *Manifesto* in fact describes Raskolnikov's reconnaissance visit to an old pawnbroker who occupies the yellow parlor, and whom he will soon murder with the blunt side of an axe. The narrative gaze of the description is thus cast quite literally with an eye to murder. When Breton concedes that "it may be argued that this school-boy description has its place, and that at this juncture of the book the author has his reasons for burdening me," his ironic understatement confirms his suppression of the text's allusion to the imminent murder.[11] There is in fact a telling gap in Breton's quotation, an ellipsis that omits precisely the element of dramatic purpose whose absence from the supposedly "empty" room he rejects. Here are the lines from *Crime and Punishment* that Breton leaves out: "'So the sun will be shining like this *then*, too! . . .' was the thought that flickered almost unexpectedly through Raskolnikov's mind, and with a swift glance he took in everything in the room, in order as far as possible to study and remember its position. But the room contained nothing very much in particular."[12] In the novel, Dostoyevsky's "school-boy description" of the yellow room indeed has its place; the banality of the room by no means reflects the banality of its description. On the contrary, the room's featurelessness registers its transformation into a site of irony and suspense by the precision of Raskolnikov's self-consciously murderous gaze. By expurgating these lines, Breton empties the larger passage of any such ominous purposiveness. As a result, the description of the room becomes little more than a fragment of narrative ornamentation, allowing Breton to transform the lack of originality of the room's decor into a symptom of the imaginative bankruptcy its representation threatens to reproduce.

Breton has, of course, performed this sleight of hand on purpose, and his careful selection of this passage from *Crime and Punishment* allows him both to conceal and to deny the privileged affiliation that literary naturalism claims to have with a "philosophical" murder such as Raskolnikov's. On the one hand, Breton's erasure of Raskolnikov's thoughts empties the passage of its access to the motive and so-called philosophy behind the murder, flattening out its psychological realism into an inventory of domestic furnishings. On the other hand, Breton's erasure of all references to the murder in *Crime and Punishment* leaves its violence with nowhere else to reveal itself other than within the ideology of naturalism itself. The violence leaves no traces in the facts of the room, instead exercising its effects, as Breton claims, upon the reader. And unlike classic locked room mystery stories, Breton's version of *Crime and Punishment* supplies no detective to reconstruct the missing psychological causality from the material and linguistic residue of its violence, since this residue is nowhere visible in Breton's version of the text. Breton thus dramatizes how the positivism and "absolute rationalism" he decries, which "[allow] us to consider only facts relating to our experience," yield a repressive condition whereby "experience itself has found itself increasingly circumscribed."[13] Neither vital nor mortal, realist expression "crystallizes" empty moments in a way that risks trapping experience within its ideological constraints, its naturalist understanding of causality as an inevitable, transcendental force of determination. In the banal yellow room of Breton's Dosteyevskian postcard, experience "paces back and forth in a cage from which it is more and more difficult to make it emerge."[14]

In the 1924 *Manifesto* Breton uses his critique of *Crime and Punishment* as a means for asserting, by contrast, the promise of surrealist and Freudian understandings of the psyche. Unlike naturalism and positivism, these contemporary modes of analysis authorize the imagination to explore "the depths of our mind" as an alternative to more hidebound conceptions of experience. But surrealism, like psychoanalysis, also relied on naturalism and positivism, even as it rejected their limitations. Accordingly, Breton's account of the mortal blow missing from *Crime and Punishment* can be found instead in an early essay dedicated to historicizing surrealism's relationship to realist modes of expression. The movement acquired its naturalism and positivism in trace form, the residue of two major technological shifts. In his catalogue essay for Max Ernst's first Parisian exhibition in 1921, which prefigures surrealism's investment in Freud, Breton makes the dramatic claim that the invention of photography in the nineteenth century "dealt a mortal blow to old means of expression."[15] Breton's Ernst essay furthermore allies the mortal blow of photography with the development of automatic writing, referring both to the poetic practice developed by poets such as Lautréamont and Rimbaud, as well as the clinical practice developed by psychiatrists such as Pierre Janet, as the "veritable photography of thought." Breton thus theorizes automatic writing, "a monologue spoken as rapidly as possible without any intervention on the part of the critical faculties," as a technological invention analogous to photography for its ability to deliver a similarly mortal blow.[16]

These technological shifts are "mortal" on two fronts. First, Breton explains, the invention of photography radically altered the conditions of artistic representation, obviating the functional need for a "purely informative" or imitative art. Suddenly making it possible to produce unmistakable, empirically verifiable simulacra virtually at the touch of a finger, the invention of photography changed the terms of how art represented the world, as much in writing as in painting. This shift, contemporaneous with the historical emergence of positivism and naturalism, promised a privileged access to the noumenal: the evidence of the real, it seemed, was also a trace of the real. Breton, however, does not privilege the photograph for its ability to "capture" reality; it might be said, rather, that he privileges the negative, the cliché, for its exhaustion of the mimetic faculty.

Indeed, Breton sees in the invention of photography a second, epistemological shift, through which naturalized ideas about "the real"—its causality, the nature of determinism, and the possibility of access to the noumenal—became suspect. Whereas photographs themselves tended to become static images (the postcards and clichés absorbed by naturalism), photography, Breton suggests, offered no such transcendental claims. Unlike individual photographs, the technological apparatus of photography did not harbor naturalism's crystallized presumptions about historical causality but instead produced simulacra that did little more than preserve "permanent and unmistakable traces of a human being."[17] As a technological form, photography represented a "blind instrument" that allowed artists "to reach with utter certainty the goal they had hitherto set themselves."[18] It was precisely in satisfying the goals of realist representation that photography's blindly mechanical production of insight inflicted its irrevocable blow: for Breton, the nineteenth-century invention of photography represented a new form of knowledge that did not so much supersede old systems as kill off their authority, rendering them outmoded ideological forms whose physical presence, and whose lingering effects and traces, were still visible at the crime scene of history.

The invention of photography in the mid-nineteenth century, like the contemporary development of automatic writing, was significant for producing epistemological discontinuity and disruption: the relationship of surrealism to these forms, however, is deeply ambivalent. For the surrealists, as for Benjamin, photography provided signification without necessarily offering anything legible, or, for that matter, anything other than a rearrangement of existing forms. As Breton writes, "Unfortunately human effort, which always varies the arrangement of existing elements, cannot be applied toward producing a single new element."[19] It would be a mistake, therefore, to presume that Breton embraced photography's mortal blow as the master signifier for the supposedly revolutionary formal quality of the surrealist movement's own aesthetic practices.[20] As with its use of automatic writing, surrealism's relationship to photography was a function of its historical application toward the pursuit of knowledge: the use of photography as an instrument of surveillance and taxonomy and its semiotic function as an apparatus for preserving permanent and unmistakable traces. This is why, in his article on Max Ernst, and implicitly in the Manifesto, Breton discusses the invention of photography itself as a historical phenomenon rather than a form of art, and as a blind apparatus rather than a way of seeing. Just as naturalism represented a form of ideological confinement within the deterministic "atmosphere" created by empirical detail, the development of juridical photography similarly yielded instruments of surveillance and pseudoscientific practices of identification that equally worked toward confinement and mastery. To the extent that surrealism inherited a mode of representation from photography, it did so only insofar as this photographic practice somehow resisted its own historical affiliation with naturalism and positivist science, deriving its significance from its potential for disrupting the very tasks to which it was put in service.

Photography's true mortal blow, for Breton, lay in reducing even the codified systems of positivism and naturalism to postcards and clichés. Just as Max Ernst's photomontages, collages, and overpaintings used stock images as the ready-made raw materials for their artistic rearrangements, the historical intervention of photography both epitomized and sabotaged the logic of positivism and naturalism. That is, from Breton's position of hindsight, positivism and naturalism were already doomed as systems for representing and reproducing an accepted understanding of the relations between empirical fact, lived reality, and historical events. In dealing these and other forms of mimesis a mortal blow, photography superseded their authority in denoting reality, leaving their ideologically determined arrangements as the residual form of an already outmoded logic.

Just as Breton privileges photography over the photograph, his notion of a "photography of thought" likewise points to an apparatus rather than a picture—an invention, like the photographic apparatus and its darkroom technology, whose primary function would be to systematize this production of obsolescence. What this suggests in turn is that although Breton explains that its practice professes a freedom from the critical faculties, the invention of automatic writing, like the invention of photography, in fact performed a critical function within intellectual history. The mortal blow dealt by photography was an epistemological murder, an assassination of old forms of thinking and understanding as well as a challenge to mimetic forms of expression.[21] The twin inventions revolutionized not simply representation but knowledge itself, insofar as they made it possible to recognize that the forms of causality that shaped experience were not inevitable, transcendent forces of nature but historical products, concentrations of human will whose power of determination became manifest within the act of representation.

This systematic assault on old forms of expression and knowledge similarly characterizes the surrealist interest in the locked room mystery. Just as ratiocinatory detective stories use the locked room as a device for generating murder mysteries, the surrealist and proto-surrealist invocation of the genre functions as an analogous mechanism for killing off naturalism and its constrictive ideology. It too delivers a mortal blow that spatializes the limits of realism as the empty husk of its own logic, much as Breton stages the emptiness of Dostoyevsky's yellow room. Without itself offering a positive model or ideology for truthful understanding (the detective genre is, like the photographic black box, a blind instrument), surrealism's recourse to the locked room mystery establishes the intellectual conditions of surrealism as conditions of epistemological violence rather than of ideological certainty or heady discovery, characterized by the genre's blind and ostensibly impartial assassination of old forms of thought.

The Locked Room and the Bloody Bed

In the May 1922 issue of *Littérature*, on the threshold of the magazine's break with Dada and its subsequent development as a surrealist journal, there appears a brief article titled "Au Clair de la lune" (By Moonlight) credited to a writer named Philippe Weil. The article is dedicated to Raymond Roussel, the reclusive author of *Les Impressions d'Afrique* (1910) and *Locus Solus* (1914), to whose poetry Philippe Soupault had devoted a critical essay in the previous month's issue. Bearing no further introductory features, the article assembles the basic elements of a locked room mystery: a corpse, a locked room, and a first-person narrator to describe them. Its resemblance to Edgar Allan Poe's "Murders in the Rue Morgue" is striking, extending to the tufts of severed hair littering the room, the straight razor used as the murder weapon, and the physical brutality of the crime itself. Yet "Au Clair de la lune" lacks the elaborate narrative apparatus of a locked room mystery like Poe's tale. Its account of the strange and bloody crime scene is distinguished by a striking lack of affect. Not only is the narrator emotionally detached from the scene, but his function is limited as well to that of a lens of perception with no independent existence, no psychological profile, no personality.

Lacking plot, analysis, or dramatic structure, the article describes the scene and its surfeit of spilled and spattered blood with an almost mechanical repetitiveness:

> The side door through which I entered had not been and could not have been opened, I was assured, except by the landlord, several hours after the event. All around me the floor and the furniture offer somewhat large and somewhat numerous traces of blood; and, first of all, of note is a couch whose back leans against the wall that faces the side door and the chimney. A night basin lies near the center of the cushion; it contains around twelve ounces of a liquid that seems to be urine mixed with blood. Bloodstains of different sizes are spread out here and there on this cushion. . . .
>
> Around a dozen little droplets of blood, more or less oblong, are noticeable on the wallpaper above the couch, as on the side of the chest of drawers that belongs with it. The marble top of the chest of drawers shows streaks of blood across its whole length.[22]

At once monstrous and monotonous, the crime scene report amasses a surfeit of evidence; its descriptive coverage of the bloodbath is as thorough as the spillage of blood itself. Yet the scene has been stripped of context and characterization, and the emotionless narrative eye neither speculates nor thinks. The exaggerated empiricism of Weil's crime report is divorced from the proceduralism of a police report, as well as from the expository logic of a detective story; whereas the latter genres strive to foreclose on the epistemological value of difference, unreason, and doubt, Weil's crime report instead multiplies this doubt through its very surfeit of evidence.

The report does not render the bloody room legible; rather it catalogues the impressions left by objects in the room in a way that isolates empirical detail from analysis and inductive reasoning. The elements of empirical reality may all be present, but their arrangement is not subject to logical reconstruction, nor does it obey the continuities of naturalist description; the details instead form a meticulous yet blindly taxonomic inventory. This primal scene of murder may know something, but it does not necessarily make any sense.

The narrator of "Au Clair de la lune" does, however, indulge in two acts of reconstruction. Less strokes of ratiocinatory logic than simple morphological connections, these interventions confirm evidence without addressing the dearth of information about the events that took place. The first is the narrator's search for "the instrument that must have caused the death: a fruitless search, since I found nothing; but a white wrapper I saw on the chest of drawers, and which the Commissioner told me they'd found the day before on the bed, held my attention." After describing the paper and its folds, the narrator is struck by the idea that the shape (le corps) preserved by the paper's folds may have been a box of razors. He then leaves to purchase a similar box, which indeed fits the paper exactly. Although it merely establishes the case's evidence, this intervention reenacts in miniature the mechanics of the article's depiction of the crime scene: the folds in the paper appear to have enclosed a body, in much the same way as the flecks and stains of blood around the room preserve the "shapes" of some kind of deadly struggle whose verifiable presence is no longer at hand. Fittingly, the narrator's further act of reconstruction involves replacing a cushion so that the bloodstains on the couch match up to their original position:

> Looking at the pillow, I notice that the bottom half of the side I found in contact with the cushion is bloody. Positioning this pillow in the place where it should naturally go, that is, along the base of the couch, I find that its lower part, which is heavily impregnated with blood, matches up exactly with the large coating of blood, which demonstrates to me that evidently the pillow was positioned this way during the action, and that, weighed down by a heavy body, it formed the obstacle that faced what the blood could pass through.[23]

In spite of its exhaustive catalogue of the room and the corpse lying dead within it, the paucity of narrative context renders this evidence evocative yet virtually illegible, resistant to hermeneutics. Whether the razor marks and tufts of hair among the bloodstains represent an act of self-mutilation, the drawn-out effects of torture, or some fantastic atrocity like the razor blows of Poe's Orangoutan, the text seems indifferent to all that lies beyond the immediate focus of description. Even the narrator's induction adds only a further degree of precision to the text's quasi-photographic documentation of how the room, its furniture, and the blood decorating it preserve the traces and impressions of the person who died and, presumably, lived within it. At the same time, though, the missing body preserved by the folds of paper poses the challenge of legibility to readers of the story: Are we, as readers, destined to become detectives?

The paucity of interpretation in Weil's text leaves the question of what its surfeit of evidence means in the context of an avant-garde magazine such as Littérature. Were this a straightforward police report, the lack of expository intervention by a fictional detective would, of course, be natural, since the faith of a Dupin, a Holmes, a Rouletabille, or a Poirot in the possibility of making evidence speak would be demanded of the reader's own powers of forensic analysis. Even so, the detail amassed and catalogued in "Au Clair de la lune" is presented in a false light, since in spite of the self-evidence of certain facts (the shapes and patterns of blood, for instance), there is little of the information necessary for solving the crime. As a proto-surrealist artifact published in Littérature, the report abandons any immediate forensic referent, any overt connection to a historically verifiable case. Instead it leans heavily for support on its literary and literal surroundings: its position in the magazine, as well as the peculiarities of its title, its dedication to Raymond Roussel, and the name of its author, Philippe Weil, who is otherwise unknown to Dada and proto-surrealist circles. These uncertainties in turn dramatize the efficacy of "Au Clair de la lune" as an apparatus for systematically reproducing the kinds of enigmas its locked room investigation refuses to solve.

The uncertainties about the status of Weil's text are further multiplied by its editorial context in the May 1922 issue of Littérature, to which it appeals for interpretive assistance. The article is flanked by two poems that play with the concept of the unknown. The mystery intimated in the title of Jacques Baron's poem "L'inconnu" (The Unknown), which immediately follows Weil's article, is compounded by the incognito of the poem that precedes Weil's piece. Introduced by an illegibly signed prefatory letter challenging readers to guess the poem's title and author, it compounds the uncertainties of Weil's text with its own riddle of authorship. At the same time, the poem itself, a formally conventional sonnet, intensifies the challenge posed by its anonymous (or illegible) sender with a salacious content that depicts a much different kind of aftermath from that of "Au Clair de la lune":

> Dark and wrinkled like a purple carnation
> It breathes, humbly crouched amidst the foam,
> Still moist with love, that trickles down the soft slope
> Of white buttocks to the verge of its rim.
>
> Thin streams like tears of milk
> Have been shed, against the cruel southern wind that drives them back,
> Across small clots of reddish marl,
> To go wherever the slope directs them

My dream often couples with its suction
My soul, jealous of more tangible coitus,
Makes it a musky tear pit and a nest of sobs.

It's the ecstatic palm and the tender flute,
The tube from which the heavenly praline descends

Womanly Canaan in sticky bloom.[24]

Readers familiar with Rimbaud's secret poetry may recognize this text as his "Idole: sonnet du trou du cul" (The Idol: Sonnet to an Asshole), which was coauthored with Paul Verlaine as part of the "Album Zutique" and only formally published in 1923. As a posthumous *trouvaille* describing the messy aftermath of a sexual "little death," in its flight of lyricism the poem lavishes so much attention on the minutiae of the body that it too becomes a sort of crime scene, though less for its celebration of the so-called crime of sodomy than for its exquisite accumulation of evidence. Moreover, when the poem is stripped of its celebrated (and celebratory) title, as it is in *Littérature*, its analogy to Weil's text becomes all the more prominent: it too fixates on the details of a scene whose actors, and whose conclusions, are left playfully indeterminate. This is not to mention that in Rimbaud's (titled) "Idole," the playfulness of this graphic love sonnet to an anus becomes instead a much more explicit fixation on the poetics of courtly love sonnets; the articulated body parts of the courtly love object are here parodied by the "inverted" sexuality of sodomy.

In its juxtaposition of Rimbaud's little death to Weil's depiction of the aftermath of a real death, the poem's position in *Littérature* suggests a deliberate editorial play whose author is almost certainly Philippe Soupault, who abandoned his editorial role shortly after this issue. The reappearance of "Au Clair de la lune" as an overheard fragment of a detective's conversation one year later, in 1923, in Soupault's novel *À la dérive* (Adrift) may not put to rest questions about the article's status as an artifact—whether it was actually written by Soupault, or whether is was an actual crime report appropriated by the author as a readymade—but it confirms the status of "Au Clair de la lune" as one of Soupault's "secret texts" which his novels adapt from earlier published writings.[25] More significantly, its publication next to Rimbaud's "secret" text, whose sonnet form rewards interpretation with its burlesque eroticism, exacerbates the resistance of Weil's text to hermeneutics. This pairing, we might say, confirms the function of the two texts as literary ephemera that take aim at the self-evidence of legible literary prose. It is worth stressing that while Rimbaud's poem, and Weil's identity, offer secrets to reveal, Weil's locked room description holds no such promise. The mortal blow of Weil's text, in other words, is less its generation of mystery than the mechanical surfeit of empirical detail its editorial framework appears to present as authorless.

The challenge to hermeneutics posed by such photographic prose is prefigured in Soupault's article on Raymond Roussel from the previous issue of *Littérature* in April 1922. In this piecemeal and rather difficult work of criticism, the systematically repeated patterns of blood in "Au Clair de la lune" are prefigured in the work of Roussel, whom Soupault celebrates as an essentially photographic writer. Like Breton in his essay on Max Ernst, Soupault identifies photography as a historical intervention, a technological form that changes the nature of both representation and, consequently, thought. Addressing how Roussel's poetry responds to a contemporary crisis in expression, Soupault explains that "to write, to describe [*écrire, décrire*], amounts to the same thing. Is it once again a question of arithmetic? You open a window upon some manuscript paper and they talk of dynamism. A likely story! And indeed, the others talk of skill, talent, and the subjunctive."[26] In opposition to the closed circuit of so-called modern writing as the work of an ordering consciousness privileging "skill, talent, and the subjunctive," Soupault cites a passage from Roussel's poem "La Vue" describing a kind of inscription that is not writing at all:

> Sight is kept inside a glass ball—
> Small but visible—that holds itself
> On high, near the tip of the white penholder
> Where red ink has left stains, as if in blood
> Sight is a very keen,
> Imperceptible photography.[27]

Though his poetry is itself attentive to minute empirical details, Roussel uses this descriptive language ironically, in order to celebrate its failures and limits. Like the accidental marks left behind by the poet's pen, the spattered blood marking the locked room in "Au Clair de la lune" can be understood as the residue of a kind of writing that is not itself legible as writing. Only in terms of photography, Roussel suggests, do such marks make sense, insofar as their relationship to meaning becomes indexical rather than hermeneutic, having more to do with evidence than with explanation. What this means, Soupault suggests, is that such writing can elude the pieties and constraints of "skill, talent, and the subjunctive."

In taking its cue from Roussel, surrealist writing could not only forestall the ideological closed circuit of literary production but also, more significantly, dislodge writing from the totalizing reach of an organizing consciousness. The solution photography offered to the modernist crisis in expression has been celebrated as a result of its power to "create the death of things and beings, if only for a second."[28] For Soupault, though, photography promised not so much to create the death of things as to create the death of authorship. Just as photography had the potential to counteract the legible, the meaningful, and the immediately comprehensible, writing could likewise be seen as but the residue of a mechanical function rather than the masterly exercise of talent or genius.

Roussel's role in shaping Soupault's understanding of photographic vision and writing is perhaps best illustrated by counterexample. In a 1929 essay eerily reminiscent of Soupault's earlier text, the novelist Pierre MacOrlan discusses an anonymous photograph of a bloody bed as a means for demonstrating photography's privileged access to what he calls "le fantastique sociale" (figure 1.2). Although the crime scene he discusses is, of course, a different one from the bloodbath in "Au Clair de la lune," MacOrlan is similarly interested in theorizing the apparatus of representation rather than in reconstructing the crime itself. Indeed he seems at first to share André Breton's "mortal" language in distinguishing photography from other forms of mimetic representation:

It is not a question here of an artist's interpretation of a fact; nor is it a question of an image that offers the equivalent of reality. It is simply a matter of the reality revealed by the provisional death of the very force that gives life to this scene of carnage. This death, this equally momentary immobility, reveals and permits the isolation of the unsettling ele-

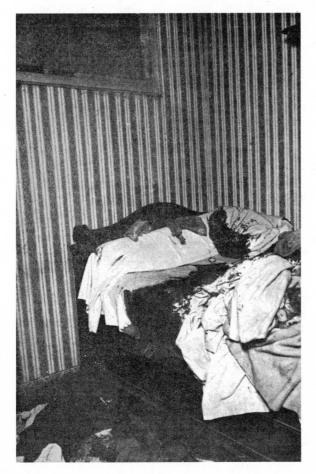

Fig. 1.2. Anonymous, illustration for Pierre MacOrlan's "Photographie: Eléments de Fantastique Social," *Le Crapouillot* (January 1929).

ment that gives this squalid and vulgar image an emotional power that acts upon the imagination, much more profoundly and much more clearly than the real sight of the room without an intermediary lens.

For MacOrlan, photographs are valuable to the modern consciousness because their "provisional death" preserves static moments that "fix the essential character" of objects and people. Photography augments rather than threatens our existing systems of representation, promising access to the "cerebral side of things," which, for MacOrlan, is composed of the "essential character of that which must constitute a fine disquiet, rich in forms, perfumes, disgust, and, naturally, in associations of ideas."[29] Though consistent with a Benjaminian understanding of photography as a preservation of "permanent and unmistakable traces," MacOrlan's analysis of the crime scene photograph differs markedly from Weil's proto-surrealist crime report in its faith in making such traces legible in a sensory, emotional, and instinctive way. Indeed his description of the bloody room furnishes the subjective emotions and affect missing from Soupault's "Au Clair de la lune":

Here, then, is a hotel room, a hotel whose four dimensions might please Francis Carco. The actors in the drama are no longer there. All that remains is the blood and all the variations of thought it inspires, from moral and physical disgust, to the detailed creation of appalling acts whose result leads us back to this simple, almost indescribable image, yet an image heavy with fear, thick with hot smells, and fraught with anxiety, once we take the trouble to think about it.[30]

MacOrlan's need to reconstruct this "nearly indescribable" quality already distinguishes his understanding of photography's "provisional death" from Soupault's: whereas for MacOrlan a photograph preserves and testifies, for Soupault photography simply accumulates. Unlike the snapshot, which allows, according to MacOrlan, a privileged access into the cerebral character of empirical reality, the photographic writing discussed by Soupault does little to intellectualize or even to comprehend the scene it represents. MacOrlan's description of how the photograph captures the blood is useful for distinguishing his emphasis on its testimonial value from the proto-surrealist use of photography to counteract the legible, the meaningful, the immediately comprehensible.

Like the photographic writing Soupault identifies in Roussel, the "photography" of Weil's description is more a mechanical reproduction of displaced evidence than a photography of information or orientation. The impact of photography on modern understanding, in other words, is a function of its automatism, its inutility rather than its scientific or commercial applicability. Discussing Roussel's fictional *Impressions of Africa* in his 1922 essay, Soupault explains that its episodes likewise "illustrate not a geographical map but a clockwork movement."[31] What he calls the "sensational machines" of Roussel's writing are photographic, he argues, in their intricacy of detail, yet they are as hermetic and obscure as a shop full of mechanical toys. Michel Foucault has similarly characterized Roussel's writings as

> the marvelous flying machine that . . . wants to say and to show forth only the extraordinary meticulousness of its construction; it signifies itself, in a self-sufficiency by which Roussel's positivism, which Michel Leiris loved to point out, was certainly enchanted. The apparatuses of *Locus Solus*, like the memorable flora of *Impressions d'Afrique*, are not *weapons* but . . . *machines*. They do not speak; they work serenely in a gestural circularity in which the silent glory of their automatism is affirmed.[32]

Roussel's writing can, in other words, be thought of as a system of machines insofar as its scrupulous description disguises, rather than constitutes, their method: its positivism is "enchanted" insofar as it is not a method but an air of method fleshing out what is otherwise a system of linguistic games.

This mechanically solipsistic quality in Roussel's work was significant to surrealism because the "silent glory" of its automatism posed a tacit yet distinctive threat to writing as we know it. As Soupault writes in the opening lines of his 1922 Roussel essay: "To find, as if by chance, the rules of the game, and to calculate without gaiety: does this permit a response to the mute interrogation of railway lines and navigation? This concern, this incredible worry that weighs upon our lives like the fear of an accident, the terror of a crowd-rush, is what I discover at every step in the *Impressions d'Afrique*."[33] Elaborating on the consequences of Breton's pronouncements about photography, Soupault's assessment of Roussel's photographic writing proposes a response to the modern conditions characterized by "the mute interrogation of railway lines."

Like photography itself, Roussel's ironic formalism, his "calculation without gaiety," makes possible a historical reflection on the systems that order mimetic representation, revealing, "as if by chance, the rules of the game." In the case of Roussel's *Impressions d'Afrique*, the lack of correspondence between sign ("Africa") and referent (the actual geographical site) is on full display: Roussel, who never once visited Africa, derived his "Impressions" from the formulaic myths and stereotypes of Africanness that had proliferated since the nineteenth century. The photographic prose of *Les Impressions d'Afrique* is a copy of these clichés, rather than a representation of any geographic or ethnographic reality. As Soupault asserts, Roussel's writing dismantles its mimetic function by basing its descriptions on the clichés of "accepted wisdom," themselves already far-fetched and ideologically suspect by-products of ethnographic and literary production.[34] The mechanical reproduction of traces, evidence, and stains, engineered through the kind of false positivism Soupault discusses in his essay and enacts in "Au Clair de la lune," is critical to early surrealist thought for its ability both to deploy and to suspend the ideologically invested tropes of realism. "Realism," however, referred no longer to the naturalized presumptions of self-evidence and continuity exercised by naturalism and positivism but rather to its material forms. Surrealism's task, in the movement's early years, would be to redeploy these forms in ways that would call attention to their epistemological function—their historical status as indices of the real—and yet suspend their totalizing function as guarantors of noumenal experience.

To Prevent an Idea from Taking Shape

Pierre Bayard, in his study of Agatha Christie's mystery novel *The Murder of Roger Ackroyd*, argues that the aim of a "whodunit" mystery is in fact "to prevent an idea from taking shape." He explains that "most literature tries to stimulate a certain idea or a certain group of images or sensations in the reader, but here we find ourselves in that original situation in which all the tension of the work is directed, through a detailed organization of invisibility, toward the prevention of thought."[35] Until the final moments of the story, such detective mysteries deliberately multiply possibilities, sleights of hand, false trails, and manufactured evidence. In the end, though, the interpretation involved in detective work represents the foreclosure of this prevented thought, a death sentence that replaces the whodunit's proliferation of doubt and difference with similarity and the semblance of reasonable truth.[36] By dismantling, even pathologizing, Hercule Poirot's solution of the mystery, Bayard advocates that the detective mystery be reevaluated as a thinking machine which, like psychoanalysis and other such interpretive systems, can be embraced for its ability to prevent ideas from taking shape. Its strength lies in its capacity for multiplying, rather than for artificially solving, difference and uncertainty.

Bayard's notion of forestalling certainty offers a useful means for approaching early surrealism's use of locked room mysteries in its formative practices of intellectual negation. As epistemological devices, such works of genre fiction advocated neither the destruction of ideas nor, for that matter, the idea of destruction but instead called for the delivery of a mortal blow to their tendency toward closure. Just as Roussel's sensational machines assassinate description with description, Soupault's "Au Clair de la lune" invokes the locked room apparatus of a detective mystery in order to assassinate the interpretive function of detection and the return to social order it promises.[37]

As I have suggested, the outmoded forms of thought and expression dismantled through such means remain present in surrealist writings and collages as the empty material traces of their ideological form. Imagine "Au Clair de la lune" as a series of snapshots. In both its systematic accumulation of evidence and its period detail and mode of dress, the article seems reminiscent of Alphonse Bertillon's *stéreométrique* crime scene photographs of the 1890s and early 1900s (figure 1.3). In addition to his more famous contributions to criminal identification and criminal anthropology—namely, the invention of the mug shot, the "spoken portrait," and the anthropometric measurement of individual bodily features—Bertillon also developed techniques for producing wide-angle photographs of interior crime scenes as well as bird's-eye views of corpses.[38] This other nineteenth-century invention made possible a formalization of evidence photographs that brought about, we might say, the entry into signification of previously unexamined and unsystematized objects and forms. This literal "preservation of human traces" contributed significantly to what Benjamin calls the era's "conquest of the incognito."[39] Beyond their identificatory significance, Bertillon's techniques were linked with the more proscriptive branches of criminal anthropology (like Cesare Lombroso's pseudoscientific measurement of criminals), whose logic the surrealist attacks on medico-legal practices would condemn. Yet as found objects in the early 1920s, *stéreométrique* photographs from the Bertillon era already preserved an excess of meaning beyond their forensic or anthropometric utility. Like Soupault's catalogue of the bloody room and its objects, Bertillon

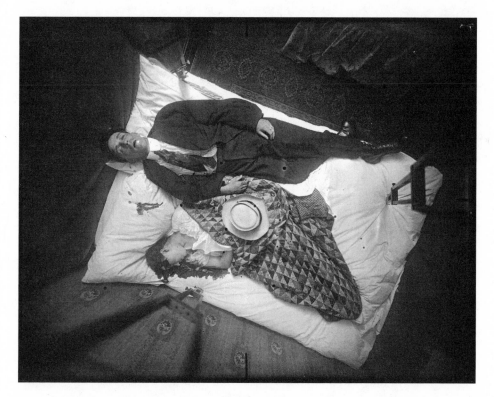

Fig. 1.3. Crime scene photograph using the Bertillon method, ca. 1914–1918. Image courtesy of the New York City Municipal Archives.

photographs are as remarkable for their presentation of lived-in petit-bourgeois interiors and nineteenth-century styles of dress—lived-in in the sense of their disarray and untidiness—as for their status as forensic evidence. Just as Weil's description of the mixture of urine and blood in the night basin reveals a rare and perhaps uncomfortable degree of intimacy, the Bertillon photographs suggest a similarly voyeuristic intrusion into a strictly private realm that has somehow been preserved through murder.

This is not to say, as MacOrlan does, that photography's "little death" allows the horror of a bloody scene to seem more real than the actual room. Instead it reveals that even the rigorously scientific application of photography bears an excess of chance detail and illegible, even insignificant traces of human existence that lie beyond its scope. This excess is what makes possible the "salutary estrangement between man and his surroundings" that Walter Benjamin lauds in later surrealist photography.[40] The preservation of photographic detail, like the historical genre of the locked room detective mystery, overwhelms the positivist faith of forensic science in the measurability—and thus the legibility—of all things. Life, the surrealists claimed, does not reside within these objects and marks. They cannot speak for this life; they can only be made to register its existence elsewhere.

A number of surrealist paintings from the 1920s appeal similarly to the "photographic" conventions of mystery fiction in order to stage Bayard's notion of the interdiction of completed thought as a visual effect. This is especially the case in the Fantômas paintings of Yves Tanguy (Fantômas, 1925) and René Magritte (L'Assassin menacé, 1926), in which the central presence of a nude murder victim supplants the erotic economy of classical nude painting with the narrative economy of murder fiction. Their iconography borrowed from the pages of cheap fiction and from the films of Louis Feuillade, these paintings exploit the exaggerated narrative conventions of the Fantômas serials, whose basic premise was the master villain's capacity for entering and escaping locked rooms and impossible situations. In both Tanguy's and Magritte's paintings, the figurative representation of crime scenes offers too much, rather than too little, evidence; their superabundance of visual detail, which recalls the false positivism of detective stories, works to suspend the visual conventions of artistic spectatorship.

Yves Tanguy's sprawling Fantômas (figure 1.4) centers on a naked corpse, who organizes and, to a certain extent, renders legible the actions and figures of the painting. The work recasts the serialized characters and events of the films and novels as elements of an oneiric landscape populated by an enigmatic collection of icons and spectral figures. Its pastiche method presents the serial's cast of recurring and minor characters simultaneously on a singular visual plane, juxtaposing easily recognizable motifs (corpses, detectives, Fantômas) with less legible forms. Whereas the pastiche elements of the composition—its exotic flora, its seven eggs, and its carnival characters—might lend it a dreamlike atmosphere of atemporality and symbolic condensation, the immediately leg-

Fig. 1.4. Yves Tanguy, *Fantômas* (1925). Private collection. Image courtesy of the Pierre Matisse Foundation, New York. © 2008 Estate of Yves Tanguy/Artists Rights Society (ARS), New York.

ible signs of violence resist the sense of reverie implicit in this atmosphere and restore the genre conventions of the Fantômas stories themselves.[41] In rendering the stories dreamlike, Tanguy's painting explores, we might say, the genre's unconscious—the extent to which its generic conventions mechanically serialized murders, investigations, and escapes as the necessary conditions of its existence.

Tanguy's early painting, completed soon after his encounter with the surrealist group, seems less concerned with rehearsing a particular Fantômas plot than with understanding how this plotting worked: like a game of chess, the characters, situations, and artifacts could be endlessly circulated, the drama and logic of each story unfolding through the relationships between each element. In this way Tanguy's painting dramatizes how these very patterns both expose and invert the ideology of naturalism; for it was the need to generate new plots that determined the social and even physical reality of the Fantômas stories rather than any belief that the laws of nature and society determined the interactions between characters and their physical environments. The painting's dialectic of legibility and obscurity, moreover, offers no resolution into a single, linear narrative but instead presents the raw materials of the Fantômas serials as an open field. The technological shift marked in Tanguy's crime landscape—the Fantômas serial's suspension of the laws of believability, linearity, and, most broadly, naturalism—is played out through the painting's carnivalesque proliferation of conceivable causes and effects, made possible by the interchangeable patterns of interaction between the figures surrounding the bleeding corpse.

René Magritte's 1926 painting *The Threatened Murderer* (figure 1.5) more concretely evokes surrealism's epistemological project. The painting transforms voyeurism into a complex puzzle of threatening demands addressed to the spectator. Unlike the tangled iconography of Tanguy's *Fantômas*, the figurative style of Magritte's painting is deceptively

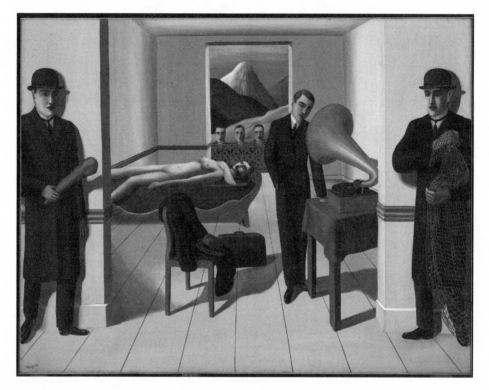

Fig. 1.5. René Magritte, *The Threatened Murderer* (*L'Assassin ménacé*) (1926). Oil on canvas, 59¼ inches × 64⅞ inches. Kay Sage Tanguy Fund. 247.1966. Image © 2008 The Museum of Modern Art/Licensed by SCALA/Art Resource, N.Y. © 2008 C. Herscovici, Brussels/Artists Rights Society (ARS), New York.

simple; yet here too the painting's voyeuristic economy resists resolution, in spite of its allusion to specific images from the Fantômas films. In Magritte's well-known painting the blank gazes of the male figures surrounding the female corpse at the center of the canvas demand an investigation into the unspoken meanings of these gazes: Does their lack of affect suggest complicity, an erasure of the distinction between murderer and policeman, criminal and viewer? The blank looks of the figures surrounding the corpse, whose gazes penetrate the fully exposed (and thus no longer locked) bedchamber, never fall comfortably back on the plot devices of the films' serial narratives (in which Fantômas, the gentlemanly "genius of crime," inevitably, impossibly, escapes).[42] The scene's disorienting lack of affect erases the figural signs that might make it more immediately legible, inhabitable by the spectator.

The details at the crime scene likewise offer little confirmation; even the murder wound is obscured, concealed by a handkerchief draped loosely across the victim's neck. There is little more than the trace of blood at the corner of the corpse's mouth to provide visual evidence of the violence that has taken place, thereby distinguishing the murder victim from a reclining nude. Magritte's scene solicits interpretation, yet the painting frustrates any singular resolution that might derive from its internal evidence. The bleeding corpse and interrogatory gazes of the police clearly demarcate a crime scene, yet Magritte renders it all blank, dimensionless. The demands of interrogation and pursuit, however, remain in play. That is, the generic conventions advertised in the painting's titular and formal allusions to crime fiction and film appeal to the need to solve the mystery. These demands are imposed on the viewer. It is not the murderer Fantômas, in other words, who is trapped by the gazes of the police who surround him but the painting's spectators. Dalia Judovitz has convincingly described this effect, writing that *The Threatened Murderer*

> stages the structure of voyeurism as a gendered gaze, since the ambiguous "assassin" and/or "policeman" in the foreground is conflated with the gaze of the viewer. This painting represents the fragmentation of pictorial perspectives or point of view through the multiplication of figures of assassins, policemen, and/or witnesses within its frame. The two "assassins/policemen" in the foreground are conflated in the figure of the man listening to the gramophone, as witnessed by three men in the background, surveying the scene from behind the balcony. The three figures look at the viewer looking. The painting sets into motion a delirium of vision, a variety of male spectators—potential assassins and policemen, organized around the spread-eagled nude. Magritte's painting, like [Marcel] Duchamp's *Given*, stages both the transgressive (assassin) and the rationalizing (policing) dimensions of the spectator's gaze.[43]

Frozen in time, presumably, at the moment before the killer's (or the policeman's) apprehension, the scene's dramatic narrative is rendered ambiguous by the delirium of vision Judovitz describes. The uncanny absence of motive or emotion in the painting only exacerbates this ambiguity: What, precisely, is being apprehended? Is there any self-consciousness, any awareness made available in the painting? Blankly multiplying the gazes of the policemen rather than appealing to their photographic capacity for surveillance, Magritte's puzzle both appeals to and yet renders useless the genre conventions of positivist investigation, which would promise a reconstruction of the murder's cause and motive from the evidence at the crime scene.

Magritte's delirium of vision, in other words, has a function. In situating itself within the familiar territory of the detective genre, the painting serves as a mechanism for superseding the legacy of positivism in visual art. Like Marcel Duchamp's readymades, Magritte's crime scene functions as a mechanism for making explicit the visual conventions that structure the way spectators view the aesthetic "content" of art. *The Threatened Murder* makes concrete, yet refuses to satisfy, the male gaze presupposed by traditional aesthetics, as well, more broadly, as the lingering positivist faith in visual representation as a guarantee of meaning. What Judovitz calls the trap of Magritte's painting hinges on the dialectical interplay between looking and insight, the two forms of visual engagement it solicits; the painting dramatizes at once the transgressive gaze of voyeurism (in which the detectives themselves participate) and the *mise-en-abyme* of investigation (in which, perversely, the Fantômas figure also participates, as he stares, in a moment of catachresis, contemplatively into the dark void of the gramophone speaker). By satisfying neither voyeurism nor the desire to render all things legible, *The Threatened Murder* derails the ideological closure demanded by the very ways of seeing it solicits.

The Mystery of the Yellow Room

The surrealists derived a similar conclusion from their reading of Gaston Leroux's popular detective novel from 1908, *The Mystery of the Yellow Room*. The group appealed to the novel for its suggestion that the manufactured evidence and false trails Bayard wished to multiply were already at work in the book's ironic relationship to the formulae of detective fiction. Soupault invokes Leroux's fiction in his discussion of Raymond Roussel, claiming that they share a similar irony in their tendency to "reveal, as if by chance, the rules of the game."[44] This irony, Soupault explains, permits the transformation of positivist description into a kind of killing machine, as is especially the case in *The Mystery of the Yellow Room*, whose spatial and textual play featured strongly in the surrealist imaginary around the time of Breton's *Manifesto*. Indeed, Leroux's *Mystery of the Yellow Room* provides a powerful counterpoint to Dostoyevsky's yellow room from *Crime and Punishment*, insofar as its self-conscious exaggeration of the locked room mystery formula exposes and parodies its own manufactured logic.

The Mystery of the Yellow Room, like Leroux's other detective novels, centers on a hermetically locked room in which the presence of a corpse does not so much interrupt the sanctity of life as establish the story's conditions for existence. The detective novel's premise presumably involves deploying the logic of detection to solve the mystery of who committed the murder, and thereby to return the novel's disrupted innocence to a kind of social order. In Leroux's novel, however, this imposition of logic is as mechanical, and indeed as solipsistic, as the "sensational machines" of Roussel's photographic writing. A function of the narrative's march toward closure, this logic performs a purely formal exercise of investigation. The result is an apparatus for the enactment of Bayard's formulation: a model for inhabiting a genre characterized, in Paul Éluard's words, by the "science of details" without succumbing to its presumptions about causality and meaning.[45]

In *The Mystery of the Yellow Room* a young woman named Mlle Stangerson has been attacked in her bedroom by an unknown assailant. Her room is locked from the inside, yet her rescuers, upon breaking into the crime scene to recover her wounded body, find no trace of the aggressor. Hovering near death during the early part of the story, Mlle Stangerson eventually recovers from her injuries. Thanks to the efforts of the intrepid young reporter Rouletabille, however, the assailant in Stangerson's room is discovered to be none other than the detective, Larsan, hired to investigate the crime. Far more interesting than the story's logical progression is its staging of the relations between its major characters as a narrowly averted Oedipal tragedy. The relations of desire between the male detective Larsan, the boy Rouletabille (like Oedipus, a foundling), and the woman whose ersatz "murder" they investigate are as tortuous as those of the classic Oedipal triangle. Its mythic traces constitute both the story's drama and the solution to its mystery: Larsan was, it turns out, secretly married to Mlle Stangerson, and it is he who turns out to have been her attacker. And the story leaves little room for doubt that the couple—the older, rival detective and his victim—are Rouletabille's lost parents, an insinuation fueled by the novel's proliferation of sons and father figures.

The principal character, though, is the yellow room itself, whose metaphorical embodiment as a gendered space, even as a kind of private female organ, transforms the novel's hypothetical murder into a violent parable of sexual penetration. The room, Leroux insists, is impenetrably locked from within, and yet somehow a man has slipped in and out without notice. Leroux depicts the violent yet non-mortal assault upon Mlle Stangerson as a kind of rape, an "abominable crime" against which she defends herself nearly to the death.[46] Yet by the novel's close, both the murder and the violation—if not the corporeal imagery—have been happily spirited away as incidental effects of the yellow room itself. Mlle Stangerson's near-mortal head wound was accidental—she fell and hit her head on the furniture while struggling with Larsan—and the bloodstains were in fact Larsan's, caused by a gunshot wound she inflicted by firing at him. The result is that the solution to the novel's mystery reduces the seemingly impossible puzzle to a relatively plausible set of circumstances. This closure accomplishes several goals, the first of which is to guarantee Leroux's claim that the locked room was truly locked. And indeed it was: Mlle Stangerson let her assailant in, since he was, after all, legally her husband, a dread secret emerging from her past. The second goal is to disarm the violence of the rape/murder and to stave off the inevitable Oedipal recognition at the heart of Rouletabille's investigation, given that Mlle Stangerson's perfume reminds Rouletabille of his lost mother's perfume. With the yellow room as its pretext, the tragedy of the novel's opening is happily returned to the more rational form of the family romance.

More significantly, in the same way that this innocence and social order are both mythical and sentimental, so too are Leroux's mechanisms of murder and detection provisional and contrived.[47] When André Breton emptied Dostoyevsky's yellow room of its mystery, he retained its furnishings and walls to indicate the ideological shape—or, in Benjaminian terms, the trace—of naturalism's positivist logic. By contrast, Leroux's yellow room, despite its formulaic show of ratiocination, already recognizes the provisional and purely functional quality of this logic, insofar as all the narrator's talk about logical method serves merely as a ruse for exposing the nexus of social relations that find their symbolic articulation in the mechanics of the locked room. Leroux's detective mystery appealed to the surrealists for its suggestion that the novel's mechanics were designed to manufacture evidence and false trails as forms of literary experience which the locked room apparatus set in play.

Such false trails, moreover, were already represented within the novel as a tangible linguistic trace. The sentence "The presbytery has lost nothing of its charm, nor the garden its brightness," which Rouletabille finds scribbled on a half-burned piece of paper, produces startling effects on the characters to whom he repeats the line.[48] Rouletabille does not know what the phrase means, but he is aware of its value as evidence, as well as its significance as the remainder of some kind of suppressed writing. Although the words never cease to function as a piece of evidence that contributes to the mystery's solution, their effects on other characters—shock, terror, surprise—give the boy reporter unexpected authority, as if the phrase were a kind of private code giving its bearer special access to the secrets of the novel's protagonists. The phrase itself is virtually meaningless except insofar as it refers to a place and time that predate the novel's actions. Less a riddle than a traumatic historical remainder (a half-burnt scrap blackmailing Mlle Stangerson about her past), the message becomes a kind of symptom, a reminder of the intractability of evidence itself. Its effects incommensurate with the eventual rationalization of its relevance to the case, the burnt scrap of paper and, by extension, the words it contains represent "enslaved and enslaving objects" of the mystery story's formal structure that nevertheless resist its normalizing tendency to repress its own ideological preconditions.[49]

As Maxime Alexander writes in his *Mémoires d'un surréaliste*, the surrealist group was fascinated by the way in which Rouletabille "is guided throughout by a combination of words that, for him, take the place of a pole star (and in 1924 the founders of the surrealist movement pasted them upon the walls of Paris)."[50] Indeed, one of the tasks undertaken by the surrealists as part of the group's activities at the Surrealist Research Bureau in 1924–25 was the printing and distribution of a collection of brightly colored fliers that made their way across Paris (figure 1.6). Reborn as a surrealist flier (*papillon*—literally, a butterfly), Rouletabille's phrase was removed from its narrative confines so that it could instead fly freely around Paris. Yet why was this phrase singled out by the group as one of its allegedly revolutionary slogans? The purpose of surrealist "research" in 1924 was hardly to incite reaction through the circulation of clever literary references. Rather, the phrase from *The Yellow Room*, and the *papillons* more generally, contributed to what might be called a surrealist theory of exteriority. Like the false trails and manufactured evidence Bayard advocates as means for preventing an idea from taking shape, the phrase similarly constitutes

JOIE ÉNORME COMME LES COUILLES D'HERCULE !
15, rue de Grenelle, Paris-7e

Le Surréalisme est à la portée de tous les inconscients
On le trouve au ...eau de Recherches Surréalistes, 15, rue de Grenelle, de 4 h. ½ à 6 h. ½

LE SURREALISME EST-IL LE COMMUNISME DU GÉNIE ?
Bureau de recherches surréalistes 15, rue de Grenelle, de 4 h. ½ à 6 h. ½

Vous qui avez du plomb dans la tête fondez-le pour en faire de l'or surréaliste
15, rue de Grenelle, Paris-7e

Si vous aimez l'Amour vous aimerez le Surréalisme
15, rue de Grenelle, Paris-7e

Ouvrez la bouche comme un four, . il en sortira des noisettes.
15, rue de Grenelle, Paris-7e

VOUS QUI NE VOYEZ PAS pensez à ceux qui voient
15, rue de Grenelle, Paris-7e

Le presbytère n'a rien perdu de son charme ni le jardin de son éclat
15, rue de Grenelle, Paris-7e

Le parapluie du chocolat est déloré. Trempez-le dans la porte et nallez
Bureau de recherches Surréalistes, 15, rue de Grenelle, de 4 h. ½ à 6 h. ½

SURRÉALISME : n. m. Automatisme psychique pur par lequel on se propose d'exprimer soit verbalement, soit par écrit, soit de toute autre manière, le fonctionnement réel de la pensée. Dictée de la pensée, en l'absence de tout contrôle exercé par la raison, en dehors de toute préoccupation esthétique ou morale.
Au Bureau de Recherches Surréalistes, 15, rue de Grenelle, Paris, de 4 h. ½ à 6 h. ½

On ne saurait rien attendre de trop grand de la force et du pouvoir de l'esprit. HEGEL.
15, rue de Grenelle, Paris-7e

APRÈS DES TENTATIVES RÉITÉRÉES POUR SAISIR L'IDÉE DE TRIANGLE, J'AI CONSTATÉ QU'ELLE ÉTAIT TOUT A FAIT INCOMPRÉHENSIBLE. BERKELEY.
Bureau de recherches Surréalistes, 15, rue de Grenelle, de 4 h. ½ à 6 h. ½

LE SURRÉALISME c'est l'écriture niée
Bureau de recherches, 15, rue de Grenelle, 15 de 4 h. ½ à 6 h. ½

PARENTS ! racontez vos rêves à vos enfants
15, rue de Grenelle, Paris-7e

Ariane ma sœur ! de quel amour blessée Vous mourûtes aux bords où vous fûtes laissée ?
15, rue de Grenelle, Paris-7e

Fig. 1.6. Collection of fifteen surrealist *papillons* (1924–25).

a resistant scrap of epistemological residue within the locked room mystery itself. By pasting this phrase at random on the walls of Paris, the surrealists attempted to integrate this little piece of resistance into the public space of everyday urban life. Even the passerby who recognized the allusion to Leroux's novel would only be reminded of the strange and uncanny effects the phrase produces within the text, a symptom of its illegible excess of meaning. The significance of the surrealist *papillons* lay in their playful multiplication of, rather than solutions to, difference and uncertainty.

Breton indicates this direction for surrealist practice as early as 1920, in his definition of Dada's erasure of the "belief in absolute space and time" in his article on Max Ernst. What holds Dada's attention, he writes, is "the marvelous ability to reach out, without leaving the field of our experience, to two distinct realities and bring them together to create a spark . . . and, by removing our systems of reference, to disorient us within our own memories."[51] Although this definition of Parisian Dada, which Breton later appropriated for surrealism, has often been read (including by Ernst himself) as a description of Ernst's collage technique, Breton's words offer a much broader theory of surrealist knowledge as a kind of encounter. The surrealist *papillons* were designed to serve as the indelible residue of this encounter, the material form of surrealism's imaginary transformation of the walls of Paris into the spaces for similar encounters. Indeed, in Leroux's novel Rouletabille can look to his magic phrase as a "polestar" because it suggests—even to him—that the truth of the locked room mystery was fictitious, or at least constructed.

The surrealist slogans aim likewise to reinscribe the inchoate "realm of our experience" as an intersubjective and textually overdetermined framework; yet rather than providing the means to ensure its logical, ordered resolution, the slogans are distributed with an aim to "deprive us of a frame of reference" in order to recast knowledge as what Maurice Blanchot has called a communication with the unknown. This unknown referred neither to the unknowable nor to the transcendental reality of the noumenon, but rather to the point at which interpretive systems break down—the limits of understanding. That is, extending the surrealist assassination of unitary logic and its ideological confines into the realm of the everyday, the activities of the Surrealist Research Bureau attempted to apply this mortal blow as a form of communication that would actually prevent any singular, unitary idea from taking shape. As Blanchot writes:

> From the unknown—what is neither the pure unknowable nor the not yet known—comes a relation that is indirect, a network of relations that never allows itself to be expressed unitarily. Whether it be called the marvelous, the surreal, or something else (that which, in any case, disavows transcendence as well as immanence), the unknown provokes . . . a non-simultaneous set of forces, a space of difference and, to speak like the first surrealist work, a *magnetic field* always free of the itinerary it calls forth, embodies, and nonetheless holds in reserve.[52]

This communication was not subjective, as Blanchot explains, but a function of what Breton calls the "disinterested play of thought." That is, it signified a dialectical recognition of the extent to which understanding occurs outside or beyond individual consciousness.

Toward the end of the *Manifesto of Surrealism*, Breton offers his most playfully literal interpretation of the kind of exteriority Blanchot describes. The best way out of positivism's locked room of circumscribed ambition, he suggests, is simply to open doors at random.

In a way that recalls the power of Rouletabille's phrase to gain him access to and egress from the crime scene, Breton cites a short story by G. K. Chesterton as a counternarrative to the banality of Dostoyevsky's yellow room with which he begins the *Manifesto*. As he writes in a footnote to his discussion of surrealist action: "Someone told me they had read in a book by Chesterton about a detective who, in order to find someone he is looking for in a certain city, simply scoured from roof to cellar the houses which, from the outside, seemed somehow abnormal to him, were it only in some slight detail. This system is as good as any other."[53] The system is as good as any other because it works. Indeed the passage to which Breton refers, from Chesterton's earliest Father Brown mystery, "The Blue Cross" (1911), reads remarkably like a section from the surrealist *Manifesto*. Describing the investigative tactics of the great detective Aristide Valentin, the passage describes a deliberate abandonment of the logical apparatus of the locked room mystery in favor of a system of chance encounters, which Chesterton's narrator defends with an almost Bretonian rigor. Chesterton writes:

In such cases [Valentin] reckoned on the unforeseen. In such cases, when he could not follow the train of the reasonable, he coldly and carefully followed the train of the unreasonable. Instead of going to the right places—banks, police stations, rendezvous—he systematically went to the wrong places; knocked at every empty house, turned down every *cul de sac*, went up every lane blocked with rubbish, went round every crescent that led him uselessly out of the way. He defended this crazy course quite logically. He said that if one had a clue this was the worst way; but if one had no clue at all it was the best, because there was just the chance that any oddity that caught the eye of the pursuer might be the same that had caught the eye of the pursued. Somewhere a man must begin, and it had better be just where another man might stop.

Chesterton's detective story thus adds a further dimension to the polestar of Rouletabille's discovered phrase in that it describes an entire system, even a cosmology, for generating chance. Co-opted as a reference point for surrealism's own practices, what Chesterton calls "the element of elfin coincidence" describes a poetic capacity within reality that "people reckoning on the prosaic may perpetually miss."[54] Chesterton's account of the detective's wisdom accommodates the phenomena that elude rational systems for determining causality; what seems to have been especially appealing to Breton about this wisdom is its systematic quality. More than a glorification of random chance alone, this method registers the symptoms of both the elsewhere or unknown that would likewise form the basis of surrealist epistemology, as well as its antithetical relationship to the rationalism that sought to suppress it or render it absurd.

Breton cites Chesterton's literary example as both a clarification and a means for demonstrating its application in the real. As Breton writes, Soupault too had explored such ways of instigating a "conversation with the unknown" through a similarly decided strategy of random strikes. Breton continues: "Similarly, in 1919 Soupault went into any number of impossible buildings to ask the concierge whether Philippe Soupault did in fact live there. He would not have been surprised, I suspect, by an affirmative reply. He would have gone and knocked on his door."[55] The results of this investigation are irrelevant, except insofar as they produce the opportunities that create an environment whereby, in Walter Benjamin's words, "every square inch of our cities" is a crime scene and "every passer-by a culprit."[56] This, in fact, was how Soupault resolved his own locked room description when he reprinted it as part of his novel Â la dérive in 1923. In the early part of the novel, David, Soupault's protagonist, happens upon a conversation between two detectives describing what one of them refers to as a "fireworks explosion of blood."[57] The conversation David overhears involves the minutiae of the crime scene, the republished text of Philippe Weil's article "Au Clair de la lune." David overhears the locked room description completely by chance, and it is by subjecting himself to this chance in the spirit of the novel's titular appeal to drifting (à la dérive) that he inserts himself into a series of random encounters by which, again by chance, he helps capture the murderer. Here too David discovers the killer's identity through an overheard revelation rather than through any examination of clues or any insight into the truth. David is never more than an aural version of Benjamin's ocular and photographic flâneur, never becoming fully interested in the murder, or its significance, even as he helps capture the killer. Cathected into the bloody drama as an itinerant yet curious eavesdropper, Soupault's protagonist resolves the case—in a manner entirely lacking closure or satisfaction—by means of his participation in this infinite conversation.

CHAPTER TWO

ON MURDER, CONSIDERED AS
ONE OF THE SURREALIST ARTS

There is a surrealist light: . . . the light of flashlights on murder victims and on love.

Louis Aragon, "A Wave of Dreams" (1924)

The comte de Lautréamont's phrase "as beautiful . . . as the chance encounter of a sewing machine and an umbrella on a dissecting table" has been memorialized not only as the starting point for surrealist experiments with language but also as a recurrent motif through which the group articulated its developing aesthetic theories. The phrase belongs to one of several litanies of "beautiful as" similes used in Lautréamont's 1869 symbolist work *Les Chants de Maldoror*; the phrase cited here describes Merwyn, the youthful protagonist of the book's sixth canto, who is abducted by the villainous Maldoror and, in the final pages of the text, flung by force across Paris and impaled atop the dome of the Panthéon.[1]

Isolated from its narrative context, the fragment exemplifies the formal techniques of early surrealist poetry and art—its experiments with collage and collage-poetry as well as its broader interest in the mechanisms of condensation and displacement in Freudian dream-work. In this sense the sewing machine and umbrella represent seemingly incompatible objects reassembled to form a surprising new image. In the context of Lautréamont's *Chants de Maldoror*, though, the simile represents less a celebration of poetic method than the textual form of Maldoror's rapacious gaze. The villain's "chance encounter" with his youthful victim registers both his aesthetic judgment and his identification of a criminal target. We are seeing Merwyn's beauty, in other words, through the eyes of a murderer. The violence of this encounter likewise inflects the surrealist appropriation of Lautréamont's phrase in ways that gesture toward the movement's later political activism and internal climate of debate.

Man Ray's playfully literal depiction of the simile in *The Enigma of Isodore Ducasse* (figure 2.1) documents the surrealist adaptation of the image, suggesting how the movement transformed Lautréamont's image into a mechanism for anatomizing aesthetic relations of judgment, authorship, and affect.[2] The photograph, which depicts an assemblage of objects covered by a heavy blanket and bound with cords, was composed in 1920 but first published, without a title, in the inaugural issue of *Révolution Surréaliste* in 1924.[3] In the image, the cords securing the blanket only begin to indicate the contours of the concealed objects—an umbrella, a sewing machine—that lie beneath, obscuring the very allusion the photograph depicts. Read allegorically, the photograph might be said to proclaim the emergence of surrealism itself, the photograph's taut cords suggesting an imminent revelation kept barely under wraps. At the same time, the image also stages *Maldoror's* "chance encounter" as an allusion to Isodore Ducasse's veiled authorial persona as the "comte de Lautréamont," whose fugitive presence in literary history has left behind only the legacy of his poetic work as its historical remainder. Indeed his mysterious identity— he died, young and unknown, in 1870, leaving little evidence of his life or appearance— compounded his interest for the early surrealists as a figure whose life was utterly subsumed by his intellectual activities.

Read as an interpretation of Lautréamont's phrase itself, Man Ray's photograph poses the "beautiful as . . ." simile as an enigma in order to interrogate its aesthetic claims: what could possibly be beautiful about this encounter between the physical objects discernible beneath the blanket? This question, I propose, is at the heart of the surrealist appropriation of Lautréamont's phrase. The "beautiful as . . ." simile was instrumental to theorizing the movement's aesthetic practices insofar as it demanded that aesthetic judgment be considered inextricable from the questions of how, and to what end, aesthetic judgment functioned. Rather than merely branding as "surrealist" certain formal techniques that had previously belonged to Dada (the use of shocking imagery, automatic writing, collage), Lautréamont's rendering of beauty as a formula would be central to the surrealist movement's self-consciousness. In the eyes of the surrealists, Lautréamont's phrase demanded that beauty no longer be considered a transcendental judgment of taste, but instead as a configuration of aesthetic relations, a "chance encounter" that positioned the artist and the work of art within a temporal and social context. Lautréamont's simile, in other words, could be inverted: "beauty" could be reinvented as the term that described the modalities of the encounter between disparate objects. To judge an object "beautiful" was both to interrogate the field of relations such a judgment rendered concrete and to nominate this field of relations as the primary object for judgment. The surrealist movement's use of Lautréamont's simile as an aesthetic formula thus rendered any "beautiful as . . ." judgment suspect, subject to interrogation. But how did the surrealists respond to situations in which the object of interrogation was not simply an anomalous sequence of object relations but a historical event or an actual act of violence?

In this chapter I examine how the surrealist group developed this instrumental use of aesthetics as a critical apparatus by studying how its writers approached the problem of aestheticizing violence. Focusing on the period in the early 1920s during which the proto-surrealist group that was affiliated with the magazine *Littérature* began to distinguish itself

Fig. 2.1. Man Ray, *The Enigma of Isodore Ducasse* (1920, remade 1972). Sewing machine, wool, and string. Object 35.5 × 60.5 × 33.5 cm. Purchased 2003 Tate Gallery, London, Great Britain. Image © 2008 Tate Gallery, London/Art Resource, N.Y. © 2008 Man Ray Trust/Artists Rights Society (ARS), New York/ ADAGP, Paris.

from Parisian Dada, I look at the way the movement dealt with actual murder cases as represented in newspapers and literary texts. The group's aesthetic self-consciousness, I argue, recognized murder as a form of cultural production that generated corpses, nominated murderers, and ideologically charged the discursive and specular realm surrounding it. Rather than projecting a fixed set of formal aesthetic principles upon the social world, surrealism's aesthetic judgments were proprioceptive; under the aegis of aesthetics, they brought about a scrutiny and analysis of this discursive and specular realm of social relations that extended to contemporary politics. As I demonstrate, the group's "aesthetic" treatment of murder and assassination generated an image of surrealism's ethical and political imperative in a way that would fuel the movement's subsequent political activism.

This chapter illustrates how the group's transition from a rebellious faction within Parisian Dada to a surrealist collective hinged on disagreements over the role of murder in the surrealist imagination, especially in differentiating the aesthetic treatment of crime from an aestheticization of crime itself. I first discuss Benjamin Péret's Dadaist invocation of aesthetic judgment to write about a recent criminal case whose horrific violence the popular media had all but ignored. Recalling Thomas De Quincey's "On Murder, Considered as One of the Fine Arts," Péret's essay prefigures the surrealist group's later political writings in its ironic adoption of an impossibly disinterested critical voice to censure the popular media for their lack of interest in the crime.

I then turn to the role of Lautréamont's violent work of experimental writing, Les Chants de Maldoror, in the somnambulistic trances introduced to the surrealist group by René Crevel in 1922. The presence of murder stories in the midst of the surrealists' early post-Dada experiments caused a scandal that provoked the group to revise its initial, primarily literary rebellion against Dada as a more ethically charged aesthetic project. This scandal challenged the group's understanding of the unconscious and the status of its amoral, egoistic desires once they become integrated as conscious elements of artistic production.

Subsequent chapters address how surrealism's increasingly politicized conception of itself would likewise be rooted in the use of aesthetic judgment as a device for analyzing murder. The movement's ever-developing ethical and political imperatives, shaped considerably by its interpretations of symbolist and Dada writings, would continue to intensify as the surrealists increased their attention to the contemporary social and political world. Indeed, Louis Aragon's essay "A Wave of Dreams," published in November 1924, memorializes the "periode des sommeils" (period of sleeping fits) in a way that shifted the terms from André Breton's mystical and aesthetic plumbing of the unconscious toward a more socially engaged experience of their new discoveries as "real phenomena" to be experienced concretely.[4]

The Crime of Versailles

In February 1920, while the French public remained fixated on the restoration of order in western Europe, Benjamin Péret took notice of a murder case that the national press seemed largely to overlook. But the tabloid newspaper Le Petit Parisien, which Péret read avidly, covered the unfolding story of what it called the "Crime of Versailles" with a tenacity that showed its efforts to raise the visibility of the incident in the face of the national events that overshadowed it.[5] Not far away from the site at which the Treaty of Versailles had been signed, and only a few weeks after it had taken effect, the mutilated body of a six-year-old girl named Rolande Leprieux was found hidden in her neighbor's house. For the writers of Le Petit Parisien, the murderer was a "vampire" whose "atrocious crime" had left the city of Versailles "in turmoil."[6] The newspaper stressed the bizarre violence of the murder, highlighting its shocking details with a combination of sensationalism and moral outrage typical of its crime reportage. Péret's Dadaist coverage of the case would invert this judgment. In an article written later that year in Littérature, Péret comments instead on the ordinariness of the crime.

Given the historical and geographical proximity to the Treaty of Versailles, it might be tempting to read Péret's claim of ordinariness as a commentary on the capacity of the so-called Great War for rendering mutilation and death practically commonplace; but Peret's report targets instead the aesthetics of the popular media, especially their tendency to conflate disinterestedness with a lack of interest, and of interest with sensationalism. For Péret, the "Crime of Versailles" was "ordinary" for its stark contrast to the sensational recent case of Henri Landru, who had been dubbed the "Bluebeard of Gambais" because of the charge that he had serially murdered an as yet unknown number of his mistresses.[7] Whereas the Landru case was notable for its almost total lack of evidence, the Versailles crime spilled forth increasingly gruesome details: the little girl, who had been missing for several days, had been raped, strangled, and cut into fifty-five pieces. The prime suspect, a mechanic named Marcel Pénisson, was incontrovertibly guilty, inculpated by physical evidence as well as by his wife's testimony; yet he firmly and repeatedly denied his involvement. And although this denial tactic would work brilliantly for Landru, keeping his case open and subject to intense speculation even after his execution in 1922, it only made the Pénisson crime seem all the more revolting and painful.

"A few months ago," Péret writes, "a gentleman, struck by a laudable ambition, wanted to make for himself a reputation 'à la Landru.'" With these words Péret begins one of the more chilling articles in surrealist and proto-surrealist writing, a Dada *fait-divers* titled "Assassiner" (To Murder). What is especially disturbing about Péret's article is that rather than adopting the moralistic language of back page stories in tabloids such as *Le Petit Parisien*, it affects the cavalier detachment of contemporary art criticism. Péret continues:

> Alas, all he succeeded in was the rape of a little ten-year-old girl whom he then cut into fifty-five pieces. (Had he only done the inverse!) After which, without a doubt satisfied as to the banality of his actions, he let himself be imprisoned like a vulgar and inept beginner. We would have liked to see this gentleman deploy some imagination in his act. To obey a sexual instinct and surrender to his desires upon a little girl has nothing in it that merits special attention; but the fact of cutting the child into fifty-five pieces permits a hypothesis about the wish to separate himself from the dark satyr who deliberately rapes children of a young age. If the girl's pieces had been received under the rubric "confectionery" by some outstanding personality (monsieur de Lamarzelle, for example), what wouldn't our admiration be for such a gesture!!!! This gentleman, calling himself the Cardinal Amette, would then have seemed the fraternal twin of the Colossus of Rhodes.

Péret's "Assassiner," published in *Littérature* at the height of the journal's affiliation with Parisian Dada, maintains a startling disinterestedness toward the gruesome sexual crime it describes. The article substitutes a searing critique of the murderer's modus operandi for any moral judgment of the crime that might have acknowledged feelings of horror, sympathy, or outrage. As if exaggerating the Dada movement's tactics of cultural negation, the article's allusion to and praise for Henri Landru seems to suggest an unvarnished endorsement of serial murder. "How," Péret continues, "could we possibly speak of Landru other than in an admiring way!"[8] Marcel Pénisson, Péret's "gentleman," merely tried to deny the overwhelming evidence that inculpated him. The Landru case, by contrast, was remarkable for its multiplication of pure speculation, relying on the traces of thought and the babble of popular speech rather than any real evidence.[9] Whereas Péret's account of the "Crime of Versailles" condemns the crime at hand, he nevertheless seems to maintain an admiration for murders of a certain distinction in which "some imagination" (quelque fantaisie) was deployed.

What does Péret mean here by "imagination?" It seems clear that he is interested in something other than the killer's powers of creativity. The focus in "Assassiner" on the murderer's paltry creative labor—whether a lapse in "ambition," subversive intention, or sublimation—condemns the absence of qualities that might have distinguished Pénisson's crime from a mere capitulation to sexual and murderous instincts. Péret argues that the rapist-murderer's "surrender" to dark instincts, like his surrender to the police, is worthy of scorn precisely because it fails to chart any new aesthetic territory: in spite of its hint of "ambition," the crime reproduces base, animal drives, and is thus as common as "two rhinoceroses who kill each other for the possession of the same female," and is "as far from curious as making babies."[10] As destructive as it may seem, the crime actually subscribes to a logic of mechanically biological reproduction. The "gentleman," in other words, is guilty of a lack of perversion.

Although Péret's article offers suggestions for what such perversions might have been—sending body parts to the right-wing royalist senator Lamarzelle, for instance—he is hardly outlining a position for Dada criminality. Instead his appeal to aesthetic judgment aims to shift the object of outrage from the horror of the crime to its banality. In contrast to the excited language and detail featured in Le Petit Parisien, Péret's article suggests that such crimes were in fact all too common, and that the desires they expressed were likewise shockingly predictable. Péret does not, of course, go so far as to attack the popular media for their complicity in reproducing such desires under the aegis of their voyeuristic moralism; the polemical content of Péret's article is clouded by its own sensationalism in appealing to shock. In its satire of contemporary journalism's moralistic attention to form, however, its aesthetic rather than moral or political assessment of the crime nevertheless forms the basis for the more militant ideological criticism Péret would later publish as a surrealist.

Reprising the parodic thesis and satirical tone of Thomas De Quincey's trilogy of essays "On Murder, Considered as One of the Fine Arts," Péret argues that the sexual killing should be grasped by what De Quincey calls its aesthetic "handle." For Péret, this aesthetic treatment offers a means for rendering the virtually overlooked crime observable and subject to analysis in ways that avoid simply fixating on the innocence of the victim or the guilt of the murderer. As De Quincey explains in the first of his essays (1827), murder "may be laid hold of by its moral handle (as it generally is in the pulpit and at the Old Bailey), and that, I confess, is its weak side; or it may be treated aesthetically, as the Germans call it—that is, in relation to good taste."[11] In what is essentially a parody of Kant's three critiques, which distinguish pure reason, practical reason, and aesthetic judgment as separate functions, De Quincey isolates the most baldly immoral act of murder as a spectacle for aesthetic consideration, divorced from the moral consideration Kant would automatically apply to it. At the same time he exaggerates the practicality of moral judgment—so-called practical reason—to the point of absurdity, explaining that it should be left to specialists, such as members of the clergy or the legal profession. Furthermore, a moral "reaction" to a crime would be possible, or practical, only if the spectator found himself in a position to do something to stop the murder in the first place. He argues that the spectator-critic's assessment of aesthetic "qualities" such as the killer's imagination or lack thereof, and details of "design . . . grouping, light and shade, poetry, sentiment," should instead become the murder's essential characteristics.[12] Peret likewise addresses the aesthetic component of the murder as its "essential" characteristic, but more as a scandal to moralistic cultural apparatuses for judging crime, I contend, than as a critique of the supposed disinterestedness of art.

Péret further complicates his position as a cultural critic of the child murder by extending De Quincey's reduction *ad absurdum* of the moral "handle" toward the legal process itself. Accusing institutional justice of reproducing the same gesture undertaken by the murderer, Péret satirizes capital punishment as a banal yet repressive imitation of criminal violence:

> If no one punishes two bulls who strike each other, why inflict a penalty on the murderer—and what possible importance do you think death attaches to this grotesque vengeance?
>
> This act toward a living being seems to us totally unjustifiable and perfectly uninteresting.
>
> The repression of crimes is nothing other than an insult to the truth. These folks are right to murder their neighbors, whereas justice punishes an assault on conventional morals with an assault on instinctual liberty.[13]

At first this anarchic call for the abolition of justice seems only further to naturalize and erase the specificity of the acts of sexual and physical violence inflicted upon the young victim of Pénisson's crime. Yet its indictment of punishment as a form of vengeance extends rather than contradicts Péret's earlier indictment of the murderer's "unjustifiable and uninteresting" acts. By connecting the logic of punishment to the logic of crime— "justice punishes an assault on conventional morals with an assault on instinctual liberty"—he suggests that the "gentleman's" desire and the social institutions that police his crime are little more than inverted copies of each other: both, Péret argues, are moral systems bound by traditionalism and banality, and both involve a mimetic surrender to base instincts. Yet whereas Péret rhetorically naturalizes the child murder as uninteresting, he depicts punishment as unnatural—an act of vengeance which, while still "perfectly uninteresting," is nonetheless grotesque and insulting. Like De Quincey, Péret trivializes the crime in order to scrutinize the formal logic of moral judgment, individual as well as institutional.

In their perverse and anarchistic isolation of practical reason from aesthetic judgment, Péret and De Quincey each suggest that morality's very promise of sustaining a social order was itself a fantasy; morality—what Kant called "practical reason"—was instead a set of conventions that eclipsed the degree to which this social order was already collapsed, or, more precisely, to which the social order reproduced its own collapse as the necessary condition for its existence. For Péret and De Quincey alike, this phenomenon became especially visible in the contemporary rise in "great" murders of an exceptionally unmotivated, culturally symptomatic nature. Such crimes—unlike Marcel Pénisson's "surrender to his desires"—suggested that this collapse in the social order was a historical reality of which the very fact of murder was a symptom.

André Breton would later theorize the role played by De Quincey's three critiques of murder in surrealist thinking. As he writes in his 1939 Anthology of Black Humor, De Quincey's understanding of murder "leave[s] aside the all-too-conventional horror it inspires," and instead "demands to be treated aesthetically and appreciated in terms of its qualities, as one would appreciate a work of art or a medical case study."[14] By expanding the category of disinterested aesthetic judgment to include medical examination as well as artistic appreciation, Breton suggests that the "black humor" (humour noir) of De Quincey's essays on murder was somehow salutary, invoking De Quincey's Confession of an English Opium-Eater to demonstrate that "no one ever showed a deeper compassion for human misery than De Quincey."[15] This very compassion fuels the antihumanism of the "On Murder" essays, since it formed the basis, Breton suggests, of De Quincey's disdain for "established reputations." Breton argues that De Quincey's aesthetic approach could serve as a critique of the conventional basis of so-called moral behavior.

And indeed De Quincey's satirical reduction of morality to a chance encounter only somewhat exaggerates the degree of alienation at stake in a public event such as a murder, in which direct moral participation by a large social body is impossible, or a conceit. For all but the immediate participants and witnesses, the experience of any such event is overwhelmingly secondhand. Sensationalized by the press, gawked at by passers-by, whispered about in hushed and horrified tones, or cited as an example for public outrage, safety, or moral benefit, murder is already subject to representation and details of "design . . . grouping, light and shade, poetry, sentiment." Maria Tatar has proposed that contemporary avant-garde depictions of sexual murder in Weimar Germany compensated for this distance or alienation between the spectator and the event through exploitative and violent relations of fantasy: identification, voyeurism, catharsis, and the experience of sublimity.[16] I contend, however, that surrealist and proto-surrealist writings like Péret's, in spite of their callous rhetoric and ironic distance, derive their "aesthetic" approach from an ethical commitment to dislodging judgment—moral and aesthetic alike—from the formalism of national myths and institutions. Writings like Péret's seek to judge murder critically as an event wherein such fantasy relations, and the ideological and psychic forces they manifest, can be scrutinized and subjected to revision. In doing so, they not only denounce the bio-mimetic logic of cultural reproduction at work in the crime and its punishment alike but also offer the beginnings of a surrealist intellectual program, a critical aesthetics with its own inherent imperative for judgment.

Whereas Péret's examination of sexual murder "considered as one of the fine arts" accuses both the murderer and the justice system of a vulgar dependence on traditional forms of representation (naturalism, mimicry), it remained far more commonplace for art critics to criminalize the avant-garde for their transgression of such formal laws.[17] Two years after the publication of Péret's essay on murder in Littérature, a review by the psychologist Raymond Meunier of Francis Picabia's entries at the 1922 Salon des Indépendants went so far as to suggest that Dada practices were themselves criminally responsible. The review, titled "Criminalité cubéo-dadaïste," compares Picabia's "bits of string and old pocket contents which, affixed to a canvas with a scatological inscription, form[ing], rest assured, a 'Dada' work of art," to the psychotic manifestations of a madman. The review extends this comparison to the entire artists' quarter of Montparnasse, in which "armed bands" of "tear-inducing canvases, incendiary newspapers, and asphyxiating books" circulated with impunity. Such transgressive practices were so infectious, claims Meunier, that they could no longer be considered only metaphorically criminal, but were literally responsible for a recent decay in morals:

> What is less laughable—though absolutely ridiculous—is the mental contagion that spreads [from the avant-garde]. A multiplication of sickness, vice, suicide, and crime, which they call intellectual. The gangrene of thought is secondary to the infection of taste: there is a direct relationship between the cubeo-Dadaist work of art . . . and certain absurdly formed crimes, such as that of the Polish woman who, last month, murdered her five-year-old daughter and killed herself, leaving this philosophico-Dadaist testament for the meditations of the police commissioner: "Neither a burst of madness, nor a blow to the head. I kill myself having reflected fully. Life is stupid. O! Spirits, help me! How can I kill my daughter! I'm nearly beside myself. Will I have the strength? . . ."
>
> She had the strength.
>
> If I cite this crime, consigned, among many, to my notes, this is because it is typical. It

is the logical outcome of the profound attacks that successive negations are making upon the soul. Life is stupid, without beauty. It no longer has any goal, it is without affirmation. And why stop at crime, when it is considered by a purely critical philosophy not to be a crime but a conception of the mind?[18]

In criminalizing Dada's transgressive practices, Meunier implicates the nihilism of Dada as both the symptom and the cause of the breakdown in postwar social values which he considers instrumental to such "absurdly formed crimes." In spite of his own moral outrage, though, he assigns Dada (or "cubeo-Dadaism") a critical philosophy fueled less by immorality than by a poisonous, contagious amorality. Dada, by construing real events as conceptions of the mind, encouraged ever more unnatural crimes as its logical outcome; this "mental contagion," Meunier concludes, had incited an epidemic of nihilism and despair that rendered murder typical.

While such charges of contagion against the avant-garde were hardly uncommon, the reviewer's alarmist characterization of Dada mischaracterizes its aesthetics as a reified set of judgments, a legitimation of specific forms of cultural production as art. Péret's aesthetic critique of Pénisson's crime was not, however, a categorical judgment: Péret was no more arguing for the aesthetic consideration of all murders than was Marcel Duchamp, in nominating a urinal for aesthetic consideration, proposing that museums invest in bathroom fixtures. Rather, Péret's analysis of murder anticipates Breton's later notion that a De Quinceyan aesthetic treatment of murder functions like a medical case study: its perverse and ironic disinterestedness seeks viable ways to transform tragedy into an object for study. As Péret claims in "Assassiner," there is something in the exceptional nature of certain crimes that makes them worth studying. He writes:

> A crime interests us only insofar as it is an experiment (a dissociation of chemical compounds). When the author has aimed at a definite target—vengeance, passion crime, etc.—this becomes not a guilty thing (it would no longer be a question of culpability against a man who kills his fellow creature, than toward two rhinoceroses, who kill each other for the possession of the same female), but something as far from curious as making babies.[19]

Even as the Pénisson murder's banal and imitative nature disqualifies it as an experiment worthy of analysis, its very rejection on these grounds establishes how Péret will use this aesthetic judgment for more than merely satirical purposes. That is, Péret's appeal to truly experimental crimes begins to outline in positive terms the proto-surrealist aesthetic apparatus equipped to deal with such horrifying acts. Péret's two opposing judgments—disdain for the "Crime of Versailles" and admiration for Henri Landru—are rooted in the same aesthetic apparatus. The difference between this developing aesthetic and the virulent "conception of the mind" of Meunier's review, I wish to suggest, is that while both the "absurdly formed" infanticide and the atrocities of Péret's killer seem to Meunier to be logical outcomes of a social collapse precipitated by Dada, they are instead for Péret the result of social reproduction. Péret's Dada aesthetics, in other words, reveal the extent to which this collapse was the product of the forms of social order through which war, crime, and punishment reproduced themselves: formalist representation, conventional morality, and institutional justice.

All the same, the young Paris Dada group that founded Littérature was known for its surveys of favorite authors, literary figures, and even murderers, suggesting anything but an abandonment of categorical judgment. Yet even the tables of numerical rankings published in Littérature in 1921, which rated writers and cultural figures according to the group's preferences—including scores for Landru, the notorious nineteenth-century criminal Pierre François Lacenaire, and Fantômas—replace the transcendental judgment of taste with their absurdly quantitative measurements of collective judgment; the figures register dissent as much as consensus. The Littérature group's preface, moreover, denies that the aim of the charts is to ascribe positive aesthetic value. As the authors explain: "This schoolboy system, which seems ridiculous enough to us, has the advantage of presenting our point of view most simply. Besides, we insist on pointing out that we are not proposing a new order of values, our goal being not to rank but to disarrange."[20] For the proto-surrealist group of Parisian Dadaists who published Littérature, aesthetics represented not an order but a critical device. However anarchistically deployed, the study of and appeal to judgments of taste or beauty was engineered as a calling-into-awareness of the conditions of judgment themselves—the encounter between objects and spectators, and the encounter between competing systems of judgment.

Péret's appeal to aesthetics in his essay on murder thus suggests the contours of a dialectical aesthetics of engagement that would increasingly characterize surrealist thinking in the early 1920s. The idea of "the beautiful" that emerges from Péret's unsettling essay foreshadows what would become surrealism's own ideas about beauty, insofar as surrealist aesthetics would define as beautiful phenomena whose very instability or "convulsive" quality would demand intellectual engagement. For De Quincey, whose work reached the surrealists largely through Baudelaire and Alfred Jarry, the notion of an art of murder remained primarily a function of its reception, as a phenomenon grasped by its aesthetic handle rather than by its moral handle.[21] The surrealists complicated De Quincey's disinterested judgment of murder by extending their critique to the crime's causes, its motives and intentions, as well as its reception as a spectacle. Péret closes his essay by emphasizing the suppression of instinct as precisely the aesthetic move found in "great" criminals like Landru and non-murderers alike: "The same instinct that makes us kill rebels against death. It requires an enormous amount of courage to suppress it, and that is really very beautiful."[22] The "courageous," paradoxically liberatory self-control

Péret describes thus foreshadows the ethical development of surrealism as a discourse on the nature of revolutionary desire and the value of the unconscious—forms of "imagination" that demanded far more than a surrender to instincts, but instead a thorough examination of the psychic processes and forms of control that mediated between the conscious and the unconscious. The surrealists would not occupy the position of exteriority embodied by De Quincey's ironic critical voice in his "On Murder" essays but would instead seek to develop a self-consciousness toward its practices that articulated the imperative for an ethical faculty within the very critique of criminal motive itself. Aesthetics would be a device in the surrealist group's intellectual work, anticipating its public engagement and even its investment in politics as well as in its analysis of culture.

Throughout the early 1920s the surrealists developed an increasingly politicized interest in the extraliterary and sociologically verifiable nature of murderous violence, as well as in the relations of fantasy, desire, hatred, and fear that murder cases revealed. The surrealists' commitment to examining these relations was both aided and complicated by their own fantasy of remaining disinterested toward social trauma; the group attempted to isolate the "chemical properties" of cultural forces and lived experience without participating in their reproduction. Even so, murder would remain a contested ground for the surrealists owing to the difficulty of studying its representation as a spectacle while still recognizing its fundamental social and physical trauma.

The spectacle of murder as a cultural phenomenon became, throughout the 1920s, a site of conflict within the surrealist movement itself. What Louis Aragon identified in 1924 as the movement's "moral thread" is considered to have been latent, at first, within the group's activities, such as its practices of automatic writing, dream interpretation, and somnambulistic trances. Only at the threshold of surrealism's birth as an intellectual movement, critics have suggested, did its ethical imperative manifest itself within its aesthetic project. This is a critical commonplace that "Assassiner" renders suspect: however terroristic its interest in murder might seem, the essay's anarchist attack on institutional morality is on full view in Péret's aesthetic apparatus. Whereas numerous critics have argued that the surrealists' turn toward "the real world" in the mid-1920s was a later logical extension of the group's antibourgeois principles of experimentation and novelty, I suggest instead that this ethical turn was produced by the movement's broader self-determination through discourse, disagreement, and scandal.[23] What would change, in other words, was less the group's position of disinterestedness than its sense of political responsibility toward the consequences of judgment. The emergence of a surrealist ethics from its aesthetics is thus both determined by and visible in the group's conflicting responses to murder as a sociological phenomenon and as "one of the fine arts."

René Crevel and the Scandal of Maldoror

> The moment for studying the moral consequences of Ducasse's work has not arrived.
>
> André Breton, "The Cantos of Maldoror" (1920)

Surrealism emerged from Parisian Dada through a series of scandals that forced the emerging movement to confirm its allegiances: its intellectual mission derived from the feuds and travesties that plagued the dissolution of the Parisian Dada group. These upheavals—whether polemical exchanges or outright brawls—would not themselves constitute surrealism's artistic practices but instead formed the basic conditions of crisis and contradiction from which the newer movement emerged. In the movement's early years these polemics tended to center on the question of consequences: What was at stake in the group's experimental aesthetic practices, especially when these deployed violent sociological material?

In the fight that erupted during a performance of Tristan Tzara's play Le Coeur à gaz (The Gas Heart) in July 1923, Paul Éluard slapped René Crevel across the face. It was certainly not the worst injury of the evening, a night of theater, poetry, and spectacle called "La Soirée du coeur à barbe" (The Bearded Heart: A Soirée). The event was organized by the group of adherents to Parisian Dada who, unlike the group of poets attached to the now post-Dada and proto-surrealist journal Littérature, refused to declare the movement dead. This included Tzara, the Romanian figurehead of the Dada movement, as well as young French writers such as René Crevel, Jacques Baron, and Pierre de Massot, all of whom would later become involved in surrealism but, on this occasion, rallied around Tzara's movement. At several points during the evening the soirée was loudly disrupted by members of the Littérature group, which included André Breton, Paul Éluard, and Robert Desnos. In the resulting outbursts, Crevel, Tzara, and Baron were slapped, and Pierre de Massot's arm was broken by a blow from Breton's cane. More fatal, though, was the blow to Parisian Dada itself, whose reputation suffered irrevocable damage.[24] Indeed the motives behind the provocation can be ascribed to the Littérature group's efforts not so much to kill the Dada impulse—for in their eyes it was already dead—as to scandalize it, in the ecclesiastical sense of debunking and discrediting it publicly, by forcefully disrupting its own economy of scandal and provocation.

The slap to Crevel's face betrayed a more complex set of motives, however, relating less to the group's disgust with Dada than to disagreements about what was soon to become surrealism. Crevel had in fact played an instrumental role in the development of this new movement by introducing Breton and his circle to mediumistic activities in September of the previous year. It was Crevel who initiated the "période des sommeils" memorialized by Breton in "The Mediums Enter" and by Louis Aragon in "A Wave of Dreams," adapting spiritualist methods of séance induction to the group's experiments with automatic writing and its budding interest in psychoanalysis. As Aragon writes, "At the seaside, [. . .] René Crevel met a lady who taught him to enter a distinctive hypnotic sleep which somewhat resembled the somnambulistic state," and which rendered its participants "like men drowned in the open air."[25] Yet in spite of his influential role in this *nouvelle vague*, Crevel broke with the *Littérature* group a few months later, critical of their reaction to and assimilation of the séances. Éluard's slap, occurring a few months after Crevel's break with the group, might therefore be viewed less as a condemnation of Crevel's participation in Tzara's play than as a delayed expression of the proto-surrealist group's censorship of his performances during the "période des sommeils."

Indeed, during this period of "sleeping fits" it was the evolving notion of surrealism that found itself scandalized by Crevel's mediumistic activity. The bloody tales of murder and suicide that Crevel described under (occasionally simulated) hypnosis confronted the proto-surrealist group with material that was neither liberatory nor new but disturbing, morally ambiguous, and obsessional. This material scandalized what Crevel criticized as the proto-surrealist group's impulse to reduce all forms of experience to occasions for poetry. Susan Suleiman, defining scandal as a derivation of the Greek *skandalon*—meaning "trap, snare, stumbling block"—has suggested that the effect of Crevel's séances on the emerging surrealist movement was to interrupt the group's automatic trajectory.[26] Even while they cited the most disturbing and morally challenging writers as influences—Lautréamont and Sade in particular—the group's participants seemed to take little interest in accounting for the manifest content of the works of such writers: namely, the rapes, torture, and murders that fill their pages. Crevel's "scandalous" tales were suppressed, I argue, because they confronted the proto-surrealists with their own reluctance to address the ethical implications of their newly developed practices. By the end of 1923 *Littérature* was no longer recording séances but instead devoted its luxurious October double issue entirely to poetry, suggesting a retreat from experimental practices. In his implicit and explicit critique of the movement's early literary use of disturbing unconscious material, Crevel thus challenged surrealism's relation to the literary and intellectual precursors it gathered. In doing so, he also questioned the very self-consciousness that Aragon would later celebrate as the reason for surrealism's difference from Dada.

In his article "The Mediums Enter," first printed in *Littérature* (1 November 1922) and later republished in *Les Pas perdus* (February 1924), Breton first presents the definition of surrealism he develops more fully in the *Manifesto* (15 October 1924). In an article devoted to the special mediumistic abilities of three members of the *Littérature* group—Crevel, Desnos, and Péret—Breton explains how "we use this word [surrealism], which we did not coin and which we might easily have left to the most ill-defined critical vocabulary, in a precise sense. This is how we have agreed to designate a certain psychic automatism that corresponds rather well to the dream state, a state that is currently very hard to delimit."[27]

The process of delimiting this word "surrealism" and the "psychic automatism" it designates—a process whose initial phase would stretch beyond the "période des sommeils"
and through the publication of the *Manifesto* two years later, only to be redefined over and
again in subsequent years—corresponds with the period of transition between the death
of Parisian Dada and the "official" birth of surrealism in the fall of 1924.

Yet what has largely been suppressed from the history of this transitional period, in
Breton's own writing as well as in subsequent critical studies of the origins of surrealism,
is René Crevel's role not only as the originator of the séances but also as a vocal critic of
how they were altered and appropriated by Breton's group. Whereas Robert Desnos's uncanny ability to speak, draw, and write in ludic poetic language and prophetic tones fascinated the group, and Breton in particular, the tales of suicide and murder invoked by
Crevel are barely mentioned in surrealist accounts of the séances. For critics and historians of the movement, as well as for members of the group themselves, Desnos's remarkable activity during this period was by far the more significant; its quasi-Freudian,
quasi-mystical atmosphere yielded a "wave" of thick, punning language and historical allusion (to Robespierre as well as to Marcel Duchamp's alter ego, Rrose Sélavy) that extended Breton's and Philippe Soupault's earlier attempts to derive a continuity between
poetry and the unconscious.

In numerous articles published after his separation from the group in early 1923, Crevel
attacked this fealty to the Desnosian current in surrealism. The movement's "discovery"
of psychoanalysis and the unconscious, he argued, was being misappropriated, merely
yielding new material for literature rather than producing truly revolutionary experimentation.[28] Even after his reconciliation with the surrealists in late 1924, Crevel would
remain critical of "automatism" and automatic writing, as well as, more tacitly, the movement's Desnosian predilection. For Crevel this was no jealous retribution but a serious accusation that revealed his commitment to understanding avant-garde experimentation as
an extension of lived experience, of politics, and of intellectual practice. For the members
of an editorial collective whose very title—*Littérature*—was intended ironically, even icon-
oclastically, the literary tendency Crevel saw in the movement risked eradicating any Dada
impulse the group might have had—such as Breton's own ideas about Dada as a "state of
mind" rather than as a stylistic platform.

Initially Crevel himself had been eager to credit the trances' exploration of the unconscious with the "absolute intellectual emancipation" promised by Breton's augury of
surrealism. In an article for the *Little Review* (published, ironically, at the height of his estrangement from Breton's group), Crevel writes: "Professor Freud by the psychoanalytic
method tries to uncover that which we force back into our unconscious. Superrealism
[sic] claims to open wide the doors; and because it really does open them, there is no con-
straint; these mysterious words arise without affected romanticism, without calculated
pose." In spite of this apologia for surrealism, which directly cites Breton's "Entrée des

médiums," Crevel admits in the next sentence that the "mysterious words" produced by surrealism's psychoanalytical methods nevertheless "have multiple reflections and it is difficult not to be carried away by their spontaneous and free current."[29] It is this aspect of getting "carried away" beyond the romantic safety of poetic inspiration that rendered Crevel's séances—and his subsequent criticism—so scandalous to the proto-surrealist group's new activities. Indeed, according to Breton's brief account of his performances in "L'Entrée des médiums," Crevel's revelations seemed to bubble forth with a ferocity that the surrealists would not fully understand until later—when, for instance, they pursued interests in hysteria and psychosis in 1928. As Crevel writes, the mysterious words that emerged from mediumistic activity had meanings and consequences that could not be written off as free play.

Determining the precise content of Crevel's improvisations remains difficult, however. In a series of radio interviews given thirty years later, Breton expressed his deep regret at never having recorded the séances on audiotape. Whereas many of Desnos's performances were dutifully transcribed, only one of Crevel's was fully recounted in Littérature, as an appendix to "The Mediums Enter" which was later omitted from reprinted versions of the essay.[30] In the later, authoritative edition of the essay in Les Pas perdus, Breton writes of Crevel's first hypnotic trance only that he uttered "a kind of defense or indictment that was not copied down at the time." The content of the slumber is relegated to a parenthetical list of distinguishing features: "(declamatory diction interspersed with sighs, sometimes going into a kind of singsong; stressing of certain words, rapid slurring of others; infinite prolongation of several endings; dramatic delivery: the story concerns a woman accused of having killed her husband, but her guilt is in dispute because she apparently acted on his wishes). Upon awakening, Crevel has no recollection of his words."[31] Breton's attention to the diction and delivery of Crevel's performance is as symptomatic as his virtual erasure of its narrative content. As the foil to the more linguistic and graphic performances in Breton's account that follow it, Crevel's crime story seems a crude sketch for Desnos's more fluid and more fully documented performances; Breton later referred to the punning language Desnos used in his transatlantic "channeling" of Marcel Duchamp's Rrose Sélavy as "words without wrinkles."[32] In the face of such performances, Crevel's subsequent trances are relegated to a footnote. Breton adds: "It should be noted that on the same day before Desnos, Crevel passed through a state similar to Monday's (another crime story, although more obscure this time: 'The woman will be naked, and it's the oldest man who will wield the ax')."[33]

Despite his obvious preference for Desnos, the motives behind Breton's suppression of Crevel's performances are neither aggressive nor entirely deliberate. The crime stories are, for Breton, more obscure and confusing than irrelevant, since they seem to elude or unsettle his ability to describe them rather than failing to capture his attention. Indeed, the manuscript of "The Mediums Enter" contains a passage in which Breton tries to articulate his aphasia in response to Crevel's improvisations. Breton writes: "I regrettably find myself unable here to reveal any of Crevel's improvisations because I would not know how to convey them as a whole, so I prefer to abstain. If I look for their equivalent in tone within literature, I find little else other than Maldoror."[34] Significantly, this passage has itself been excised from the final version of the essay, as if guaranteeing the aphasia it describes. Moreover, its allusion to Lautréamont's *Chants de Maldoror*, while partially satisfying Breton's efforts to find an "equivalent in tone" to Crevel's séances, only implicitly addresses why he finds them so difficult to reveal. How can we account for this inability to describe Crevel's crime stories? They certainly lacked the helpful graphic evidence and epigrammatic economy of Desnos's puns and prophecies. More significantly, their concentration on murder and suicide revealed the extent to which the séances' recourse to psychic automatism did not simply manufacture liberatory free play or anarchic unrestraint but could also instigate violent, obsessive desires, as well as a cruelty whose articulation challenged Breton's assumptions about intellectual liberation and the "thirst for the infinite."[35]

It would be difficult to overestimate the significance of *Les Chants de Maldoror* in the development of what would become surrealism. In "Une Vague de rêves," Louis Aragon explains that the proto-surrealist group turned back toward literature, if only temporarily, in order to instill a conceptual rigor into a Dada praxis (that is, the Parisian Dada championed by Tristan Tzara) that was becoming limited as much by its lack of concepts as by its lack of political imperative. This recursive focus on literature was contemporaneous with the group's dawning interest in psychoanalysis, through which it began to appreciate the unconscious as a text-producing mental function. This interest was particularly evident in the surrealists' admiration for the comte de Lautréamont, whose "discovery" by André Breton, Louis Aragon, and Philippe Soupault during the First World War both predated and survived their tenure with Paris Dada. *Les Chants de Maldoror* has rightly been understood to prefigure surrealism's aesthetics through its poetic construction as a kind of breathless, automatic writing. But Lautréamont's text is as significant to surrealism, as I have suggested, for the narrative pose of disinterestedness it affects toward its graphic depictions of murder, torture, and disfiguration. Lautréamont's avowal of a "thirst for the infinite" in the face of this disinterestedness would, paradoxically, help configure the surrealists' revolutionary but originally anarchic sense of ethics.

By comparing the impact of Crevel's performances during the séances to that of *Maldoror*, Breton grants them a significance that renders his abstention from describing their content all the more peculiar. As Crevel suggested in the polemical essays he wrote against the surrealists' appropriation of the séances as poetic raw material, what was at stake in Breton's expurgation was the refusal of the nascent surrealist movement to acknowledge manifest representational content. Such a refusal might be amusing when representation itself was the object of discussion. But as Crevel insisted, to dismiss manifest representational content in favor of stylistic pyrotechnics became a problem as soon as this manifest content referred to acts of horrific violence: it implied complicity. Herein, I argue, lay the symptomatic nature of Breton's inability to describe Crevel's séances. They confronted the participants with the more violent moments in Lautréamont's text in ways that could not, as with Desnos's more formally suggestive performances, be so easily assimilated as purely aesthetic experiments. Not only did Crevel's performances cast suspicion on the group's use of Lautréamont as a precursor, but they complicated the movement's celebration of its own experimental practices as well. This suspicion, and the polemics it brought about, were instrumental in transforming the nascent movement's self-consciousness about its relationship to the historical and sociological content of representation, suggesting the impossibility of a wholesale rejection of figural realism. Crevel's séances thus helped articulate the movement's relation to aesthetics as a means of both analyzing and rendering suspect the cultural fields it interrogated.

A more revealing source of information about Crevel's improvisations is the series of letters from Simone Breton to her cousin Denise Lévy, which provide an almost daily account of the "période des sommeils." As André Breton's biographer Marguerite Bonnet has explained, Simone Breton shared her husband's difficulty in describing the tales.[36] Beginning her first letter on September 25, the evening of the first séances, she was unable to finish it until the fifth of October. Nevertheless, Simone's first letter manages to articulate her anxiety about describing the events as well as to furnish the tales themselves with considerably more detail and narrative color than her husband's accounts:

> The voyage continues, so absorbing that I was not able to write you, in spite, as always, of my daily desire. My dear, incredible things are happening here. But it worries me terribly to write them down. I am going to stiffen or deform everything. You could only really understand by being there. And these things will charm and horrify you too much. Spiritism isn't the word. The fact remains that certain of André's friends have discovered mediumistic abilities in themselves which evidently resemble no other. Here at 42, rue Fontaine, fantastic séances have taken place, the dramatic fighting it out with the touching. It is dark. We are all around the table, silent, hands tight. Barely three minutes later Crevel is already heaving up husky sighs and formless cries. Then, in a strained and declamatory tone, he begins a monstrous tale. A woman has drowned her husband, but he asked her to do it. "Ah! The frogs! Poor madwoman. Maaaadwoman. . . ." Distressing and cruel tones. Ferocity in the slightest image. Some obscenity, too. What would you think to hear him, this little boy, so gentle and so feminine. Nothing's quite abominable enough. The most terrifying passages from Maldoror would give you only an idea.[37]

Simone Breton's breathless expressions of awe in response to the séances seem commensurate with her fear of distorting the events. Surpassing the mere titillation of spiritualist parlor games, Crevel's performances burst onto the scene as both unexpected and out-of-place phenomena: like her husband, Simone Breton can only sketch the incidents—which she does at some length—and give an idea of their "abomination" by citing Lautréamont's *Chants de Maldoror*.[38]

Unlike André Breton, though, Simone Breton does not cite Maldoror as a general allusion, either to the entirety of Lautréamont's novel or to its eponymous villain, but rather specifies its "most terrifying passages." She thus passes over the more formalist passages such as the famous "beautiful as . . ." litanies so critical to surrealist aesthetics, instead gesturing toward the scenes of torture, rape, and murder that take place in the book. Indeed, among its scenes of self-mutilation, random assassination, and vampirism, by far the most abominable passage in the *Chants de Maldoror* occurs in the third canto, an eruption of sexual violence and genital mutilation that disrupts the text's already explicit economy of violent and destructive imagery. Might this be the passage Simone had in mind? Certainly it challenges André Breton's more semiotic readings of Crevel's séances, uncannily and nightmarishly fusing the intellectual ancestor of Bretonian surrealism with a figure reminiscent of the "dark satyr" of Péret's 1920 article on the sexual murderer Marcel Pénisson. Lautréamont's narrator introduces a madwoman who, amidst her ravings, drops a scroll of paper that testifies to the atrocities which drove her to madness. A stranger, who turns out to be Maldoror himself, picks up the scroll and recognizes it as an account of his own long-forgotten acts. It describes how the villain, walking with his bulldog, finds the woman's young daughter asleep under a tree; he then

> undressed rapidly, like a man who knows what he is about. Naked as a stone, he flung himself upon the young girl's body and pulled up her dress to attempt her virtue . . . in broad daylight! Not at all embarrassed, not he! Let us not dwell on this foul deed. His mind discontent, he dressed hurriedly, glanced cautiously at the dusty, deserted track, and ordered the bulldog to choke the bloodstained child with a snap of its jaws. He pointed out for the mountain dog the spot so as not to witness the sharp teeth sinking into those rosy veins, . . . and this wolf with monstrous muzzle in turn satisfied himself by violating this delicate child's virginity. The blood from her lacerated abdomen ran once again down her legs and on to the meadow. Her moans mingled with the animal's whining. The maid held up the gold cross she wore around her neck, so that he might spare her; she had not dared exhibit it to the savage eyes of him who had first thought of taking advantage of her tender years.[39]

Here, though, the narrative does not retreat into Sadean repetition in a way that might defamiliarize or de-realize the violence of its double rape. Nor for that matter does it attempt to restore a kind of moral order by invoking celestial or vengeful justice, as might be the case in a novel by Eugène Sue or Zola. Instead the testimony remains defiantly literal, extending the initial violations through an escalating series of genital mutilations whose specificity—and verifiable historical possibility—defy abstraction:

Maldoror (how loathsome to utter the name!) heard the death pangs and was amazed that the victim was so hard to kill and was still not dead. He approached the sacrificial altar and saw the behavior of his bulldog. . . . He kicked the dog and split open one eye. The crazed bulldog raced off across the countryside dragging after him . . . the little girl's dangling body. . . . Maldoror drew from his pocket an American penknife with ten or a dozen blades serving diverse purposes. He opened the angular paws of this steel Hydra and, equipped with one like a scalpel, and seeing that the greensward had not yet disappeared—dyed by so much spilled blood—readied himself without blanching to grope bravely inside the unhappy child's vagina. From this enlarged trough he removed the inner organs, one after the other: intestines, lungs, liver, and finally the heart itself were ripped from their roots and pulled out through the frightful aperture into the light of day. The sacrificer perceived that the girl—a drawn chicken—had died long ago.[40]

What does it mean that Crevel's quasi-unconscious crime tales called to mind such passages as this? Certainly there is not enough information in Simone's account of the ferocity in Crevel's "slightest images" to account fully for how his tale of a man drowned by his wife might directly evoke the sexual viciousness and gruesome mutilations of *Maldoror*. A particularly troubling aspect of this passage is its disruption of the radically experimental and oneiric imagery of the *Chants* with a realism whose sadistic attention to detail evokes the sensationalism of nineteenth-century crime reports, yet whose sexual violence defies any retreat into symbolism. The narrative's status as a found text further demarcates it from the poetic economy of the *Chants*, suggesting that this horrific incident may bear a more concrete set of references, whether to an actual crime case or to fantasies of sexual violence that implicate the book's author, Isodore Ducasse, through the veil of his authorial alter egos. Moreover, in the time between the book's publication in 1868–69 and its surrealist reception in the 1920s, such scenes had become all too true to life, verified by the notoriety of famous serial killers such as Jean-Baptiste Tropmann, Joseph Vacher, Jack the Ripper, and, more contemporaneously, Marcel Pénisson and Henri Landru.

Simone Breton's allusion suggests that Crevel's performances, despite their dreamlike syntax, bore a similarly intransigent kernel of figural realism that complicated the "psychic automatism" of the séances. However oneiric Lautréamont's text or the proto-surrealist séances might have appeared, the murderousness of such passages could not be dismissed as simply the manifest—and thus metaphorical—expression of more latent "real" desires. Even though Maldoror recognizes his deed as archaic and part of a dimly remembered past, the minuteness of the detail employed in the madwoman's scroll resists the suppression of these events. The incident emerges as a text whose historicity can no longer be ignored.

Crevel's séances likewise refused assimilation within the surrealists' atmosphere of mystery, where "the dramatic [fought] it out with the touching"; unlike Lautréamont's text, though, Crevel's performances seemed to bear within them an accusation, implicating their audience within their scandalous violence in a way that conflicted with the more palatable marvels of Desnos's mediumistic activities. More significantly, they also threatened to compromise the group's appropriation of fierce and controversial writers such as Lautréamont and Sade as intellectual precursors. Indeed, in this context André Breton's allusion to Maldoror seems symptomatic of another aphasia, his similar inability to address fully the totality of Lautréamont's work itself.

The nature of Breton's interest in *Maldoror* becomes clear, as Marguerite Bonnet writes, in the passages he copied out for his friends Louis Aragon and Theodore Fraenkel in letters from 1920, namely, passages such as the famous "beautiful as . . ." litanies from which the brutality and murder of the book are absent in any literal form. Bonnet writes: "This choice [of passages] invites several observations: in the first place, he [Breton] does not, as we see, address the stories in which the demons and furies of eroticism and cruelty are unleashed. . . . In the other fragments he retains, the habitual means of action—murder and torture—are nearly absent."[41]

Noting that Breton tended to return throughout his career to the same passages he copied out for Aragon and Fraenkel, Bonnet argues that the *Littérature* group's reading of Lautréamont during the period of the séances similarly absorbed the violence represented in the text within more metaphorical notions of disruption and assault. Such proto-surrealist forms of epistemological violence, as Bonnet writes, railed against "the *imposture* inherent within language which, making a screen for our existential dissatisfaction—let's not forget that for Lautréamont metaphor renders immense service 'to human aspirations toward infinity'—we insidiously adapt to the disorder of the world."[42] Thus directing its violence against the linguistic and imaginary boundaries that block such "aspirations toward infinity," the Bretonian Lautréamont of the early 1920s was still primarily an avatar of poetic negation, of "revolutionary" violence directed toward imaginary aims. It did not, in other words, raise a question of real ethical practice—for indeed, as Breton later wrote in his article on *Maldoror* in *Les Pas perdus*, "the moment for studying the ethical consequences of Ducasse's work has not arrived."[43] This reluctance, however eschatologically Breton may have intended it, is Crevel's primary object of scorn in his scathing 1924 review of Breton's book in the journal *Les Feuilles Libres*, where he calls Breton a "victim of words, [who] does not realize at all that they have a meaning, a value, that they engage what they pronounce."[44] Crevel's reconciliation with Breton and the emergent surrealist group that same year was largely contingent on the group's acknowledgment of this imperative.

In his other critical writings from this period, Crevel directs his suspicion of the Littérature group's exploitation of the somnambulistic performances toward a broader theory of intellectual practice which significantly reshaped the role that psychoanalysis would play in the surrealist movement. In the aftermath of the "période des sommeils," Crevel became disgusted with what he considered the proto-surrealists' enchantment with unconscious (or mediumistic) imagery *as* imagery, and not as a true conduit for self-exploration, which would demand the anxiety and discomfort that lay in the expression of the "subterranean work of thoughts." He recalls "certain spiritualist séances repeated to [the point of] tedium in which [Breton] did not know how to find anything other than literary nourishment."[45] Crevel articulates this position more fully in an essay titled "Après Dada" (After Dada), ostensibly a review of an article by Marcel Arland about the "new mal de siècle," but really a hostile response to Breton's own "After Dada" article in *Les Pas perdus*. As Crevel writes, the avant-garde movements of the postwar years were characterized by a new spirit that "surpasses . . . the domain of art." This spirit "is not systematically in books like a Buddha in the middle of a fireplace; it is in life, and it is that which demands the revision of values, the destruction of idols, a new faith. From a literary point of view it is the sworn enemy of this frivolous poetry, which Pascal compared scornfully to the work of embroiderers." The "new mal de siècle," which for Arland describes a general postwar malaise in literature and morals as a result of the "absence of God," is rehabilitated by Crevel as a "virile unrest."[46] Arland's response to this contemporary crisis in consciousness is to call for a resurgence of literary moralism: "Thus morality will be our primary concern. I do not conceive of literature without ethics. No one doctrine can satisfy us; but the absence of doctrine torments us."[47] Crevel, like Arland, recognized both the necessity of ethics and the failure of doctrines; yet unlike Arland, Crevel agreed with the surrealists that formalisms and doctrines were to be destroyed rather than mourned.

Any criticism Crevel might have had of Arland's nostalgic formalism, however, was directed toward what he called surrealism's "quest for the absolute" insofar as this apparently total lack of doctrine risked becoming another aesthetic system in spite of itself. "Already," Crevel writes, "certain literary types would like to assimilate themselves to the search for the absolute: there are the false prophets who establish puerile systems, there are those who wonder at their own unconscious as they would a miracle. They all bestow complete faith in spiritual experiments whose pretentious dupes they really are. They bring out big words, talking of surrealism."[48] Elaborating on this mockery of early surrealism's fascination with the marvels of the unconscious, Crevel continues, marking his distinctions in the language of racial primitivism: "They have all the ingenuity of a Negro who gazes at an electric lamp because he has no idea how light is to be made from it. Yet the Negro is at least logically consistent and doesn't profess to a critical spirit. Intellectual anguish demands more than unconscious or spiritual stirrings in order to appease itself; true boldness comes from never stopping at appeasement, but in always going further."[49] In a way that reveals the workings of his own "colonial unconscious," Crevel charts the surrealists' discovery of the unconscious on a quasi-Hegelian racial timeline that stretches from primitive enchantment to modern technological mastery.[50] Accusing the surrealists of reveling naïvely in empty mysteries while smugly professing their boldness, Crevel argues that a true avant-garde would dedicate itself to discovering causes and means—seeking less to glory in the lamp itself than to comprehend the electrical forces that produce the lamp's magical light. Likewise, the surrealist exploration of psychoanalysis, automatic writing, and mediumistic activity should not, Crevel argued, simply highlight the beauty and intrigue of psychoanalytic symptoms, the products and projections of unconscious processes; these practices should rather demand an encounter, however difficult or traumatic, with the desires and motives that guide them. The "virile unrest" Crevel advocates as an avant-garde ethos fundamentally shaped the movement's tireless interrogation and development of psychoanalytic thought, and would continue to condition Crevel's contribution to surrealism throughout his life. This ethos of unrest would also drive Crevel's political thinking, not only in characterizing its shift from the primitivist racism of his 1924 review to the fierce anticolonialism of his later writings, but also in animating his efforts to reconcile psychoanalytic practice with Marxist theory.

Crevel's attacks against what he considered surrealism's tendencies toward abstraction and aestheticism stressed that the unconscious is not a treasure trove but a dangerous mechanism; its recourse to the absolute is made possible only by its terrifying and terroristic intimacy with desire and death. As the madwoman's scroll in *Maldoror* makes all too evident, Crevel argued that the manifest products of the unconscious, once committed to language, gain a historical presence and verifiability no longer subject to the amoral egoism of dreams but invested with real ethical and social demands.

Crevel's writings from the early 1920s return persistently to this problem, exploring through polemic as well as through tireless self-critique the demands of taking responsibility for the determining causes and unconscious desires dredged up by surrealist experiments. Indeed, the tenuous margin between murder and suicide that Crevel's séances explored was all too familiar in his own life, and would become a recursive theme in his writing: at age fourteen Crevel allegedly witnessed the corpse of his father, who had hanged himself. According to his biographer Michel Carassou, Crevel's mother forced her adolescent son to look at the dangling body "so that he could take away the moral of this horrible spectacle," a confrontation whose repercussions are rehearsed throughout Crevel's early novels.[51] In his first novel, for instance, the quasi-autobiographical *Détours* (1924), the protagonist's father commits suicide by inhaling gas from an unlit oven. Having discussed this method of suicide with his father the previous evening, Daniel, the protagonist, becomes aware of his own unconscious complicity in his father's suicide. Daniel reflects:

> By dint of looking to understand the subterranean work of my thought, my feelings, and their secret reasons, in a desire to go further than consciousness, I assumed responsibility for that which was done beyond the control of my will. I believed that I had discovered

an intention that I had not been able to clarify spontaneously. If I had chosen the heading "suicides" in the *faits-divers*, this was not simple chance. Rebelling against my father, feeling toward him not the indifference I tried to feign but a hatred I did not dare proclaim, I had, without admitting it clearly to myself, but by the fault of what I thought deep down, really deep down, that is, by my fault, resolved to read such a heading.[52]

Just as Daniel recognizes that his interest in suicide *faits-divers* was motivated rather than coincidental, his self-implication reflects Crevel's own belief that unconscious desires are no longer amoral or innocent once they have been recognized and rendered conscious.

Daniel's inculcation of the "subterranean work of thoughts" in *Détours* by no means alienated Crevel from the work of Freudian psychoanalysis, which was only then beginning to become recognized in France. As early as March 1922, Crevel wrote in a book review that "psychoanalysis has taught us to find the truth about ourselves in the language of dreams, of which each utterance is an image, a concrete symbol of intimate thought, whereas in waking life we no longer know what is the exact expression of precise thought or simply a word, nothing more."[53] For Crevel, then, the importance of recognizing the work of the unconscious was less a matter of mining the liberatory material it promised than of fulfilling the ethical responsibility to short-circuit the production of evil enabled by its repression.

Such an ethical application of psychoanalysis foreshadows Crevel's later attempts to fuse Marxism and psychoanalysis, in which he argued that true social revolution required not a liberation from oppressive material conditions but a recognition of the latent desires of the proletariat. Crevel would reject the orthodox Marxist opinion that psychoanalysis was a curative system of policing the bourgeois social order; he instead advocated its value as a means for studying the subterranean workings of thought instrumental to generating great liberation and beauty as well as tremendous evil. Evil, Crevel claimed, is perpetuated through the ignorance and suppression of personal responsibility for such forces; beginning in *Détours*, he would accuse conscious memory of complicity in this repression, on account of its inability "always [to] go further."[54] A letter written by Daniel's professor in *Détours*, ironically dismissed by Daniel as boring and philosophically insignificant, reads: "I accuse memory. Evil comes from what we ignore . . . so that memory is in reality a hallucination. In order to grant faith in its revelation, we situate far from us that which is its object. A fine excuse for not taking the trouble to exercise any control!"[55]

Just as memory became surrealism's excuse for originally repressing the scandalous revelations of Crevel's séances, one of the most problematic aspects of *Maldoror* is that the villain bears no responsibility for his actions: upon reading the scroll of his atrocities, he realizes that he has forgotten them. "Great beauty," however, is made possible for Crevel by the traumatic and disturbing encounter with responsibility, an encounter made possible but not satisfied by the ability of aesthetic judgment to render concrete the unconscious forces guiding one's behavior, actions, and imagination. Maldoror, Lautréamont's fictional villain, may be an amoral construction; but as a reader of the text narrating his atrocities, Crevel emphasized the need for the surrealists to recognize their own collusion with Maldoror's acts of forgetting whenever they attempted to escape into pure poetic language. This is why Louis Aragon, in "Une Vague de rêves," lauds Crevel's somnambulistic trances for producing "utterances of great beauty." This great beauty, as Péret proposed in 1920, and as Crevel vehemently reminded the surrealist group in 1924, came from the courage to face—rather than simply to marvel at—the violence of individual instincts and unconscious desires. It was only at this point that a surrealist revolution could begin.

CHAPTER THREE

GERMAINE BERTON AND
THE ETHICS OF ASSASSINATION

Absolute liberty offends, disconcerts.

Louis Aragon, *La Révolution Surréaliste* (1924)

ouis Aragon's affinity for the "great beauty" of Crevel's Maldororian utterances extended beyond their shared insistence that the experimental languages of the avant-garde had "a meaning, a value, that they engage what they pronounce."[1] Like the troubling material that emerged from Crevel's mediumistic performances, Aragon's own writing from this transitional period in early surrealism is notable for its rhetorical excess and its hostility to conventional morality. Dogged in its assault on ideologically overdetermined forms and beliefs, Aragon's writing is also critical of the ways in which such assaults tended to become reified as moral systems, or as sets of formal techniques.

Aragon, like Crevel, heeded Tristan Tzara's early Dada proclamation that the "the absence of system is but another system."[2] However stridently the postwar avant-garde may have lashed out against existing systems of control and order, it never failed to impose new systems in their place. This was most recognizably the case with the surviving Italian futurists who, after the war, ended up backing Mussolini; but it was also the case with Dada, whose provocations risked solidifying into a doctrine of "scandal for scandal's sake." In light of this problem, Crevel and Aragon redefined the intellectual mission of surrealism in ethical rather than aesthetic terms. Rather than justifying shocking artistic developments on a moral or political basis, Crevel and Aragon envisioned surrealism as a system whose aesthetic means could produce the salutary forms of crisis and contradiction that accompanied real historical events. These upheavals would be the impetus, in turn, for the explosive and liberating forms of thought that surrealism demanded.

The challenge facing surrealism, according to Crevel and Aragon, was thus to develop intellectual and aesthetic practices capable of generating such explosive effects, yet without privileging individual works of violent art or violent public acts as institutionalized sources of revolutionary meaning. To what extent, they asked, was it possible to produce epistemological violence without reproducing real violence? The uniqueness of Crevel's and Aragon's thinking lay in recognizing that the surrealist movement's answer to such questions, and its intellectual mission more broadly, would rely as much on its judgment of real acts of violence as on its judgment of aesthetics.

Crevel, as we have seen, was in fact deeply suspicious of the avant-garde's tendency to aestheticize the explosiveness of historical acts of violence. As he argues in his pointedly titled essay "Which Way?," published in a 1923–24 issue of *The Little Review*, "many a person has manufactured a bomb to destroy detestable monuments and has then been content simply to place his bomb on the mantelpiece, make a thousand copies of it which he puts on sale like the Venus de Milo in cheap plaster."[3] Crevel's complaint invokes the bomb-throwing turn-of-the-century anarchists such as Ravachol, Émile Henry, and the Bonnot gang, whose notoriety and terrorist tactics fascinated many of the early surrealists.[4] Such anarchist attacks provided spectacles of revolt, but beyond their initial impact, there wasn't much to prevent them from becoming little more than spectacles in the end, aestheticized in spite of their violence.

Yet whereas Crevel's essay advocates transforming such plaster casts back into bombs, it does not do so to embrace their return to deadly force. Instead, Crevel contends that the deadliness of real-life acts of terror demands of their perpetrators a serious ethical choice, which their assimilation as historical spectacle renders abstract and insignificant. The magnitude of this choice is itself explosive and real, and the experimental literary and artistic movements of the postwar avant-garde would do well, Crevel suggests, to recognize this. Nevertheless, his gesture toward historical anarchism serves only as a metaphor for the commodification that obliterates any such ethical dilemma from its purview. Anarchist bomb-throwing is not, in other words, the basis for any real political platform; Crevel instead resorts to aesthetics in order to foreground the imperative for ethical judgment that the more incendiary artists and writers of the avant-garde might otherwise ignore.

Crevel's own aesthetic system demanded a recognition of the danger and power of any linguistic or imaginary "explosive" that would "distinguish whosoever has the courage of wishing to profit by it."[5] For Crevel, as would become the case for the surrealists more broadly, aesthetic relations were a conduit for ethical relations. Dada's attacks against form and restraint remained significant to the surrealist group as strategies for exploring the deep recesses of the unconscious, as well as for creating shocking images whose value lay beyond good and evil. The results of such endeavors, Crevel stressed, were alive with psychic and cultural meanings whose consequences could not be ignored or spirited away, for to do so would do more than betray the group's sense of novelty; it would participate in the very repression it attacked.

Aragon's approach to the "explosive" quality of the avant-garde, though couched in more inflammatory language than Crevel's critical writings, also instrumentalized aesthetic judgment as a strategy for demanding intellectual engagement. Unlike Crevel, though, Aragon did not consider real criminal violence as the historical limit against which avant-garde aesthetic practices were to be measured. For him the phenomenal excesses of murder and other crime cases epitomized the kind of event that most fully demanded involvement. Not only were such cases already subject to aesthetic judgment by the fact of their public reception and media representation, but also, as Benjamin Péret suggested in 1920, as disruptions of the social order they often revealed the forces of moral, legal, and ideological control at their most inflexible. In his earliest surrealist writings Aragon maintained that disturbing aesthetic phenomena could be transmuted into forms of historical action by bringing about an ethical call to thought, and not, as many have claimed, by one's simply embracing their transgressive relation to existing laws. It is here that Aragon's thinking reflects Crevel's: the ethical imperative of surrealism lay in its commitment to heeding a demand to think independently. That is, its practices sought both to obey and to propagate the command of thinking itself, rather than to heed predetermined moral laws or to obey transcendental principles of "experimental" or "practical" judgment.

The Congratulations of the Jury

Surrealist thinking about ethics in 1923 and 1924 was profoundly shaped by the notoriety of the anarchist assassin Germaine Berton, whose disruption of the social order would test the group's commitment to independent judgment. Berton was a frail yet outspoken twenty-year-old woman who, on January 22, 1923, killed Marius Plateau in his offices at the ultra-right-wing newspaper *Action Française*. Later that year, while she was awaiting trial for her crime, her media presence inspired the suicide of Philippe Daudet, the son of the newspaper's chief editor, the prominent royalist intellectual Léon Daudet. The sixteen-year-old Philippe, himself a habitué of anarchist circles, was allegedly infatuated with Berton, and his suicide was seen by many as a desperate form of tribute. His royalist father accused the anarchists of a conspiracy, since the elder Daudet had, according to Berton's testimony, been the assassin's primary target. The irony of Philippe Daudet's suicide was that it made it seem as though Germaine Berton's attack had somehow managed, however circuitously, to reach its mark. The surrealists immediately professed their strong admiration for Berton's actions. For Aragon, Germaine Berton became a beacon of "absolute liberty"; her portrait later formed the centerpiece of the surrealist group photograph published in the first issue of *Le Révolution Surréaliste* (figure 3.1). This suggested not only the centrality of Berton to the movement's self-conception in the early

La femme est l'être qui
projette la plus grande
ombre ou la plus grande
lumière dans nos rêves.
Ch. B.

Fig. 3.1. Surrealist group portrait surrounding Germaine Berton, *La Révolution Surréaliste*, 1 (1924). Image courtesy of the Pennsylvania State University Special Collections Library.

1920s but also the significance of the thought process through which the group justified her act of violence.

What catapulted the Berton affair into the national consciousness—and the surrealist imagination—were Berton's actions following the assassination. Having fatally shot Plateau, Berton then shot herself. Upon her recovery she maintained that her actions had been deliberate and that her motives were clear. Her individual action had been prompted by her intense hatred of the right-wing group and, she argued, could be considered a form of delayed retaliation for the assassination of Prime Minister Jean Jaurès in 1914. This logic was strengthened by the fact that Marius Plateau was not only the editorial secretary of Action Française but also a founding member of the *camelots du roy*, the ultra-right group of royalists who had encouraged Jaurès's assassination.[6] On the basis of this peculiar logic of retribution, the anarchist assassin, no longer simply an agent of historical violence, soon became an object of intense media scrutiny, both reviled and eroticized by the press. Berton's cultural impact extended her influence well beyond her own individual agency: she was by turns a siren, a femme fatale, and a deranged killer. The surrealists, following Aragon, recognized this impact as a largely aesthetic phenomenon, motivated by popular judgments of beauty, taste, and disgust. Yet rather than fashioning Berton as a heroine or muse for surrealism, Aragon's analysis and justification of the assassination, which differed radically from that of the anarchist and right-wing media alike, significantly reordered the emerging movement's aesthetic relations in a way that instead foregrounded the ethical questions so pointedly raised by Crevel.

In an essay published in the same issue of *The Little Review* as Crevel's "Which Way?" Aragon seems to anticipate the outcome of Germaine Berton's trial later that year, in which the admitted assassin was, perversely, acquitted of murder. Aragon's essay, titled "A Man," ironically celebrates the changing moral temper of the age, at first proposing, and then seriously entertaining, the possibility of the moral collapse that Berton's acquittal likewise seemed to represent. Aragon writes: "A hundred years ago crimes of passion were punished with death; under the influence of romanticism they are no longer dangerous for their perpetrators. In fifty years, under the influence of DADA, patricides will be acquitted with the congratulations of the jury."[7] He thus appears to forecast Berton's similarly unlikely acquittal, which occurred in December 1923, shortly after the publication of the essay. There had been no reasonable doubt that she committed the act, since she not only shot Plateau in the offices of the *Action Française*, surrounded by witnesses, but also admitted full responsibility for the killing. Although Berton was hardly congratulated by the jury, the acquittal indicated that her act had somehow been excused, sanctioned as a form of retaliatory justice against the right-wing group Plateau represented. This proved a surprising turn of events even for Aragon, who remained fascinated by the case for nearly two years. Aragon's own justification of the case would champion Berton's judgment— her decision to commit an act of political murder—without supporting the act itself.

Wishing to isolate this decision as the basis of his own understanding of ethical judgment, Aragon described it as a coming-into-consciousness "of the monstrous inequality, of the vanity of all speech before the aggrandizing power" of "those who threaten the liberty that remains for others."[8] Explaining that the provocation for this coming-into-awareness emanated from "those who threaten . . . liberty," Aragon suggested that Berton's decision to assassinate Plateau originated in her recognition of his power; in turn, the surrealists would derive their own ethical priorities from their recognition of Berton's unique power as a public figure.

Aragon's brash prophecy of Dada's influence on contemporary morals in his *Little Review* essay was hardly an apology for justifiable homicide. Like De Quincey's essays on murder, Aragon's parodic voice harbors a sincere claim about the significance of observing and analyzing acts of public violence such as Berton's. Aragon depicts an explosion of psychic and moral constraints, represented by a hypothetical Man whose social relations have been divested of all moral judgment. For instance, the essay exposes Oedipal taboos, among other moral laws, as contingent: "No one," Aragon writes, "conceals his incestuous loves any longer."[9] Completing his Oedipal parody, Aragon reduces the moral law to an absurdity—to the extent that he makes the phrase "IT IS BETTER TO KILL ONE'S FATHER THAN TO EAT NUTS" interchangeable with the catachresis "IT IS BETTER TO EAT ONE'S FATHER THAN TO KILL NUTS."[10] Indeed, Aragon so fully dismembers the moral relations of his hypothetical Man ("let us call him M to simplify it") that M exacts this dismemberment upon others in turn: "M has no neighbor. He cuts up men and puts them in water to ornament his apartment. He kills as he can at random. He robs, he rests, he fornicates, he reproaches no one, he breaks bodies for his pleasure, he has already said that he is good."[11] Far from the bomb-throwing anarchists Crevel invokes, Aragon depicts M as an aesthete, for whom pure, disembodied aesthetics—a kind of "art for art's sake" exaggerated toward horror—takes the place of all moral and social constraints. And by having M call himself good, Aragon ironically naturalizes the imagining of murderous atrocity as an extension of libertarian pleasure.

The apocalyptic irony of Aragon's essay, however, registers the danger of the absurd violence that results. The explosion of social relations, unconscious desires, and cultural values that M brings about represents not the negation of these social constraints but their apotheosis. Indeed the article ends with a sudden change of tone as Aragon more straightforwardly faces this danger. He writes, "The day when someone will have found the explosive which will destroy the world, someone will be found to use it, in spite of laws, century old, dictated by the fear of this unique event. That is why I think."[12] This new explosive suddenly poses a very real threat: no longer a metaphor for experimental art, it introduces the real possibility of mass destruction as an independent historical phenomenon. Dada transgression is no longer the cause of this destruction; instead its shocks cry out for a recognition that the law is no protection against this apocalyptic threat. Like

Péret's 1920 essay on the child murderer Maurice Pénisson, "A Man" invokes and naturalizes the sociopath's arbitrary relationship to moral relations. Aragon's diagnosis of the
fragility of social laws short-circuits both the conservative fear of social dissolution and
the anarchist appeal to total collapse. In their place Aragon posits a demand for judgment
itself, supplementing this Dada cry of alarm with the added imperative to think consciously and independently. Rather than advocating transgression—or worse, the murderousness that logically extends from it—the essay sets in motion the thinking it
ultimately demands, as a substitute for the "century old" laws that inevitably fail.

But what does Aragon mean by thinking? In "A Man" he seems to limit his attention to
an assault on existing systems of law and morality. Yet if there is a glimmer of his surrealist future within this late Dada invective, it can be seen in the degree to which the very art
or artifice of scandalizing existing systems itself constitutes a way of rendering conscious
the givens of conventional reasoning. Aragon's text does not so much subvert the existing order (this is scandal's artifice, not its result) as surprise individual subjects into an
awareness of their repressed or repressive habits. Unlike the more weighty phenomenon
of the sublime, which overwhelms the senses and judgment in order to reaffirm the power
of reason, Aragon's surrealist scandal more sarcastically replaces reason with doubt and
unease. That is, it represents the systematic reification of a scandalous object that resists
sense, order, and law—in this case M himself, as well as the terrible trophies he uses to
ornament his apartment, the bits and pieces of other people. The hyperbolically aestheticized object relations of Aragon's murderous sociopath, which invite but suspend moral
reaction, collapse the distance between murder and art, the human and the inanimate.
The scandal of this collapse demands, but does not impose, a new set of object relations.
Thinking, for Aragon, takes place as the subsequent experience of unfreedom in the face
of such an aesthetic object, the heeding of a demand for moral, and no longer merely aesthetic, judgment.

For Aragon, and for the surrealists in turn, Germaine Berton would epitomize this new,
explosive set of object relations. What made Berton especially significant was that the
politicized and eroticized aesthetic relations configured around her in response to her assassination of Plateau were themselves, in turn, the cause of another death. Less than a
month before her curious acquittal for murder, Berton became the symbolic cause of the
assassination by proxy represented by Philippe Daudet. Indeed René Crevel's anxious fascination with assisted or even murderous suicides found its real-life counterpart in November 1923, when sixteen-year-old Philippe apparently shot himself in a moving taxicab,
"just as the taxi was passing in front of the Saint-Lazare Prison where Germaine Berthon
[sic] is."[13] In a breathless letter to Denise Lévy written shortly thereafter, Aragon re-
marked on this coincidence, as well as what we might call its poetic justice. He calls the
suicide a "perfect destiny," and remarks that "[Philippe Daudet's] poems in Le Libertaire
are extraordinary; it would be great enough without that, but there is this as well."[14] The

coincidences in Daudet's suicide were indeed startling. For one thing, Berton's original target had, she confessed, been Philippe's father, the Action Française writer Léon Daudet.[15]

Philippe's suicide was such a remarkable coincidence that the Action Française suspected a conspiracy: the anarchists were attacking Léon Daudet by gradually bumping off his intimates. Or perhaps Philippe's death was an outright murder; the right-wing press insisted that his death was the product of a deadly complot between the anarchist union and the police, organized by the editor of the anarchist newspaper Le Libertaire, Georges Vidal. It was Vidal's anarchist ideology, they argued, that had armed Berton in the first place. The suicide incited a furious volley of attacks and accusations between the Action Française and the anarchist newspaper, for indeed Le Libertaire offered a very different set of allegations. Announcing with a front-page story "THE TRAGIC DEATH OF PHILIPPE DAUDET, ANARCHIST," it revealed that the young Daudet, himself an anarchist and poet, was hopelessly in love with Germaine Berton.

According to Vidal, Philippe Daudet had spent his final days working incognito alongside him at the offices of Le Libertaire, impressing the editor with his anarchist fervor. After the suicide Vidal realized the identity of his young visitor and immediately published the papers he had left behind as part of the original story: a suicide note addressed to his mother (published in facsimile), and a number of quasi-Baudelairean poems reprinted on the second page. While the poems testified to Daudet's literary promise and amorous sensibility, the suicide letter became Le Libertaire's evidence that the young anarchist had fully rejected both the ideology and the love of his militant right-wing father. The note, as Vidal sharply pointed out, was addressed only to Philippe's mother. The suicide itself, and its "dedication" to Germaine Berton, became the final stroke in this family drama. Under the banner "EXPLANATION OF THE SUICIDE: Philippe Daudet Wanted to Kill His Father," the paper's editors wrote:

> It was on the boulevard Magenta, while passing in front of the Saint-Lazare prison, that Philippe Daudet killed himself.
>
> Is this a coincidence? Is this not instead the supreme homage that the little anarchist wished to pay to the woman imprisoned for her action? Is this not the final lesson, the most cruel of lessons, given by Philippe to his father, Léon Daudet?[16]

This suicide was no mere coincidence, Le Libertaire suggested, but a deliberate act of filial rebellion whose consequences bore national significance. The scandal was a fortuitous one for the anarchist paper, since its connection both to Berton and to the newspaper were salutary for the struggling paper's circulation. By the time this article appeared, Germaine Berton had become such a central figure in the newspaper's public profile that it was not even necessary to mention her name. The so-called coincidence of Daudet's suicide was thus all the more remarkable because Berton's cause was already being used to sell news-

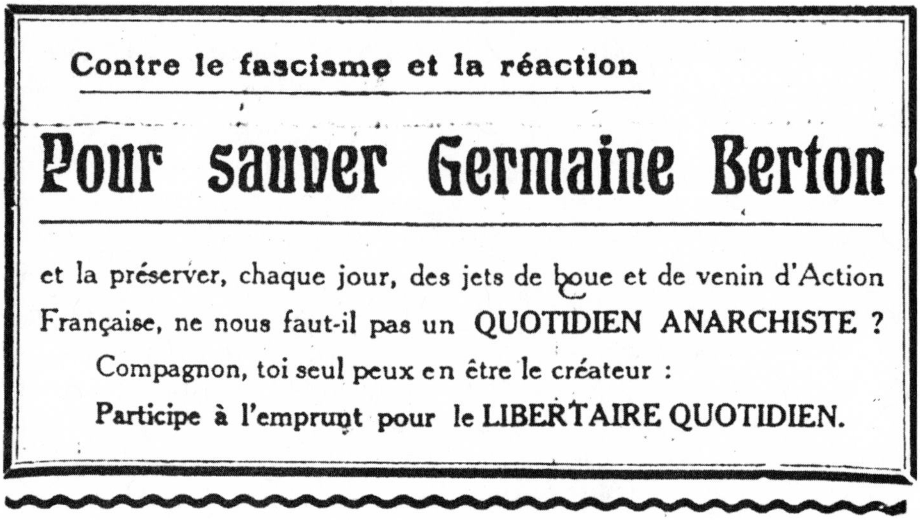

Contre le fascisme et la réaction

Pour sauver Germaine Berton

et la préserver, chaque jour, des jets de boue et de venin d'Action Française, ne nous faut-il pas un QUOTIDIEN ANARCHISTE ?

Compagnon, toi seul peux en être le créateur :

Participe à l'emprunt pour le LIBERTAIRE QUOTIDIEN.

Fig. 3.2. "Pour Sauver Germaine Berton!" *Le Libertaire*, 21 September 1923.

papers. *Le Libertaire* had in fact timed its shift from weekly to daily publication to coincide with the date of the upcoming trial, promoting daily subscription as a blow "against fascism and reaction" and a means "to save Germaine Berton and preserve her, each day, from the mud-slinging and venom of the *Action Française*" (figure 3.2).[17] The possibility that a sixteen-year old boy would believe so fervently in this cause that he would kill himself only further dramatized the anarchist newspaper's efforts to mobilize its readers under the banner of Germaine Berton.

Even if *Le Libertaire*'s role in the Berton-Daudet affair was decidedly an interested, self-advocating, and possibly even underhanded one, what impressed the proto-surrealist group was how close the suicide came to fulfilling Berton's original intention of killing Daudet *père*.[18] This interpretation was largely a product of *Le Libertaire*'s campaign against the *Action Française*. It was *Le Libertaire* that dramatized the affair as an Oedipal crisis brought to fruition by Philippe's suicide: by falling under Berton's spell, the youth had acted out his unconscious desire to kill his father. Germaine Berton's bullets had, thanks to Philippe Daudet and Georges Vidal, become increasingly metaphorical. Yet they had also become more accurate. For one thing, the suffering and deadly effects were no less real; they merely arrived through a more circuitous route—by way of an intermediate victim whose significance was overdetermined by his ties to the warring causes in whose name he was killed. Berton's agency had become dislodged from the immediate material necessity of her physical actions. Indeed, what was particularly impressive to the surrealists was Berton's ability to commit political murder through her aesthetic reception as an object of desire and media attention. Her second attack upon the *Action Française* required no direct agency, only the ability to influence others by means of what might well be considered a form of intoxication.

You Can Kill This Man in Peace

Philippe Daudet was not the only one to think of himself as having fallen under Berton's spell. The mainstream conservative press was likewise overwhelmed by its feelings—albeit far less amorous—toward the assassin. Of the most immediate concern was Berton's scandalous, inexplicable acquittal; though press photographs of Berton after the verdict were staged comically (figure 3.3), the judgment had the disturbing effect of excusing, even ratifying, the assassination of Plateau as the final gambit in the bloody confrontations between the *Action Française* and its political enemies. In response, the

Fig. 3.3. Anonymous press photograph of Germaine Berton after her acquittal (1923). Collection of the author.

outraged editors of the center-right newspaper Le Figaro lambasted the verdict as a legal carte blanche, citing Victor Hugo: "You can kill this man in peace."[19] It would have been one thing to have found the defendant guilty and to have suspended her sentence or even pardoned her; it was another, Le Figaro argued, to abandon the machinery of justice to chance and whim. The acquittal marked "a critical date in the history of political and social morals," wrote one reporter, hoping that "in the end, the disorder of spirits and the weakness of the public powers do not lead to troubles in the street."[20] The threat of an outbreak of "legalized" anarchic violence was second only to Le Figaro's moral outrage against Berton's own sense of entitlement.

Louis Aragon, it seems, was all too eager to fuel this outrage. As Maxime Alexandre, a close friend of Aragon's during this period, recalls in his Memoirs of a Surrealist:

> The day after the acquittal, I have a rendezvous with [Aragon], near 11 o'clock, in the basement of Café Select, avenue des Champs-Elysées. Beforehand, as usual, I skim through Le Figaro, where I notice a drawing by Forain: a disheveled shrew [mégère], a smoking revolver in hand, standing in front of a corpse, with the caption: "When's the next one? . . ." Aragon arrives. Barely had I shown him the drawing than he gets up, says, "Wait for me!" and heads for the stairs. I see him a few seconds later, in front of the telephone box, on the landing between the basement and the ground floor, and he calls me over. He looks in the directory, then he asks for a number and pulls me in to hear.
>   —"I desire to speak with Mr. Forain, please," he said; "it's Louis Aragon speaking."
>   I hear Forain's voice:
>   —"What is it?"
>   —"This is Louis Aragon. I welcome you to take this down: Louis Aragon, 18, rue Saint-Pierre, in Neuilly . . . I wish to inform you that the next one will be you!"
>   —"To hell with you."
>   —"The feeling is mutual."[21]

The image to which Alexandre refers, Jean-Louis Forain's editorial cartoon about the verdict, is titled "Le Prochain pour 1924" (In Line for 1924; figure 3.4). The image depicts Berton standing over a corpse with a gun in her hand, leaning against a wall in a pose of deep satisfaction. The caption, referring to the excited crowd gathered to witness this spectacle, reads: "Well, now, what's this? The Seine jury is there, for once!" intimating that Berton would have to be caught red-handed by the jury in order to be convicted. Berton, as both the title and the smug, almost sexual satisfaction on the assassin's face attest, will kill again. Who will be next?

Aragon's implicit death threat in response to Forain's image—"the next one will be you!"—is significant for a number of reasons. The hostility of his response suggests that his telephone call, far more than being a simple prank, stages a counterattack against

— Eh bien ! quoi ?... Le jury de la Seine est là pour un coup.

Fig. 3.4. Jean-Louis Forain, "Le Prochain pour 1924," *Le Figaro*, 30 December 1923. The caption reads: "Well now—what's this? The Seine jury is there, for once!"

Forain's moralistic portrait of Berton, itself likely a parody of the press photographs of Berton reading the news of her acquittal. Alexandre's misremembered account of Berton's portrayal as a "shrewish" woman in Forain's cartoon hardly accounts for the paroxysm of sexual enjoyment she seems to take from the act of killing. Though ostensibly a commentary on the confusion of the jurors, who have stumbled upon the murder scene, the cartoon's real prediction for the coming year seems to be that there will be little to stop the enraptured Berton from continuing to kill for pleasure. To represent Germaine Berton as a "disheveled" and sexually excited killer was, Aragon implied, an act of political suppression that could only partially repress the real danger of her historical presence. The threat she posed was more real than people cared to imagine: Aragon's telephone call also made it clear that the danger did not have to come from the barrel of Germaine Berton's revolver, or even from a revolver at all; it could spring from the unpredictable reactions of angry newspaper readers like Aragon himself. Reinterpreting Forain's cartoon, Aragon implies that the lawless, anarchic social phenomenon to fear was not the serial repetition of individual—and individualist—assaults but a dissemination of the potential for assassination across a broad cultural field.

Philippe Daudet's suicide made this dissemination all the more visible since it was not Berton who pulled the trigger but (presumably) the boy himself, an avid reader of *Le Libertaire*, whose role in Philippe's suicide, whether sinister or not, was curiously bound up with his editorial and literary involvement in the newspaper. What this suggests is that Germaine Berton's greatest danger lay in the reactions she provoked. For the surrealists, her power as an assassin was largely a function of the reception and judgment of her act even more than of the individual deadliness of her act itself. Consequently, in its responses to the events, the group strove to recognize her action as a legitimate form of revolt and yet to shift attention away from her agency in the killings. In place of Berton's own fully articulated, individualist motives for assassinating Plateau, the surrealists conflated the two deaths and attributed them to a multiplicity of causal factors. This overdetermination was structured as a nexus of human relations: erotic, narcotic, and aesthetic all at once.

Fusing attraction, judgment, and causality, this reinvention of Berton's individualist strain of anarchism as an intersubjective field of object relations is precisely what made her such a critical figure in the ethical and political development of the surrealist movement. Carolyn Dean has suggested that the male surrealists rehabilitated "so-called deviant women" like Berton in order to embrace their transgression of taboos and to purge them of criminality, thus affirming what they wished to have in common with them. This identification, in turn, provided access to a transgression of taboos and the release of a desire that "constituted the origin of art."[22] But the surrealists did not embrace Berton for the "transgressiveness" of her act of violence; they instead saw her as the signifier for the relations between politics, journalism, history, and desire that provoked questions of responsibility and choice necessary for imagining "absolute liberty." Rather than providing a wellspring for artistic creation, then, the surrealist "rehabilitation" of Germaine Berton borrowed the principles of aesthetics—judgment, objectification, fascination—in order to work through what were essentially ethical problems.

As Aragon's writings on Berton attest, she was never a rehabilitated criminal for the surrealists at all. Instead they viewed her as a figure who stood for political action—a symbol—but also as an agent of violent historical change whose motives were more significant than her actions.[23] Aragon's legitimation of Berton's motives continued the appeal to critical thinking he voiced in "A Man"; only in Berton's case, the coming-into-consciousness he advocated as an intellectual response to crime he now cited as the source of Berton's motives as well. Though no less aestheticized and objectified by the surrealist group, in other words, Berton herself also became the bearer of an ethical consciousness that Aragon considered vital to the movement's own emerging self-consciousness.

Soon after the assassination of Plateau in January 1923, Aragon published a brief article in *Littérature* that justified the killing as a legitimate and even necessary act. The complete article reads:

> It is impossible for me to consider the death of Marius Plateau as anything other than an occupational hazard in the exercise of a profession for which I feel only contempt. A man's service record during the war does not seem to me by any means to legitimate the actions he has been able to carry out in peacetime; I deny, even formally, the merit of such an argument on whatever occasion it might be invoked. The cowardice of the whole so-called leftist press on the present occasion would fully justify, in my eyes, and with no further information, the act of Mademoiselle B. In an era when all liberty has been left to a faction, blackmailed by sentiments that flatter what is most sordid in a nation, in order to express everywhere and in all terms an arbitrary and dictatorial doctrine, the provocation emanates from those who, at every moment, threaten the liberty that remains for others; and if an individual becomes conscious of this monstrous inequality, of the vanity of all speech before the aggrandizing power of such a faction, I hold this individual to be more than authorized to resort to terrorist means, in particular to murder, in order to safeguard, at the risk of losing everything, that which seems to him—rightly or wrongly—to be precious beyond everything else in the world.[24]

The first part of Aragon's essay echoes the logic of *Le Libertaire*'s contemporaneous coverage of the affair, which similarly attributes Plateau's assassination to a kind of occupational hazard. As one headline quipped, "He Who Lives by the Sword Shall Die by the Sword."[25] *Le Libertaire*'s justification framed Berton's act within the same economy of terrorist action engaged in by the *Action Française*, wherein the victim was responsible for his fate. Aragon's essay distances itself, however, from the depiction of Berton as a mere instrument of this fate, absorbed within an economy of violence and armed by the anarchist cause. For Aragon, Berton's assassination was an act of warfare, the result of a coming-into-awareness that broke with the pieties of postwar nationalism through which Daudet was honored as a war hero. The excesses and imbalances of power enforced by the *Action Française* were, Aragon argues, truly scandalous; Berton's murderous impulse sprang from her recognition of that scandal. Her actions arose from her awareness of "the vanity of all speech before the aggrandizing power" of a faction represented by the *Action Française*, whose hegemonic blackmail of the mainstream press and mainstream opinion was enforced by its quasi-military organizational wing, the *camelots du roi*.

Yet even as Aragon attempted to justify Berton's consciousness, he nevertheless abstracted her faculty of judgment from her actual agency in Plateau's murder. Berton, her name reduced to a gendered initial, "Mademoiselle B.," becomes a function once again; but her function is no longer simply to carry out an isolated act of killing (an occupational hazard) but rather to enact the thinking that authorizes it. The paradoxical nature of this thinking, as I have suggested, is that it is both free and obligated; it is not the property of a subject but the response demanded from a subject by the object relations that call it into being. Although Aragon lauds Berton's judgment, he does not himself share it; instead Berton herself becomes another of the scandalous aesthetic objects by means of which Aragon works through his own ethical system.

Aragon's claim that he could defend Mademoiselle B.'s act "with no further information" was reflected in the surrealists' collective interest in Berton, who championed her cause even before they understood why. Following Le Libertaire's publication of the news of Philippe Daudet's death, the Littérature group (including André and Simone Breton, Paul and Gala Éluard, Aragon, and Péret), sent a letter of support to Georges Vidal, editor of the anarchist newspaper, which reads: "We openly congratulate you for your article 'The Tragic Death of Philippe Daudet,' which appeared in Le Libertaire. We do not belong to your circle, which does not prevent us from admiring the courage you are showing. Our thoughts are with Germaine Berton and Philippe Daudet: we value the merit of any true act of revolt."[26] What, though, do the authors of this letter mean by a "true act of revolt?" How did Berton's action, or Philippe Daudet's, constitute a truer act of revolt than the anarchist bombs and attacks of the Belle Époque, which, in Crevel's words, risked becoming cheap plaster casts? Even in its support for the newspaper's cause, the letter to Vidal does not go so far as to advocate Berton's assassination, or Daudet's suicide, in their specificity; the Littérature group values the "truth" of these actions, judging them positively as specimens of revolt without necessarily adopting them as surrealism's own. The letter did not, in other words, enshrine the assassination and suicide as transcendental forms of revolt that could serve as models, or as a categorical imperative. In fact, it was the very impurity of the Berton-Daudet case that attracted the surrealists' attention in the first place. To the extent that the Berton affair perverted pure anarchist violence with questions of taste and consciousness, the surrealists embraced this perversion as a collapse of a priori standards of moral judgment.

Powers of Derangement

Aragon's advocacy of the open-endedness of thought describes the surrealists' reaction to the Berton affair as a whole; indeed their position toward the assassin and her actions was more intuitive than scientific. The group's correspondence, in fact, suggests that the surrealists changed their minds about Berton, tempering their initial enthusiasm for her violent actions. André Breton, for one, wished at first to isolate an abstract absolute quality of revolt in Berton's assassination. Working against such a search for purity, though, were not only the details of the case itself but also the changing nature of surrealist thought as it developed collectively in the early 1920s. Under pressure from René Crevel to resist commodifying their admiration for acts of revolt, the surrealists gradually reimagined their notions of a "pure" form of revolt as a construct, an artificial paradise whose effects in fact multiplied the scandals and distortions of the case. As Daniel Cottom has suggested, the artificiality of what might be called surrealist purity—as opposed to truth, by contrast "a concern of cops, judges, priests, and intellectuals"—lay precisely in the notion that this so-called purity was "not defined by reason but by antagonism, organization, affection, and association; and so its enemy was not error but slackness, an absence of discipline."[27] Rather than precipitating the group's rejection of the Berton affair, this notion of pure revolt as collective and institutional made the case all the more significant to the group. For it was in the unorthodox nature of her politics, and in the extremity yet intransigence of her allegiances, that Germaine Berton stood as a figure for surrealism's own desire to dedicate itself utterly—yet in a nondoctrinaire fashion—to the demands of independent judgment.

Berton's own statements about her assassination of Plateau are quite modest as to any purity her motives might have contained. Citing her hatred and anger toward the *Action Française*'s support for acts of terror through the years, Berton's letters and statements in defense of her action represent the assassination as an expression of disgust and rage rather than the exercise of a political imperative. As one such statement reads:

> Among the enemies of the proletariat, I've always particularly hated the royalists and their agents provocateurs; it is with a barely contained rage that I recall the abject attitude of M. Maurras and M. Daudet toward workers' organizations. The articles and the press campaign of the *Action Française* in 1920, when the *camelots du roi* made themselves strike-breakers; the incessant calls for force; the shameful slander against certain anarchists and communists, the threats of repression and fascism. Toward the end of 1922 I'd had enough; I would have been a coward if I didn't have the courage to proclaim, in my way, my rancor and disgust.[28]

Although she emphasizes the courage it demanded of her, Berton explains the killing more as a form of expression than as a political act, a proclamation made in the face of what Aragon called "the vanity of all speech." But what happened when this murderous proclamation, as well as the testimony explaining it, was ratified by the court? Could this still be considered a "true act of revolt"? The writers for *Le Figaro* certainly disagreed, writing that the jury's acceptance of ideological rhetoric in place of evidence had the result of "glorifying her crime which, in the current language of the court, is no more than a gesture. The decay of sound legal judgment to a matter of taste has prompted the court to up-hold the paradox of Thomas De Quincey: 'Murder considered as one of the fine arts.'"[29] A court of law, the writer implies, is no place for an aesthetic appreciation of murder.

All the same, Berton's acquittal decriminalized her act of assassination. According to Simone Breton's letters to Denise Lévy, André Breton lost interest in Berton soon after she was acquitted (though not before he, Simone, Aragon, and Max Morise sent a bouquet of roses and carnations with the note: "For Germaine Berton, who did what we did not know how to do").[30] As Simone Breton wrote on the day after Berton's acquittal in December 1923, paraphrasing André Breton's loss of interest in the case: "A gesture ratified by a jury is no longer an act of revolt. She is in accord with society, since, as someone who has been acquitted, she longer interests them. Because of this she is no longer an anarchist; she is less than what she was a year ago, and will become a victim of what we hate. Here her action, all that she represented, ceases and dies."[31] The paradox here is that the surrealist support of Berton's actions as a form of revolt did indeed seem to rely on the lingering criminality and scandal of her presence as a public figure. And yet Berton's acquittal did not end the surrealists' interest in the anarchist assassin. The act of killing Marius Plateau, as well as the inner workings of Berton's own subjectivity, may have lost their immediate appeal for the surrealists—or at least for André Breton—after the court's decision, but her disruptiveness as a media presence and an object of outrage did not.

Nearly a year later, the inaugural issue of *La Révolution Surréaliste* published a second article by Aragon dedicated to Berton, as well as the full-page photo collage of the surrealist group in which Berton's portrait forms the central image (figure 3.1). This group portrait offers the most definitive statement of the assassin's function within surrealist thinking; it demonstrates not only the degree to which the Berton affair haunted the movement but also the function of her image as an aesthetic object that organized the surrealist group's thinking about its responses to worldly political events. Or, more accurately, it shows how Berton's image served to disorganize surrealist thinking, that is, to intrude upon it and disrupt it.

The photograph of Berton at the center of the surrealist group portrait is reprinted from a front-page article in *Paris-Soir* that appeared the day before the trial opened in December 1923.[32] It is but one of the countless images of Berton's face that flooded the press in 1923, yet its strange, twisted affect is so vividly depicted that it seems to reflect an aberration in Berton's physiognomy rather than an aberration in her expression. Why did the surrealists choose such a distorted image? The photograph chosen as the centerpiece for their collective portrait was in fact part of what *Le Libertaire* claimed to be a slanderous media campaign aimed at vilifying the assassin on the basis of visual evidence of her constitutional degeneracy. As an editorial addressed "To Women" argues against the assassin's negative portrayal in the press: "The public papers misrepresent her life. The anthropometric negatives disfigure her face."[33] Aragon was, as we have seen, likewise outraged by

Jean-Louis Forain's similarly vituperative physical representation. Although it might be tempting to add this "deranged" portrait to the gallery of détraquées and madwomen who haunt some of the most famous surrealist texts—the photographs of Jean-Martin Charcot's hysterics reprinted in La Révolution Surréaliste in 1928, or the characters in André Breton's Nadja[34]—the surrealists used the photograph neither to condemn nor to celebrate speculations about her mental or moral aberration. Instead, they selected this particular photograph, I contend, in order to represent her powers of derangement over others.

As she insisted in the statements she made on her own behalf, Germaine Berton claimed full responsibility for her assassination of Plateau. In a testimonial printed in Le Libertaire soon after Plateau's death, Berton stated that "neither material poverty nor psychological deficiency had any influence upon my act."[35] Though uncompromising about her motives, Berton was less successful in managing the numerous interpretations of and reactions to her action, which at once expanded her influence and escaped her control. Aragon, in a short article published in the same inaugural issue of La Révolution Surréaliste, scorned those—himself included—who applauded Berton's act while it served them but abandoned her in the face of "what they call her lapses, her inconsistency."[36] Instead, in this later, surrealist assessment, Aragon suggests that Berton's power lay in the certainty that she would compromise her partisans.

The composition of the photo collage is striking for the way it frames Berton's strange, twisted expression as its organizing motif. As the centerpiece of the group portrait, Berton's photograph—by far the most recognizable—seems to cast the surrealists as her partisans. At the same time, her distorted features invite speculation about the logic of her inclusion: her expression might be said to describe the group's appropriation of her image for their own purposes, their distorted view of the assassination case expressing their beliefs rather then hers. Berton is less a surrealist in her own right than the object of the group's attention.

More accurately, though, the surrealists surrounding her are organized in a way that suggests it is they who are subject to her "distorting" influence. This format—we might think of it as a map or almanac of the male surrealists and fellow travelers of the moment[37]—recalls an earlier surrealist composition that similarly organizes the group around a collective influence. A section from Robert Desnos's early work Nouvelles Hébrides, titled "The Cemetery of the 'Semillante'" (figure 3.5), represents the individual members of the Littérature group as if they had been buried as the communal victims of a shipwreck.[38] The image is thus a map of their headstones, a list of epitaphs. The map imagines the deaths of the individual surrealists, a frequent theme of Desnos's automatic séances, in a way that dramatizes their collectivity as fellow passengers. Here Desnos emphasizes this collectivity by plotting the individual headstones in relation to a central common grave containing the movement's intellectual precursors: Lautréamont, Rimbaud, Jarry, Apollinaire, and Baudelaire, among others. If the arrangement seems ominous, it is

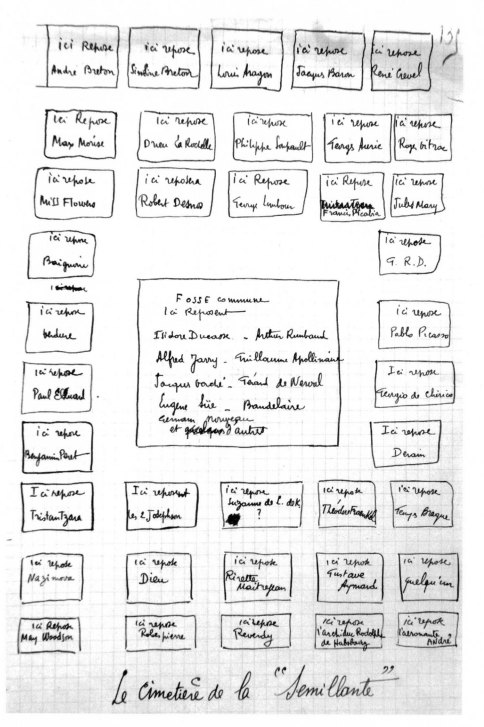

Fig. 3.5. Robert Desnos, manuscript of *Le Cimitière de la "Semillante"* (1923). Photograph by Suzanne Nagy. Image courtesy of the Bibliothèque Littéraire Jacques Doucet, Paris.

perhaps due to the way in which Desnos's homage to these figures is strangely inverted: whereas the precursors' mass grave brings a meaningful order to the surrealist cemetery as a whole, its own crowded ranks subsume its tenants within their entombment as an intellectual genealogy.

The photographic version of these headstones in the first issue of *La Révolution Surréaliste* in 1924 achieves a similar effect, except, we might say, that it imagines the surrealists as victims of assassination rather than shipwreck. By arranging their portraits around a photograph of Germaine Berton, the surrealists impose a similarly influential, yet similarly de-individuated, value on the young assassin's portrait. If they become her metaphorical victims, then equally, Berton's actual, historical role as Plateau's assassin and as the object of Philippe Daudet's desire is likewise rendered metaphorical. Both Berton's individuality and her individualist politics have become assimilated as the figure of the surrealist group's coming-into-being. Indeed, as David Bate has noted, Berton's face both stands for and enacts the rhetoric of association through which the surrealist group imagined itself as a collective.[39] No longer an autonomous political reactionary, Berton has been made into an object to which others react. As I have suggested, this transformation is critical to surrealist praxis more broadly: such an objectified, aestheticized figure becomes a spur for the derangement of systematic thought rather than a model for imitation. This, I propose, is how it became possible for Germaine Berton to serve as both an object and an influence for the surrealist group.

The nature of Berton's influence is more explicitly addressed in the caption chosen by Paul Éluard to complement the group portrait. The caption, an excerpt from Charles Baudelaire's dedicatory preface to *Les Paradis artificels*, reads, "Woman is the being who casts the deepest shadows, or the strongest light, in our dreams."[40] In Baudelaire's original usage the passage explains the logic of dedicating a book on narcotics to a woman, whom Baudelaire addresses only as "J.G.F." Woman, Baudelaire writes, is a natural source of altered consciousness, whereas his book on narcotics examines its artificial sources, hashish and opium. Both, however, are significant to human understanding, since they at once excite and prove the existence of a greater "thirst for the infinite." The surrealists borrow this association of gender with intoxication in order to conceptualize the strange and paradoxical forms of agency they attribute to Germaine Berton. As Baudelaire writes, "Woman is inevitably suggestive; she lives from a life other than her own; she lives spiritually in the imagination, which she haunts and nourishes."[41] A woman, Baudelaire implies, has no interiority of her own; supplemental and parasitical, she exists, like a drug, only for her effects on others. Here Baudelaire revises one gender stereotype in order to create another: rather than an empty vessel or a blank screen, infinitely prone to suggestion, a woman as he imagines her is nothing other than an agent of suggestion. Applied to Germaine Berton, such an argument flies directly in the face of the young individualist's expressed principles of political action. Whereas Berton attributed her actions to disgust and anger, the surrealist group photograph instead foregrounds her powers of derangement and suggestion. In doing so, the surrealists transform the anarchist assassin into a figure of "absolute liberty," an aesthetic object whose intransigence could be witnessed but not possessed. Berton no longer judges; she is instead the object through which judgment takes place.

The surrealist incarnation of Berton—no longer the flesh-and-blood assassin but the woman who cast the most light and the most shadow in surrealist dreams—was manufactured to serve the movement's ends. Germaine Berton's "act of true revolt" was surrealism's own artificial paradise, a real historical phenomenon refashioned, by coincidence and revisionist intervention, to resemble the causality of dream activity. That is, Berton could cast shadows or light on dreams because she represented, in the historically present domain of everyday reality, the lawless agency of wish fulfillment. Yet to the extent that the surrealist movement dedicated itself to realizing the power of this agency—recalling André and Simone Breton's homage to the assassin as someone who achieved what the group only wished it could do—this did not mean that the surrealists sought to promulgate Berton's actual acts; they were interested, rather, in their effects. The assassination, in other words, represented an impossible solution that nevertheless articulated the seriousness of real ethical choices and lingering political divisions.

The paradox here is that the surrealists made Berton stand for the resistance to serving a cause—even a surrealist one. To the extent that she demanded and even exemplified a new form of surrealist thinking, it was in her refusal of any orthodox affiliation that she demonstrated her greatest influence on the group. Louis Aragon, in his brief article accompanying the surrealist group portrait in the first issue of La Révolution Surréaliste, denotes this quality of compromise as the human manifestation of the "stumbling block" of scandal which he discussed in his writings from the previous year. Her individualism spirited away, Berton becomes an agent of surrealist collectivity through her appropriation as a kind of aesthetic, erotic object who, paradoxically, symbolizes her own resistance to appropriation. The complete article reads:

Absolute liberty offends, disconcerts. The sun has always wounded the eyes of its worshippers. Remember that Germaine Berton killed Plateau, and the anarchists applauded—and with them a very small number of men, myself included. But that's because she then served, it seems, their cause. As soon as her life prevailed, who followed her in what they call her lapses, her inconsistency? It's a sure bet that she will *compromise* her partisans. And of course the anarchists exalt life and condemn suicide, which is, as we know, a cowardly act. So it is that they introduce me to shame: they leave me nothing else than simply to prostrate myself before this woman, *admirable in every respect*, which is the greatest challenge I know against slavery, the most beautiful protest raised to the whole world against the hideous lie of happiness.[42]

Berton serves no cause. What remains, Aragon writes, is to admire her "beautiful protest," and thereby to design a cause around the paradoxes and inconsistencies she represents. By doing so, and by placing Berton's "deranged" photograph at their center, Aragon and the surrealists reorganized the assassin's image as a master signifier for their own developing understanding of moral judgment and historical agency.

Surrealism, in other words, served Germaine Berton's cause in the same way that Philippe Daudet did: by invoking her as a calling, as a command to organize the movement's intellectual praxis around the compromise of principles. In its approach to difficult cultural material, the surrealist group's collective function would not rest on transcendent principles or on the enshrinement of specific practices as its ethical basis, as Aragon and Crevel both warned; rather in enshrining—or entombing—Germaine Berton, the surrealists appealed instead to the shifting and fugitive nature of revolt, of the disconcerting and offensive nature of "absolute liberty." This was no longer to praise the absolute liberty of offense, as they claimed Dada had—that is, to institutionalize the subversive appeal of scandalous acts and works of art. Rather, surrealism's collective organization came fully into being around the ethical imperative Berton symbolized, a call to thought that necessarily represented an embrace of error, changes of opinion, and disagreement.

CHAPTER FOUR

DIME NOVEL POLITICS

Assassins, bandits, pirates—you were the first revolutionaries.

Robert Desnos, "Description d'une révolte prochaine" (1925)

In the spring of 1925 the French army launched an offensive in the Rif sector of Morocco in an effort to suppress a major anticolonial uprising in the Spanish protectorate. The rebellion, fronted by the Berber leader Mohammed Ben Abd el-Krim, had begun as a war against Spanish imperialism in the early 1920s. But in 1925 the Rif rebellion became a French concern when France declared war against Abd el-Krim's government in order to protect its own "Oriental" colonial interests in Morocco. In the wake of French military action against the uprisings, the surrealists vociferously supported Abd el-Krim and increasingly turned their attention to revolutionary politics.

This political turn was not unique to surrealism. In the mid-1920s French intellectuals deliberated on the question of their political responsibility after the brief period of relative intellectual autonomy following the First World War. As a survey published in *Cahiers du Sud* in January 1925 asked, "Can intellectuals of our time, whether *littérateurs* or artists, still confine themselves to an ivory tower, or should they be involved in public affairs?"[1] The war in Morocco made this question all the more urgent. Yet even in the context of this shift in sentiment, surrealism's political involvement was remarkable for its comprehensiveness, as the group virtually reinvented itself in the years that followed. As André Breton wrote in his 1926 tract justifying the movement's leftist engagement, "Légitime Défense" (Self-defense), surrealism had committed itself to "mobiliz[ing] all the powers of the imagination" in order to transform the social and economic—no longer merely the spiritual or cultural—conditions of European existence.[2]

The political commitment that would lead to the movement's involvement with the Communist Party in the wake of the Rif War came about, Breton writes, as a call to arms that reshaped the group "from the outside in" as well as from "the inside out." It was an "unprecedented summons, by virtue of which we are chosen . . . to preside over a kind of dizzying exchange" of political discussion.[3] Accordingly, the surrealist movement's engagement in leftist politics was both far-reaching and collective, forged largely through the group's relationships with other intellectual groups, journals, and political organizations of the mid-1920s. It emerged most directly as a collaboration between the writers and artists affiliated with *La Révolution Surréaliste* and the young communist intellectuals affiliated with the journals *Clarté* and *Philosophies*, who came together in support of the anticolonial politics of the Rif uprising. These intellectual relations constituted the immediate field of inquiry from which surrealism's political thinking emerged. Moreover, the very nature of these relations was itself a theoretical concern for the surrealists as they reshaped their assumptions about the nature of collective action and the function of intellectual labor in a revolutionary context.

Surrealism's political thinking in the years immediately following France's entry into the Rif War is tied up, I argue, with the movement's struggles to distinguish itself from the literary and cosmopolitan periodicals that published and reviewed surrealist work but were no longer ideologically in step with the movement's increasingly leftist ties. As the press reviews published by Benjamin Péret and Paul Éluard throughout the existence of *La Révolution Surréaliste* attest, the surrealists remained avid and critical readers of contemporary periodicals, whether leftist (*L'Humanité*, *Le Libertaire*, *Clarté*), right-leaning (*Le Figaro*, *L'Intransigeant*), or literary (*transition*, *La Revue Européenne*, *Les Feuilles Libres*, *Les Cahiers du Sud*).[4] Their awareness of the ideological positions of such publications was acute. In 1925 and 1926, as the group began to focus attention on its political initiative, the relationship of surrealism to the literary and popular media soon became polarized. Whereas surrealist writers such as Philippe Soupault, Antonin Artaud, and Roger Vitrac maintained the validity of addressing their work to a general readership, others, such as Breton, Aragon, Péret, and Éluard, directed their efforts toward the more theoretical task of formulating the intellectual and spiritual exigencies of revolutionary political change. After a long series of formal discussions about the movement's political future, which took place at the *Clarté* offices as well as at the cafés Cyrano and Le Prophète, the first set of writers (Soupault, Artaud, Vitrac) were excluded from the movement for their unwillingness to formalize their political affiliations. These exclusions, I wish to suggest, yielded divergent understandings of surrealism and its demands for intellectual responsibility: writers such as Soupault and, later, Robert Desnos cultivated a more public set of intellectual and cultural affiliations than the group that surrounded Breton, Aragon, Péret, and Éluard.

This chapter measures the effects of surrealism's politicization by studying the group's written work during its first militant phase; it focuses on the group's exclusion of two of its founding members, Soupault and Desnos, who were each dismissed for their "counterrevolutionary" literary activities and admonished for the true crime stories they published. At stake in the exclusions of Soupault (in 1926) and Desnos (in 1928–29) was not simply the question of what kind of literature could be deemed appropriate to the group's turn toward communism but also a broader theoretical question about the forms of political agency this commitment required. Both questions, I argue, hinged on the surrealist movement's changing ideas about the political value and conceptual function of popular crime writing.

Surrealist political thought of this period derived much of its polemical energy from its discussions and arguments about collective action, which invoked dime novel villains and other fictional criminals. The resistance of these figures to discipline and co-optation might have seemed to make them anathema to any viable political understanding. Such pulp criminal figures were central to surrealist political thought, however, rather than exceptions to it—whether Desnos's fascination with Fantômas and Jack the Ripper; Soupault's interest in Edgar Manning, the black criminal dandy of his novel Le Nègre (1927); Breton's obsession with real and fictional deranged women in Nadja (1928); or Crevel's tragic pursuit of the elusive Arthur Bruggle in La Mort difficile (1926). The appeal of such characters was in part their privileged access to urban underworlds, as well as their ambiguous status as figures of "absolute liberty." These texts pose the question whether such fugitive figures somehow embodied rebellion, or whether their inability to embody rebellion demanded a more rigorous pursuit of revolt itself. The surrealist group's use of pulp genres changed in response to the intellectual climate surrounding the Rif War, as I will show, shifting from a means of exploring urban modernity to a literary device for negotiating the contemporary field of intellectual discourse about French colonialism, intellectual responsibility, and political agency. In this same light, I also discuss the surrealist game of "exquisite corpse," a collective game developed simultaneously with the group's introduction to leftist militancy, which playfully interrogated the extent to which agency could be embodied at all.

The group's disagreements about the revolutionary or counterrevolutionary status of its crime writing hinged on the ways these texts approached the problem of politicizing surrealism more broadly. The group's members scrutinized the literary and intellectual periodicals in which their work appeared, measuring their ideological positions toward Marxist and anticolonial politics. Was collective action presumed to be an intrinsic quality within avant-garde writing, or was it an effect, something a text strove to make possible in an extraliterary political sphere? The surrealists' debates and exclusions in response to this question manifested a tendency toward polemicism that would continue to animate surrealist thinking in the decades to come. This extraliterary quality of disagreement was itself key to the movement's politics. Indeed, even as its leftist turn demanded a greater call to order, the movement continued to summon the convulsive forces of dissent and discussion around which the group had come into being.

The Death of Nick Carter

In November 1926 Philippe Soupault was excluded from the surrealist movement. This event took place after a series of meetings at the Café Le Prophète in Paris, themselves the fruit of more than a year of organized discussions about political action and collective discipline. As the notes from the café meetings record, the surrealists claimed that Soupault's literary activities—his prolific output of novels and contributions to "bourgeois" literary journals—had rendered his participation in surrealist circles increasingly sporadic; his dedication to helping the group impose collective discipline was thus compromised. Max Morise and Benjamin Péret attacked Soupault's literary activities as "louche," claiming that his plans to join the Communist Party were only for show and that his membership would consequently be worthless.[5] Moreover, as Pierre Naville, the group's most vocal communist, attested during the meetings, Soupault's novels and other activities "come from and reinforce bourgeois culture rather than tending toward its destruction."[6] Even though Soupault insisted that his writings sought to demoralize the bourgeoisie and thus served a leftist cause, Naville argued that they more readily demoralized his surrealist friends. Soupault was upbraided for his ideological non-evolution, and his literary work was branded as counterrevolutionary, anathema to the group's emerging political project.

To a certain extent Péret and Naville were right: Soupault had remained aloof from the surrealists' recent ties to leftist intellectual journals such as *Clarté* and *Philosophies*, whose members—Marcel Fourrier, Victor Crastre, Jean Bernier, Pierre Bernard, and Camille Fégy among them—were in attendance at the café meetings. He instead favored cosmopolitan modernist journals such as *transition*, the *Nouvelle Revue Française*, *Les Feuilles Libres*, and especially *La Revue Européenne*, where he worked as an editor. And thus, even though *La Revue Européenne* had published texts and reviews by and about Breton, Aragon, Crevel, Vitrac, Éluard, Leiris, Desnos, and Artaud through 1926—most notably Aragon's *Paysan de Paris* and portions of Desnos's *Liberté ou l'amour!*—Soupault's affiliation with such cosmopolitan literary journals now underscored surrealism's radical change of direction. Indeed, unlike the majority of the other surrealists, who sacrificed their growing stature in contemporary French literature for the sake of politics, Soupault refused to abandon his affiliations with internationalist journals and presses.[7]

The ostensible reason for Soupault's exclusion from the surrealist movement was the publication of one of his short stories in the Franco-Italian journal *900*, edited by Massimo Bontempelli and Curzio Malaparte, in the fall of 1926. Malaparte was at this time a member of the Italian Fascist Party, and thus, in spite of the journal's publication of notable modernist writers—including James Joyce, Pierre MacOrlan, Max Jacob, Blaise Cendrars, Ivan Goll, and Georges Ribemont-Dessaignes—the surrealists decried the journal as fascist. As Aragon wrote in an article in *Clarté* attacking both the journal and Soupault's decision to publish in it, 900 was "a journal fed by state funds and supported by fascist banks, toward the pure and simple goal of pan-Italian propaganda." Even though the French literary press had hailed the journal as representing a "universal diplomatic language," Aragon argued that its contributors "think only of gold. They have sold out and are forever for sale."[8] Citing the generous compensation the magazine offered for contributions, Aragon argues that the journal's real ties to the Italian Fascist Party expressed the truth of all so-called internationalist literary periodicals: their cosmopolitanism was but a pretext for their commercialism, which meant that seemingly apolitical journals like 900 could become a haven for any political opportunist with enough ready cash. As Aragon writes, "In every country, such money-grubbing schemers find and recognize their fellow creatures, who, for a few cents, will always help them."[9]

Yet the problem of Soupault's publication in 900 revealed as much about the surrealist group's own radical change in intellectual affiliations as it did about Soupault's allegedly counterrevolutionary tactics. As it sought to transform itself from an experimental literary movement into a leftist intellectual collective, the group's real issue with Soupault was the ideological difference between the internationalist catholicity of the journals in which Soupault published and the relative theoretical rigor of the leftist journals (such as *Clarté* and the daily communist newspaper *L'Humanité*) with which surrealism had affiliated itself by late 1926. Even so, Soupault's fiction from this period also reveals his own distance from the movement's conceptual and political orientation: while the other surrealists attempted to mobilize literary activity toward political ends, Soupault made no claim to the revolutionary power of literary activity. In fact, Soupault explicitly critiqued the movement's revolutionary pretensions at the Café Le Prophète meeting during which he was formally excluded. "Surrealism," he testified before the group, "cannot lead to an effective revolution."[10] Soupault instead considered experimental literature a device for championing the intransigence of "life" over either revolutionary politics or organized surrealist practice.

The short story that Soupault published in 900, "The Death of Nick Carter," made no overt political claims. Its citation of Nick Carter invokes the American dime novel detective serials, about which Aragon and Soupault had each written as early as 1921; turning away from contemporary politics, Soupault's story might seem a nostalgic look backward to such boyhood stories of the prewar era, as well as to an earlier moment in surrealism itself. The story does, however, outline a more frontal response to the intellectual and political upheavals of the mid-1920s, registering Soupault's ideological distance from the other surrealists even as he continued to share many of the group's aesthetic and ethical preoccupations. For Soupault, race would trump politics as the mode of lived experience toward which writing could appeal for historical agency. This position, which Soupault would articulate more fully in his 1927 novel *Le Nègre*, is visible in his earlier adaptation of the dime novel form in "The Death of Nick Carter." Unlike the thousands of installments of the Nick Carter series published in the United States and France from the 1880s through the 1920s, Soupault's modernist update of the dime novel franchise recasts Carter, the white American detective, as the agent in an oneiric narrative of pursuit in which Carter dies. No longer in possession of the miraculous ability to cheat death at the end of each tale, the white detective pursues but cannot apprehend the mysterious Albert Martel, the black American fugitive who supplants him in triumphantly reading about Carter's death in the next day's paper.

The significance of this very brief experiment in genre fiction lies in its use of the dime novel genre to propose a narrative of racial supersession that articulates the cultural position on American blackness which Soupault proposed in a number of his other published writings. This work would culminate in a 1928 study of jazz, as well as in Le Nègre, which celebrates the "absolute liberty" of its titular black villain in language reminiscent of the other surrealists' admiration for writers such as Lautréamont, Rimbaud, Baudelaire, and Sade, as well as for the real-life anarchist Germaine Berton. Soupault's argument for African Americanness as a quintessentially modern form of being was also significant within the French colonial discourse of the 1920s for its deliberate and violent substitution of American blackness for European whiteness. As we will see, Soupault's literary efforts to privilege an essentialized notion of American blackness derived from an understanding of insurrectional agency which Soupault originally shared with the other surrealists, but which the rest of the group had since modified under the aegis of communism. Whereas the group, along with fellow travelers from the Clarté group, now theorized revolution as a radical form of political change that could, by definition, be practiced by the European proletariat, Soupault's writing posited revolt as a form of agency essentially alien to white Europeans.

"The Death of Nick Carter," which marks this distinction, begins in medias res with a late-night phone call to Carter's apartment, describing an investigation already under way. Soupault writes:

> Four o'clock in the morning.
> Nick Carter was asleep but was listening even in his sleep.
> The ringing of the telephone scarcely woke him.
> He was expecting the voice of his assistant, Patsy.
> —Hello—Nick?
> —365—it's I.
> —I looked it over—without much luck.
> —Let's hear it.
> The house opens like an oyster. You have to push with all your might to get in, a shoulder isn't enough. In the anteroom are fourteen tables side by side according to size. On

the first is an orange and a knife, on the second a green feather-duster, on the third two sea-shells, on the fourth a new Spanish penny.[11]

Soupault's tale begins with a blank cataloguing of physical evidence characteristic of his earlier fiction (see chapter 1); Patsy's minute description of the house's contents continues until the assistant recounts how a mysterious man, "a negro, very tall, dressed in evening clothes and white gloves," springs up and flees the scene.[12] Without ever divulging the purpose of the investigation, the narrative then shifts to a second house, a clinic, in which Patsy interviews a doctor about a black former attendant named Albert Martel. In the story's third act a new attendant arrives at the clinic, where he encounters a man named Albert and, after a brief pursuit, tumbles with him to the ground. Revolvers are pulled, whereupon the detective's assistants, disguised as tramps, scale the walls of the institution. Chaos breaks out inside the asylum. In the aftermath, there are three corpses: Carter's two assistants, Chick and Patsy, as well as Nick Carter himself, who had been disguised all along as the new attendant. The story closes with a cinematic image of Albert Martel receiving the news of Carter's death:

About seven o'clock in the evening the newsvendors on the boulevard were yelling.
DEATH OF NICK CARTER
A negro with a bandaged hand bought a paper and gave a hundred franc note to the newsboy: "Keep the change," he said.[13]

In a story in which the titular hero's only actions are to listen and to die, the conditions of Carter's death in a madhouse riot present this final scene as Martel's triumph, insofar as he has escaped his pursuers without revealing, even to readers of the story, anything of his identity.

In spite of its dime novel origins and almost total lack of disclosure, "The Death of Nick Carter" functions as a true crime story, insofar as the detective's fictional death marked the historical deaths of the dime novel series' original authors, who had each written under the pseudonym "Nick Carter": as Régis Messac notes in his 1929 study of detective novels, the writers John Russell Coryell, Thomas C. Harbaugh, and Frederik Van Rensselaer Dey all died between 1922 and 1924.[14] These successive deaths uncannily replicated the serial's symbolic economy of killing off Nick Carter in every episode, only to have him miraculously resurrected in the next. Real flesh-and-blood writers, however, are unresurrectable, as Messac notes, and thus the peculiarity of "Nicholas Carter" dying more than once points tellingly to the industrial production of the serials themselves, in which both authors and stories were essentially interchangeable. Soupault's own heady literary output suggests his kinship with this dime novel productivity. The industrially produced weekly magazines such as the Nick Carter series, as well as the *Fantômas* novel and film serials of the immediate prewar years, represented a mode of artistic production Soupault considered analogous to that of surrealism, as well as to his own frenetic literary career. Dime novels were the products of a kind of automatic writing, Soupault claimed, composed almost mechanically and characterized by a near-absolute degree of spontaneity.[15]

In addition to providing a historical reflection on changing conditions of modern authorship, Soupault's Nick Carter tale also functions as a true crime story insofar as the figure of Albert Martel presages the more fully developed character of Edgar Manning in Le Nègre. In this later novel, the titular black character is modeled on the real-life Edgar Manning, a drug dealer and occasional jazz drummer notorious for his ties to the deaths of a number of English film starlets. "The Death of Nick Carter," significant enough to appear in a 1926 anthology of new French prose, and again in English in Eugène Jolas's transition magazine in 1927, thus outlines Soupault's developing interest in popular American modernism, and especially in African American blackness.

Soupault's attention to American, and particularly African American, popular culture emerged during a period of crisis in France's colonial imagination when increasingly militant groups of young French intellectuals sought to distinguish themselves not only from the nationalist policy of colonial absorption and imperialist progress championed by the right, but also from the melancholic pacifism tentatively adhered to by an older generation of leftists. These young intellectuals, whose ideas were rapidly becoming visible in the explosive rise of little magazines and literary periodicals, looked for solutions to this intellectual and political impasse. For Soupault, these periodicals—and their exploration of experimental writing and American popular culture in particular—were themselves valuable for exploring forms of modernity that both rejected French imperialism and supplanted a moribund European style of life. The other surrealists, however, reconciled the political tensions of the French left much differently, rejecting cosmopolitanism, and rejecting Soupault, too, in favor of the revisionist form of Marxism they would develop during their discussions with the Clarté and other leftist groups in 1925 and 1926.

The historical crisis French intellectuals faced in the mid-1920s had less to do with either the United States or France's own "Negro" colonies in sub-Saharan Africa and the Caribbean than with its "Oriental" colonies—that is, in North Africa and Asia. The real emergency lay in Morocco, when, as we have seen, in the first months of 1925 France became involved in suppressing an anticolonial insurgence in the Rif region of the Spanish protectorate in Morocco. Then as now, the violent North African uprising and its equally violent suppression lent an immediacy to a longer-standing postwar discourse about the future of European imperialism and the so-called decline of the West. In early 1925 the journal Cahiers du Mois published an inquiry, "The Call of the Orient," with other periodicals following suit.[16] A number of French studies of Oswald Spengler's 1919 work The Decline of the West furnished this discussion with a metaphorical language reiterated throughout the periodical literature of the 1920s: the Occident represented the "civilized"

European nations whose recent world war was symptomatic of Europe's moral and intellectual decline, while the Orient, by contrast, represented the formerly great imperial civilizations whose empires had already decayed, leaving a residual barbarism whose influences were now spreading back toward the West. These terms, though not the values assigned to them, were used by the left as well as the right to signify a variety of cultural positions, from the most eugenicist to the most revolutionary. Soupault's dime novel paean to African American culture would similarly borrow from this language of Occidental decay and Oriental volatility, albeit in ways that would clash with the other surrealists' relation to Orientalism.

Positioned between the metaphorical vagaries of Occident and Orient and the immediate historical conditions of real anticolonial insurgence, left-leaning postwar intellectuals were divided in their political stance. The surrealists, even before their exclusion of Soupault, were no exception. At first the group appealed explicitly to the disruptive power of "Oriental" influences as an antidote to French imperialism and bourgeois subjectivity alike, writing in essays such as Breton's "Introduction to the Discourse on the Paucity of Reality" (1924) and the anticolonial group tract "The Revolution First and Always" (1925) that it was "the Mongols' turn to set up camp in our squares."[17] This Orientalism reached its peak in the "Open Letter to Mr. Paul Claudel, French Ambassador to Japan," a tract distributed in July 1925, which asserts, "We hope, with all our might, that revolutions, wars, and colonial insurrections will come and annihilate this Occidental civilization, whose parasites you defend in the Orient; and we appeal to this destruction as the least unacceptable state of affairs for the mind."[18]

The initial surrealist imperative for "Oriental" revolution—repeated in a series of such open letters and proclaimed at a number of public events—was so strongly phrased as an appeal to barbarism that it elicited a barrage of angry responses among the literary intelligentsia. Louis Aragon's friend Pierre Drieu La Rochelle, for instance, published in *La Nouvelle Revue Française* his essay "La Veritable Erreur des surrealistes," lampooning what he considered the movement's sad turn in grafting an anarchic literary avant-garde onto a fixed ideological position. Addressed to Aragon, Drieu's essay questions why surrealism would put its faith in anything, and is especially contemptuous of the "feeble" surrealist statement that light comes from the East. "How," Drieu writes, "can anyone prefer the East to the West? As for me, I believe the Russian sociologists no more than I believe the American economists. And as for the undergraduate Chinese or Hindu, please!"[19] Drieu attacks the surrealists' credulity in using older civilizations as models, mocking their fascination with a "cramped terrain, cluttered with old corpses and gibberish from another century."[20] As if anticipating his later shift from libertarian Dada to right-wing cynicism, Drieu's assessment of surrealism's politics essentially accused the movement of associating with the wrong people. As he writes: "In politics as in literature, here you are once more gathering up a bunch of old cigarette butts [mégots]: images, Freud, Einstein, Caligari, literary painters, *poètes maudits*, all that is rationalist mysticism—and today it's neo-Orientalism.[21] Aragon's response to Drieu's essay the following month points out that the object of Drieu's scorn was as much the German nationality of the *mégots* that surrealism was collecting—not just Freud, Einstein, and Caligari but Marx and Hegel as well—as the neo-Orientalism he derided as the group's latest cheap thrill. However accurately Drieu might have characterized the movement's brief faith in the concept of the Orient, Aragon's response reasserts that the surrealists deployed their Orientalism to resist the xenophobia at work in Drieu's portrayal of German intellectuals as trash and of "Oriental" thinkers as nameless quacks and undergraduates.[22]

Similarly hostile responses to surrealism's initially Orientalist politics appeared in the two magazines that published Soupault's story "The Death of Nick Carter." In "The Occident," published in *transition* in 1927, the future filmmaker Jean-Georges Auriol disparages the general sympathy of young French writers toward the metaphorical appeal, if not the actual politics, of the Rif insurgency. "At present," writes Auriol, "it is customary to believe firmly that the young French literature is turned entirely toward the East, and that it looks to the Orient for rejuvenation, clarity, and happiness."[23] Auriol, however, argues that "the assimilation of an Asiatic spirit and culture can bring nothing but disorder, hate of life, and impotence of manifest creative reaction, and a passive inactivity and shrinking which tends toward nothingness." He wishes instead to distinguish his own understanding of avant-gardism from this orientation, asserting that "there is a whole generation of young men in France who, unlike their immediate seniors, await salvation from the West."[24] The position taken by Massimo Bontempelli in 1927 in the editorial statement for 900 was even more virulently anti-Orientalist. As he writes in the journal's first issue: "We are Occidental down to our toes. We profess an innate and treasured mistrust for the Orient. I detest belly dancing and Asiatic revelation. If the desire strikes me to believe in metempsychosis, I would rather receive it from Pythagoras' own hands."[25] Bontempelli's unrepentant anti-Orientalism was hardly a fascist ideological position in itself, Aragon's exposé notwithstanding. But in the context of the Rif War, such calls for classical renewal were antithetical to the surrealists' initially pro-Oriental position. More problematically, whereas the surrealists had, by the time of 900's publication, shifted the terms of their own anticolonial politics, Bontempelli's editorial statement exaggerated the East-West binary in a way that situated European modernism—and especially the metempsychotic project of a writer such as Joyce—as the antithesis of anticolonial insurgence.

Auriol, however, argued that the solution to European decline and "Oriental" disorder alike could be found in what he calls the "brutal influence of America." It is the "adventurous, violent, and touching" literature and cinema of American modernism, Auriol writes, "that will save us, because it presents us with a primitive force which properly belongs to us."[26] Unlike Soupault, who would revise Auriol's modernist America by attacking Fordist capitalism and privileging jazz, film, and African American culture, Auriol appealed to the American West in neocolonial terms. His United States was a white America, the Wild West to the West of western Europe, which could be mined for its rejuvenating spirit.

Soupault's own response to the Orient-Occident debate was more complex, targeting the bankruptcy of European culture, and of Western capitalism, without erecting monuments to the East. Although he maintained that his affiliation with 900 was not an ideological one, Soupault remained similarly convinced that European culture could not simply be revitalized by a sharp dose of Orientalism. Nor, however, could it merely delve into its own classical past for renewal. Europe, he writes, is a "shoddy garden covered with corpses."[27] In his contribution to the *Cahiers du Mois* survey on "The Call of the Orient," Soupault lambastes the will to domination he finds in Henry Ford, Jesus, and the Standard Oil Company as characteristic features of "that immense, prodigious, and unqualifiable vanity" that divides the West from the East, and which has now given way to an "enfeebled, demoralized spirit" under the shadow of death.[28] In a manner that in many ways reflected his surrealist affiliation, Soupault's writings maintained that European culture was moribund and required demolition rather than revitalization.

The source of this radical gesture, though, was neither the Orient nor the revolutionary agency of the Communist Party, but the intransigent modernity of American popular culture—and of African American blackness in particular—for which the experimental writing represented in internationalist avant-garde magazines such as *transition* and *La Revue Européenne* could serve as conduits. For Soupault, writing did not represent simply a highbrow attachment to belles lettres, as the surrealist attacks against his "louche activities" insinuated. Rather, these pursuits were for Soupault a style of life, inextricable from a mode of being that included not only the vigorous literary production his dime novel tastes reflected but also the noctambulism and racial longing featured in his autobiographical fictions. Revolt, Soupault's fiction implied, existed as a fugitive property of the modern city and its criminal and racial underworlds; the promise of experimental writing lay in its dedication to bringing to light the intransigent modes of existence this underworld presented.

In his 1925 novel *Le Coeur d'or*, for instance, Soupault narrates his efforts to uncover the secrets of a town in which he has lost himself, in an effort literally to escape his own bankrupt bourgeois subject position. "Like a detective," Soupault writes, "I look for traces, signs, a trail. I pursue the phantoms of a crowd. My path, my trail, is scattered with corpses. Over here is a dead train station, the lifeless center square; over here is the market where the wind scatters papers, knocks over trash cans, and stirs odors."[29] Soupault's detective story metaphorics are suffused with the very sense of European decline that Auriol claims the genre resists; the detective trope articulates the vexed relationship of the narrator to the "scattered corpses" of European city life, scrutinizing it from the perspective of a privileged outsider.[30] More significantly, albeit less self-consciously, Soupault

Fig. 4.1. Cover of *Nick Carter Detective Library*, no. 1 (1891). Image courtesy of Stanford University Library Special Collections.

also borrowed the dime novel's promise of infinite imaginary access to the criminal as well as social underworld. As an early masthead for the Nick Carter series renders visually (figure 4.1), the great American detective solved crimes primarily through his keen knack for disguise—disguises that often took the form of ethnic impersonation. The forms of transgression and alterity this proffered were part of what gave the Nick Carter series its appeal, and Soupault's fiction leading up to "The Death of Nick Carter" often fantasized about such possibilities.

Soupault's Carteresque penchant for impersonation stems from his Dada period, which was characterized as much by bodily performance as by writing. His dynamic "practice of life" brought about endless walks through Paris, as well as the disruption of theatrical events, and extended to racial cross-dressing as well. Matthew Josephson, an American observer of surrealism's early years, recalls Soupault's racial impersonation as a formative part of his avant-garde persona. Calling Soupault a "regular ball of fire," Josephson writes that "loving all things African, he collected records of Negro spirituals and jazz tunes, and once posed as an African when he appeared at a Dadaist soirée, his face daubed with burnt cork, and splendidly costumed as the president of the Liberian Republic."[31] What is artificially and parodically "African" about Soupault's blackface costume of the early 1920s becomes, by 1926, an essential quality of racial otherness that Soupault can only admire from a distance. This shift is announced in "The Death of Nick Carter," wherein Soupault fictionally dispenses with the dime novel tactic of ethnic impersonation in favor of "real" American blackness. Although, as we will see, Soupault's more explicit fictional treatment of blackness in Le Nègre bears its own peculiar form of racial essentialism, the earlier short story nonetheless revises the popular French fascination with "African" primitivism as the framework for characterizing American blackness. For Soupault, African American blackness provided an alternative to the rhetoric of "Occident" and "Orient" that characterized a large part of contemporary political discourse.

Even though Soupault would soon abandon the notion of a barbarous and generalized Orient, the language of violent supersession lingers in his fiction and would be developed most explicitly in Le Nègre. The Orientalist language of "revolutions, wars, and colonial insurrections," would linger, too, in the surrealist group's polemics, as well as in the intensity of its brief period of communist engagement.[32] Yet whereas Soupault staged his literary politics as the violent encounter between American blackness and bourgeois European decline, the surrealists, under the influence of the Communist Party, began to focus more rigorously on the nature of revolutionary change itself.

The Reign of Freedom

In a way that would come to define the surrealist movement's political thinking by the time of Soupault's exclusion in late 1926, the radical left rejected the metaphorical generalizations of "Occident" and "Orient" which public intellectual debate tended to privilege, and which at first had been central to surrealist definitions of revolutionary action. The left instead viewed events such as the Rif War as colonial crises with immediate economic and political ramifications. In a heated contribution to the journal *Europe*, for instance, Marcel Fourrier—a leading writer for *Clarté* and one of the animating figures in the surrealist group's political discussions—challenged its readers:

> When the French planes bombarded Riffian villages, scattering bombs over marketplaces under orders from French generals and killing women and children by the hundreds, most of you put forward the great word "civilization" in finding a shameful excuse for this crime. . . . And what is already cropping up is the idea of a possible defense of European civilization (which is only the end of bourgeois civilization) against Barbarism and the Orient (which represents the logical revolt of oppressed people against that famous bourgeois European civilization that carries out its actions, even murder and collective theft, behind its men of letters and intellectuals).[33]

As Fourrier's language suggests, the young left's response to the Rif War was not only to oppose the notion of "revitalizing" Occidental civilization through Oriental contact but also, increasingly, to resist the metaphorics of "Occident" and "Orient" altogether. This represented a significant shift in the avant-garde's political rhetoric, since many of the same writers who had appealed to "the Orient" in early 1925 were suddenly adopting the communist rhetorical tactic of identifying Western capitalism with state terror, and were now organizing their artistic activities according to an established communist platform.

This sudden shift, too, received criticism from the more traditional left. A long article by the Leninist (and later Trostkyite) writer Marcel Martinet, "Contre le courant" (Against the Grain), attacks both the arrivism and, in particular, the abstraction of young avant-gardists who summoned "revolution" in ways that had nothing to do with the proletariat. Whereas Martinet hopes that the avant-garde might produce "some honest boys who will one day merit their place in the workers' ranks," he admits that for the moment the revolutionary interest of groups such as the surrealists remains "a Marxism for use in nursery schools." He continues, in language that directly implicates the surrealists: "Their surintellectuality resolves to a weak little form of thinking, wherein all the edginess of our Lenins-in-short-pants' assertions can't sharpen their rudimentary and disordered ideas, which would make even the thickest workers laugh, were it not forbidden for cooped-up workers to think and laugh. These infantile exercises will count little."[34] Martinet's dismissal of "sur-intellectualism" has a conceptual as well as a derogatory point: the neo-revolutionary position adopted by surrealism and other such groups was mistaken in its attack on European nations and civilizations, alienating the very populations it sought to rally. More damningly, these young writers and artists couched their political appeals in terms of violence, at the expense of the intellectual tradition upheld by the French left since the days of the Dreyfus affair. As Martinet writes:

> It's "down with intelligence," another inanity committed by these kids, whose only baggage is the two cents' worth of rhetoric they picked up in school, but where, once more, we have to admit our share of the blame. We listened all too well to our Sorel, once so rightly admired, when he rejoiced that the Russian Revolution was carried out—and this is far from being true—to the cry of "Death to the intellectuals!" . . . This cry, in the recesses of the popular imagination, was immediately translated, in effect, as "Down with intelligence!" And thus comes about bad action, both against the civilization without which the revolution is nothing but a vain and bloody farce, as well as against the workers who carry out revolution only with and for civilization.[35]

For an earlier-generation Marxist such as Martinet, the mistake made by avant-garde groups like the surrealists was less that they harbored abstract notions of the Occident and the Orient than that their ideas about revolutionary change, and especially about revolutionary violence, were equally abstract. Breton would later defend surrealism's political involvement against Martinet's patronizing reproaches in his 1926 essay "Self-Defense"; yet what is remarkable about the surrealists' meetings of 1925 and 1926 is the extent to which the group in fact heeded Martinet's critique.

One of the reasons for this is that the group discussions of 1925 and 1926 reflected the presence and influence of the communist intellectuals from the journals *Clarté* and *Philosophies* who, like Fourrier and Martinet, maintained that the rise of the proletariat and the overthrow of capitalism was a logical and "civilized" rather than barbarous historical process. Like Martinet, too, the *Clarté* and *Philosophies* groups demanded not that intellectuals abolish intelligence but that they slough off the accessory role into which their cultural position had cast them. The collective discussions of 1925 and 1926 strove, indeed, to change the terms of contemporary intellectual debate about political action and collective organization. For one thing, the focus of the left's attention was no longer to be the binary relation between the West and the East (or between Occidental order and Oriental barbarism), but instead the historical demands of the global proletariat. Second, these political discussions questioned the vague, transcendental notion of historical causality implicit in popular ideas about European decline and regeneration; they redefined revolutionary action in Marxist-Leninist terms rather than in the language of overthrow and rampage.

Some of the strongest pressure on the surrealists to adjust their thinking was in fact exerted from within. One of the more active participants in the group discussions between the surrealists and the Clarté-ists was Pierre Naville, who published a tract in early 1926 titled The Revolution and Intellectuals: What Can the Surrealists Do? urging the surrealists to adopt a more rigorously Marxist platform. As Naville explained in his memoirs, his tract was an attempt to dislodge surrealism from its early Orientalism, whose tangled metaphorics reflected the movement's lack of clarity about its revolutionary aims. "I was worried," Naville writes, "about the ways we were making free with the real Orient, on behalf of a badly drawn figure, more in accordance with our own drives than with itself, modeled on everything from Montesquieu's Lettres persannes to Malraux's Tentation de l'Occident; it was a symbol of our doubts and upheavals, and no longer of the revolution we strove to achieve."[36] Naville's pamphlet urged the surrealists to recognize the sociological nature of revolution, and to acknowledge the historical reality of the human populations that intellectuals had recently been turning into symbols. As Naville wrote, echoing the Clarté group's imperative: "In a Marxist vision of the global situation, Asia and America can by no means be considered symbols of a reality in consciousness. They are at the present time the expression of an actual state of affairs, measurable in terms of quantity and quality, from the point of view of the extreme development of capitalism and the revolutionary crisis that must permit the birth of socialism."[37] As a recognition and interruption of the surrealists' tendency to mythologize the Orient, Naville's pamphlet remained consistent with the group's professed dedication to breaking up such reified systems of belief. More immediately, though, its critique of surrealism's conceptual language—scorning the reduction of geopolitical actuality to "symbols of a reality in consciousness"—suggested that the group needed to rethink its basic assumptions if it privileged the latter "reality" over the former.

The yearlong commingling of the surrealists and their fellow leftists soon altered the movement's rhetoric. By the fall of 1926 the majority of the group declared itself in favor of a definition of revolution grounded in socialist terms. More difficult than this rhetorical shift, however, were the theoretical adjustments the group would have to make with respect to its own activities: How would it be possible to separate the work of intellectuals from the kinds of historical mythmaking that Naville condemned? At the heart of the surrealists' resulting discussions was the question of how writing and art could be assimilated into a leftist political project. What was to be the role of writing and publication in an idea of revolutionary action based no longer on "a state of mind" but on a real set of material circumstances?

There has been no shortage of writing about surrealism's involvement with commu-

nism and its brush with political militancy.[38] And to a large extent this writing has use-
fully emphasized the collective nature of the group's leftist turn, as well as the seriousness
of its political intentions: the surrealists no longer toyed with the notion of revolution as
a metaphor for avant-garde provocation but, as a statement by the Clarté writer Jean Bernier
attests, defined it explicitly as "the violent overthrow of capitalist society through the establishment of the dictatorship of the proletariat, and the maintenance of this dictatorship, not as an end but as a means."[39] It is important to note, however, that Bernier's
synthesizing statement about the Clarté and surrealist groups' project to define revolution
already reveals its distance from communist orthodoxy in the way it stresses the instrumental nature of the dictatorship of the proletariat. As the end result of the group's yearlong discussions, Bernier's statement privileges the "superior phase" of communist
society, during which class would disappear in favor of a currently inconceivable state
wherein, Bernier writes, citing Engels, "humanity will leap from the reign of necessity to
the reign of freedom."[40] As traditionally Marxist as this might sound, Bernier's definition
in fact downplays the utopian necessity of a postrevolutionary classless society, instead
making this "reign of freedom" the conditional end of revolutionary activity: liberty is not
the logical consequence of revolutionary violence but its singular purpose, to be remembered constantly. What this meant was, first of all, that other forms of liberatory activity—
especially intellectual work, poetry, art, and psychoanalysis—were intrinsic to a revolutionary project that was nonetheless organized economically and socially. Second, as the
group's judgment of Soupault revealed, it meant that the role of writing and art was not
simply to represent social upheaval or postrevolutionary society but to participate in the
revolutionary project of total liberation.

While the majority of surrealist writers turned their theoretical attention toward carry-
ing out this project, Soupault's immediate response was to augment—rather than to interrogate—his literary affiliations and writerly output. Absent for the large part of the
group's political meetings, Soupault defied the pressure to conceptualize revolution on
strict historical-materialist grounds. The cosmopolitanism of Soupault's editorial work
and the peripatetic nature of his fiction seemed to offer solutions to the problems surrealism faced; his fictions, composed quickly in terse, cinematic language, clung to the
promises of spiritual and cultural revolt that characterized the movement's pre-Marxist
thought. As he explained during the 1926 meeting at which the case for his exclusion was
discussed, Soupault considered his writing to be continuous with his understanding of
surrealism as a way of life, not as a line of praxis.[41] To this end he channeled American-
ism as a living, anarchic alternative to European thought, looking to the dime novel as
both a model for his prolific artistic production and an apparatus for structuring the metaphysical wanderings of his semiautobiographical novels and stories. At the same time, the
dime novel's sensationalized exploration of the criminal underworld remained a means
for him to pursue the demoralization of bourgeois culture. Soupault's "louche" persis-

tence in employing the literary figures of European decline and non-European revolt so firmly rejected by the left derived from his insistence on approaching revolutionary change as a transformation in lived experience; this transformation, Soupault claimed, existed as a modality of being rather than as the historical result of political struggle. Whereas the other surrealists shifted their focus to the rise of the global proletariat, Soupault claimed that the origin of revolutionary change would be African American.

The Corpse of Europe

Soupault's 1927 novel *Le Nègre*, written largely during his surrealist period but published after his exclusion from the group, radicalizes his notion of American blackness as a form of life antithetical to Occidental, European decay. The novel opens with a chapter titled "The White Negro, or, the Bad Example," which frames the novel's notions of blackness within a historical account of anticolonial uprising. Whereas the body of Soupault's novel is set in contemporary Europe, the opening chapter recounts the dramatic rise and fall of Faustin Soulouque, the former slave and revolutionary hero who became emperor of Haiti in 1849, only to be overthrown, ridiculed, exiled, and reduced to poverty by the time of his death in 1867. Soupault's opening chapter first appeared in magazine form in *Les Feuilles Libres* in late 1925 as "Histoire d'un nègre" (Story of a Negro); in the political climate of 1925, Soupault's tale of Soulouque's violent rise to power might have been read as a parable of anticolonial uprising published in response to Abd el-Krim's leadership in Morocco. The problem such uprisings faced, Soupault's story suggested, was the problem of exemplarity: at stake in Soupault's parable of revolutionary energy run amok was not the legitimacy of anticolonial violence itself but the historical form such uprisings took. Under the guise of satirizing emperors, that is, Soupault's story satirizes the imitative nature of revolution itself; the parable thus offers a response to the surrealist group's discussions with the *Clarté* group about the nature of revolutionary action.

In Soupault's account, Soulouque gains visibility in the successful Haitian revolution of 1803 and rises through the military ranks. When the time is right, he poisons the revolutionary president and becomes president himself. Soulouque then begins exterminating his real and perceived enemies in a campaign Soupault likens to the Terror, modeling himself increasingly on Napoleon. Demanding a throne and a crown, he becomes, in turn, "Faustin Soulouque, Faustin the 1st, Emperor Faustin," following Napoleon's own rise to emperor and eventual exile and downfall.[42] In Soupault's text, Soulouque's self-fashioning as a Napoleonic European satirizes the imitative nature of Soulouque's political aims, as well as the similarity of their defeats; more broadly, the comparison disparages the ambitions of both historical figures. Unlike Soulouque's treatment in the nineteenth-century press as a caricature of Napoleonic gallantry, Soupault's version of Soulouque suggests that he was a "bad example" for anticolonial uprising because his downfall revealed the extent to which his ambitions were modeled on European notions of imperialism. Anticolonial insurgence, Soupault suggests, needed to break away not only from European colonial power but from European forms and ideas as well.

Renamed "The White Negro, or, the Bad Example" for its inclusion in Le Nègre in 1927, the account of Soulouque's imitation of white Empire presents a stark historical contrast between the revolutionary logic of the nineteenth century and the contemporary story of its titular black protagonist, Edgar Manning, which follows. Contrary to the "bad example" of Soulouque, Edgar Manning "needed no illusion, no consolation"; whereas Soulouque's life was parodically bound to the historical figure of Napoleon, Manning's life "centered on the present, on the very moment in which he lived."[43] For Soupault, the "White Negro" chapter might thus be read as a commentary on the fleeting and ultimately episodic circularity of revolutions themselves, critiquing less the hubris of Soulouque than the similarly autocratic results of the Haitian and French revolutions. What Le Nègre posits instead, in the form of Manning, is a figure who replaces the concept of revolution altogether, representing instead a form of "absolute liberty" inadmissible to, and inassimilable within, the historical and epistemological forms of European whiteness. Published in the wake of Soupault's exclusion from the surrealist group, the novel conceptualizes Soupault's alternative to the movement's leftist reorganization as a line of praxis.

Like Albert Martel in "The Death of Nick Carter," Manning's presence in the text signals the collapse of Europeanness as a viable style of life; yet unlike the fictional Martel, Manning participates in this collapse, rendering literal the earlier story's substitution of blackness for European whiteness as a violent physical act. At the center of Soupault's novel is Manning's murder of a white prostitute named Europe, an act whose allegorical overtones render explicit the geopolitical narrative sketched out in "The Death of Nick Carter." At the same time, like Breton's Nadja and Crevel's lover Eugene MacCown, the model for Arthur Bruggle in Difficult Death, Soupault's Manning is based on a real historical figure, one whose life story was serialized in the World's Pictorial News in 1926.[44] The novel's structure as both an autobiographical fiction and a true crime narrative thus suggests that its appeal to a criminalized blackness in place of an impoverished European whiteness was more than simply an allegorical gesture. Soupault made a single, historically grounded character the living embodiment of the "absolute liberty" he located within American blackness; the ideas about revolutionary politics embraced by the surrealists therefore remain metaphorical in Soupault's work, characterizing a "spirit" of liberty rather than an organized program for radical social change. Soupault's own thinking about radical political change still rested, as with the surrealists, on the question of how writing related to the social realities of historical agency. Yet unlike the surrealists,

Soupault refused the mantle of intellectualism, using his writerly pursuits to document his own estranged relationship (as a white European) to the racialized form of being, of which he considered this agency an essential characteristic. That is, for Soupault, violent agency was an ontological rather than a theoretical concern, a real if fugitive presence to be encountered within the practice of everyday life, and not simply an idea to be discussed within the realm of theory.

Georges Ribemont-Dessaignes's 1927 review of Soupault's novel in *Les Feuilles Libres*, the journal in whose pages its opening chapter first appeared in 1925, explicitly situates *Le Nègre* in terms of the East-West discussions of the previous years. The timeliness of Soupault's book lies for Ribemont-Dessaignes in its ability to unearth "blows against the old world" that had not been dulled by imitation or popular consumption.[45] While satirizing the Parisian trend of negrophilia into which Soupault's novel emerged, the review in fact distinguishes *Le Nègre* from the consumption of all things black, claiming instead that it resists this commodification of blackness. As Ribemont-Dessaignes explains, *Le Nègre* is the first novel in which a white soul inhabits, rather than devours, a black soul; at the same time, he continues, this white soul discovers that it is itself inhabited in turn by a second black soul. Through this interpenetration, Ribemont-Dessaignes writes, "the Orient's ancient heyday renews itself."[46] This renewed heyday refers not only to the utterly non-European modality of being which Soupault articulates throughout his paean to American blackness, but also to the "Oriental" violence through which this way of life manifests its sovereignty.

As Ribemont-Dessaignes's review suggests, the novel's central concern is the "interpenetration" of Soupault's white narrator and *Le Nègre*'s black hero. Unlike a number of similar contemporary novels and accounts cataloguing white people's fascination for and romanticization of blackness—from Blaise Cendrars's *Anthologie nègre* (1921) to Carl Van Vechten's *Nigger Heaven* (1926) and Paul Morand's *Magie Noire* (1928)—Soupault's novel documents the narrator's encounters with a singular figure. The novel is structured as a romance, insofar as the narrator's pursuit of Manning renders acutely his alienation from the agency and mystery Manning embodies. This alienation, too, is central to Soupault's distance from surrealism's political orientation, as it permits *Le Nègre* to portray its titular black criminal hero as a figure of "absolute liberty" while intimating the impossibility of ever fully grasping this fugitive quality.

Soupault's characteristically autobiographical narrator begins his story by leaving a cream yellow house on the rue Fontaine that closely resembles André Breton's studio at 42, rue Fontaine; from there he enters the Tempo-Club, a nearby jazz bar, at which a band called the Syncopated Orchestra is playing. While noting the proximity of Breton's studio to the jazz clubs, strip clubs, and cabarets of the Pigalle district, Soupault's narrator tacitly marks the novel's exploration of blackness as a departure from Breton's circle. At the Tempo-Club the narrator contemplates his black friendships, reflecting on what he considers the capacity for black people to laugh and, at the same time, to maintain a faraway look that "gives me a kind of fright. They see," he explains, "what I cannot see, that which I can never see."[47] Soupault's novel might be considered a meditation on this paradoxical combination of laughter and mystery, which his text inscribes, to the point of absurdity, as an intrinsic racial characteristic.[48]

Manning's status as a figure of romantic revolt is carefully developed through the narrator's intermittent encounters with him over more than a decade. The real Edgar Manning, whom Soupault's narrator recalls having met in a London boardinghouse before the war in 1913, was in fact a drug dealer and jazz drummer whose arrest in 1923 for drug trafficking was linked by the press to the fatal overdose of the British actress Billie Carleton.[49] In Soupault's novel a young pastor writes the narrator a letter describing the arrest and criminal career of the narrator's boardinghouse acquaintance, the "very well dressed Negro who left his room every night and returned only at dawn." The pastor's letter condenses much of the contemporary press coverage dedicated to Manning's arrest:

> I learned that the young Negro Edgar Manning was just sentenced to three years in prison. I am sending you the enclosed newspaper clipping that I cut out especially for you, in the hope that it would serve as a lesson, or should I say, put you on your guard. . . .
>
> He claimed to be a musician in a jazz band and, from time to time, just to keep up appearances, he could be found in some trendy dance club, beating drumsticks against some more or less sonorous objects while hollering out those guttural shrieks that usually accompany ultramodern dances.
>
> But the bulk of his income came from two other sources: first, the shameless exploitation of the unfortunate girls he terrorized, and then from selling cocaine, opium, and all the other drugs that are so popular in that strange world of debauchery, where people die of boredom amid the artificial pleasures they seek out.
>
> Edgar Manning always wore the latest fashions and was dressed to the nines. His poor girls, from whose earnings he cut a share for himself, knew that he always hid a razor and a Browning in the pockets of his elegant tuxedo.
>
> He was known as the "Dope King."[50]

Soupault's narrator relishes rather than heeds the pastor's account, choosing to cherish what he remembers as Manning's "indefatigable melancholy." "By melancholy," he explains, "I mean everything that is indefinite or undefinable."[51] Whereas the English press referred to Manning as an "evil Negro" and as a "Dope King," Soupault's Manning is memorialized instead as "master of a kingdom without borders."[52] Far from rehabilitating Manning, Soupault's novel elaborates the lawlessness and limitlessness he represents.

In contrast to the language of the pastor's letter, Soupault's narrator eulogizes Manning's criminality in a passage that anticipates their next chance encounter in a Parisian jazz bar:

> Let me be clear about this: Edgar Manning is not a common, blue-faced killer with sweaty, trembling lips; he is not one of those cat burglars who is betrayed by his stealthy movements; nor is he a calculating thief. No, I want to be clear: the painfully clenched hands about to strike; the revolting beady-eyed stare; the petty, conniving mind—these are not attributes that could ever be ascribed to him. He is fearless.
>
> I recognize my friend Manning because he is as alive as the color red, and as quick as a catastrophe. He appears and disappears. He moves in a rarified air, in unfathomed waters, in a fire more generous than a lamprey, and he inhabits that noble world punctuated by bursts of laughter and bull's blood.[53]

As the ecstatic Maldororian language of this eulogy suggests ("as alive as . . ."), Soupault's true crime hero epitomizes the spirit of rupture Soupault admired in surrealist precursors such as Lautréamont, Apollinaire, and Rimbaud, each of whom Soupault wrote about in 1926 and 1927 as similarly fugitive and lawless figures.[54] Like Rimbaud, who "simply pursues his life" and whose "shadow guides him toward infinity, the thirst for which is an atrocity, a painful sickness," Edgar Manning both rejects and reveals the moribund state of white European life.[55] Manning, though, can actually smell the decay. As Soupault writes of Manning's prison term: "Prisoner 523 sniffs. The stench of a corpse precedes the daily sound of footsteps in the hall. This is the man they call the jailer. For Edgar, he reeks of death, like all whites. Once he has brought some soup, he locks the door. But his disgusting odor, and its mauve stench, fills the cell for several hours afterward: a dark, rotting shadow."[56] For Soupault, as for Edgar Manning, the decline of the West was as much a palpable state of disgust as a set of historical patterns; throughout Le Nègre Soupault's language shifts similarly from the most abstractly metaphorical to the most concretely physical. Manning's sensitivity to this stench of decay derives, Soupault suggests, from his total distinction from Europeanness, as an ontological function of his blackness, at once mythical and bodily. Manning consciously and physically rejects the "putrescence" of Soupault's Occident, even though, as Soupault later declares, Manning has at least learned to understand Europeans.[57]

In the novel's pivotal scene, Manning's physical sense of revolt at the "smell of blood" in Europeans takes its most violent form. While in Barcelona, Manning meets the prostitute named Europe—a name he laughs at initially—and becomes her client. Whereas their sexual contact is at first purely physical, nearly wordless, she soon "tries to amuse him and tell him stories."[58] Europe's narrative of her life and ambitions, however, awakens Manning's contempt; on a subsequent visit her simultaneous solicitation of multiple clients increases his rage, which continues to mount as he pays her once more for sex.

Their intercourse is punctuated by Europe's cries of "You're taking so long," her impatience provoking, it would seem, Manning's criminal outburst. As Soupault writes: "'That does it! It's time.' Just as she is opening her mouth to say, 'You're . . . !' he turns abruptly and senses his knife jabbing into his thigh. It says: 'I am here,' and Edgar understands. The angel of blood has finally given him the signal. With a stealthy movement of his fingers, he pulls the knife from the bottom of his pocket. The knife is ready."[59] In an orgasmic burst of violence, Manning stabs Europe in the heart, steals her money, and flees Barcelona for Lisbon. The scene charts Manning's evolution from hateful rage to violent sexual pleasure, an outburst sparked largely by the call of Manning's knife; the murder somehow emerges from this imperative. At the same time, the graphic physical detail of Soupault's account of the murder overwhelms the scene's otherwise unambiguous allegorical overtones: Manning's murder of Europe is neither a liberatory gesture of anticolonial violence nor a revolutionary act. Any sense of revolt it bears refers more to disgust than to insurgency; Manning's contempt and pleasure alike stem from the psycho-erotic economy of his relations with Europe and his knife rather than from Europe's Occidental overtones or her symbolic ties to European imperialism. This physicality is nonetheless essential to Soupault's allegorical panegyric to Manning's violent capacity for revolt: Manning experiences his murderous rage *as* rage, not as a symbolic attack against the paucity of the Occidental spirit.

In the episode that follows the murder scene, however, the allegorical significance of the crime returns—and with it Soupault's renewed logic for exalting all that Manning represents. For the revolt against Europeanness and whiteness that Soupault documents is not Manning's murderous act but his ensuing struggle with the "European disease" of despair and memory. Aboard the ship bound for Lisbon, Manning writes to the murdered woman, describing in a letter, never to be delivered, how her memory haunts him. Manning's thoughts "swarm like flies around the corpse that is starting to become a memory."[60] Instead of ignoring his crime, as Soupault suggests he might otherwise have done, Manning "let himself be consumed by the persistent heat that gnawed at his eyes and attacked his hands," yielding himself to the Lisbon weather as well as to "his sadness, or what others mistake for sadness, [which] is really a lingering, mellow, and faded drunkenness."[61] In the symbolic economy of Soupault's novel, this intoxication by memory and sadness amounts to a form of colonization: Manning, however fleetingly, has fallen victim to Europeanness. Later, in the company of the narrator, the "triumphant Negro" returns when he regains his ability to "draw force from the swiftly passing time," insofar as he has the power to forget the past, to crush it "diamond against diamond, into flecks of memories."[62]

A second violent event shows a similar dynamic at work. Upon the narrator's arrival in Lisbon, Manning witnesses the failed revolt of early 1927 against Lisbon's military dictatorship, a failure that at first sends Manning into a state of despair. Soupault writes of Manning's initial reaction to the suppressed uprising, "For the first time, I had caught a glimpse of Edgar's weakness, when he had given in, for a moment; when, sick from disappointment, he seemed European."[63] As with his "weakness" toward the memory of the prostitute he murdered, Manning's quality of despair becomes for the narrator a symptom of his immersion in, or his infection by, Europeanness. Whereas immediately after the failed revolt Manning is at his most European, he soon masters his remorse, with Soupault rejoicing in the return of his power to slough off these affiliations. He writes: "I searched [Manning's] voice for its true melody, the melody that rose above all of us who seek refuge from the day. But he simply laughed like someone who had lost and accepted his defeat. He was saved, nevertheless, and he knew it."[64]

In the book's closing passages Soupault writes of Manning's final departure in near-epic terms that celebrate Manning's triumphant fugitivity. On his way to Africa, Manning gains a perspective on Europe in a sweeping historical gesture that registers his emancipation from it. Soupault writes:

> From atop the headland, Manning observes the staggering course of events, with his right eye closed. A great precipice, with what's commonly called a gaping void, slowly opens like the lips of a slumbering man. And, to the other side, he sees himself living in the past. He has made no plans, no decisions. He has traversed his native land, America, and discovered Europe by taking advantage of laws he knew only by name and customs that seemed to him to be older than the world itself, more outdated than all the rest, and a decayed and putrefied way of thinking. He has wended his way across these systems, sweeping away, with a brush of the hand or a wink of the eye, the mountains of haze that seemed to paralyze with fear those whites who were so proud of their audacity.
>
> All of the great works erected by the Caucasians' ancestors and grandchildren over the centuries have cast a propitious shadow on those who want to remain invisible.
>
> For Edgar Manning is as powerful as a man who is perfectly invisible. . . . He is invisible because he is as free as an emancipated slave or a wild horse, because he has refused to accept the "handcuffs forged by the mind," because he did not construct his own prison, because he did not inherit all the shackles passed down from father to son by the whites living in rich lands, because he owns nothing.[65]

What Georges Ribemont-Dessaignes called Soupault's "hymn to liberty" praises the power of Manning's invisibility, his physical and spiritual fugitivity, which Soupault raises here to a transcendental property. In tacit yet total opposition to the organizational rigor and theoretical practices of the surrealists, Soupault creates in Manning a monument to romanticized blackness, an emancipatory form of being—of "life" rather than revolutionary praxis—whose extremes of cruelty and laughter represent, for Soupault, a refusal of European ideology.

What remains insuperable for Soupault is, however, his own distance from this monument to absolute liberty. Manning's racial distance from the narrator is as definitive as the historical gulf that separated the living Soupault of the 1920s from the dead literary heroes whom he similarly addressed as friends: Apollinaire, who died in 1918; Rimbaud, who died in 1891; and Lautréamont, who died in 1870. With regard to Manning, Soupault's narrator admits that he cannot adequately gauge or describe the black man's "absolute liberty"; in writing of Manning, and in trying "to define his strength," he fears that he "will only prove [his] own weakness" and bring Manning down to his level. Manning's superiority, Soupault writes in the novel's final lines, "escapes me. It seems mysterious. I am only a white man, and I resemble the other pale faces."[66]

In his review of Le Nègre, Ribemont-Dessaignes praises this admission of irreconcilable difference in the face of Soupault's exclusion from surrealism the previous year. Ribemont-Dessaignes, himself a former Dada writer at odds with the surrealist movement's turn toward organized politics, cites Manning's freedom from European knowledge and memory as the key to Le Nègre's distinction from the movement. He writes:

> There are people who, having read Soupault's book, will respond: a hymn to liberty is insufficient; you must make your liberty real: set out after it.
>
> This is false. There's Edgar. There's us. Edgar leaves without baggage; he possesses nothing. To know: this is what plagues us. Alone in the desert or in the equatorial forest, we, however, are not free, because we know. We know why through Edgar, and we know why we leave. He didn't know this. It's not enough to paint oneself black to give a white woman black babies. Liberty is also a chain.
>
> Soupault, thank you; the answer is written in the stars.[67]

Citing Le Nègre's final line—"the answer is written in the stars"—Ribemont-Dessaignes suggests that Soupault's novel writing supersedes the surrealist movement's focus on "making liberty real" through its rejection of theory. Knowledge, even the knowledge of liberty, may be "written in the stars," but freedom itself cannot be known because it consists precisely in the abandonment of knowledge, memory, and the accumulated bolus of Western culture that characterized European despair.

Ribemont-Dessaignes's and Soupault's hymns to liberty privilege being over thinking—whether in Soupault's essentialist notion of race or in Ribemont-Dessaignes's proto-existentialist primitivism—in a way that responds not only to surrealism but also to the logical Marxism of traditional leftists such as Marcel Martinet. Indeed, in Le Nègre Soupault champions the "down with intelligence" charge Martinet decried, to the extent that this intelligence derived from the very body of dead European knowledge that

Soupault sought to discard. The revolutionary promise of Marxism, toward which sur-realism gravitated in the aftermath of the Rif War, was itself an intellectual and historical product of Western knowledge; the dictatorship of the proletariat was yet another bad ex-ample to be discarded. Liberty, both Soupault and Ribemont-Dessaignes suggested, could only be pursued; it could not be organized or harnessed without becoming an imitation of itself. Even in its most essentialized forms—as violence, as blackness, as murder—it remained, as Soupault writes, a "kingdom without borders."

The Exquisite Corpse Will Drink the New Wine

Soupault was hardly the only surrealist—excluded or otherwise—to invoke "all the shackles passed down from father to son by the whites living in rich lands," or to depict Europe as a corpse.[68] In a composite series of articles on religion and the state published in La Révolution Surréaliste in March 1926, the Clarté writer Victor Crastre addressed the cur-rent status of European life by asking: "What secret power, what all-powerful demon has blown this icy and fatal wind upon us? We are no more than living corpses—living, alas![69] Paul Éluard continued Crastre's rant against the "decomposing corpse of the West" by at-tributing this death to what he considered the new postwar cult of dead military heroes, "a religion still more absurd and more ugly than the others: that of the dead."[70] For Élu-ard, this religion referred both to the general conditions of European spiritual life, as well as to the specific postwar tendency toward imperial patriotism, nationalism, and the adu-lation of war heroes. Éluard argued that to honor the old and dying heroes of the Great War (such as Maréchal Foch, against whom Benjamin Péret directed his slanderous poem "Life of the Murderer Foch")[71] was to pay homage to men who were "subservient to all the lies, all the commandments of a society based on mankind's lowest reality, having proved their powerlessness to disobey, and having confirmed that they, as heroes, were no more than the sycophants of death and the good servants of their masters."[72]

Though reminiscent of Soupault's claim in Le Nègre that white Europeans "smelled like corpses," such anti-Occidental rhetoric differs from Soupault's in that the antidote to such conditions of death was, by 1926, neither racially essentialized black America nor "the Orient" but the moral and political imperative for revolution. Defining the nature of this revolution, as I have suggested, became the central theoretical concern in the Clarté and Révolution Surréaliste group meetings throughout 1925 and 1926. The surrealist group never questioned Soupault's disdain for the European bourgeoisie as a mode of life, nor did they doubt his intentions of joining the Communist Party. Soupault's allegorical treat-ments of anticolonial uprising—in the form of Nick Carter's death and Edgar Manning's murder of the prostitute Europe—were unsatisfactory because they reduced the problem of political change to events narrated within literature and, however romantically, rendered criminal. Perhaps most significantly, as the actions of racially marked fugitive heroes forever beyond the reach of his narrative identifications, Soupault's attacks on a moribund European social order refused the mantle of collective organization. Soupault's isolation and estrangement of historical agency as a modality of Manning's race was anathema to the political ambitions of the other surrealists, insofar as it rendered praxis impossible. The other surrealists, by contrast, sought forms of collective practice that could reconcile the spiritual freedom Soupault championed with the political actuality promised by party communism.

Indeed the result of the group discussions was a mandate to disentangle surrealism's political thought from the implicit romanticism of Soupault's fiction, and instead to specify the terms of revolution according to the tenets of Marxian socialism: the violent overthrow of capitalism and the establishment of the dictatorship of the proletariat. This did not mean that all surrealist writing and art was to become instrumentalized in the service of "effective" revolutionary praxis; instead the group mobilized its experimental energies toward broadening the theoretical basis of communism. The surrealists, in other words, proposed nothing less than to dislodge revolutionary politics from the narrowly doctrinaire, an intellectual project they would defend against Stalinism in the decades to come.

One of the fruits of the group's Rif War period of communist allegiance was the parlor game of exquisite corpse, which at first glance seemed far less attuned to the movement's political fervor than Soupault's investment in popular literature. Although it represented a far different set of collaborative practices than the "violent overthrow of capitalist society" mandated by the surrealist and Clarté groups' statements on revolution, the game nevertheless constituted a form of theoretical activity insofar as it involved speculating about collaborative labor, cause and effect, and historical becoming. Indeed in the game of exquisite corpse the vexed question of surrealism's powers of collective action became institutionalized as a playful form of praxis.

The game of exquisite corpse was invented in 1925 at the shared residence of Yves Tanguy, Marcel Duhamel, and Jacques Prevert at 54, rue du Château, during roughly the same period as the group's more heated political meetings in response to the Rif War. The game, in which sentences or images are composed by participants unaware of what the other contributions look like, produces results that are at once humorous and monstrous. The composite phrase or drawing that results forms the hybrid "body" whose logic seems entirely fortuitous, the product of a ludic yet systematized invocation of chance (figure 4.2). The game and its composite products are named after the first phrase composed through its method: le cadvre / exquis / boira / le vin / nouveau (the exquisite corpse will drink the new wine). The focus on corpses in the inaugural game suggests the residual traces of the group's Rif War–era rhetoric: the cadaverousness of European imperialism and the futurity of revolutions. Indeed, suggesting a prophetic, even apocalyptic agency, the game

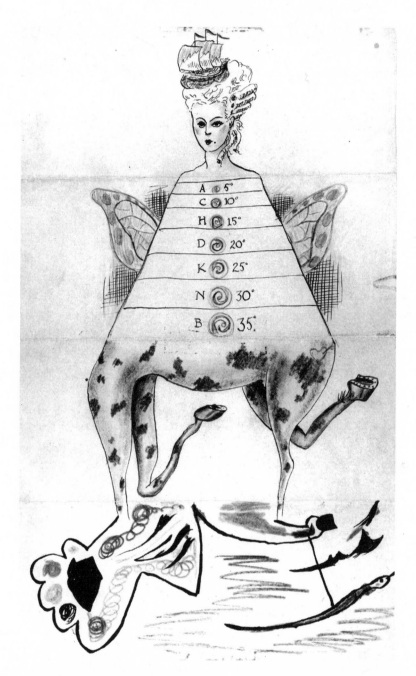

Fig. 4.2. Joan Miró, Man Ray, Yves Tanguy, and Max Morise (from bottom to top), *Exquisite Corpse* (1927). Game of paper folded in four, each artist working on his section without seeing the other sections and knowing only the title. Private Collection, Paris. Image © 2008 Snark/Art Resource, N.Y. © 2008 Successió Miró/Artists Rights Society (ARS), New York/ADAGP, Paris. © 2008 Man Ray Trust/Artists Rights Society (ARS), New York/ADAGP, Paris. © 2008 Estate of Yves Tanguy/Artists Rights Society (ARS), New York.

reveals the degree to which the "corpses" it produces are not dead at all but animated and composite.

Yet the game of exquisite corpse represented more than an impression of surrealism's political discourse on the group's more playful activities; its composite verbal and visual bodies stage the necessary inconsistencies of the game's multiple authorship as its determining logic. Where one might expect to find chance, in other words, there is instead overdetermination, a surfeit of artistic agency. The exquisite corpse's exaggerated play of cause and effect thus demonstrated that surrealist collectivity did not entail subservience to a law or principle of communal practice, but instead exercised a form of group activity that multiplied the interferences of its participants.

The exquisite corpse's perversion of cause and effect can be read as a parody of the assembly line; as Hal Foster has suggested, the blind assembly of parts by multiple hands both replicates and satirizes the alienated labor of automated industrial production.[73] But the difference is that the finished industrial product of the surrealist assembly line was not the artifact—the work of art—but the game itself, which functioned as a machine for eliminating alienation. Though hardly "political" in itself, the game was significant to surrealist political thinking for its gamelike structure: it staged theory—speculation about the revolution's final form rather than about its instrumental use of violent uprising alone—as a collective practice. In place of a doctrinaire Marxism or a static set of political principles, the game yielded a form of theoretical activity subject to the dynamism of a group as well as to the bits and pieces of drawings and phrases it spawned. As Breton wrote in a footnote to the *Second Manifesto of Surrealism* in 1929, a surrealist parlor game like exquisite corpse "brought out into the open a strange possibility of thought, which is that of its *pooling*."[74] The original French term is *mise en commun*, literally, a sharing or making common, which alludes to the synthetic result of the exquisite corpse's collection of individual efforts and parts but does not name it as an actual synthesis. Breton continues: "The fact remains that very striking relationships are established in this manner, that remarkable analogies appear, that an inexplicable factor of irrefutability more often intervenes and that, in a nutshell, this is one of the most extraordinary *meeting grounds* [*lieux des rencontres*]. But we are only at the stage of suggesting where it is."[75]

As both a process and the artifact of this process, the exquisite corpse embodied the group's theoretical and practical inquiries into political agency and historical causality. The sentences and images produced by the game did not solicit comparison to real, living bodies, except to invoke bodily logic as a kind of syntax whose lingering traces in the exquisite corpse (head-body-legs) remained primarily as a reminder of the collective way in which the game was played. As Maurice Blanchot has written, this *mise en commun* may have been collective, yet it never resolved into a single, unified understanding: "The surrealist affirmation . . . never coincides with the understanding that individuals, grouped around a faith, an ideal, or a labor might sustain."[76] The game of exquisite corpse thus voiced, in the form of a game, the surrealist movement's distance from party politics: the possibility of a "reign of freedom" that exceeded anything imaginable under the moribund conditions of Occidental, capitalist existence, demanded speculation in the prerevolutionary present.

In a later essay, "The Exquisite Corpse: Its Exaltation" (1948), Breton writes that the most successful of the composite word and image games were those that "produced in us the strongest sensation of disorientation and strangeness."[77] Like the parlor game of "Consequences" he claims it resembled, the exquisite corpse derived its disorientation and its humor alike from the havoc its composite syntax wreaked upon standard conceptions of cause and effect—even more so than by its assault on any bodily logic the corpse might call to mind. Invoking causality as an overdetermination so multiplicitous as to name even chance as one of its determinants, or as what Maurice Blanchot calls "the indeterminant that indetermines," the game resulted in a synthesis that did not unify or resolve its contributions. For the corpse formed by the collected fragments was not a decomposition of previously recognizable parts but rather an amalgamation of individual automatic drawings or writings whose totality became legible as a disordered body.

As Catherine Vasseur has suggested, Breton understood the game of exquisite corpse in the same way that he understood historical materialism: both were processes that strove "to construct a world on the immense scale of mankind." History, Vasseur claims, "rests entirely upon this construction. History no longer progresses; it becomes *incarnate*."[78] The point was not, in other words, that the dismembered, reassembled body of the exquisite corpse represented either surrealism's principle of causality or, as another critic has written, its categorical imperative.[79] Instead the game practiced as well as articulated the collectivity that formed the basis of surrealist politics—a coming together of individual acts of creativity that constituted an event through which the possibilities for postrevolutionary liberty could be hypothesized and experimented with in the prerevolutionary world. In the context of the Rif War in Morocco, the reality of organized violence was at hand; what the exquisite corpse kept in play, under the aegis of a simple game, was the practicability of other forms of collective thought and activity. This, I contend, helps explain the game's popularity among the surrealists, even as the group worked to formalize its collective political engagement.

Breton's theoretical work between 1926 and the *Second Manifesto of Surrealism* of 1929 might be considered the elaboration of the exquisite corpse game's essential insight about the salutary indeterminacy of collective praxis. Breton's first major defense of surrealism's political efforts, the 1926 tract *Légitime Défense*, makes use of the exquisite corpse's language of disorientation and indetermination, describing surrealism's coming-into-politics as "an unprecedented summons" through which the group was "chosen . . . to preside over a kind of dizzying exchange."[80] The tract addresses the conceptual and pragmatic difficulties of surrealism's entrance into organized politics, refusing to distinguish between the movement's continued intellectual and aesthetic pursuits and its support for a Marxist-Leninist definition of revolution.

In response to Pierre Naville's challenge for the surrealists to choose between the anarchic experimentation of their early years and the formal Marxism they were contemplating after the Rif War, Breton argues that such a choice, between what he calls the "inner" (psychic, poetic) and "outer" (socioeconomic, activist) appeals of liberty, was based on an artificial distinction. As an implicit response, too, to Soupault's claim that surrealism could never lead to an effective revolution, Breton rejected the so-called practical irreconcilability between organized political action and the imaginative labor of pursuing absolute liberty. In place of this false distinction, Breton appealed precisely to the sensation of "disorientation and strangeness" he admired in the game of exquisite corpse. He writes:

> It is time . . . for the mind to revise certain purely formal oppositions of terms, such as the opposition of act to speech, of dream to reality, of present to past and future. The basis of these distinctions, in the deplorable conditions of European existence at the beginning of the twentieth century, even from the practical point of view, cannot be defended for a moment. Why not mobilize all the powers of the imagination in order to remedy this situation?[81]

The imperative to "mobilize all the powers of the imagination" defined the surrealist movement's political commitment in the years following the Rif War. To this end, the form the movement's artistic exercises took—crime tales, tracts, poetry, or parlor games—mattered less than the writer's or artist's participation in the development of collective practices that would foster a dialectical tension between the impetus of social revolution and the practice of thought. As Breton explains: "To write—I mean to write with such difficulty—and not in order to seduce, and not (in the sense in which it is ordinarily meant) in order to live, but, rather, at best to be adequate to oneself morally, and being unable to remain deaf to a singular and tireless appeal—to write in this way is neither to play games nor to cheat, that I know of."[82] Breton is attempting here to redefine writing itself as a practice that obeyed more than a single imperative: not only did surrealist writing follow the dictates of an individual consciousness, but also it heeded a "singular and tireless appeal" from without.

Soupault, though one of the first surrealists to be dismissed for "cheating," arrived at a similar conclusion in his fictions dedicated to pursuing the relations of longing and fugitivity between white narrators and romanticized black men. Yet Soupault's approach to this "singular and tireless appeal" remained firmly entrenched in the realm of fiction and embodied within the ontological fabric of individual characters. The example of the exquisite corpse, like the group discussions with the *Clarté* intellectuals that took place during the same period, stressed instead that such an appeal derives from the social world: the empirical realm of economic and political relations, and the collective body of surrealist intellectuals themselves.

Coda: Robert Desnos in the Shadow of Jack the Ripper

Robert Desnos, one of the most dedicated early surrealist writers, would resist Breton's understanding of the collective, and procedural, nature of surrealist politics. Whereas for Breton, group activities—even games—provided a means to approach writing as both an individual and a collective form of intellectual engagement, Desnos chose instead to pursue a more popular direction for his cultural politics. On January 29, 1928, the first installment of Desnos's serial article on "sadistic crimes" appeared in the daily *Paris Matinal*.[83] "The recent criminal affair of the Saint-Denis woman cut into pieces," he writes, "has brought sadistic crimes back to mind."[84] Having reported previously on the discovery of several horribly mutilated corpses found on the outskirts of Paris, Desnos begins the special series by advertising how it would be "curious" at this time to relate "two great criminal epics from the last century" for comparison. The first of these "epics" was the story of Jack the Ripper, who terrorized the Whitechapel district of London from April 1888 to February 1891; the second was that of Joseph Vacher, the French "Ripper," who confessed to raping and murdering at least eleven people throughout the French countryside roughly ten years later.

The article's curiosity about these two serial killers is striking for its curt dismissal of the contemporary murders in Saint-Denis in favor of crimes that were by then over thirty to forty years old. Likewise, Desnos's article on "sadistic crimes" dismisses surrealism's contemporary interest in proletarian revolution in adopting a mode of crime reportage reminiscent of Péret's "Assassiner" article eight years earlier (see chapter 2). Part sensationalist journalism, part hagiography, the article, in its catalogue of Victorian-age atrocities, amplifies the already numerous tributes to Jack the Ripper that appear throughout Desnos's surrealist writing.[85] Yet even in contrast to his earlier writings, Desnos's 1928 article does more than articulate an amoral fascination with an uncapturable genius of crime; it argues for the aesthetic consideration of sadistic crimes in a way that more subtly expresses Desnos's rapidly evolving position toward the surrealist movement.

Although his rupture with surrealism would take place three years later than Soupault's, and under different political circumstances, the principal object of contention between Desnos and the group revolved similarly around questions of literary production. As in Soupault's case, too, such literary disagreements hinged on divergent understandings of intellectual and political agency. Desnos had taken part in the political discussions of 1925 and 1926, yet like Soupault he jealously guarded his journalistic career in the face of the surrealist movement's increasing pressure toward collectivization. By 1928 Desnos was more and more at odds with the group's collective discipline and commitment to the Communist Party, as well as with Breton's antagonism toward his "individualist" career in journalism. Desnos not only insisted on the financial necessity of supporting himself as a professional writer but also stressed that the "revolutionary" potential of an individual writer was only better served by his connection to the broader agency of the public. Although relations had not yet reached the overt hostility of the anti-Breton tract Un Cadavre (1930) or Breton's response in the revised version of the Second Manifesto (1930), Desnos had, by the time of his Paris Matinal articles, grown estranged from the group and its formal ties with communism. Nevertheless, he continued to champion the movement's early promise to change life, albeit through aesthetic rather than strictly political means.

In the earliest years of the surrealist movement Desnos had looked to crime and adventure films such as Fantômas, Les Vampires, and the Mysteries of New York as sites at which "the desired life"—or the life of desire—was represented as it is in dreams. In his numerous writings from the early 1920s he articulated how film, and crime film in particular, could provide a passport to the fugitive "regions where the heart and the mind finally free themselves from the critical and descriptive spirit that binds them to the ground."[86] Desnos defined the marvelous experience of film in similar terms to Soupault's paeans to blackness or surrealism's broader tributes to the Orient; this notion of the marvelous could, at its best, realize the "supreme goal of the human spirit ever since it took possession of the creative power conferred on it by poetry and imagination."[87] At first Desnos seemed to be celebrating little more than sensationalism. "Love," he writes in a 1923 article, "and the spirit of adventure, are what make us fond of the murderer in detective novels; it's poetry itself that follows the actions of revolutionaries, and it's our senses that vibrate with those beautiful men, those adorable women, who dare to commit that which fear prevents us from perpetrating."[88] Yet it soon becomes clear that Desnos was more interested in the spectacle of the screen for its fantasy of an amoral realm of infinite possibility than for its ability to manufacture transgression. Like Freud's depiction of the dream-work as the condensed and distorted projection of unconscious wishes, Desnos's poetic and cinematic marvelous eluded the conventional censorship of commercial narratives. It described instead a space beyond good and evil that Desnos attempted, in turn, to reconcile with the real. This reconciliation, he argues in a 1924 essay, is the "revolutionary" goal of surrealism, and, more specifically, of surrealist ethics as "the sense of life and not the observance of human laws."[89] Yet whereas Breton argued for the inextricability of socioeconomic revolution from a surrealist liberation of the mind, Desnos's understanding of revolution privileged the latter aim. Indeed, in the wake of surrealism's political activism Desnos was increasingly willing to experiment with alternative means for making such imaginative conditions real.

In the context of the surrealist group's collective political discussions of 1925–26, Desnos tried at first to politicize this marvelous poetry of criminality in terms similar to the other leftists'. In "Surrealism's Revolutionary Meaning," published in *Clarté*, Desnos argues that surrealism was misconceived by many of its critics as a bourgeois individualist movement, whereas it actually lent itself naturally to communism. In support of this point Desnos performs an exegesis of Breton's first definition of surrealism in the 1924 *Manifesto*, showing how a political direction was already implicit in the movement from the beginning: surrealism's revolt "against the reprehensible exploitation of the mind that favors the current régime" fights a composite enemy and thus requires collective action. Desnos writes:

> They are a gang—from the priest to the professor—who invoke the spirit, who make a living from it, and who make it serve the lowest ends. It's against them, and against this deformed spirit, that the *surrealists* mean to fight.
>
> "You claim to ruin bourgeois painting and yet you make paintings. Go and destroy the Louvre," people told me on the way out of the surrealist exhibition.
>
> If we destroyed the paintings in the Louvre we would be individualists. Likewise you don't just go out and shoot fascist delegates. But you fight the capitalist spirit. Right now it's less a matter of carrying out revolution than of preparing for a battle of opinion.[90]

Desnos's focus on the "spirit" of capitalism is consistent with his use of pulp-fiction and film criminals to gain access to "regions where the heart and the mind finally free themselves." But Desnos grew increasingly weary of the surrealist movement's disciplinary practices, finding them too close to the critical spirit he considered anathema to the cinematic marvelous. Following the dismissals of Soupault, Antonin Artaud, and Roger Vitrac, Desnos increasingly distanced himself from what he considered a surrealist orthodoxy that defined political activism negatively—not to mention hypocritically—as a prohibition from publishing fiction and journalism.[91]

Insofar as his Ripper articles strove to present sadistic crime not just as "one of the fine arts" but as a distinctly surrealist art, Desnos's crime reportage suggests an alternative to the movement's Marxist definitions of revolution in terms of class struggle. In a deliberate shift away from the *Clarté* and surrealist groups' attempts to accommodate themselves to communism, Desnos's murder reportage organizes its political charge by concentrating on its popular affect. Rather than following the theoretical direction in which writers such as Breton, Aragon, and Naville pursued their revolutionary intellectual labor, Desnos's aesthetics embraced collective struggle on the level of the reception of images. In terms of surrealism's own history this was a deliberate step backward: it was through the kinds of poetic imagery Desnos had previously celebrated in the cinema that Jack the Ripper could, in 1928, be invoked as a surrealist historical presence. Far from sanctioning the serial rapes and murders that took place in Victorian England, in his true crime reportage Desnos attempted to confront his readers with the phenomenal experience of imaginative awakening which he hoped would arrive through reading about the crimes.[92] As the name given to the uncaptured murderer, Jack the Ripper was an invention; Desnos's article provided this invention with a physical presence, both recalling the "dark and handsome face" dreamed about by Victorian sleepers and, scandalously, publishing a drawing of Jack the Ripper himself on the front page of *Paris Matinal* on the morning of February 7, 1928. For Desnos, such a confrontation with the imagery disseminated by popular media such as newspapers and the radio represented a liberating, even revolutionary experience that for him not only matched communist organizational rigor in significance but surpassed it in viability as well: as he would later write in his polemical "Third Manifesto of Surrealism" (1930), "Surrealism exists only for non-surrealists."[93]

What made Desnos's newspaper article particularly significant to his poetic and polemical work from the same period is its attribution of a genre to the historical killings. The article refers to Jack's string of murders as an "epic" of criminality, and later to Vacher's as the more prosaic "bloody novel," or romance, of his life, though it occasionally strays from or conflates its categories. To assert the epic quality of Jack the Ripper's crimes is to insist on their historical, even mythical, significance as a form of poetry: they are not only acts of "real horror," as Desnos writes, but also works of art in the De Quinceyan sense. Just as Desnos's film writing championed serial "epics" such as Feuillade's *Fantômas* and *Les Vampires* for their suspension of moral considerations in favor of "absolute action," in this serial article he extends the *morale du cinéma* into the sphere of history's grasp on the popular imagination.[94]

Desnos's invocation of De Quincey's essays on murder was, like the understanding of surrealism Desnos promoted, rooted in a preference for the movement's pre-communist period, to whose exploratory, amoral environment his own linguistic and mediumistic experiments had been so central (see chapter 2). This preference corresponds, too, with Breton's attacks on Desnos's journalism, which not only abandoned leftist politics in favor of populism but also guarded nostalgic images of prewar criminal heroes such as Fantômas and Jack the Ripper in order to preserve the fantasy of their sublime power. Yet Desnos's *Paris Matinal* articles also share one of De Quincey's insights about the tendency for aesthetic and moral responses to acts of violence to become indistinguishable historical events unfolding in such a theatrical way as to conflate appearances and being.[95] In its use of De Quincey's aesthetic handle to describe the phenomenal experience of mass participation in a murderous spectacle, Desnos's notion of the marvelous as a "mass experience" differed dramatically from the communist surrealists' ideas about collectivity. Whereas Breton would strive to prove that socioeconomic and imaginative liberation were indivisible, Desnos, in his return to De Quincey, strove to demonstrate the extent to which they were interchangeable. That is, Desnos believed that the public, through its spectatorial participation in such crimes, both shaped their reality as historical events and were affected by them in turn.

Desnos also redeploys the De Quinceyan notion of moral and aesthetic handles as a way of establishing the difference between Jack the Ripper and the more distasteful Vacher. While both Jack's and Vacher's tales may indeed be epic in their scope, violence, and lasting effects on the national consciousness, for Desnos it is Jack the Ripper for whom the notion of "a seductive novelistic hero considering, like Thomas De Quincey, murder as one of the fine arts" seems to "come closest to reality."[96] Desnos compounds his allusion to De Quincey by drawing an analogous distinction between the two halves of his article, the "aesthetic" first part, discussing Jack the Ripper, and the "moral" second part, relating the more prosaic "bloody novel" of Vacher the Ripper—who, unlike Jack, was captured, subjected to scientific scrutiny, and executed. This juxtaposition allows Desnos to differentiate a murderous artist from a mere homicidal maniac.[97]

And for Desnos, Jack the Ripper's distinction from Vacher, in turn, foregrounds the poetic value of his crimes, insofar as their command of the Victorian imagination represented an irruption of the marvelous, in however inhumane a fashion, into everyday life. Desnos's counter-surrealist move in his *Paris Matinal* articles derives less from lionizing Jack the Ripper as a surrealist presence than from appropriating this disturbing historical force as an express function of his own writing. Unlike Soupault, for whom writing was forever inadequate to the task of representing the singularity of his black criminal heroes, Desnos embraced the power of popular literature. Although he champions Jack the Ripper early in the article for his ability "victoriously [to] den[y] the forces of law and ordinary morality," the article multiplies this defiance throughout its imagery. The description of how Jack literally cut into the bellies of his victims "with as much facility as one cuts, every Sunday in English households, the traditional plum cake" performs this irruption poetically, the simile transforming puddings into corpses and the everyday use of knives into ritual acts of murder.[98]

Similarly, describing the recent case of a corpse found in pieces over a period of several days, Desnos notes that the body was disarticulated in a manner that was indeed rough but which displayed that Jack the Ripper "was as familiar with anatomy as a maître d'hôtel who knows how to carve a chicken."[99] The killer need not have been previously trained as a doctor or butcher, as many speculated; his anatomical expertise was a function of the experience that came with the repeated expressions of his "terrible desire." Desnos's addition of culinary detail to this insight addresses the taste, and not just the critical faculties, of the reading public. Indeed Desnos's detailed descriptions provoked the disgust of at least one reader, who, in an unpublished letter to the editor, wrote to cancel his subscription to the newspaper, "in which I find a bad religious tendency, and in which certain articles are profoundly immoral—Why relate in detail the ancient crimes of Jack the Ripper and now Vacher's old crimes? Do you not find that there are enough crime stories each day in the newspapers? Would you please respond to this letter, and no longer send me your newspaper, which is harmful for my children to read."[100] Although the real object of this reader's disgust, as he explains elsewhere in the letter, is the fact that he never received a promotional watch promised him with his subscription, his expression of moral outrage seems to be based less on the celebration of murderers than on the graphic detail Desnos uses to describe their acts.

What may be most disturbing about Desnos's poetic language is that it reminds its readership that Jack the Ripper's crimes, like the poetic marvelous, were alarming for their infusion throughout everyday experience. Their linguistic appropriation of common culinary objects alters the function of such objects within the symbolic economy of one's morning routines. By contrast, what was ultimately uncompelling about the recent crimes in Saint-Denis was their divorce from everyday possibility—whether clinical, legal, or moral. The marvelous nature of Jack the Ripper's crimes was a function of their inveterate possibility, of the fact that they could have been committed, at any time, by virtually anyone.

The result of this open-endedness is a perverse and discomfiting participation in the killer's pathological fantasy.[101] Desnos seems here to be making an essentially Duchampian point—that the spectator completes the work of art by becoming part of its aesthetic apparatus.[102] Desnos is less interested in showing Victorian society's complicity in the "terrible desires" of a serial murderer than in framing his article as a trap for its contemporary readers, soliciting their participation—by means of their aesthetic and moral judgments—in order to transform their reading experience into an encounter with the marvelous.

Stylistically, too, Desnos's newspaper article multiplies the disruptiveness of Jack the Ripper's historical presence. Distinguishing his journalism from the prosaic naturalism of sensation fiction and romans feuilletons, Desnos portrays the villain's enigmatic persona as a disruption, rather than as a product, of his urban environment. Desnos marks the contrast between the "tragic atmosphere" of Whitechapel's "labyrinth of streets, alleys, and passages" and Jack the Ripper's ability to commit his crimes without discovery, "without ever being seen, without ever being worried."[103] The enigma of Jack the Ripper is not, in other words, represented sociologically as an emanation of the streets of London in all their gaslit mystery, poverty, and prostitution. While steeped in details of Victorian everyday life, Desnos's portrayal of the Whitechapel atrocities focuses on the Ripper's invisibility, noting how people going about their morning routines fail to see him at work. His crimes, in other words, are something that gaslit London's routines fail to notice.

Desnos's writerly agency expresses itself through the confrontation of Paris Matinal's readership with this overlooked violence. Having described the mutilated corpse of the Ripper's fourth victim, Desnos writes, "Above, in the tender sky, the everyday sun continues its regular ascension and will come to touch on the ridge of the sullen pit in whose depths the diabolic exploit has just come to pass."[104] Desnos's imagery marks the blind continuity of the city's diurnal routines while also emphasizing how the poet, or the poetic image, can turn this obliviousness on its head by charging it with a visceral sense of what it represses. The sky is tender, like the ruptured inner organs Desnos has just described in his account of the victim's mutilated body. Desnos's article multiplies such transformations in a way that denies the possibility for space to remain inert or for the reading public to remain innocent. The killer and his murderous impulses lurk everywhere, suffusing everyday life, and the language used to describe it, with an aura of the horrible and supernatural.

Desnos's journalistic experiment in popular surrealism extended its aesthetic system beyond this description of the nineteenth-century crimes, inflecting his portrayal of Jack the Ripper himself. In a manner that both returned his readers to the immediate present and highlighted the gymnastics of his own authorship, Desnos published a drawing whose caption declares it to be an actual portrait of Jack the Ripper, drawn by the killer's mistress (figure 4.3). Near the conclusion of the story's third installment Desnos prints a notice that responds to a letter from a certain "W.W." and solicits a rendezvous. This mysterious W.W. claims to know about "the life and the personality of him whom you have called the 'genius of crime,'" and furnishes Desnos with an image.[105] As a result, the "criminal epic" of Jack the Ripper becomes a drama of Desnos's encounter with this mysterious friend of the murderer.

Scrupulously preserving his incognito, W.W.'s enigmatic initials and veil of secrecy extend the aura of mystery, if not the violence, that Desnos previously attributed to the killer himself. Like the figure who haunts the narrator in Edgar Allan Poe's "William Wilson," W.W. emerges from the abyss of history with a special knowledge that promises to recast the Ripper epic as a contemporary problem. For Desnos, this uncanny knowledge provides a welcome intrusion of the marvelous into everyday life. As he writes in anticipation of their rendezvous: "Romantic incidents are, alas, too rare in life. On my part, I attach the greatest tenderness to the mysterious moments I can spend: unforeseen encounters, extraordinary coincidences, sentimental emotion, melancholy, desire. But rare are the adventures where the terrestrial marvelous consents to manifest itself in an imperative form."[106] W.W. thus not only returns the Ripper murders to the present moment but invokes Desnos' poetic imagery as part of this process as well.

In his account of their actual meeting, Desnos invokes this "terrestrial marvelous" in a manner reminiscent of his description of the Whitechapel murders, although he revises their cannibalistic imagery as a more conventionally romantic irruption: "We walked in silence up to the rue Guynemer, whose bituminous sidewalk was resplendent, a mirror of the play of streetlamps it reflected. This familiar landscape suddenly seemed to me mysterious and as if consecrated, in spite of the Luxembourg's trees, with all the splendor of a uniquely mineral country."[107] Removed from the historical violence of the crimes, this

Les extraordinaires révélations d'un ami de Jack l'éventreur à "Paris-Matinal"

par ROBERT DESNOS

Le ciel était brouillé. Il bruinait encore. Sur l'asphalte étincelante se reflétaient les réverbères. Les tours de Saint-Sulpice se perdaient lourdement dans une brume d'humidité Je me retournai vers celui qui venait de poser sa main sur mon épaule, ne doutant pas un instant que ce ne fut celui que j'attendais.

J'étais en présence d'un homme d'une soixantaine d'années, de forte taille, de figure rouge et tannée comme si le sang avait été figé sous la peau par l'action du soleil et de l'alcool. Il était enveloppé dans un vaste pardessus marron foncé, quadrillé de

JACK L'EVENTREUR à *dix-neuf ans.*
(Dessin exécuté en 1888 par sa maltresse)

Fig. 4.3. Anonymous, "Jack the Ripper at Age Nineteen (Drawing Executed in 1888 by His Mistress)," *Paris-Matinal*, 7 February 1928.

scene unfolds with an almost gleeful air of gothic suspense. W.W.'s revelations are nevertheless disturbing precisely for their chilling account of the killer's unremarkable origins. W.W.'s revelations redouble and render literal Desnos's more figurative intimation that Jack the Ripper could have been anyone.

W.W. explains that he knew Jack when they were students in Edinburgh and that the future murderer—as young and elegant as the dandy speculated about in Desnos's article—committed the first crime on a dare: for a wager of three pounds he copied another murder, the misattributed first "Ripper" killing of December 1, 1888. Rather than establishing a definable motive for the crimes, this confession performs the inverse, charging this allegedly disinterested act of murder with an alarming excess of enjoyment: regardless of his original impetus, Jack the Ripper continued to kill and mutilate prostitutes with an increased facility and enthusiasm.

Most important, the drawing printed in the article renders literal Desnos's depiction of Jack's "dark and beautiful face" in the dreams of Victorian sleepers, transforming this psychic apparition into an actual artifact and publicly reproducible material presence. Again, the (fictional) circumstances of its origin complicate this effect: attributed to the Ripper's mistress a month before the fatal wager, this portrayal of the murderer's face is presumably still innocent of the atrocities to come. If, however, we can read the cruelty and horror of the murders into the dark eyes, unearthly pallor, and strange, pronounced features of the profile, the possibility that this monstrous disemboweller of women was all the while in female company suddenly charges their intimacy with a devastating irony.

As a hoax that would later be cited as evidence by the surrealists who denounced Desnos's recent work, this irony becomes the article's masterstroke, a joke that expresses Desnos's evolving theories of authorial agency.[108] For the portrait of Jack the Ripper printed in *Paris Matinal* bears a striking resemblance to Georges Malkine's 1927 portrait of Desnos (figure 4.4). Like William Wilson in Poe's famous tale, W.W. provides Desnos not only with a likeness but with an uncanny double as well. As Desnos's doppelgänger, W.W. provides an authorial stand-in for Desnos's invented history of the Ripper's origins; at the same time, the suddenly materialized figure of Jack the Ripper appears as a thinly veiled portrait of the author. Such tongue-in-cheek gestures express Desnos's ideas about authorship as a kind of impersonation or, as Katharine Conley has suggested, as a form of public transmission modeled after the broadcasts of wireless radio.[109] Recalling the mechanics of his early dream-trances and transatlantic "correspondence" with Duchamp's Rrose Sélavy, Desnos's contact with Jack the Ripper is made possible by the intervention of a medium. In the context of his growing estrangement from surrealism, moreover, such jokes about authorial alter egos reveal Desnos's notions about forms of public intervention achieved directly through writing—and not, therefore, through organized political stances alone. Desnos's aim was thus less to fool the public into accepting his narrative at face value than to invoke the present as a medium, as a moment of possibility in which such an encounter with Jack the Ripper could occur.

A letter to the editor of *Paris Matinal* dated February 6, 1928, responds to Desnos's encounter with W.W. in a manner whose generous acceptance for the article suggests how little readers of *Paris Matinal* might have been expected to take Desnos's story at face value. "As an assiduous reader of *Paris Matinal*," the letter reads, "I find your articles on Jack the Ripper truly interesting, but you mustn't abuse it. Sherlock Holmes is dead, sir, and likewise my credulity. What are your motives for writing like Maurice Leblanc?"[110] Whether the writer of this letter is deliberately conflating fact and fiction in his claim that "Sherlock Holmes is dead," the credulity with which she or he is willing to entertain other fiction has not been aroused by Desnos's elaborate fancy. It seems, however, that the point of Desnos's rendezvous with W.W. is less to perpetrate a hoax (or, for that matter, to report an actual encounter) than to raise the stakes of his own attempt to lure readers into considering murder as one of the fine arts.

As Marie-Claire Dumas has suggested, the iconography of the criminal genius epitomizes Desnos's understanding of myth as a collection of images representing otherwise inexpressible desires. Such "masters of crime" as Jack the Ripper and Fantômas command a whole corpus of mythic figures in the Desnosian imagination who deny "hierarchy [and] authority in the name of a community founded otherwise."[111] While Dumas helpfully emphasizes Jack the Ripper's uncapturable and faceless embodiment of silenced desires, it is Desnos's article in *Paris Matinal* that assumes the mantle of the marvelous in rendering Jack the Ripper visible. In replacing an invisible source of public horror and outrage with an iconography of elegance and beauty, Desnos compels his readers to recognize that the Ripper's power over the imagination could be harnessed, conscripted for popular consumption as a function of its reception as a work of art. This is not to say that Desnos confronts the public with a desire to commit violent sexual crimes; rather he presents the experience of transcending the systems of morality and social order that might otherwise characterize the public's repose. It might be said that in translating his enthusiasm for the poetic and cinematic marvelous into a form of journalism, Desnos's deployment of a De Quinceyan "aesthetic handle" offers a means for the public to sidestep, and even to become aware of, its own moralizing tendencies and ideological presuppositions. Contrary to surrealism's recent efforts to define revolution as the product of organized political action, this forced encounter with aestheticism in the morning paper contends that an equally powerful challenge to bourgeois life could be seen in the shocking dreams of Victorian sleepers and contemporary newspaper readers alike, a kind of political unconscious waiting to be teased into awareness.

The other surrealists regarded Desnos's interest in popularizing surrealism with hostility, as the language of Louis Aragon's vitriolic review of Desnos's 1930 poetry collection, *Corps et biens*, makes apparent. Aragon, writing in response to Desnos's equally vitupera-

Fig. 4.4. Georges Malkine, *Portrait of Robert Desnos* (1927). Image courtesy of the Bibliothèque Littéraire Jacques Doucet, Paris. Photograph by Suzanne Nagy. © 2008 Artists Rights Society (ARS), New York/ADAGP, Paris.

tive *Third Manifesto of Surrealism*, portrays Desnos as a writer who has sabotaged his intellectual integrity by resorting to tricks, hoaxes, and doggerel in order to pander to a mythical public. That same year found Desnos publishing as poetry the linguistic and mediumistic experiments of the "période des sommeils," which in 1922 and 1923 had instead been "clinical documents for the study of hysteroform crises"; likewise Aragon finds Desnos's journalism to be little more than muckraking and lies. As Aragon writes: "The man who claimed to have received the confidences of Jack the Ripper, not to mention the telepathic messages to which he is wont, is a professional liar who gets away with attacking all that is pure, in raking up and seasoning with his drool the most malicious gossip and the poorest inventions."[112] However humorless Aragon's distaste for Desnos's journalistic trickery may seem, the broader issue in the surrealists' rejection of Desnos's later writing was its investment in the status of authorship as a gateway to transformative experience; for Desnos, "revolution" became relegated to a form of cultural politics. As

Katharine Conley has stressed, Desnos's distance from Bretonian surrealism was itself a product of his journalistic work; his relationship to language "sprang more from a desire to communicate clearly with others than from a wish to see what happens when language is allowed to play freely and with a certain narcissism in the imagination."[113]

In the years following the Rif War and the group's political mobilization, however, the surrealism Desnos rejected was less a haven for free play than a movement seeking to yoke even its most frivolous experiments to the theoretical and practical demands of organized leftist politics. For all the group's admiration of Desnos's writing, it was his celebration of his own authorial influence that the other surrealists considered narcissistic. Even so, as the object of surrealist polemics shifted from discussions about the danger of metaphorical appeals to the Orient to debates about the relationship between revolutionary politics and intellectual labor, Desnos's emphasis on writing for a public would remain a stumbling block in surrealist thinking.

CHAPTER FIVE

X MARKS THE SPOT

> All our ideas are representations of objects that strike us. . . . [E]very
> principle is a judgment, every judgment the outcome of experience,
> and experience is only acquired by the exercise of the senses.
>
> D. A. F. de Sade, "Yet Another Effort, Frenchmen,
> If You Would Become Republicans" (1795)

In a late 1930 issue of his journal *Documents*, Georges Bataille printed a review of the American pamphlet *X Marks the Spot: Chicago Gang Wars in Pictures*, which had been published anonymously earlier that year. The review includes a selection of crime scene photographs from the pamphlet, which documents the trail of assassinations that marked Al Capone's rise to power in Chicago (figure 5.1). The editorial apparatus of this Prohibition-era shock journalism is remarkable for its use of uncensored photographs as well as the tough-sounding banners and captions that frame them. The pamphlet's public mission is explicit. Heralding an insurrection against organized crime, *X Marks the Spot* takes as its precedent the nationwide publication of crime scene photographs of the Saint Valentine's Day Massacre in 1929, a publicity campaign through which "public indifference to Gangland's crimes came to an abrupt end." The pamphlet continues:

> The work of destroying organized crime in Chicago began determinedly, coldly, sternly. To use a phrase borrowed from Gangland, the exponents of the "gat" and the machine gun are today being "pushed around" by Decency and Integrity, and they must surely fall into the abyss of oblivion. What has brought about this uprising? More than any other single factor has been the wide and unceasing publicity given to Gangland's activities.[1]

The "wide and unceasing publicity" advocated by *X Marks the Spot* refers both to the distribution of crime scene photographs as propaganda in the war against crime and to the images' full disclosure of the aftermath of gangland violence. Bataille, while in favor of violent imagery, nevertheless questioned the assumption that uncensored photographs of murdered gangsters could "driv[e] home the lesson that the underworld has present day

X marks the spot

Here you have the first actual photographic story ever published of the world famous beer wars of Chicago Gangland. It begins with the murder of "Diamond Jim" Colosimo at the dawn of prohibition, and it continues on up through the years, death by death, until the killers of Gangland finally graduated from murder to massacre on St. Valentine's day, 1929, and more recently hit one below the belt by assassinating Alfred "Jake" Lingle, a newspaper reporter. ✗ With the country-wide publication of the massacre photograph, public indifference to Gangland's crimes came to an abrupt end. The work of destroying organized crime in Chicago began determinedly, coldly, sternly. To use a phrase borrowed from Gangland, the exponents of the "gat" and the machine gun are today being "pushed around" by Decency and Integrity, and they must surely fall into the abyss of oblivion. ✗ What has brought about this uprising? More than any other single factor has been the wide and unceasing publicity given to Gangland's activities. ✗ It was this fact that gave the authors the idea for this book. Newspaper reporters of long Chicago police experience, they realized that any book showing the criminals of Boozedom as they really are would necessarily be one of brutality and blood and horror. Only in such a book could it be done. ✗ X Marks The Spot is the result. In its terrible Truth, this book will become of tremendous value in obliterating gangsters from the Chicago scene. The publication of death pictures in newspapers is becoming more common every day. Editors have at last realized the terrific force a death picture can exert, particularly in driving home the lesson that the underworld has present day civilization in its grip. ✗ The ultimate good of the death picture far outweighs the shock that it may have on a certain delicate emotional segment of the newspaper readers. A famous New York newspaper editor commenting in Editor & Publisher recently on the publication of the Valentine massacre picture, declared that "it was a more powerful example of the defiance of law and order by the underworld than could be drawn by twenty-five columns of editorials." ✗ In Chicago the tendency to publish death pictures, particularly of slain gangsters, is definite and growing. And the result is the passing of the gangster. It is interesting to speculate on what the effect might have been on crime in Chicago if this tendency had manifested itself on page one four or five years ago. ✗ X Marks The Spot publishes those pictures for the first time. The body of the gangster which was blotted out and an X substituted is restored as the camera saw it. You have read the story in countless volumes, now, for the first time you can see it. You will see Chicago crime "put on the spot."

Fig. 5.1. Frontispiece from *X Marks the Spot: Chicago Gang Wars in Pictures* (1930). Image courtesy of the Ryerson and Burnham Libraries, the Art Institute of Chicago.

civilization in its grip."[2] The pamphlet deliberately removed the "X" of censorship that traditionally replaced actual corpses in published crime scene photographs; yet this explicit gesture was itself censored, Bataille suggests, by the editorial blinders inherent in the pamphlet's status as propaganda. That is, the photographic gaze that claimed to function "determinedly, coldly, sternly" was in fact motivated and blinded by the forces of Decency and Integrity in whose name the images were distributed.

Composed at a healthy remove from the Chicago gang wars, Bataille's review offers an alternative reading of the pamphlet's photographs. In opposition to the pamphlet's idealistic language of civic mission, Bataille argues that in face of such images, "the desire to see ends up prevailing over disgust or fear."[3] For all the pamphlet's strivings toward propaganda, it could instead be said to sanction voyeuristic contemplation. The photographs, after all, depicted the wounds and suffering of hardened criminals: these were images to be consumed. Bataille embraces this implicit capacity for enjoyment. In reading X Marks the Spot in terms of a morally unproductive "desire to see," moreover, the review articulates two significant features of Bataille's thinking in 1930, at the height of his disagreement with the surrealist movement. First, the review forms part of his broader critique of institutional justice for its unacknowledged participation in such voyeurism. Second, it reproduces, in condensed form, Bataille's more general critique of surrealism—a movement that, like X Marks the Spot, seemed on the verge of collapsing beneath the weight of its idealistic social and political project.

Unlike other contemporary critics of surrealism, who tended to dismiss its theoretical work as either dangerously reactionary or naïvely intuitive and hostile to rigor, Bataille instead criticized the all too deliberate logic through which surrealism grounded its politics. The group's call for revolution had more to do, he felt, with the philosophical appeal of dialectical materialism than with the reality of violent rebellion. Most broadly, Bataille's critique of the movement's "idealism" attacked the incorporating dialectic through which poets such as Breton and Aragon, instead of rejecting orthodox Marxism outright, attempted to reconcile its formal principles with the group's artistic practices. This is why, in his contribution to the 1930 anti-Breton pamphlet Un Cadavre, Bataille lambastes Breton for purveying a "mythical liberty" by "concealing his religious enterprise under a feeble revolutionary phraseology."[4] Bataille criticized surrealism, in other words, for the same disavowed moralism he saw in X Marks the Spot, and for the same vagueness for which older Marxists such as Marcel Martinet had disparaged them several years previously in calling them "Lenins-in-short-pants." For Bataille, though, the social reality the surrealists were guilty of abstracting was neither that of American gangsters nor that of the global proletariat, but the brute violence Martinet had accused them of courting. The surrealists had heeded Martinet's critique all too earnestly, Bataille suggested, eagerly refashioning themselves as leftist intellectuals at the expense of acknowledging the "bloody farce" of real insurrectional violence.[5]

By 1929 the surrealist group was in the midst of a profound critique of its own interpretation of the nature of historical, political, and empirical change. During this period the surrealists and their fellow travelers interrogated the consequences, and not merely the promise, of their communist affiliation; the group likewise reevaluated its intellectual genealogy—in liberatory figures such as Lautréamont, Rimbaud, Freud, Hegel, Sade—in response to the increasingly orthodox cultural program of the Communist International.[6] And while Breton would claim in the *Second Manifesto* that "this frame of mind which we call Surrealist . . . seems less and less to require any historical antecedents," this did not mean that such figures ceased to play a role in the actuality of surrealism's political thinking.[7] It meant, rather, that the movement's precursors remained relevant insofar as they could be recapitulated as living elements within contemporary surrealist thought. The marquis de Sade in particular was one of the most contested theoretical figures in the movement's debates about leftist politics. Facing the hypothetical question of whether Sade, "in a plenary session of the National Convention, commit[ed] a counterrevolutionary act," Breton responded that such an "interrogation of the dead" was sterile and represented a form of "spiritual highway robbery"; the movement should "hold the cult of men in deep distrust."[8] He instead urged the movement to recognize "the impeccable integrity of Sade's life and thought" as a function of Sade's "heroic need . . . to create an order of things which was not as it were dependent upon everything that had come before him."[9] Breton works, in other words, to distinguish the historical Sade from the surrealist Sade, depicting him as the embodiment of a revolutionary pessimism that cast suspicion on the tendency for thought, even revolutionary thought, to become inflexible.

The disagreements over the political direction of surrealism which erupted toward the end of 1929 revolved largely around the nature of this "heroic need." The question of how literally Sade's works could be read figured prominently in the movement's most serious ideological rifts during its communist period. Sade did not, in other words, represent simply the pornographic antithesis of political responsibility; his work took part in the fundamental articulation of this commitment. Even Bataille's critique of the movement was grounded in an investigation of Sade as a historical figure; so too were the political theories of numerous surrealists. Hegel, Engels, Marx, and Heraclitus may have formed the philosophical basis for the movement's understanding of dialectical materialism, but it was Sade who called attention to the limits and blindnesses of revolutionary ideology. For the surrealists, Sade's life and works confronted organized politics not only with the excesses of horror and violence toward which Bataille directed his attention, but also with the extremes to which revolution had to be pursued in order to avoid unconsciously reinstating the forms of power it sought to overthrow.

The present chapter examines Sade's role in surrealism as both an object of contention and the intellectual figure whose works fostered what the painter André Masson called a "physical idea of the Revolution."[10] This "physical idea," I argue, represents surrealism's response to dialectical materialism; it derives from the movement's efforts during the late 1920s and early 1930s to reconcile itself with Marxism, as well as, under pressure from Bataille, to distinguish itself from communist orthodoxy. Masson's notion of a "physical idea of the Revolution," which dates from 1923, was conceived as a break with "Occidental civilization" in grounding revolutionary thinking in direct bodily experience rather than in ideological constructs that were themselves European products. Pursued more broadly throughout the 1920s and early 1930s, Masson's "physical idea" points to the group's ongoing collective interrogation of political agency and political expression, which challenged the naturalist assumptions of party communism about the relationship between thoughts and deeds and between desire and action. The surrealists, in effect, heeded Sade's critique of the French Revolution in *Philosophy in the Boudoir*: the Revolution's descent into Terror meant not that the Revolution had gone too far but that it had not gone far enough; it left unchallenged presumptions about the sovereignty of law, the family, God, the Catholic Church, and, most broadly, the bourgeoisie. Bataille's review of *X Marks the Spot* makes a similar claim in its impatience with the residual idealism of the pamphlet's hard-boiled images of dead gangsters.

In light of Sade's critique, in this chapter I examine the surrealist group's attempts to pursue such physical ideas of the Revolution, tracing the genealogy of what might be considered a Sadean materialism. The chapter begins with a discussion of Sade's place in the political discussions of 1925–26. It then turns to the development of the group's means of political expression, focusing on the shift in Breton's thinking between *Nadja* (1928) and the *Second Manifesto of Surrealism* (1929). Whereas *Nadja* invoked cold-blooded murder as the "simplest form" of political expression, Breton revised this claim to emphasize the need for a "crisis in consciousness" fundamental to any truly revolutionary form of political action. Salvador Dalí further systematized this notion in his writings on paranoia-criticism; by contrast, Aragon's 1931 poem "Red Front" embraced violent propaganda as a form of revolutionary expression that sought to prevent, rather than to incite, any such crisis in consciousness, abandoning surrealist poetics in favor of the instrumental language of Soviet socialist realism. The chapter concludes with a discussion of the efforts of the Martiniquan surrealist Jules Monnerot to redefine Breton's and Dalí's "crisis in consciousness" in the wake of Aragon's propaganda poem.

The Anatomy of Destiny

Jailed for roughly thirty years of his life "in various bastilles, fortresses, or keeps of the Monarchy, then of the Republic, of the Terror, of the Consulate and of the Empire," Donatien-Alphonse-François de Sade would have seemed intolerable to any regime.[11] His constant imprisonment might be understood in either of at least two ways: as a response to the threat he posed as a revolutionary, or as a reaction to his toxic presence as a libertine and writer of monstrous works. The surrealists, with Baudelaire and Apollinaire before them, were among the first to share Marcel Hénaff's assertion that "it is utterly ludicrous to take Sade literally, to read his fictions as programs for crime and perversion."[12] But what did it mean not to take Sade literally? Could the extremes of Sadean crime, perversion, and scatology really be read as the imaginative form of a moral philosophy determined to abolish laws and limits? The surrealists, though among the first to look beyond the atrocities catalogued in Sade's works, were also among the first to recognize the extent to which their sexual violence frustrates any philosophical system they might seem to set in play. This recognition, I maintain, forced the group to confront its own position toward violent action, whether linguistic or physical, even as its members evoked this violence in the name of revolutionary socialism. Only in this conflicted way could Sade's works contribute to André Masson's directive for the surrealists to develop a "physical idea of the Revolution."

The surrealist interest in Sade developed in tandem with the movement. Yet it was in 1925 and 1926, when Maurice Heine began to republish Sade's lesser-known works and letters, that Sade began to emerge fully as a philosophical figure in the surrealist imagination.[13] These rediscovered works augmented the group's understanding of Sade as a writer and philosopher; more significantly, they transformed the movement's investigations into religion, sexuality, gender, and ideology. The surrealists' direct appeal to Sade as a political figure emerged in late 1925, when the group expressed its solidarity with Abd el-Krim's insurgence in the Rif (see chapter 4). Insisting that a dissolution of the moral values of patriotism and nationalism was essential to opposing France's imperialist efforts to suppress the Riffians, the surrealists called for "liberty, but a liberty modeled on our most profound spiritual needs, on the strictest and most human demands of our flesh (in truth it is always others who are afraid). The modern age has had its day. The stereotypical cycle of Europe's gestures, acts and lies has completed the cycle of disgust."[14] In calling for a liberty modeled on the demands of the flesh, the surrealists sought an abolition of the alienated modern relations through which, "for over a century, human dignity has been reduced to the level of exchange value."[15] They refused to participate in European capitalism's "cycle of disgust"; yet they recognized, too, the extent to which this disgust had already penetrated the flesh, and had exercised a determining influence on the very demands that opposed it. Modeling liberty on the demands of the flesh thus could not involve simply an embrace of anarchic individualism, since these very demands were themselves determined by ideological apparatuses that reproduced relations of power: religion, the family, the state, the police, and reproductive sexuality. As Angela Carter later wrote in The Sadean Woman, "Flesh comes to us out of history; so does the repression and taboo that governs our experience of flesh."[16]

In this context Sade came to embody a total revolutionary project that saw direct political action as only the starting point for a more fundamental critique of the laws and ordering principles governing the experience of the flesh. Sade, in other words, violated the
laws left unquestioned by those groups that heeded the demands of political expediency
alone. Paul Éluard articulates this synthesis in an article titled "D. A. F. de Sade, a Fantastic and Revolutionary Writer," published in La Révolution Surréaliste in 1926. The article defends "the spirit of Sade," which, Éluard argues, challenges the "mockery" of Christian
morals with "all the appetites of the body and mind that rise up against it."[17] According
to Éluard, Sade's writings offer a dialectics of their own, wherein the liberation of appetites functions as a critique of the moral and social laws that police them. This critique
in turn demanded a broader conception of liberation as an upheaval of the ideological
structures that govern human experience, and no longer simply as an exercise of bodily
appetites.[18]

As both a historical figure and the author of obscene works that systematically catalogued their perversion of natural and moral laws, Sade offered an equally systematic
means for perverting the increasingly bureaucratic tendencies of communism, especially
with regard to the politicization of cultural work.[19] Sade's writings, in both their obscen-
ity and their direct challenges to religion, the family, and the state, threw into high relief
the epistemological and methodological shortcomings of French (and, more broadly,
Stalinist) communism's definitions of human liberty. Was the communist revolution content merely to overthrow the socioeconomic bases of bourgeois power without taking into
account the institutions that perpetuate its moral, psychological, and ideological influence? Were the conditions for intellectual and artistic freedom to emerge only after the
final victory of the revolution and the end of history? Breton, in the Second Manifesto, argued
to the contrary that "the problem of social action . . . is only one of the forms of a more
general problem which Surrealism set out to deal with, and that is the problem of human expression in all its forms."[20] In this respect Breton's manifesto might be read as an update of
Sade's "Yet Another Effort, Frenchmen, If You Would Become Republicans" in its rhetorical extension of "revolution" to the most elemental facets of social and intellectual
existence.

In an essay published in La Révolution Surréaliste in 1926, André Masson reiterates his
earlier appeal to Sade to provide surrealism with "a physical idea of the Revolution." In
"Tyrranie du temps," Masson defines this idea as a process of liberation that would entail
not just the bloody overthrow of colonial and state power but also, more important, a
recognition of the extent to which those institutions wielded ideological power over the
very revolutionaries who sought to overthrow them. This is why Masson rejects even the
idea of dying in a blaze of glory as a revolutionary's goal. He writes that "the blood of revolutions, the blood of victims," is little else than a snare, when considered as a motivat-
ing tactic or as an end in itself. Martyrdom and glory are ideological constructs, Masson

argues, urging instead that "we must believe, like Saint-Just, that a revolutionary will know no rest before the tomb—and with Sade, flatter ourselves that we will disappear from the minds of men."[21] Masson, citing Sade's "Last Will and Testament," invokes Sade's memory to reject the value of satisfaction, and even of memorialization itself, as extensions of the egoistic logic of bourgeois capitalism. Masson's "physical idea of Revolution" is more, in other words, than simply an appeal to revolutionary effectiveness; it invokes Sade both as an embodiment of a political imperative and as a means for critiquing the ideological construction of real bodies, whether living, dead, or in revolt.

Although Masson's surrealist attack on nationalism and revolutionary piety might seem to anticipate Bataille's argument against the ideological blindnesses of a crusading document such as X Marks the Spot, Bataille criticized the surrealist appropriation of Sade as what he considered a "foreign body." The group's relationship to Sade, he argued, resembled "that of primitive subjects in relation to their king, whom they adore and loathe, and whom they cover with honors and narrowly confine."[22] Bataille's criticism suggests that this paradoxical glorification and erasure of Sade's specificity was already symptomatic of the movement's ambivalence, or even blindness, toward the true violence of his works. Without discounting Bataille's perceptiveness, I contend that this ambivalence derives from the surrealists' tendency to champion Sade as a means for distancing themselves from orthodox communism. It is this ambivalence that makes the confrontation between Marxism—as a political philosophy dedicated to the liberation from oppression—and the works of Sade—which endlessly multiply acts of torture, murder, and rape—something other than a fatal contradiction.

Bataille, however, insisted that there was a contradiction. Not only did the surrealists disavow that Sade was fundamentally inassimilable within any Marxism, whether orthodox or not, but also they suppressed Sade's moral difficulty beneath an idealized abstraction of his philosophy. They developed what was, for Bataille, merely an elaborate form of idealism; he contended that their "physical idea" presumed the autogenesis of concrete reality through little more than the unfolding of concepts. Bataille's critique was in fact perceptive: Aragon had certainly been enchanted with nominalism in his early writing, and Breton's interest in the Rimbaudian "alchemy of the word" suggested, too, an appeal to the power of language to invoke real physical transformations. But even if the surrealists had not fully worked out their relationship to philosophical idealism before Breton's Second Manifesto, the group subsequently revised their presumptions about the causal power of speculative concepts and imperative language, largely in response to Bataille's critique.

Cold-Blooded Murder

One of the ways the surrealists conceived of "a liberty modeled . . . on the strictest and most human demands of our flesh" was through the physical means the group used to voice its demands. What did they mean by making a demand physically? In the program that accompanied Luis Buñuel and Salvador Dalí's film L'Âge d'or in 1930, the collective group essay on the film cites "the blasphemies screamed by the divine marquis through his prison bars" as a form of political expression to which the surrealist film could be compared.[23] Sade's screams, the program claims, lashed out against "the triumphant bourgeoisie's inexorable physical and moral repression" in a way that invited speculation about "the development of this pessimism in the struggle and triumph of the proletariat."[24]

The film, which closes with an image drawn directly from Maurice Heine's recently published edition of Sade's 120 Days of Sodom, imagines numerous similar sequences that conflate or condense depictions of bodily suffering with scenes of love and sexual pleasure. This filmic experience, as the group tract published in the program states, represents a "most desperate struggle against all artifice, subtle or vulgar." Buñuel "smashes, he sets to, he terrifies, he ransacks. The doors of love and hatred are open, letting violence in. Inhuman, it sets man on his feet, snatches from him the possibility of putting an end to his stay on earth. Man breaks cover and, face to face with the vain arrangement of charm and disenchantment, is intoxicated with the strength of his delirium."[25] The program suggests that the film's means of expression were as physical as its effects on an audience: like the gut-wrenching corporeality of Sade's blasphemies, the surrealist film was itself a form of violence.

The surrealists, of course, were not above using violent language when it suited their rhetorical purposes. A number of the movement's initial interventions into the field of politics maintained the rhetorical and occasionally physical violence of the group's Dada period. At a banquet in honor of the poet Saint-Pol-Roux in July 1925, Breton, Soupault, Leiris, and others let fly a salvo of anticolonial and antinationalist pronouncements such as "Victory to the Rif!" and "Hail the worker's paradise!" which sparked an outbreak of fistfights and arrests typical of earlier proto-surrealist brawls, such as the Coeur à barbe incident in 1923 (see chapter 2).[26] By the late 1920s, though, such outbursts had become both more premeditated and more hypothetical. When read as the pronouncements of a left-wing intellectual movement, such language might seem tailored to instrumentalize its power to shock and terrorize. Indeed, surrealism's recourse to shocking language has tended to overshadow the subtlety of the movement's thinking.

Such was the case, certainly, with Breton's use of murderous language in Nadja as an attack on the institutional violence of psychiatric clinics. Toward the end of the text Breton contemplates the fate of his lover, Nadja, who has been institutionalized. Sanitariums, Breton writes, exercise "the most pernicious influence" on those they shelter, and are analogous to prisons in the oppressiveness of their disciplinary function. "All confinements," explains Breton, "are arbitrary. I still cannot see why a human being should be deprived of freedom. They shut up Sade, they shut up Nietzsche; they shut up Baudelaire."[27] In response to the legal incarceration of mental patients, Breton writes that if he were institutionalized, he "would take advantage of any momentary period of lucidity to murder in cold blood one of those, preferably the doctor, who happened to come my way. At least I would be put into a cell by myself, the way the violent patients are. Perhaps they would leave me alone."[28] Breton is not simply lashing out here against the fate of his incarcerated lover; his attack on the clinic forms part of a broader reflection on human emancipation. As Breton states: "Human emancipation—conceived finally in its simplest revolutionary form, which is no less than human emancipation in *every respect*, by which I mean, *according to the means at every man's disposal*—remains the only cause worth serving."[29] Breton's notion of emancipation applies both in the abstract, as a liberation from "logic, that is . . . the most hateful of prisons," as well as in the concrete, as an overthrow of institutions of reform. In the context of his proposed act of murder, Breton's earlier assertion that the simplest revolutionary form of human emancipation demanded "the means at every man's disposal" here announces a fundamental recourse to violence. Breton makes no claim to overthrow the psychiatric institution; he is simply reacting to the conditions it imposes. Murder, the text suggests, demonstrates the degree of desperation required for revolutionary commitment; but the act itself is little more than an egoistic gesture, to which Breton would later refer as the simplest of surrealist acts.

Upon the publication of Nadja by Gallimard in 1928, Breton's statement became the occasion for a clinical discussion about the dangers psychiatric doctors faced in their encounters with violent patients, and consequently about the inflammatory nature of a surrealist text such as Breton's. In a colloquy published in the *Annales Médico-Psychologiques* and reprinted as the preface to Breton's *Second Manifesto of Surrealism* in 1929, a number of leading psychiatrists debated the significance of Breton's attack on their profession. In the report that prompted the Société Médico-Psychologique's discussion, Paul Abély writes of Breton's statement that "if it is not tantamount to inciting to murder, then nothing is. We can only react to it with complete disdain, or with utter indifference."[30] Dr. Gaétan Gatian de Clérambault, the eminent psychiatrist and mentor of Jacques Lacan, agrees with Abély in characterizing Breton's statement as a symptom of the surrealist movement's moral extremism and intellectual bankruptcy. Unlike his colleague Pierre Janet, who claims that the surrealists are "men obsessed, and men who doubt," Clérambault derides the movement, explaining that such antisocial "tendencies" as Breton's incitement to murder were the result not of any psychological defect but of an epistemological short-sightedness. He accuses the surrealists of a "methodism" that "consists of saving oneself the trouble of thinking, and even more of observing, so as to rely upon a method or pre-determined formula in order to produce an effect of itself unique, schematic, and conventional: thus one produces rapidly, with some semblance of style, and avoiding the criticisms that a similarity to life would facilitate."[31] Clérambault accuses Breton of resorting to inflated rhetoric in place of reasonable judgment and reasoned intellectual discourse.

Yet Breton's call to murder in Nadja was a calculated formula for reciprocity: his statement was based on a logic of self-defense which claimed that psychiatric institutions were themselves murderous in the degree to which they created madmen and monsters. A sanitarium, Breton argued, "requires a certain degree of adaptation. Unless you have been inside a sanitarium you do not know that madmen are made there, just as criminals are made in our reformatories. Is there anything more detestable than these systems of so-called social conservation."[32] Breton would soon abandon terms like "cold-blooded murder" in voicing his critique of such detestable systems, instead insisting more forcefully on the criminality of the institutions whose repressive effects surrealism strove to combat: institutions of nationalism, totalitarianism, and colonialism. Colonialism, in particular, legitimated insurrectional violence as a form of self-defense against the exercise of what the surrealists identified in 1932 as a "murderous humanitarianism."

Reprinting the Société Médico-Psychologique's discourse as the preamble to the Second Manifesto allowed Breton to frame his 1929 text as a rebuttal of Clérambault's charge of methodism. Here, though, Breton's rebuttal raises the stakes of Nadja's momentary recourse to cold-blooded murder in stating that "the simplest surrealist act consists of dashing down into the street, pistol in hand, and firing blindly, as fast as you can pull the trigger, into the crowd."[33] Breton's claim transforms the implicit reciprocity of his earlier statement about cold-blooded murder into a mandate: if you have not at least dreamed of using such violent means in the service of revolt, Breton argues, then you have "a well-defined place in that crowd, with [your] belly at barrel level." His point is not to advocate such acts of random violence but instead to reiterate his claim in Nadja that human emancipation, "conceived finally in its simplest revolutionary form," will use any means at its disposal. The difficult part of revolution is not its violence; indeed, Breton suggests that violence is all too simple. What is difficult is the full realization of a project of emancipation that extends to all facets of life, and that places the most extreme demands on its practitioners. Revolution, Breton writes in the Second Manifesto, requires the kind of commitment to the overthrow of bourgeois capitalism that can be experienced only as a despair so strong as to render extremism imaginable. Anyone who believed in surrealist politics as little more than a gleefully metaphorical pursuit, "without truly sharing this despair, would soon be revealed," Breton writes, "as an enemy."[34] Breton's most notorious statement, in other words, invokes murder not as an extension of surrealism's alleged methodism into the field of political violence, but as the hypothetical extreme that Breton claims to be the measure of surrealism's refusal to operate simply as a method, whether aesthetic, epistemological, or political.

Nevertheless, Clérambault's attack on the likely consequences of Breton's murderous rhetoric has continued to color the critical reception of surrealism as an intellectual movement. This negative reception, which began in 1925 with journalistic speculation about how the poetic movement would find itself stranded on the shores of politics, continues through Jean-Paul Sartre's admonishment of the movement's rhetorical violence after the Second World War, and lingers in the movement's critical legacy. At stake in such critiques are the consequences, moral as well as political, of defining a "physical idea of the Revolution" in terms of violent speech.

George Bataille's criticism of the movement was, however scathing, antithetical to such self-righteously alarmist attacks on surrealism's use of violent language. Unlike the psychiatrists of the Société Médico-Psychologique, Bataille scorned the surrealists for the extent to which they did not really mean what they said: their violent written and visual rhetoric, he argued, was circumscribed by a conceptual idealism that, for all its attempts to embody the idea of revolution physically, was not truly physical at all. The antidote for such conceptual idealism, Bataille claimed, was a form of critical practice derived from Sade. The surrealists praised Sade's prison screams as a mode of political expression directed against the repressive institutions of an aristocratic social order; Bataille, by contrast, championed the fundamentally inarticulate nature of any such cries, asserting that they nevertheless had prompted the masses to storm the Bastille.

In questioning surrealism's assumptions about what he called "the use-value" of the marquis de Sade, Bataille's critique also prompted further surrealist attention to the ideas about causality implicit in any Sadean materialism. Unlike Georges Sorel, the surrealists did not posit spontaneous acts of violence as the determining impulse for revolutions; instead, Bataille's critiques demanded that the movement consider all the more carefully how it understood the relationship between violence and the patterns of historical change. In spite of the polemics between Bataille and Breton, Bataille's critiques were deeply influential to surrealist thinking, compelling the movement to concentrate as much on its own guiding assumptions about political expression as on the objects of its political critique.

The Police Eye

Bataille first launched his attack on surrealism's implicit self-censorship in an article that appropriated, rather than criticized, some of the more overtly Sadean surrealist works. In his 1929 essay on the eye as a "cannibal delicacy," he invokes the eye-slashing scene from Salvador Dalí and Luis Buñuel's recent film Un Chien andalou, arguing that the scene proved that the film should be "distinguished from banal avant-garde productions, with which one might be tempted to confuse it."[35] Dalí and Buñuel no longer belonged to the surrealist movement, he implies; they instead belonged to the group of former surrealists who had migrated to Bataille's journal Documents in 1929: Robert Desnos, Michel Leiris, Raymond Queneau, André Masson, and Roger Vitrac. The eye-slashing scene did not merely abandon avant-garde "banality" but did so by pursuing an interest in "very explicit facts" toward the "extreme seduction [which] is probably at the limit of horror."[36] That is, Dalí and Buñuel do not use the eye solely as a metaphor for vision or visionary experience sharply emancipated from, say, the narrative logic of film; they express both fascination and horror with the eye itself as a physical object. This attention to the seductive power of "explicit facts" is for Bataille a Sadean practice, through which Sade defines his own materialism as a recognition of the ineluctable physicality of matter.

In response to Bretonian surrealism's efforts to develop a "physical idea of Revolution" through language whose violence challenged the formal, ideological, and institutional limits of revolutionary activity, Bataille abandoned the language of emancipation altogether. He instead favored the libertine's bonds of attraction and fascination as the basis of his critical practice. As a way of illustrating his distance from surrealism, Bataille reprinted one of Dalí's recent paintings alongside his "Eye" essay, the spectacularly gruesome Honey Is Sweeter Than Blood, which he juxtaposed with images from the pulp magazine L'Œil de la Police (The Eye of the Police; figure 5.2). Bataille frames his commentary on this presentation as a series of Socratic questions: "Why . . . on the masthead of a perfectly sadistic illustrated weekly, published in Paris from 1907 to 1924, does an eye regularly appear against a red background, above a bloody spectacle? Why isn't the Eye of the Police—similar to the eye of human justice . . . —finally only the expression of a blind thirst for blood?"[37] What rescues L'Œil de la Police from abject blood lust is, counterintuitively, its sadism, the same interpretive lens that rescues Dalí's painting from avant-garde banality. That is, the sadistic embrace of voyeurism—the "desire to see" which Bataille similarly highlights in his 1930 review of X Marks the Spot—divorces even an exploitatively sensationalist pulp magazine like L'Œil de la Police from either a desire for pure violence or an idealistic set of guiding principles.

Bataille further elaborates this position on voyeurism several months later, in December 1929, when he returns to Dalí's Honey Is Sweeter Than Blood in an essay on Dalí's better-known painting The Lugubrious Game. Inverting the title (perhaps deliberately) as "Blood Is Sweeter Than Honey," Bataille interprets the painting as a similar pursuit of "very explicit facts"; what impresses Bataille is the "sweetness" he sees in the painting's bloody depiction of violence. He notes "the body with the head, hands, and feet cut off, the head with the face cut, the ass, symbol of grotesque and powerful virility, lying dead and decomposed, the systematic fragmentation of all the elements in the painting." In Dalí's paint-

L'Œil de la Police, pages de la couverture en couleurs. — 1908, Nº 26.

Salvador Dali, Le sang est plus doux que le miel (1927).
Barcelone, Coll. privée.

Fig. 5.2. Page from *Documents 4* depicting *L'Œil de la police* and Salvador Dalí's *Honey Is Sweeter Than Blood* (September 1929). Image courtesy of the Ryerson and Burnham Libraries, the Art Institute of Chicago.

ings, Bataille maintains, "a new and real virility is found . . . in ignominy and horror themselves."[38]

It is here, in this proliferation of bloody detail, that Bataille situates a principle of historical change. Whether he calls it power, virility, or sovereignty, he argues that the causal principle of revolt is a property not of concepts or collective agency but of material things as they exist within a network of social and psychological relations. As he writes in his essay on *The Lugubrious Game*: "Little by little the contradictory signs of servitude and revolt are revealed in all things. The great constructions of the intellect are, finally, prisons: that is why they are obstinately overturned."[39] The "great constructions of the intellect"— whether concepts such as Revolution, Justice, "Decency and Integrity," or movements such as surrealism and communism—are never truly revolutionary or shocking because their aim of imposing a conceptual order fails to indulge the "desire to see" that resurrects *L'Œil de la Police*, and even *X Marks the Spot*, from their idealism. Whereas human life, Bataille claims, "always more or less conforms to the image of a soldier obeying commands in his drill," the inverse is true of spectacles of horror. The "sudden cataclysms, great popular manifestations of madness, riots, enormous revolutionary slaughters" all manifest an inevitable backlash against this image.[40]

In this context Sade becomes the true revolutionary to the extent that the "desire to see" which is exercised in his works is as cataclysmic and as unredeemable as the madness of crowds. Mapping this idea onto Sade's own life, Bataille proposes, somewhat facetiously, that the storming of the Bastille may have been the result of Sade's mad scream from the bowels of the prison. Unlike the surrealist version of this anecdote in the *Âge d'or* program, Bataille's thoughts about the revolutionary attraction of such an abject outcry privilege the voyeurism of the crowd outside the prison: the Revolution was not the product of rhetoric or intentional political speech but the consequence of a collective desire to participate in Sade's scream. This scream, broadcast through a sewage pipe, "practically the scream of an old *rentière* with her throat slashed at night in a suburb," was not intended to do anything; yet it nevertheless mobilized the crowd.[41] The screamer, according to Bataille, had truly stared into the darkest recesses of horror without seeking refuge in a "prison" of intellect, and this scream was itself seductive in turn. Bataille's response to Dalí's painting serves as a refrain to this anecdote about Sade: Bataille's desire "to squeal like a pig" before Dalí's canvases is meant to reveal his own recognition and repetition of what he considers to be their true, noncommunicative horror.[42]

Revolutions, Bataille, argues, function similarly. They do not require a "physical idea" but instead take place as spectacles that solicit the complicity of their participants. As Bataille writes in "The Use-Value of D. A. F. de Sade," written but not published during roughly the same period as his articles on Dalí:

> Without a profound complicity with the natural forces such as violent death, gushing
> blood, sudden catastrophes and the horrible cries of pain that accompany them, terrify-

ing ruptures of what had seemed to be immutable, the fall into stinking filth of what had been elevated—without a sadistic understanding of an incontestably thundering and torrential nature, there could be no revolutionaries, there could only be a revolting utopian sentimentality.

This notion of complicity suggests how Bataille considered the "desire to see," discussed in his *X Marks the Spot* review, as a voyeurism designating what was ultimately an erotic bond. Sade's use-value comes into play here through his reception as the theorist of an "ever more shameless awareness of the erotic bond that links [human beings] to death, to cadavers, and to horrible physical pain."[43] Bataille's interpretation of Sade is crucial to this system of complicity and participation: Sade's works, Bataille argues, replace the reproductive organs with a proliferation of natural forces, bodily parts, and substances that function perversely, through the processes of excretion (the emission of sperm, blood, urine, vomit, or excrement) and assimilation (penetration, incorporation, drinking, eating, swallowing). This reading allows Bataille to dislodge Sadean sexuality from what Angela Carter has called the "graffiti" of pornographic sexuality and toward a broad and pan-cultural notion of heterology that accounts for the organization of heterogeneous elements—bodies, body parts, animate and inanimate objects, collectives—within a general symbolic economy.[44] This, for Bataille, is what it meant to have a sadistic understanding; without it, there could be only a revolting utopian sentimentality.

One of the more unsentimental illustrations of Bataille's notion of heterology is Alberto Giacometti's *Femme égorgée* (Woman with Her Throat Cut; figure 5.3), a sculpture that signals how certain surrealists would respond to Bataille's theories in the early 1930s. Composed after Giacometti's period of involvement with Bataille's *Documents* group and his subsequent affiliation with the surrealists, the 1932 sculpture explores Bataille's Sadean theories of voyeuristic participation within the immediate physical context of murderous violence. In the sculpture, which depicts a splayed female figure writhing in agony, this violence is overdetermined, multiplied through its bodily affect rather than explained or mastered. The titular cut throat is oddly minimized, represented as a small notch in the figure's equally dwarfed head. And while the mouth is indeed open in an arrested scream, the figure's arched body instead becomes the primary means of expression. The contorted limbs double as pools of spilled blood, and the jagged right leg resolves into a double row of sharp points: the teeth of a trap, perhaps, or the bared bones of a broken rib cage. Even as the sculpture's title beckons toward the cut throat overshadowed by the body's spatial composition, Giacometti's titular isolation of the throat disguises the more gruesome possibility that the figure has also been disemboweled, *éventrée* as well as *égorgée*, for the jagged points along the spine—which has been displaced onto the figure's right leg—suggest a second order of violence unmentioned in the title.

As Mary Drach McInnes has suggested, Giacometti's sculpture recalls the serial mur-

Fig. 5.3. Alberto Giacometti, *Woman with Her Throat Cut (Femme égorgée)* (1932, cast 1940). Bronze. 9⅛ × 35¹⁄₁₆ inches (23.2 × 89 cm). The Solomon R. Guggenheim Foundation, New York, Peggy Guggenheim Collection, Venice, 1976. 76.2553.131. Photograph by David Heald © 2008 The Solomon R. Guggenheim Foundation, New York. © 2008 Artists Rights Society (ARS), New York/ADAGP, Paris.

ders of Desnos's Jack the Ripper articles from 1928 (see chapter 4), with which the sculptor may have been familiar through their mutual participation in the *Documents* group.[45] More broadly, Giacometti's 1932 sculpture pursues Bataille's Sadean discourse in its physical representation of noncommunicative horror. Invoking Bataille's description of Sade's prison outburst as the scream of an "old *rentière* with her throat slashed," Giacometti's sculpture abandons the rhetoric of liberation or revolution, instead configuring itself as a spectacle of victimization and suffering. The figure's disrupted bodily economy—with its multiple sites of violence and displaced body parts—emerges from the Sadean project outlined by Bataille as the exploration of complicity in spectacles of violence: here the spectator is caught up in the sculpture's overdetermined violence as if in a trap, arrested in and by one's "desire to see." Composed, however, during Giacometti's period of affiliation with Breton, the sculpture intimates the extent to which the surrealist group was receptive to Bataille's Sadean notions of complicity.

The more militant leftists within the surrealist group, however, opposed Bataille's critical practice of finding the evidence of subversion and heterogeneity within spectacles of power. They instead began targeting popular culture for its police function, its hostility to any elements that might be considered subversive. Bataille courted voyeurism as a way of seeing that could dislodge publications such as L'Œil de la Police and X Marks the Spot from their ideological functions, and espoused sadism as a form of understanding that acknowledges one's complicity in the "natural forces" of violence. But the surrealists also began attacking popular incarnations of the "police eye" for their repressive actions against the forms of perverse and liberatory expression they identified as Sadean. These attacks would take two divergent forms. Certain surrealists—Giacometti, Masson, and Dalí among them—continued to champion Sade, and to heed Bataille, in confronting bourgeois and communist ideology alike with the moral and psychic conditions they left unacknowledged. A second group of increasingly Stalinist surrealists, who would soon break with the movement in favor of communism—Aragon, Georges Sadoul, Pierre Unik, and Maxime Alexandre—targeted instead the physical repression exerted by the police as an instrument of censorship against leftist intellectual work.

Georges Sadoul, in his 1929 article "Bonne Année! Bonne Santé!" (Happy New Year! Be Well!), attacks the popular sensationalist press—and in particular Détective magazine—for demonstrating "such servility, such eagerness to execute the dirtiest work of the lowest police."[46] Sadoul's article joins a number of militant surrealist attacks on "the spirit of the police" published in the final issue of La Révolution Surréaliste in 1929, as well as in early issues of the group's subsequent magazine, Le Surréalisme au Service de la Révolution, in 1930. Sadoul's essay is by far the most paranoid, arguing that the popular appeal of magazines like Détective extended the reach of the powerful right-wing police chief Jean Chiappe. Read, Sadoul claims, by everyone on the Métro, and without protest, such magazines were "agent[s] provocateur[s]; and the murders they will drive people to commit will serve to make the police richer and stronger."[47] Sadoul argues that this complicity, far from yielding the sadistic understanding Bataille advocated, amounts to nothing less than fascism. Sadoul writes: "I can't help smiling when they talk to me about fascism, in France where the cop is king and the chief of police is chief justice, in America where Pinkerton Agency detectives beat down workers, and even in Austria where the Heimwehfen provoke the dictatorship of the chief of police."[48] Citing the work of the Pinkerton National Detective Agency—whose insignia, depicting an ever-vigilant staring eye, advertised surveillance rather than the voyeurism Bataille celebrated in L'Œil de la Police—Sadoul stresses that such private police forces were designed to protect the interests of capitalism. And indeed, agencies like the Pinkerton agency were still very active as strikebreaking and anticommunist forces in the Prohibition-era United States. For Sadoul, the law was merely the pretext for a conspiracy of police forces, whether professional, amateur, or journalistic: "the police," Sadoul writes, "is the function of the industrial power of a bourgeois nation; whoever says rationalization says police."[49]

As David Walker has pointed out, Sadoul's article reproduces extracts from Détective magazine that focus on police brutality, "implying a degree of collusion between the authors and the miscreants they are reporting on. Quoting from a number of editorials,

Sadoul alleges that the magazine is in favour of severe sentences on minors and capital punishment for women, and that it encourages criminals to become police informers."[50] Walker argues that Sadoul thus grossly oversimplifies and quotes out of context the intentions of the *Détective* writers. Yet it hardly seems that Sadoul's goal is to discredit *Détective* alone; rather his intent is to suggest the complicity of even this widely read magazine (he cites a circulation of 800,000 readers per week) with the ideological function of police activity. This function is fascist, Sadoul argues, to the extent that participation in the surveillance and pursuit of so-called criminals is less a question of desire than an automatic function of the state. And yet *Détective* was hardly the sordid pulp material of *L'Œil de la Police*; Sadoul keenly notes its respectability (it was published by the highbrow *Nouvelle Revue Française*). This was, in fact, the very problem: the sensationalism Sadoul decries represented not a liberation of desire or an explosion of perversity but, as Aragon similarly expresses in his "Introduction to 1930," the "revenge of censorship on the unconscious."[51]

Aragon, like Sadoul, attacks "the exaltation of the cop" in police magazines like *Détective*, *Jazz*, *Vu*, and their ilk. His sense of urgency for this attack also looks toward the future, and Aragon closes his "Introduction to 1930" with an ultimatum: "Will you accept that everything you love will, in the future, be visible only from a point of view dictated by a billy club, and that your whole life, all your thoughts, and all your force, will one day be seen by common folks as a little too *Chiappe*, and the name will mean nothing? I ask this question to all those who can respond to it."[52] For Aragon, as for Sadoul, the growing conspiracy between the press and the police under Jean Chiappe was logic enough to reinforce their own communist militancy; after their visit to the International Writers' Conference at Kharkov in November of the following year, this militancy would place the Stalinist-leaning surrealists (Aragon, Sadoul, Alexandre, and Unik) at a remove from surrealism itself.

Kill the Cops, Comrades!

In December 1930 an early public showing of Buñuel and Dalí's new film, *L'Âge d'or*, met with violent protests that would temporarily maintain an alliance between the militant communists and the less orthodox members of the surrealist group. At the first public presentation of *L'Âge d'or*, at Studio 28 in Montmartre on November 28, 1930, the film played without incident. The Spanish filmmakers had secured a French visa for the film, which, according to its own brochure, would derive its "use-value" from "the satisfaction of the need for destruction within the oppressed and perhaps also from the flattery of masochistic tendencies within the oppressor."[53] Six days later, representatives of the League of Patriots and the Anti-Jewish League disrupted the screening during one of the film's many sacrilegious scenes which depicts a Roman Catholic monstrance lying in the gutter. The incident is well documented; it was reported widely in the press, as well as in a surrealist pamphlet published in response to the disruption. Shouting, "We'll see whether there are still any Christians in France!" and "Death to the Jews," the extremists threw ink at the screen, lit smoke bombs, herded spectators out of the theater with billy clubs, and destroyed the numerous surrealist paintings and texts on display in the theater's foyer (figure 5.4).

The violence of this reaction found its counterpart in the legal aftermath of the attack; in the days that followed, the chief censor, under orders from the police and the city council, demanded cuts in the film. A few days later a censorship board decided instead that the entire film should be banned and that its director should be jailed. On December 12, 1930, the police department of the Grandes Carrières quarter (eighteenth arrondissement) seized all copies of the film, which would not be shown publicly again in France until 1949, and not distributed commercially until 1981. Here, it seemed, was a manifest symptom of the repressive, proto-fascist collusion that Aragon and Sadoul had written about the year before. As the surrealists wrote in a questionnaire printed at the end of their pamphlet publicizing the details of the Âge d'or affair: "Since when does one not have the right, in France, seriously to question religion, its foundations, the morals of its representatives, etc.? Since when are the police in the service of anti-Semitism? Is the intervention of the police, sanctioning the pogrom of the League of Patriots, an official encouragement for the establishment of fascist methods in France?"[54] The essay printed in the program for L'Âge d'or had argued that the film's Sadean "use-value" derived from its pessimistic negation of bourgeois values and its embrace of love as "the principle of evil within the bourgeois demonology, which asks one to sacrifice everything—job, family, honor—but whose failure within the social organization introduces the sentiment of revolt."[55] The questionnaire published in the later pamphlet, however, was forced to recognize that a much different sentiment of revolt had been awakened within youth groups such as the League of Patriots and the Anti-Jewish League; the surrealists had to face the fact that any Sadean dialectic of revolt targeting religious and moral limits would meet with increasingly real opposition.

The surrealists were less surprised by the vandalism and scare tactics of the reactionary bourgeoisie, however, than alarmed by the sudden and overwhelming collusion of the police and the censors with the radical right in destroying the film. This was, the surrealists claimed, an opportunity contrived by the reactionary right wing to exercise its power. As the psychoanalyst Jean Frois-Wittmann warned the surrealists in his response to their questionnaire:

It comes as no surprise that all these wise, idealist, and right-thinking ladies and gentlemen keenly maintain, through moral hygiene, a "return of the repressed" as periodic and as regular as a bowel movement; and that they use this to uphold by any means necessary

L'analphabétisme chrétien ———▶

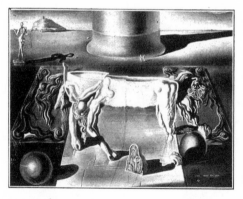

Lion, cheval, dormeuse invisibles

Tableau de SALVADOR DALI

Ce tableau, après le passage de jeunes bourgeois français respectueux de l'art et de la
propriété. ——————————▶

Fig. 5.4. Page from surrealist pamphlet in response to the *Âge d'or* affair showing damage to the theater and to Dalí's painting (1931). Image courtesy of the Ryerson and Burnham Libraries, the Art Institute of Chicago.

their wars, capital punishment, prostitution, banking and commercial theft, the exploitation of slaves, and other precious advantages of capitalist society—and let's not forget the Lynch Law, which the other day may only have caused the ravaging of the work on display at Studio 28, but in whose name you will soon be targeted as well.[56]

As Frois-Wittmann's notion of a periodic "return of the repressed" suggests, the Âge d'or affair revealed a tendency for European bourgeois culture to justify its own recourse to violence as a necessary and regular purgation of subversive elements. The surrealists would later address the logic of lynch laws and colonial exploitation more fully in their response to the massive Colonial Exposition of 1931; in 1930 the official suppression of Buñuel and Dalí's film provided an object lesson with regard to the bourgeoisie's implicit potential for violence in asserting its prowess on the ideological front.

The Âge d'or affair temporarily reconciled two diverging tendencies in surrealist practice, a split that Maurice Nadeau, in his History of Surrealism, locates between Aragon and Dalí, representatives of the movement's "two parallel paths: that of the political revolution, that of the ever widening exploration of the unknown forces of the unconscious."[57] The distinction between these two parallel courses was more subtle, however, than Nadeau recognized; what guaranteed any such "split" was not simply the competing disciplines of Marxism and psychoanalysis but the group's shifting ideas about political expression, and about political confrontation as well. Aragon's increasing orthodoxy would culminate in his break with the movement in 1932, following the legal and intellectual fracas surrounding the publication of his propagandistic poem "Red Front" in 1931. Conversely, the resistance to orthodoxy expressed by writers and artists such as Crevel, Dalí, Breton, Giacometti, and Tzara signified an unflagging commitment to revolutionizing intellectual as well as social conditions. Whereas Sadoul and Aragon would emphasize the literal, institutional complicity of the popular media with police work, these other surrealists would instead stress ideological complicity as the target of revolutionary labor. Drawing on Breton's call, in the Second Manifesto, for surrealist activity to prompt a crise de la conscience—meaning both a crisis of conscience and a crisis in consciousness—there emerged a counter-Stalinist tendency in 1930s surrealism, which would insist on the Sadean pursuit of revolutionary action on the ideological front, and not merely on the social front. This meant an interrogation of the most intimate structures of human consciousness, pursued not in opposition to organized political action but as an extension and a possible modality of it.

The best-known development during this period was Dalí's invention of paranoia-critique, a response to Bataille's critique of surrealism that was designed to counteract what Aragon identified as "the revenge of censorship on the unconscious." In Dalí's paranoia-critique, André Masson's early notion of a "physical idea of the Revolution" found a new incarnation as a psychic mechanism whose "revolutionary" potential Dalí advocated in an essay printed in the first issue of *Le Surréalisme au Service de la Révolution* in 1930, titled "L'Âne pourri" (The Rotting Donkey). Dalí's theory of paranoia heeds Bataille's claim that it is through participation in spectacles of violence, rather than through grand ideals or "prisons of intellect," that it becomes possible to overthrow existing ideological frameworks. Yet Dalí strongly disagreed with Bataille's presumption that such spectacles were natural occurrences that could be experienced without idealism or fancy concepts. Dalí argues that the Bataillean effect of spectacular participation could instead be produced through the capacity of paranoia for generating simulacra whose presence vies with other "images of reality"; as a result, one's ideologically overdetermined confidence in such images would begin to self-destruct.

In "The Rotting Donkey," Dalí theorized his synthesis of surrealist and Bataillian ideas, explaining that the revolutionary potential of paranoia lay in its power to train artists to become "idealists without participating in any ideal. The ideal images of surrealism in the service of the immanent crisis in consciousness [conscience], in the service of the Revolution."[58] In what is certainly a reference to Breton's *Second Manifesto* and the group's crisis of 1929–30, Dalí subjects the revolutionary impulse of *Surréalisme au Service de la Révolution* to the immanent crisis of conscience/consciousness that surrealism needed to undergo in order to be of service. Rather than targeting popular magazines or specific bourgeois cultural institutions—what Sadoul called "the function of the industrial power of a bourgeois nation"—Dalí targeted la *conscience* itself as an ideological apparatus policing bourgeois class relations.

Marcel Fourrier makes a similar point in his article "Police, haut les mains!" (Hands Up, Police!), published several months previously in the final issue of *La Révolution Surréaliste* in 1929; Fourrier writes that "to destroy the police without abolishing the *spirit* of the police would be work done in vain."[59] "The police" did not, as many revolutionaries tended to assume, designate simply the armed body of civil servants contracted to preserve order in the streets. Rather, Fourrier argued that the police stood for a broader function, representing "essentially the state of mind of the bourgeoisie."[60] Surrealism's immediate "service to the Revolution," as both Fourrier and Dalí each suggest, lay in its ability to overturn the repressive order perpetuated with and by this "state of mind," as a necessary extension of organized social action.

Fourrier's essay remains firmly within the purview of historical materialism in implicating cultural workers, intellectuals, religious figures, and politicians as the professional basis of the bourgeois state of mind he targets; Dalí's theory of paranoia, by contrast, takes the notion of a bourgeois state of mind literally: Dalí wishes "to at least advance the point that our images of reality themselves depend on the degree of our paranoid faculty."[61] Paranoia, Dalí argues, systematizes a mental crisis which is analogous to hallucination, yet which expresses itself instead in terms of recognizable and empirically verifiable evidence. As paranoia calls on the exterior world to validate its obsessive ideas, its troubling power derives from its exacting particularity; as Dalí writes: "Paranoia uses the external world to assert the obsessive idea, with its disturbing characteristic of making this idea's reality valid to others. The reality of the external world serves as illustration and proof, and is placed in the service of the reality of our mind."[62] Dalí notes the "inconceivable subtlety" of paranoiacs, who take advantage "of motives and facts so refined as to escape normal people" and thus "reach conclusions that are often impossible to contradict or reject." As a result, these "conclusions," in the form of simulacra, can at their most powerful compete with, and even displace, reality itself. "It is because of their failure to cohere with reality," Dalí writes, "and because of the arbitrary element in their presence, that simulacra can easily assume the form of reality and that reality, in its turn, adapts itself to the violences committed by simulacra."[63]

Unlike what Breton would call the surrealism of its mid-1920s "rational phase," Dalí's paranoia-critique no longer relied on accurate critique to expose the ideological excesses of contemporary society. Instead it mechanically—yet critically—misinterpreted reality in order to provoke a "crisis in consciousness" that would dislodge contemporary thinking from its ideologically overdetermined sense of the real. The significance of Dalí's discussion of paranoia as a psychic mechanism lay in the painter's insistence that it permitted "an idealism without . . . any ideal," a reflection of Bataille's injunction to perform critical work without falling back on utopian abstractions or philosophical idealism. This is true of Dalí's method as well as of surrealist discourse more broadly. Dalí's strong presence in the movement after 1929 both signaled and extended the group's own ideological disruptions, as well as its warring priorities about multiplying such disruptions on the political front. These disagreements would soon erupt in the form of the "Aragon affair" of 1932, which hinged on opposing interpretations as to whether Louis Aragon's violently insurrectionist poem "Red Front" constituted "pure" political violence or was simply the rhetorical form of Aragon's ideological platform.

Aragon's 1931 poem is characteristically viewed as the poet's act of conversion to Stalinism, a rejection of surrealist poetics in favor of the emerging Soviet literary program set forth by the party leadership at the Second Congress of Revolutionary Writers at Kharkov in November 1930.[64] "Red Front" is a manifestly pro-Soviet work of propaganda, and the legal and intellectual fallout over the poem certainly did finalize Aragon's break with the surrealist movement. It is worth noting, though, that the poem is also an extension of the group's anti-police discourse of 1929 and 1930, in its recasting the surrealist attacks on "the police spirit" of bourgeois culture in poetic form. Yet the very fact that it did so marks its break with earlier surrealist thinking about the possibility of developing a "physical idea of the Revolution," since unlike earlier critical writings, but like his own "Introduction to 1930," Aragon's poem no longer seemed to harbor any concern for ideas at all. In positioning itself as an instrument of propaganda, "Red Front" represented a form of revolutionary consciousness, presenting the shift from prerevolutionary pessimism to revolutionary action as a ready-made necessity. Whereas Breton would attempt to defend the poem by referring to it as the incarnation of an idea, Aragon himself made it clear that "Red Front" was conceived as a political instrument in and of itself.

The poem opens with a satirical portrait of the bourgeoisie ordering "something nice for my dog" at the fashionable restaurant Maxim's in Paris. The poetic voice then shifts abruptly to a reminiscence of recent demonstrations of political unrest in the city, summoning France's political memory as the poem builds to a revolutionary crescendo:

> Hey Belleville and you Saint-Denis
> where the kings are captives of the reds
> Ivry Javel and Malakoff
> Call them all with their tools
> the galloping children bringing the news
> the women with the heavy buns of hair the men
> coming out of their work as though out of a nightmare
> feet still unsteady but eyes clear
> There are always armorers in the city
> cars at doors of the bourgeois
> Bend the lampposts like wisps of straw
> Send the kiosks dancing, the benches, the fountains
> Kill the cops
> comrades
> Kill the cops[65]

The structure of Aragon's poem—which, in spite of its significance to the history of the surrealist movement, as well as to the fate of communism in France, is rarely discussed in its specificity—is rhetorically crafted to dissolve the separation between the mindless chitchat of the bourgeoisie and the seething unrest their lives are designed to ignore. Beginning with its account of the bourgeoisie's repression of political inequality, the poem moves toward a heroic and violent return of the repressed. Aragon's poem recalls Frois-Wittmann's statement about the bourgeoisie's prophylactic recourse to the return of the repressed, yet in "Red Front" this return overwhelms the police function of the bourgeoisie, gathering strength as a violent overthrow of capitalist society.

The poem's structure characteristically reflects this return of the repressed; the poem's refrain, for instance, begins as polite banter about Russia but develops later into a violent hymn to the Soviet Republic. This banter begins as a conversation about a breach in etiquette:

The princess is really too kind
For all the gratitude it brings you
You're lucky if they thank you
It's the example of the Bolsheviks
Poor Russia
The USSR
The USSR, or as they say the SSSR
SS what that SS
SSR SRR SSSR o darling please[66]

In this early stanza the speakers ponder the "example of the Bolsheviks" and the sad fate of "poor Russia" as a hyperbolic instance of the ingratitude of the poor. The conversation then turns to the Soviet Republic, as the unnamed speakers ponder its official name, asking whether to call it the Union of Soviet Socialist Republics (USSR) or the Soyuz Sovetskikh Sotsialisticheskikh Respublik (SSSR). Here the reiterations of the republic's name are as abstracted from historical reality as the bourgeois world described in the early stanzas of the poem. The banter is little more, at first, than idle wordplay. By the poem's close, however, Aragon's poetic consciousness has restored the historical memory absent from these early conversations. The poem cites facts, names, and events in an effort to render the revolutionary present both concrete and immanent. The early conversation about the SSSR, in a late refrain, becomes a revolutionary anthem:

Those who wait with clenched teeth
to carry out at last their vengeance
whistle a tune that speaks volumes
a tune a tune US
SR a tune joyful as steel SS
SR a burning tune it is
hope the tune SSSR it's the song the song of October with its
brilliant fruit
whistle whistle SSSR SSSR SSSR patience
won't wait forever SSSR SSSR SSSR[67]

As the "burning tune" described here suggests, what is ultimately more surprising than the poem's famous calls to murder ("fire on Léon Blum / Fire on Boncour Frossard Déat / Fire on the trained bears of social democracy") is its nostalgia. In spite of the call for violence in the present, through its revolutionary consciousness the poem directs its historical memory as a panegyric to the USSR, the "brilliant fruit" of the October Revolution of 1917. Herein lies the poem's true Stalinist turn: the Soviet Republic is the revolution, a state to be defended against its enemies. Aragon thus proscribes "Death to those who endanger the October conquests" and "Death to the saboteurs of the five-year plan." The bourgeoisie—any bourgeoisie—is the enemy of the revolution, and this logic of persecution becomes, in turn, the guiding logic for the poem's call to violence.

This nostalgic reduction also extends to Aragon's caricature of dialectical materialism, whose incarnation he celebrates in the Red Army. Aragon writes:

> The universe must hear
> a voice shouting the glory of materialist dialectics
> marching on its feet on its thousands of feet
> shod in military boots
> on its feet magnificent as violence
> holding out its host of arms bearing weapons
> to the image of victorious Communism
> Glory to materialist dialectics
> and glory to its incarnation
> The Red
> Army
> Glory to
> The Red
> Army[68]

Here, as in the poem's Stalinist allegiance to past (rather than future) revolutions, lay Aragon's final break with surrealism. Dialectical materialism was no longer, for Aragon, a means for describing historical causality; it was historical causality itself, insofar as it could be incarnated in a concrete historical body like the Red Army. What is curious about this formulation is the extent to which Aragon's "materialist dialectics" is no longer either materialist or dialectical but a purely idealist abstraction, a spirit of historical becoming incarnated in physical form. Aragon's poem dramatizes the transformation of ideas into the concrete reality of revolution, culminating in an "image of victorious communism" to which the poetic voice sings its praises. In doing so, Aragon's paean to the USSR recalls Bataille's critique of the surrealist Sade as a foreign body covered with honors but confined to a static image. Yet whereas the response of the other surrealists to Bataille's critique was a dramatic reconsideration of their reliance on fixed ideas, Aragon's idea of revolution had become all the more monolithic. His poem implies that there is no such thing as revolutionary thought; there is only action, guided by an operative consciousness of the revolutionary past.

The demand of Aragon's poem that its readers "kill the cops, comrades, kill the cops" met with strong legal and intellectual repercussions. Aragon risked a five-year prison sentence for its publication, and the resulting "Aragon affair" sparked debates among lead-ing writers and intellectuals over whether "Red Front" was to be considered art or propa-ganda. Could the poem's straightforward advocacy of assassination in the name of political change be considered a metaphorical speech act, or was it really an incitement to murder? André Breton's defense of the poem, in his 1932 essay "Misère de la poésie" (The Poverty of Poetry), begins by attacking the powers of bourgeois justice in language similar to the terms of the Âge d'or affair. Breton writes, "If bourgeois 'justice,' in the pro-fascist period through which we are now passing, becomes daily more savage and ex-peditive . . . this cannot be a reason for us to abandon all critical spirit to the point of mistaking the profound meaning of the poetic act."[69]

Breton's essay defended "Red Front" against the charges of sedition and incitement to murder leveled against it by the French authorities. But in doing so, his argument was fa-mously double-edged: while aimed principally at the "villainous laws" that sought to dis-tinguish literal, and thus punishable, language from metaphorical language, it also sought to dislodge the literal-mindedness of Aragon's own propagandistic ambitions. Breton contended that the poem "is to be judged not on the successive representations it makes, but on its power to incarnate an idea, to which these representations, freed of any need for rational connection, serve only as a starting point."[70] Distinguishing poetry's "power to incarnate an idea" from prose's capacity for representation, Breton argues that poetry has survived historically because it cannot be abolished within the prosaic. Aragon's poem would be nothing more than close-minded propaganda, and flatly anti-communist propaganda at that, if its call for the proletariat to shoot up the city and chant hymns to the Red Army were read literally as prose.

In stressing that the poem instead incarnates an idea of class warfare distinct from the poem's literal content—that it offered its own "physical idea of the Revolution"—Breton makes the case for poetry's service to the revolutionary cause in its power to "wrench it-self from the habits of ordinary thought, which prefers the indifferent and the acciden-tal."[71] Breton cites Hegel here in order to champion the surrealist practice of generating crises in consciousness as a corrective to the reductive idealism to which even revolution-ary Marxism could, and did, succumb.[72] Indeed, in defending Aragon's poem against its own idealism, Breton's tract expands upon the political significance of poetry's tendency toward intransigence. Breton's title invokes Karl Marx's 1847 text The Poverty of Philosophy, a polemic against the rigid socialist philosophy of Marx's former ally Pierre-Jean Proud-hon; similarly, "The Poverty of Poetry" asserts that to judge "Red Front" as a work of po-litical realism, whether in condemnation or in praise, would impoverish poetry and politics alike. As Breton argues, the very nature of poetic language is to elude conscious delimitations of its utility and authority, just as it is the nature of Marxian political econ-omy to elude the rigid conceptual determinism and formalism Marx criticized in Proudhon. Breton thus suggests that Aragon would be a bad Marxist, and a bad poet, if he believed that the nearly infinite suggestiveness of poetry could be harnessed as propaganda. Scorned by both the Communist Party and Aragon alike as counterrevolutionary, Breton's essay failed to lure Aragon away from Stalinism. It did, however, articulate many of the principles of the surrealist movement's continued efforts to theorize its own political militancy on the margins of the Communist Party.

In the Name of Self-Defense

A more collaborative effort to maintain an anti-Stalinist allegiance between surrealism and Marxism developed concurrently with the Aragon affair. In the wake of the surrealists' opposition to the massively popular Colonial Exposition of 1931, a group of Martiniquan university students studying in Paris, which included Jules Monnerot, René Ménil, Étienne Léro, and Pierre Yoyotte, launched the fiery but quickly suppressed magazine *Légitime Défense*. The venture yielded only a single issue in the summer of 1932, containing polemical essays and poetry, before the magazine was shut down by censors for its radical Marxist content.[73] The journal's explicit target was the assimilated black bourgeoisie of the French Caribbean, against whom the journal's contributors stated their intention "as traitors of this class—to take the path of treason so far as possible."[74] As René Ménil notes in his 1978 introduction to the magazine's republication, however, this antibourgeois militancy has been overestimated as the magazine's singular political tactic. More broadly, *Légitime Défense* aimed to heed the surrealist call to address and overthrow the ideological forces that perpetuated class relations under colonialism. As the journal's inaugural declaration states:

> Of all the filthy bourgeois conventions, we despise more than anything humanitarian hypocrisy, that stinking emanation of Christian decay. We despise pity. We don't give a damn about sentiments. We intend to shed a light on human psychic concretions similar to that which illuminates Salvador Dalí's splendid convulsive paintings, in which it sometimes seems that lovebirds, taking wing from assassinated conventions, could suddenly become inkwells or shoes or small morsels of bread.[75]

Recalling Bataille in its praise for Dalí's paintings, the journal maintains a crypto-Bataillian position by preferring "psychic concreteness" over abstractions and ideals. The journal's title also lays claim to a surrealist genealogy: *Légitime Défense*, denoting the legal term for self-defense, certainly evokes the journal's polemical content. It also alludes to the surrealist pamphlet of the same name published several years earlier, in 1925, announcing that in addition to accepting communist discipline, the journal would "unreservedly accept surrealism with which our destiny in 1932 is linked."[76]

The nature of this synthesis, and of the ensuing collaboration between the European surrealists and the Martiniquan intellectuals of *Légitime Défense*, would be to propose new forms under which the Bretonian crisis in consciousness could gain revolutionary utility. The earlier "Légitime Défense," written by Breton, had been a by-product of the surrealist group's support for the Rif uprising. An act of self-defense in itself, the 1925 pamphlet asserted the right of surrealism to participate in the political arena without sacrificing its artistic aims or its interest in psychoanalysis. Breton's "defense" took shape, though, as a full frontal attack against the literary wing of the French Communist Party. In particular, Breton disparaged the communist newspaper *L'Humanité* for its "secret resignation to what exists, with the concern to keep the reader in a more or less generous illusion as cheaply as possible."[77] In language that anticipated his later contribution to the Aragon affair, Breton denounced this "secret resignation" for its tendency to succumb to "the errors of a propaganda method which seems to me deplorable." Breton never ceased to maintain that the surrealist commitment to communism was one "of enthusiastic principle," yet he qualified this commitment by suggesting that communism was not in itself a principle but "in our eyes a minimum programme."[78]

Breton's heavily qualified allegiance to communism is revisited and redirected in the pages of the Martiniquan *Légitime Défense* of 1932. As the journal's prefatory manifesto states, "We believe unreservedly in [communism's] triumph because we accept Marx's dialectical materialism freed of all misleading interpretation and victoriously put to the test of events by Lenin."[79] At the same time, the authors champion surrealism and Freud as similarly essential platforms for "dissolving the bourgeois family" and "ris[ing] up against all those who don't feel suffocated by this capitalist, Christian, bourgeois world, to which our protesting bodies reluctantly belong."[80] This juxtaposition of communism with Freud—whom the Soviet Union rejected in 1930 for his individualism and minimization of the class struggle[81]—already suggests the Martiniquan group's qualification of any orthodox position. Indeed, this negotiation between communism's historical and political Marxism and surrealism's bodily Marxism already indicates the significance of the Martiniquan group as revisionist Marxist writers.

The Martiniquan journal's "self-defense" is directed most broadly as an attack against colonialism. This attack is twofold; it addresses the relation between colonizer and colonized as a class hierarchy that determines the relations not only between the French bourgeoisie and black colonial subjects but also between the colonized black bourgeoisie and the native black workers. These colonial relations permeate the French Caribbean, where, as Jules Monnerot writes, "in the fields, the blacks continue to cut cane and it still hasn't occurred to them to cut off the heads of those who continually betray them."[82] This colonial hierarchy also characterizes relations of race in the United States. Indeed, the over-whelming majority of articles in *Légitime Défense* cite the travesty of justice of the Scottsboro case, the notoriously mishandled rape trial of nine African American teenagers in Scotts-boro, Alabama; the group argued that the legacy of state-sanctioned lynchings, whose racist logic of mob violence carried over into the legal trial, revealed the true face of Amer-ican "civilization." In their coverage of the Scottsboro trial, too, the journal's writers con-demned the black American bourgeoisie for remaining criminally silent about the case. As Étienne Léro writes in "Civilization": "The coloured press in America, in the pay of whites and prisoner of its class interests and political ideals, has hushed up the incident. The Association for the Advancement of Colored People, having to tiptoe around the crim-inal justice system of American capitalism, acknowledges that it is incapable of assuming the victims' defense."[83] Deliberately conflating the murderous enforcement of segrega-tion in the United States with the allegedly humane French policy of colonial assimilation, the writers of *Légitime Défense* adopt the communist position that colonial exploitation is coextensive with capitalism's exploitation of the proletariat. Overt violence toward the colonized population is supported and extended by the cultural institutions that strive to absorb and "civilize" it.

This was essentially the position maintained by the surrealists in their protests against the Colonial Exposition, whose pavilions celebrating the breadth and extent of the French colonial empire occupied the Parc de Vincennes from May through November 1931. As with the *Âge d'or* affair, the surrealist group suspended its growing internal divisions, as well as its differences with Soviet policies, to organize a counterexhibition titled "The Truth about the Colonies" in collaboration with the Communist International. In a re-cently rediscovered polemical tract written for the International, Paul Éluard describes how "in front of the great parade of the Exposition Coloniale, we can see the bourgeois parties together, from the Royalists to the Socialists, beaming with admiration for the plunder and crime that have been done."[84] Éluard and the surrealists argued that the im-mensely popular exposition, which paraded the "success" of French colonial ventures in Africa, Vietnam, and the West Indies, tacitly extended the legacy of "villages pillaged and destroyed, crops burned, massacres from a hail of bullets, bombardments from the air, men working chained like beasts, women serving the amusements of commissioned louts."[85] The reconstruction of colonized countries as pavilions to be visited by tourists in Paris represented the culmination of the colonial project, which began with violence and completed itself by suppressing this violence beneath images of happy natives and colonial leisure.

In this context the notion of self-defense returned as a response to this thinly veiled exploitation and outright murder. While Monnerot, Ménil, Léro, and Yoyotte invoked "légitime défense" as a justification for their attacks on colonial ideology writ large, the co-authored tract "Murderous Humanitarianism," written during the same period but

first published in English as the surrealist contribution to Nancy Cunard's 1934 Negro anthology, develops this legitimation of political and poetic violence most explicitly. Not
only were the historical forms of colonial domination murderous, but so too were the
more recent "humanitarian" attempts to erase this violence in the guise of assimilation.
Written in the wake of the Scottsboro case, the tract inculpates the latent means through
which imperialist power is most broadly exercised: the "humanitarian" institutions of European and American capitalism, the imitative forms of thought and belief structuring the
ideology of the black bourgeoisie, and even writing's very claim to individual expression.
In fact, these ideological apparatuses become the most deliberately articulated facet of
Jules Monnerot's broad attacks on what he calls the "civilized" mentality.

In his prose contribution to *Légitime Défense*, Monnerot specifically targets the black
bourgeoisie and its "humanitarian hypocrisy." In an essay that could be considered proto-
Fanonist were it not for its concentration of rage toward his own class, Monnerot writes,
"The bourgeoisie is one and indivisible, and in their conformism these grandsons of
slaves—like those in Dijon, Boston and Bremen—would be unable to conceive of themselves without that individualism which is both that conformism's cause and its effect."[86]
This conformism, Monnerot continues, is a product of European forms of education,
style, and morality that find their most legible symptom in the local arts. Dislodging this
"civilized mentality," Monnerot argues, requires a crisis in consciousness of the most fundamental nature. Likewise, Étienne Léro's article titled "The Poverty of a Poetry" attacks
Caribbean poetry for its tendency to uphold the moral and aesthetic values of the French
classical tradition as well as of the existing social order. Léro's response to this "poverty,"
unlike Monnerot's, anticipates the internationalism and essentialism of Senghorian *négritude* in offering hope that "the wind rising from black America will quickly cleanse our
Caribbean of the aborted fruits of a decrepit culture. Two black revolutionary poets,
Langston Hughes and Claude MacKay [sic], bring us, soaked in red alcohol, the African
love of life, the African joy of love, the African dream of death."[87] Léro develops a counter-
genealogy, based in the poetry of the Harlem Renaissance, to supplant the poetics of medi-
ocrity that flatter the existing social order.

Monnerot's response to this problem of poetry as an ideological apparatus differs from
Léro's in its ideas about what it is that makes poetry "revolutionary." Rather than isolat-
ing a mythical "African love of life," we might say, Monnerot instead isolates the "red
alcohol" soaking the poems of Hughes and McKay. That is, Monnerot's revolutionary poetics refers neither to a positive, empirically verifiable quality, nor to an abstract ideal, but
instead to a potential for dissolution operating within poetic language itself. Heeding Breton's Hegelian claim in "The Poverty of Poetry" that poetry "wrenches itself from the
habits of ordinary thought," Monnerot develops a poetics of negation antithetical to the
propagandistic literalism of texts like Aragon's "Red Front." Monnerot evokes this potential in an untitled prose poem in *Légitime Défense* in which the revolutionary moment to

which he refers as "very long-awaited" will be attained "when the time for cries of sick hatred will speak no further either morning or night, when those who were black and those
who were white will all be hung from the same hopes. . . . When I will be allowed to forget that I have always slept the life of others, when the word DEAF, drawn by the faraway
smoke of a fire whose author will never be discovered, will knock upon doors in blows of
silence."[88] In imagining a future beyond race, Monnerot's poem divulges the Marxist es-
chatology at its heart, the revolutionary dream of a classless society. But its "blows of silence" also suggest the real force of political action as well; yet if so, it is an action that
comes about through not saying, an action that supersedes the overt force of "cries of sick
hatred" with its banner of deafness written in smoke.

Monnerot pursues his theory of revolutionary poetics in a 1933 article "On Certain
Common Characteristics of the Civilized Mentality," which further distinguishes his contribution to surrealism from Aragon's Stalinist idealism. Monnerot's essay, published in
the fifth issue of Le Surréalisme au Service de la Révolution in 1933, argues that the concrete
forms of capitalist power—whether the cops Aragon demands the proletariat fire upon,
or the cafés along the Champs-Élysées he demands it occupy—are not the only organs of
domination. As in Légitime Défense, it is the humanitarianism of the bourgeoisie, even humanism itself, that forms Monnerot's primary target. The bourgeoisie's very sense of reality, he writes, is a mask, and "positivism—a submission to what was there before they
existed—is one of the ideological tricks the bourgeoisie uses to perpetuate its existence.
It considers 'facts' as taken for granted, neglecting the dialectic law of their becoming by
which alone they can assume a meaning."[89] Poetry's role in the anticolonial struggle thus
takes shape in Monnerot's article as a total decolonization of the mind, and even as an
abandonment of the notion of thoughts, ideas, and individuality as private property. He
writes:

> In France . . . there is nothing about which we cannot ask the indispensable, ignoble,
> sacramental question "Who owns it?" Consciousness itself is only ever conceived there
> as the property of a subject. Books and other publications invariably speak of the thought
> of Mr. So-and-so, of the mind or spirit of a particular individual, nation, corporation, fam-
> ily, or landscape. I will take it upon myself, because this is the place to do so, to churn out
> the following propositions: the person who writes does not express his thought, but
> thought, in other words what is thought and of which he can consider himself only the most
> temporary location. The thought passing through me cannot to any extent be considered
> as mine. It comes to me from what is not me, it is a use-value for the world.[90]

In this 1933 essay Monnerot advocates treating psychic private property similarly to the
way Sade advocated treating sexual private property: by abolishing the guiding laws and
assumptions that held them in place. Monnerot was not, of course, arguing for the blind

submission to ideology in his notion that human subjects are temporary locations of thought; instead he was attempting to redress the traces of "individualism, nationalism, imperialism, colonialism" within civilized thought most broadly, from Aragon's guiding poetic consciousness to the Stalinist cult of personality. In order to do this, Monnerot proposes a poetry without language.

That is, in attempting to isolate the poetic principle that best accommodates itself to this task, Monnerot looks not only past communism but beyond the contemporary preoccupations of surrealism as well. He suggests that the revolutionary action Aragon calls for in "Red Front" is delimited not just by "facts" but also by words; even the best surrealist poetry "is still distanced from dreams by all that brings it close to discourse (syntax, words bullied by education, memory)."[91] If the Marxist promise of a classless society may be considered modernity's dream, Monnerot argues that "the slightest dream is more perfect than the best poem because it is by definition concretely adequate to the dreamer for whom it is an individually historical fact." Toward the realization of this dream, he claims that what will be required is something akin to Georges Bataille's theory of heterology, a means of pursuing the ways in which "directed thought, science, and industry will be able to serve as vehicles for dream." Distribution, he explains, is the key to this new political economy, even though "the means by which we will lay hands on the levers controlling the *changes of state* are not known."[92] It is, for Monnerot, a question of the dialectical reinvention of what he calls sorcery—not magic but a kind of sacred collective experience to whose sociological analysis Monnerot subsequently devoted himself. Indeed, having read Bataille's work from the early 1930s, Monnerot began to work toward an extensive sociological study of forms of sacred experience that bring forth such "waking dream states" as group phenomena. In opposition to communism's rigorous ideological system—which, later in his life, he would equate with fascism as equivalent "illnesses" of totalitarian mind control—Monnerot helped Bataille found the Collège de Sociologie in 1937, as a means to isolate a social principle of "dream" that would manifest itself as both a collective experience and "an individually historical fact." Monnerot's emphasis on the collective experience of a poetics without language would help to bring about the eventual reconciliation of the surrealists with Bataille in the mid-1930s, under the ever-increasing pressure to invent, in the face of fascism, new ways of conceiving revolution as a physical idea—and as a theory with blood stakes.

CHAPTER SIX

SURREALISM NOIR

The quiet life, dull and slow. The cocoon-like house, the muffled rug, the staircase which turns at the end of the hall, the rooms full of old family furniture, the chest of drawers under lock and key, the linens and the jam in the cupboard. The calm bourgeois dwelling of a sleepy country town.
And, inside, drama. A dark drama.

Maurice Coriem, "Histoire d'un drame passionnel:
'Le Crime des Soeurs Papin'" (1933)

In the smoldering political climate of the early 1930s, André Breton's "simplest surrealist act" of randomly firing a pistol into a crowd encountered its opposite: the mobilization of a crowd that threatened at any moment to fire back. In Germany, such crowds testified to fascism's terrifying rise to power; in Paris, their allegiance to a discernible party or cause suddenly became a pressing political concern. Louis Aragon's demand for readers of his poem "Red Front" to "kill the cops / comrades / kill the cops" sought to incite mass violence in the name of a communist overthrow of bourgeois society. The right wing's tactics were no less incendiary: three years later, on February 6, 1934, an armed demonstration of nationalist and pro-fascist organizations against Édouard Daladier's Republican government erupted into a bloody riot at the Place de la Concorde, triggering the downfall of the government and a state of emergency among leftist groups.

Both events provoked deep fissures within the surrealist movement. Aragon's poem precipitated surrealism's definitive break with orthodox communism, as well as Aragon's exclusion from the group. The fascist riots of 1934 prompted a massive antifascist campaign among surrealist writers, yet this too was marked by upheaval and tragedy; the collapse of the group's efforts to reconcile with communist organizations concluded with René Crevel's suicide in 1935, on the night after André Breton was barred from speaking before the Congress of Writers for the Defense of Culture.[1]

Yet in the years that separated these ruptures, the question that animated the communist left and the nationalist right alike of how to mobilize a crowd, or even how to use violence effectively, seemed less important to the surrealists than the status of Aragon's poem as propaganda. Though ambivalent about the artistic value of Aragon's "Red Front" (see chapter 5), Breton and the surrealists nevertheless defended the poem's legality. They insisted that since it was a poem and not a political tract, its incitement to murder was the result of a form of poetic conception whose "exalted" language necessarily exceeded its immediate content. And indeed for the surrealists, who broke with Aragon on account of this, the poem was disastrous less for its rhetoric than for its instrumentalization as propaganda: the group claimed that the Communist International was using poetry's access to the mind simply to goad the public into action rather than to promote class consciousness or to liberate the imagination.

Both Aragon and the Communist Party, however, decried the surrealist defense of "Red Front" as a counterrevolutionary espousal of art for art's sake. The resulting "Aragon affair" exploded the already turbulent relationship between surrealism and communism, which, since the late 1920s, had been fraught with disagreements over the political role of intellectuals. Particularly at stake in the Aragon affair was the question of whether the surrealists, who defended their interest in such bourgeois cultural forms as psychoanalysis and literature, could possess the ability to mobilize the proletariat against a reigning capitalist order. And indeed, in the wake of the Aragon affair, the surrealist movement appeared to retreat from active political engagement following a brief renewal of its communist militancy. As Breton wrote in a 1933 letter to Paul Éluard, "I believe more and more in the necessity of a brilliant rupture with these commies and the resumption of the most intransigent surrealist activity."[2]

It is clear that by "intransigence," Breton could not have meant autonomy: in spite of the movement's rupture with Aragon and the French Communist Party, numerous surrealists—such as Breton, Éluard, Cahun, Crevel, and Tzara—fought to maintain relations with the Association des Écrivains et Artistes Révolutionnaires (AEAR), although Breton was expelled, first in July 1933, and again, more disastrously, in 1935.[3] Moreover, the group's flagship journal, whose very title suggested the movement's eagerness to harness its activities to the leftist cause, Le Surréalisme au Service de la Révolution (hereafter SASDLR), foundered after the two issues published simultaneously in May 1933. In what must have seemed a dramatic shift in priorities, the group started to contribute to the Belgian art journal Minotaure, which, according to Éluard, began to succeed as a properly surrealist journal with the appearance of its double issue 3–4 in December 1933.[4] The intransigence to which Breton refers thus became, in Éluard's words, a function of the parallel course of surrealism's "political aspirations" and "the free exercise of experimental surrealism." "I am," Éluard writes in a 1933 letter to Dalí, "provisionally for this separation of surrealism's tasks."[5]

The transition from the overtly Marxist SASDLR to the luxuriously illustrated Minotaure reflects surrealism's political migration from a "red" period of communist activism to what I call its "noir" period. Characterized by a renewed interest in formal innovation, mental aberration, and automatism, surrealist activity of this period, as reflected in Minotaure, privileged the group's affinity for historically noir art forms such as symbolism and the roman noir, or gothic novel. This critical attention to noir forms centered on their historical function: what gave *l'écriture noire* its contemporary relevance was that its emergence, always in times of historical turmoil, brought about sudden changes in the ways in which art represented political upheaval. Designating a break in the stylistic transparency of realist representation, the mannered proliferation of stylistic motifs in *romans noirs* and symbolist poetry, as well as in certain interwar crime films, exceeded its own formalism in order to evoke the terror and social dissolution at work in historical reality. These effects became a guiding interest for the surrealists in 1933, as they suggested the role to be played by psychoanalysis and art alike in confronting and diagnosing the historical pressures at work in the present moment.

This change in the group's tenor constituted neither an "exasperated" retreat from politics nor, for that matter, a failure of the movement to establish an effective political platform.[6] Instead this noir period accomplished what might be considered a negation, rather than an abandonment, of the group's overt political activities, a return to earlier surrealist interests such as automatic writing and the interpretation of dreams for the sake of understanding more fully their value as theoretical tools.[7] The political use-value of this dialectical return lay in its reassessment of the moral and epistemological bases of surrealism's political platform, in response to a historical moment rapidly becoming—to cite the title of an article in *Minotaure* 3–4—an "Age of Fear."

In this chapter I examine how the surrealists read the political universe of the early 1930s in terms of the forces that threatened it: its motives, its ritualized patterns of behavior, its terrifying outbursts of violence. As Gérard Durozoi has suggested, the first "surrealist" issue of *Minotaure* can be described overall as articulating a similarly dystopian theme: "the diverse ways in which behavior and invention escape the control of attention and reason."[8] In spite of its gothic or decadent interest in stylized forms of representation, surrealism's noir period was nonetheless driven by a serious political imperative, insofar as this dystopian theme performed analytical work toward the group's changing political philosophy. Increasingly suspicious of the dangers of stylizing real political violence, the surrealists made style itself the terrain for better understanding the "superior reality" of the historical, social, and psychological facts that conditioned lived experience and determined political change.

The methodical character of the surrealist investigation into the nature of causality became clear in the group's responses to two major criminal cases of 1933. The surrealists, for the most part, steered away from the most sensational political scandal of 1933 and 1934, the "Stavisky affair," whose scandalous intrigue of fraud and suicide incited the right-wing rioting of February 1934 and toppled the Daladier government.[9] Instead they found political meaning—and discovered the seeds of fascist tendencies in French culture—in two murder cases whose crimes were domestic rather than explicitly political. In both instances the gender of the murderers, as well as their questionable motives and sanity, catapulted the cases into the national consciousness. Beginning in February 1933, the

"Papin affair," the criminal case involving two housemaids from Le Mans, Christine and Léa Papin, who slaughtered their employers, focused attention on the relations between domestic servants and the families for whom they worked. The case already bore gothic overtones: if the quiet demeanor of two maids could conceal the potential for horrible atrocities, how could a bourgeois family possibly know the true nature of the people living and working within their walls? What evils haunted the minds of the murderers, even as they appeared to go about their daily labors? For the surrealists, the public response to the affair dramatized the insufficiency of conservative, communist, and even medical-legal understandings of motive and madness. As a result, the incident formed a critical case study for theories of paranoia that had been developed, almost simultaneously, by Salvador Dalí, René Crevel, and Jacques Lacan.

In December of the same year a second major murder case, the "Nozière affair," shifted the surrealists' attention from paranoia to sexual abuse as the primary object of speculation about the governing motives of the crime and its punishment. The case concerned the poisoning murder of a railroad engineer by his daughter, Violette Nozière, who claimed after her arrest that her father had been sexually abusing her for nearly six years. Yet for a public who refused to believe that the murderer—a sexually prolific eighteen-year-old woman—was anything other than a vampiric femme fatale, the forces of degeneracy lurking within the bourgeois household had become even more intimate: the real "poison" was, to cite one journalist, "in her blood."[10] In the eyes of the surrealists, the gothic family drama of the Nozière affair revealed the press's and the legal system's misrecognition of the sources of social degeneracy and moral sickness; in its response to the crime, the group strove both to remedy this interpretive fallacy and to uphold the potential for poetic language to perform the work of analysis. Violette Nozière's poisoning murder of her sexually abusive father sparked a renewed attack on the ideological privilege of the bourgeois patriarchal family; this ideology was complicit not only with a repressive logic of rape and incest but, the surrealists claimed, with the rising threat of fascist sympathies in France as well.

Part One: Papinorama—The Papin Sisters and the Paranoiac 1930s

The full-page double portrait of Christine and Léa Papin (figure 6.1), printed at the back of the fifth issue of Le Surréalisme au Service de la Révolution in May 1933, is as remarkable an illustration of what would be known as the "Papin affair" for what it does not show as it is for what it shows. In February 1933 the Papin sisters, cook and housekeeper in a haute-bourgeois household in Le Mans, brutally, almost ritualistically, slaughtered their employers, Mme and Mlle Lancelin. While the victims were still alive, the sisters gouged out

AVANT

APRÈS

« *Sorties tout armées d'un chant de Maldoror...* » (Voir page 28).

Fig. 6.1. "Before/After" photographs of Christine and Léa Papin, *Le Surréalisme au Service de la Révolution* 5 (1933). Image courtesy of the Pennsylvania State University Special Collections Library.

their eyes with their bare hands, bludgeoned them to death with a hammer and a pewter jug, and then hacked at their legs with knives. For the local and Parisian press, the murders provided a spectacle of domestic terror and class conflict whose clearly antibourgeois significance seemed immediately and unmistakably clear. How else to explain the virulence with which the atrocities were committed? The surrealists, however, rather than co-opting the murderers as allegorical political figures or interpreting their crimes in terms of class conflict, focused on the clinical aspects of the crime: that is, on the sisters' enigmatic motives and their obvious but officially undiagnosed insanity.

The surrealists' attention to the unrepresented elements of the Papin affair is suggested by the composition of the double portrait, which was printed, virtually without explanation, in the back of SASDLR The top image, a posed studio portrait, shows two young woman in formal dress smiling at the camera; its caption reads "Before." The bottom image, marked "After," shows two women, dressed in kimonos, with wild, unkempt hair and blank expressions; they look almost nothing like the women in the first image. The twin photographs bear a legend at the bottom of the page that reads, "Sprung forth fully armed from a canto of *Maldoror*," and gives a page reference to an article by Paul Éluard and Benjamin Péret earlier in the issue. Yet in spite of these captions, the twin photographs do not so much illustrate the murders themselves as omit it, or even suppress it. The photographs invoke the historical fact of the murders only through their absence, as the unrepresentable event that has caused the transformation of the women depicted in the photographs. Indeed, what the surrealist composition privileges instead is the transformation in affect of the murderers themselves, which registers the unspeakable cruelty of the crime through the way it changed even the killers.

The transformation in affect between the two photographs is largely the product of their juxtaposition, the orientation of two seemingly incompatible images in terms of their temporal references to the murders: "before" and "after." Most viscerally, the comparison plays upon the possibility that the sisters, in their kimonos—the only clothes they were wearing as they were taken to prison—somehow manifest the crime's sadistic urges in a language of sartorial and physiognomic signs. Dull-eyed and degenerate, the Papins of the second photograph look like murderers. The comparison, however, also performs a reversal of this superficial reading, casting suspicion on the "innocent" first picture: Are there not signs of murderous urges in the "before" image? The ironic possibilities of this studio portrait were first exploited by *Détective* magazine, which, a week after the murders, printed it on its front cover with the caption "Two angels? No! Two demons."[11] When the images are placed together in SASDLR, however, this irony gives way to the simple, terrible fact of the sisters' transformation. Although it is clear what has happened in the time between the photographs—the crime is "written all over their faces"—the murders are inscribed in no definitive way within the pictorial language of the photographs.

This effect of this photographic juxtaposition thus does more than sensationalize the crime's emotional or psychic burden; its disjunction invokes motive as a question instead of citing any significant physical trait as its answer. The juxtaposition itself reveals the disastrous fact that the sisters are the same people without in any way resolving the disparity into a unified image. The blank space between the photographs, in its mute resistance to the formal assimilation of the two images, thus suddenly "speaks" as an allegory of the crime and the enigma of its cause.[12] Maintaining the breach between the photographs, this space exceeds the formal duality of the images in its exoteric reference to the murders, the unrepresented act between "before" and "after" manifested only as a change in the sisters' appearance.

The second, "afterward" image is, in fact, a photomontage designed to exacerbate precisely this juxtaposition. The sisters, separated from each other at the time of their arrest, were not photographed together; the image is a collage assembled from two separate mug shots, pasted together to form a mirror image of the studio portrait. Such practices were hardly uncommon in the popular media, especially in composing collective portraits of criminal groups after their arrests; the surrealist composition, in pairing the studio portrait with the later montage, invents very little. And yet, in opposition to magazines like Détective, which tended to use only one of the images to illustrate the Papin affair, the surrealist composition dramatized what the photographic evidence of the case could not possibly establish: both formally and metaphorically, the manufactured doubleness of the paired images insists all the more forcefully on the breach between the "before" and "after" images. In disavowing the actual separation of the sisters in prison, it further dramatizes the incompatibility of the docile "before" picture and the decadent "after" picture and invokes once again the violence at the root of this transformation. But what was the cause of this violence? How could such horrific outbursts be reconciled with the narratives of class conflict promulgated by the provincial and national press? Were these murders a sign of things to come?

Unlike the more celebrated surrealist images of the early 1920s, this composition invokes, through absence, the disruptive violence of the Papin murders for analytical rather than affective purposes. Its aim is no longer to "disorien[t] us in our own memory by depriving us of a frame of reference," as Breton wrote in 1921, but rather to orient.[13] Indeed by 1933 disorientation and disillusionment were no longer simply the watchwords of surrealist activity but had instead become conditions of political life under the threat of the seemingly incomprehensible rise of fascism. In this context the surrealist image offered a new frame of reference for political judgment; yet its value as theory would derive less from philosophy or logic than from the clinical study of paranoia, whose challenge to the naïve realism at the core of communist thinking would provide the epistemological grounds for a renewed surrealist commitment to political resistance, directed explicitly against fascism.

Covered in both SASDLR and Minotaure, the Papin affair sprang forth fully armed into surrealist discussions of mental illness and paranoia, which had long played a central role in the movement's approach to automatic writing, but which had begun to feature strongly in its political thought as well. From Breton and Éluard's book *The Immaculate Conception* (1930) and Salvador Dalí's essay "The Rotten Ass" (1930) to Dalí's and Jacques Lacan's essays in *Minotaure* (1933) and René Crevel's "Notes Toward a Psycho-dialectic" (1933), paranoia increasingly offered, as Steven Harris has written, a form of thought that "was both autonomous and critical," and "could destabilize a consensual understanding of the real."[14] The Papin affair reveals the extent to which surrealist thinking about paranoia was, by 1933, less interested in simulating the illness as an alternative to propagandic art than in coming to terms with the analytical potential that paranoia gained through its psychoanalytic study.

In particular, the Papin murders raised the question of what such an outburst revealed about motive, desire, and violent agency. By addressing how the sisters' ferocity could stem from causes that were incomprehensible even to the killers themselves, the surrealists attempted to determine the use-value of the paranoiac imagination as what Lacan defined as "a coherent structure of immediate noumenal apprehension of oneself and the world."[15] This analytical turn was an extension of the group's more general efforts to understand the relationship of the unconscious to historical and political change. At the same time, this examination of motive necessarily entailed a new theory of representation; paranoia's access to "immediate noumenal apprehension," however delusional, claimed a privileged relationship with things-in-themselves, as opposed to signs or representations. Yet whereas a paranoiac might claim to have an unmediated relationship with things-in-themselves, the disease itself could be read and understood as a representation of the aggregate factors that produced it, such as the subject's social conditions, case history, and structures of unconscious desire. As Jacques Lacan argues in the first of the two articles he published in *Minotaure*, paranoia's systematic distortion of a subject's relationship to the real provided a "new syntax," a system of representation that offered a model for better understanding the nature of causality in the first place.[16] Paranoia's "new syntax," the surrealists suggested, was already a representation of complex structures of social and psychological determination that could be mobilized for the sake of political understanding.

Coins of Red-Hot Iron

> Interested in human destinies and their simple and secret causes, I had at first wanted to judge rashly: hatred, hatred of their employers, hatred slowly accumulated in the minds of two animalistic girls. And, one day, the

explosion . . . the aggression, the eyes torn out . . . the horror that testified
to a stored-up rancor.

And yet! no. . . . That's not it.

Maurice Coriem, "Histoire d'un drame passionnel:
'Le Crime des Soeurs Papin'" (1933)

As the crime scene photographs attest, the murder of Mme Lancelin and her daughter
by their servants on February 2, 1933, was committed with a ferocity that mystified and
fascinated the popular press. Although the photographs were not made public until much
later,[17] equivalently graphic eyewitness accounts of the crime scene injected substantially
more sensational detail into Parisian newspapers than the usual *faits divers*. What made the
violence particularly compelling was not only its symbolic character but the irony of its
context as well: exploding the tranquility of a bourgeois household in the equally tranquil
town of Le Mans, the murders were committed by two seemingly docile servants (soon
baptized "the enraged ewes" by *Détective* magazine).[18]

The image of bourgeois domesticity rent furiously asunder was promulgated even in
the earliest descriptions of the murders, inflecting their language with political or mock-
political overtones. As the American writer Janet Flanner writes in her *Paris Journal*, cap-
turing the tone of contemporary accounts: "On the third step from the landing, all alone,
staring uniquely at the ceiling, lay an eye. On the landing itself the Lancelin ladies lay, at
odd angles and with heads like blood puddings. Beneath their provincial petticoats their
modest limbs had been knife-notched the way a fancy French baker notches his finer long
loaves."[19] Borrowing its language from the original reports in the local Le Mans newspaper, *La Sarthe*, Flanner's depiction of the bodies as bourgeois comestibles—blood puddings, fine bread—not only invites disgust in evoking their formal similarities to food but
also reflects the degree to which the butchering was treated by the press as a critique, however nominal, of bourgeois life. Indeed, echoing the more overtly politicized language of
Parisian journals like the weekly *Détective* magazine and the communist daily newspaper
L'Humanité, Flanner writes of the Papin affair that "it was not a murder but a revolution. It
was only a minor revolution—minor enough to be fought in a front hall by four females,
two on a side. The rebels won with horrible handiness. The lamentable Lancelin forces
were literally scattered over a distance of ten bloody feet, or from the upper landing
halfway down the stairs. The physical were the most chilling details, the conquered the
only dull elements."[20] Flanner's account, written after the trial in late 1933, represents
particularly well how the media first presented the murders as an especially gruesome
form of petty class warfare. L'Humanité's coverage was, in fact, even more literal in its interpretation of the affair, transforming the cynical tone of Flanner's "minor revolution"
into more adamantly political terms. Without in any way questioning the reliability or psychology of the Papin sisters' own testimony, L'Humanité published two short articles on

February 4 and 5 under the headlines "Christine and Léa Papin Give the Reasons Why They Mortally Beat Their Mistresses" and, more straightforwardly, "The Murderesses of Le Mans Are the Victims of Exploitation and Servitude." The latter article derives "a distinctly social character" from the murders, explaining decisively that "poverty, isolation, continual confinement, servitude, doubtlessly working upon a hereditarily bad terrain, produced this double monstrosity."[21] Though not exactly presenting the revolution Flanner describes, L'Humanité's version of the murders sentimentalizes the killers' motives as it portrays Christine and Léa as the real victims of the crime.[22]

The surrealist response to the Papin affair, by contrast, is remarkable not only for its relative quiescence but also, more significantly, for its rejection, even parody, of the terms set out by the communist L'Humanité and the bourgeois press alike. Indeed the surrealist response seems directed more toward the press's sentimental Marxism than toward the Papin sisters themselves, insofar as it takes issue with the vulgar reduction of the crime's motive and significance to an emblem of class struggle. In two articles—the first by Éluard and Péret, the second by Jacques Lacan—as well as in the photographic illustration discussed earlier, the surrealists address the mysterious causality of the crime; each aims to specify the role of the unconscious in an act whose political significance was not comprehensible even to the women who committed it.[23] The articles, like the illustration, address the murders in a language deliberately abstracted from the press's literal reading. Without ever advocating the Papin sisters' crimes, the surrealist response to the affair attempts to reconcile the group's earlier positions toward revolutionary violence with the methodological necessity of acknowledging unconscious desire as a motive for human action.

In the May 1933 double issue of SASDLR, Éluard and Péret compiled a series of brief "reviews of the press" that lambaste the bourgeois press for its disavowal of class conflict and social tension in its coverage of current events. The final segment about the Papin sisters seems to invert the terms of this media critique; when read alongside other accounts of the murders, Éluard and Péret's article is striking for its distance from the sudden willingness of the press to politicize the murders, a manifestation of the politics it all too readily ignores elsewhere. The review reads in full:

> The Papin sisters were raised in a convent in Le Mans. Then their mother placed them in a "bourgeois" house in the same town. For six years they endured remarks, demands, insults with perfect submission. Fear, fatigue, and humiliation gave birth slowly to hatred within them, that alcohol, so sweet, which consoles in secrecy because it promises to supplement its violence, sooner or later, with physical force.
>
> When the day came, Léa and Christine Papin repaid the currency of evil in coins of red-hot iron. They literally massacred their mistresses, tearing out their eyes, crushing their heads. They washed themselves carefully and, released, indifferent, went to bed. The

thunder had struck, the woods had burned, the sun had been definitively put out.

Sprung forth fully armed from a canto of *Maldoror*.[24]

Although it certainly does not ignore the determining role of domestic servitude in the murders, the article's representation of economic conditions is mediated by additional rhetorical and imaginative conditions, for which Lacan's article would later account theoretically. For one thing, Éluard and Péret cite emotions—fear, fatigue, humiliation—in place of *L'Humanité*'s emphatically material list of conditions, "doubtlessly working upon a hereditarily bad terrain," which "give this horrible drama a distinctly social character." Éluard and Péret do not so much ignore the material conditions faced by the Papin sisters as suggest that their motives are better accounted for in psychological terms.

Describing hatred as a kind of alcohol, Éluard and Péret indicate an unreason, an intoxication behind the crimes, distancing their account from the headlines in which the sisters lucidly "give the reasons" for their atrocities. The mannered, mythology-laden style of Éluard and Péret's writing further complicates the "doubtless" causality of the murders. Moreover, whereas the notion of paying back evil in coins of red or red-hot iron (*fer rouge*) may sound like a stroke of quasi-communist rhetoric, its inflated metaphorical language satirizes the banal circumstances under which, according to Christine Papin, the murders occurred: the Lancelins, returning home, rebuked the sisters for a blown fuse caused by a hot iron (*un fer à repasser*). Rather than struggling to make sense of the affair as a gruesomely literal "eye for an eye" retribution for the evils of class oppression, Éluard and Péret poke subtle fun at the press's acceptance at face value of Christine Papin's "reasoned" account of the murders as an act of reciprocity. In the article's final line they instead invoke the gratuitous evil of Lautréamont's *Chants de Maldoror*, whose "fully armed" offspring the Papin affair becomes: significantly, the allusion to Athena—or perhaps even to the figure of Sin in Milton's *Paradise Lost*—implies that in spite of their Maldororian alienation from reason, the murders promise a "sign portentous," a perverse kind of wisdom.

The direct mythic lineage established here between the Papin affair and Lautréamont's *Maldoror* has been interpreted as evidence of the Papin sisters' place within the surrealist pantheon of revolutionary heroes, alongside its other female criminal "muses" such as the anarchist Germaine Berton and, as we will see, the poisoner Violette Nozière. Yet the group never paid explicit collective homage to the Papins, nor did it rally in defense of their crimes, as it did for Berton in 1924 (see chapter 3) and, albeit in a much different way, for Nozière later in 1933. Instead the Papin murders were significant precisely because they complicated any efforts to legitimate their violence as revolutionary or heroic. So too would fascism's precipitous rise to power severely challenge any idea that acts of terror, whether random or massively organized, could be harnessed unproblematically in the service of revolution. The surrealist movement's earlier positions on violence would, moreover, be further tested by the Papin sisters' resistance to any clear understanding of their motives or actions. Christine's continued psychotic outbursts in prison, for instance, exploded the possibility that their motives might become either more conscious or more comprehensible in the months following their crime.

The Papin case marked a corresponding shift in surrealist thinking, as the group largely turned away from the investigation of the political and ethical possibilities of violence that had characterized Aragon's work and turned instead toward clinical analysis of the causes of violence. Indeed Jacques Lacan's writings on paranoiac crime, and especially his diagnosis of the Papin sisters as paranoiacs, made possible the application of psychoanalytic theories of paranoia toward surrealism's understanding of political change. In particular, Lacan's understanding of paranoia as an illness that develops over time, and whose symptoms come about through the subject's social and psychic development, meant that the disease itself could be studied as a representation of unconscious and conscious forces of determination.

Paranoiac Theory

As early as 1923 Louis Aragon had begun to define, in anarchist and individualist terms, the ethical position toward violence that he would later maintain in "Red Front." He writes that "if an individual becomes conscious of the monstrous inequality, of the vanity of all speech in the face of the growing strength of a certain faction, I hold this individual to be authorized, moreover, to resort to terrorist means."[25] By the early 1930s Aragon had tailored this radical individualism to the collective rigor of the Communist Party; yet its emphasis on consciousness remains crucial to the poem's call for political violence, as well as to the Communist Party's own ideological platform. The majority of the surrealists, themselves fully committed to the overthrow of a bourgeois order, were nevertheless critical of Aragon's assumption that this revolutionary consciousness could be fully manifest as a ready-made form transmittable through literary expression. It was not the recourse to violence that was under debate; the true object of contention was the possibility that violence could be wielded as a political instrument, called for and authorized in unmistakably transparent language. In response to this crisis, the Aragon affair—which began as a debate over poetry—occasioned the rise of what we might call surrealist theory, in the Althusserian sense of a systematic expansion of the fields of Marxist inquiry beyond its own orthodox presuppositions.

René Crevel's 1933 essay "Notes toward a Psycho-dialectic" makes precisely this theoretical move. Published in the same issue of *SASDLR* as Éluard and Péret's review of the press coverage of the Papin sisters, Crevel's article uses Jacques Lacan's recent doctoral thesis on paranoia to articulate how psychotic crime could provide a means for better understanding political expression. Crevel thus revises Aragon's justification of violent in-surrection as a function of "visionary" class awareness, instead describing proletarian rev-olution as a gradual process of increasing consciousness as a subject. As Crevel writes: "The best quality of a proletariat is its class consciousness. Thanks to this, it turns from an object into a subject. It is no longer an instrument in a stranger's hand. It is its own in-strument. Its eyes urging it, it sees clearly. It looks only to demolish the walls that confine its life, its view, in order to construct houses made of light."[26] Although it confirms or-thodox communism's moral ground as a function of "clear vision," Crevel's methodology tempers its concept of awareness with a psychoanalytical notion of subjectivity at odds with party-line communist thinking. Crevel's Marxian depiction of workers as tools em-phasizes the passage from object to subject as constitutive of the proletariat's "clear vi-sion." Such psychoanalytical models of consciousness were, however, explicitly excluded from communist ideology in the early 1930s. At the 1930 writers' conference in Kharkov which was especially influential for Aragon, the Soviet directors rejected Freud, claiming that the ultra-individualist character of his work veils and minimizes the significance of class struggle: "The wave of Freudian enthusiasm which has passed through Occidental Europe is a wave of bourgeois reaction against materialism, a wave of decadence."[27]

Fittingly, Humanité's coverage of the Papin murders reflects—to a fault, as Éluard and Péret suggest—this predilection against the "pessimistic" operation of instincts and un-conscious drives. The communist paper's ideological premise, that the social character of the crime is self-evident, so clearly assumes a willfulness behind the sisters' "savagery" that the justification of its extremity requires an outmoded notion of hereditary degener-acy, the biological terrain that exacerbated the effects of servitude. In contrast, it was the Papin affair's challenge to the possibility of explaining, or justifying, such violence as something fully conscious that made it so significant to surrealist political thought.

Crevel's own response to this problem of comprehending the significance of uncon-scious motives to Marxist thought is counterintuitive. Rather than confronting party com-munism with its rejection of psychoanalysis, Crevel challenges the French psychiatric industry to advance its own dialectical and materialist science of the unconscious. Through this, he writes, psychoanalysts can, like materialists, "regain contact with life and study it in its contradictory manifestations." This would mark "a return from the ab-stract to the concrete. Movement is restored to the disintegrated, ossified, and paralyzed parts. Man regains the potential for acting upon his universe."[28]

Lacan's 1932 thesis on paranoia was appealing to Crevel because it allowed him to ex-pound a materialist theory of unconscious development, which stressed the social rather than the constitutional, genetic, or even instinctual development of paranoia's delusional system. Lacan's study of paranoia stands in opposition to the two major French theories of the illness: the notion of automatism, which understood the mind as series of auto-matic functions, and of constitutionalism, which understood the mind as organically fixed in its irregularities.[29] Lacan's theoretical breakthrough was to propose instead that paranoia is a delusional system with an emphatically social basis, a condition brought about through the dialectical interplay between the subject and other people.[30] Lacan's theory of paranoia does not simply reject the patient's delusional structure, through which the subject strikes out against her own ego-ideal in the form of a persecuting enemy, as a false or alien theory of persecution; it understands the illness as already a synthesis of conscious perception and unconscious judgment. By studying the real social conditions that contribute to paranoia, Lacan thus structures his own theory as a dialectical extension of the illness itself. For Crevel, this theory of psychotic illness was significant because it showed the possibilities for using psychiatry to reconcile further the science of dialectical materialism with the science of psychoanalysis in ways that could better account for the psychodynamics of political persecution.

The idea that paranoia offered a theory of persecution that could be used, rather than simply applied as a diagnosis of a pathological condition, is a central and largely unrecognized factor in the surrealist reception of Lacan's thesis. As numerous Lacanian scholars have noted, Lacan's thesis was both directly and indirectly influenced by surrealist literary experiments with "schizography" and simulations of paranoiac writing.[31] Crevel is less interested in discovering the influence of surrealism in Lacan's work, however, than in offering Lacan's work on paranoia as a critical response to the political situation of the movement in the early 1930s. By the time of the Papin affair, the surrealist movement found itself facing the irreconcilable confrontation of opposed interests. For one thing, the movement's serious problems with orthodox communism were becoming increasingly conspicuous, on both organizational and theoretical grounds. Moreover, the surrealists were fighting to promote awareness of the impending threat of fascism in France—not just in Germany—a threat shielded by popular nationalism and the French tendency to consider Nazism an alien peculiarity.

Indeed it was self-consciously in the wake of Hitlerism that Crevel looked to what he called Lacan's "nascent theory of personality" as a possible way to bolster Marxist dialectical materialism with an acceptable theory of the unconscious. Crevel saw modern Europe immersed in a mortal struggle between fascism and revolutionary Marxism. In "Notes toward a Psycho-dialectic" he argues that the immanent disruptions of violent social upheaval, whether fascist or revolutionary, could never be understood, condemned, or, for that matter, justified without recourse to the unconscious. He thus strives to advance a theory that explains both political action and psychological motive in terms of a dialectical synthesis between the "thesis" of consciousness and the "antithesis" of the unconscious.

The imperative for such a synthesis became apparent in the wake of two significant crises in surrealist thinking to which Crevel responds in his "Notes." The first is the rift between the surrealist movement and the French Communist Party that culminated in the legal and literary backlash against Aragon's "Red Front." The second and more ominous event to which Crevel's essay responds is the League of Nations' broad international publication of a pamphlet titled "Why War?" which consisted of a series of letters between Sigmund Freud and Albert Einstein on the current state of Western culture. Through a grim stroke of irony this correspondence was published in 1933, after Hitler's appointment as German chancellor not only threatened the safety of the two Jewish intellectuals but also seriously undermined the pamphlet's adamant pacifism. For Crevel, the pamphlet's espousal of pacifism and international cooperation signified how limited the capability of Freudian psychoanalysis was to diagnose on its own the "unconscious" political forces of persecution and aggression to which Freud had otherwise been so sensitive on the level of the individual subject.

There is a sense, then, in which Crevel does in fact heed the Soviet rejection of Freud; by discussing the coming into being of class consciousness in terms of "clear vision," he is responding directly to the explicitly anti-Marxist (and implicitly anti-dialectical) overtones of the Einstein-Freud correspondence. In particular, though, he rejects the quietism of Einstein's lament that the masses have been reduced to "blind instruments" of power. Whereas Einstein does indeed deplore such conditions in terms of the mechanics of state control, Crevel insinuates that Freud accepts this disempowerment as a necessary consequence of culture itself. Indeed Crevel attacks "the incredible loss of energetic thinking in Freud, even in the course of this very short letter to Einstein," arguing:

We see the deaf ass's ear of idealism burst when Freud writes: "All that works toward the development of culture also works against war."

But what culture, what civilization, are we talking about? . . .

In 1933 it seems that the culture and civilization of capitalist Europe are conceivable only through their opposites. What we might imagine Freud to mean by culture and civilization has worked toward nothing other than the preparation for war. . . .

Einstein, who assumes the examiner's role, notes that his publisher, the League of Nations, has obviously not freed mankind from the threat of war and, moreover, that war makes the fortunes of arms dealers.

We may have suspected this.

For a start, the minority of leaders (it's Einstein who so politely calls them this. We would more readily say the minority of exploiters, profiteers, and war profiteers) has the schools, the press, and all the religious organizations in the palm of its hand (here, Freud, is your culture, your civilization).

"It is through these means," according to Einstein, "that it dominates the great majority, who become its blind instrument."

Blind instrument. We have qualms about making this expression our own, when it now is the very time to reject it.

Crevel does not merely reject Einstein's expression about the "great majority" as a blind instrument; he also rejects the increasingly conservative science of Freudian psycho-analysis, "fully shut, metamorphosed into a house of illusions," that supports this ex-pression.[32] Whereas Einstein represents the masses as pawns in the game of war, Freud increasingly portrays the masses as unwitting instruments of their own unconscious drives, conflating the "civilizing" constraints of culture with the repressive forms of power themselves.

Lacan's doctoral thesis on paranoia was significant to Crevel, and to surrealist theory more broadly, because it examines a subject whose case history seemed to illustrate, in broad and violent strokes, the struggle between unconscious and conscious motives that "Why War?" reduces to a repressive formula. Lacan's thesis is based on the case study of a patient, "Aimée" (Marguerite Pantaine), who had assaulted a well-known actress under the delusion that she threatened the safety of Aimée's child. Rather than considering this persecution fantasy as either a hereditary defect or a purely psychogenetic condition, La-can traces the development of Aimée's illness as a process, a function of her development as a subject. Lacan's developmental theory suggested that the illness itself was a synthe-sis of unconscious and conscious processes; the patient's symptoms—interpretive delir-ium, persecution mania—were both the product and the expression of the subject's interiorization of a form of self-punishment.[33]

Crevel, too, notes how Aimée's paranoia manifested itself as a means of expression; he describes "the affective complexes and mental images that haunt her," as well as "the elo-quence, the grand and subtle allure of her writings, [which] testifies to a poetic value so intransigent that it can only exaggerate the initial discord between the creature and the world, which she deems detestable enough to want to recreate."[34] For Crevel, Aimée's crime is, like her writing, a significant form of expression that made her something more than the blind instrument of her repressed desires and aggression. Referring to her stab-bing attempt as a "homicidal gesture," Crevel writes: "In the case of a sexual or murder-ous exhibitionism, how do we judge it, unless we go back to the repression at its origin? The beauty of certain assaults on modesty or on life is that they accuse, with all their vio-lence, the monstrosity of laws and the constraints that make monsters."[35] Although this passage seems to present a straightforward justification of murder as beautiful, Crevel is hardly interested in presenting revolutionary violence in aesthetic terms of disinterested judgment and contemplation. Instead, like Lautréamont's famous definition of beauty as an encounter—"as beautiful as the fortuitous encounter of an umbrella and a sewing ma-chine upon a dissecting table"[36]—Crevel's appreciation of "assaults on modesty and life" is based on how they function as events characterized by discontinuity and trauma.

The beauty of paranoiac crime derives, in other words, from the idea that the traumatic encounter it stages between the interior structure of unconscious motive and the exterior world actively "accuses" an otherwise invisible third element. This third element, according to Crevel, consists of the social forces of repression that both unite and divide the subject as a social being. Insofar as the paranoiac engages in a form of self-punishment, striking out at her own ego-ideal in the form of another person (the famous actress stabbed by Aimée; the two Lancelin women murdered by Christine and Léa Papin), Lacan's thesis allows Crevel to argue that she is in fact lashing out against the idealized image of bourgeois subjectivity that determines the ego. The paranoiac's self-punishment is thus also a punishment of the self as a social construct. Such an encounter enables the application to political theory of what Crevel calls a "psycho-dialectic," a model of revolutionary empowerment made possible by the working class's coming-into-consciousness of repressed desires and repressive forces.

For Crevel, Lacan's thesis was promising to the left for its understanding of paranoia as a psychotic structure that systematically accuses the very ideological forces signified by Freud's notion of "culture." This culture was repressive not simply because it beat back the death drive but because it represented the full force of bourgeois social conditioning which, in the France of the early 1930s, was beginning to take on a frighteningly discernible shape: an attachment to so-called family values that sanctioned patriarchal privilege and a rampant homophobia; and an ever-present xenophobia and anti-Semitism whose deep roots in twentieth-century French culture only strengthened what Crevel and the surrealists considered to be a growing fascist sympathy among the French bourgeoisie.

The "accusation" performed by murderous exhibitionism thus does not canonize the psychotic as a revolutionary figure; insofar as the physical illness represents the moral illness that produces it, Crevel's structuralist notion of behavior as a representation allows his further ideas about political illness and oppression to be a matter of extension. That is, the shift from a developmental illness produced in the unconscious by oppressive conditions, to a physical illness—outbursts of violence and crime—is valuable for the curative value of the manifestation itself. As Crevel asks: "Does not the organic illness itself at all satisfy the self-punishing drive? . . . For those who have looked for or found the material conditions of illness, this physical illness will be the moral illness's chance for recovery."[37] Crevel is not actually interested in the nosology of mental patients (and seems misguided in thinking that the organic illness provides any satisfaction for the subject, except insofar as it allows the analyst to diagnose her). Yet Crevel's version of political and psychological causality structured as a "fortuitous encounter" is particularly useful to surrealism insofar as it rethinks the causality not only of presumably legitimate revolution but of the most inexplicable, brutal, and regressive of events as well—whether domestic murder or the growing domestic appeal of fascism. Indeed the truth of France's complicity in the spread of Nazism would not become consciously, physically manifest until the pro-fascist demonstrations in Paris on February 6, 1934, spurring the surrealists toward a more active antifascist campaign.

At the time of the Papin affair, Crevel and the surrealists were already interrogating the motives behind France's attempts to repress the rise to power of fascism by portraying it as either a temporary fluke or an utterly alien terror. This was not, Crevel insisted, a time for pacifism or, as Freud claimed in "Why War?," for "resting on the assurance that whatever makes for cultural development is working also against war." On the contrary, it was a time for further encouraging "the healing power of moral illness, shock, and organic illness" on the level of the state as well as on the level of ideological critique: a time, as Crevel wrote, for civil war.[38]

Motifs of Motive

When *Minotaure* 3–4 appeared in mid-December 1933, the Papin sisters had been tried and, in Christine's case, sentenced to death. The trial and official psychological diagnosis of the sisters as "sane" and thus "responsible" did little, however, to answer questions about the motives behind such acts of violence. In the meantime, reports had begun to circulate about the sisters' peculiar, almost catatonic, behavior during the trial, Christine's psychotic outbursts in prison, and the fiasco of their having been found "perfectly sane" by psychiatric experts.[39] According to Article 64 of the French Penal Code of 1810, as legally sane they were fully punishable and thus subject to the death sentence. Breton had himself railed against the injustice of the Penal Code article in 1932, calling it "philosophically incomprehensible."[40] Lacan's article on paranoiac style in *Minotaure* 1 (1933) echoes Breton's outrage in its critique of the Penal Code, and of academic psychiatry more broadly, urging:

> We must not misrecognize that the interest in mental illness is born historically from needs that are juridical in origin. These needs appeared at the time of the establishment, formulated on the basis of law, of the bourgeois philosophical conception of man as gifted with an absolute moral liberty and a responsibility proper to the individual. . . . Since then the major question landed practically on the science of psychiatrists has been, artificially, that of an all-or-nothing of mental forfeiture (article 64 of the Penal Code).[41]

Lacan's attention to the historical basis of psychiatry is meant to dislodge the practice of diagnosis from questions of criminal responsibility or irresponsibility, which risked reducing definitions of insanity to a moral choice policed by the state. Lacan instead stressed the importance of determining the motives for the crimes committed by the mentally ill. This was not, of course, to authorize them but to understand the forces and conditions that contributed to their development. Lacan's abandonment of the clinical as well as ideological foundations of psychiatry is especially evident in his diagnosis of the Papin sisters as paranoiac. In his second *Minotaure* article, published in the December 1933 double issue, he extends to this difficult case a methodology attuned to the opacity of the crimes, and inflected by the difficulty of understanding paranoia's own complex structure of related social and psychological processes.[42]

Reflecting their accordance with Breton's and Lacan's objection to Article 64, a number of journalists published articles challenging the official diagnosis of and verdict against the two sisters. Jérôme and Jean Tharaud, writing for the daily *Paris Soir*, and Maurice Coriem, writing for the weekly *Police* magazine as well as for the glossy crime review *Scandale*, express doubt about the ability of psychiatric experts adequately to define and detect madness, and thus legitimately to make "comprehensible" their values for determining legal responsibility.[43] As Lacan explains in his own reading of the Papin case (by way of the Tharaud reports), mere judgments of insanity would fall short of escaping the "bourgeois philosophical conception" that structures such all-or-nothing decisions. Paranoia confounded the categorical distinction between reason and madness, both in its development as an illness and in its heavily rationalized delusional system.

The Papin sisters posed an unusual problem for the psychiatric community, owing as much to the courts' failure to recognize the nature of their insanity as to the extremity of their "murderous exhibitionism." Christine and Léa were themselves unable to provide "any comprehensible motive, any hatred, any grief" of their own; likewise, the judge, jury, and all but one of the experts testifying to their accountability similarly failed to notice anything unusual about their behavior or their past.[44] Yet Lacan, like the Tharauds and Coriem, enumerates several such peculiarities: a suspicion of their incestuous lesbianism, which was voiced by a number of witnesses and supported by their fierce attachment to each other; Christine's psychotic episodes in prison, during which she tried to tear out her own eyes; and a family history of sexual abuse, given reports that their alcoholic father had raped their other sister.[45] However "sociological" these overlooked factors may have been, they suggest that the conditions that influenced the Papins' behavior were less measurable, and more deeply buried in the formation of the unconscious, than the jury and most of the press were willing to acknowledge, even in their eagerness to ascribe to the crime an antibourgeois political meaning. Lacan's work strives to render comprehensible the motives that were unavailable or invisible to the legal system and to the Papins alike.

Lacan's methodology in diagnosing the Papin sisters, in contrast to those of the psychiatric experts in the case, drew from multiple fields of inquiry: his very definition of paranoia in the 1933 article challenges existing psychiatric models of the illness and, more provocatively, refines Lacan's own earlier explanation of paranoia in terms of style. For Lacan, the disciplines brought together in *Minotaure*—artistic, psychiatric, and theoretical—were all necessary to the study of mental illness, since paranoia reveals the work of signification and imagery in the formation of subjectivity, and not just within the fields of cultural and artistic production alone. Lacan's work on the Papin sisters builds on his description, in the first issue of Minotaure, of paranoiac lived experience as an "original syntax," a mode of symbolic expression that could be at once intentional and yet still determined by real social tensions.

The work of surrealism is useful to Lacan here for its understanding of psychiatric symptoms as viable forms of expression in themselves. The classic symptoms of paranoia described by Freud—interpretive delirium, fantasies of grandeur and persecution, outbursts of aggression—simulate intellectual behavior without corresponding to reason or logic; such symptoms, according to Lacan, are not a retroactive attempt by the reasoning mind to explain its attacks of dementia but the product of paranoia's organization as "a coherent structure of immediate noumenal apprehension of oneself and the world."[46] That is, the illness, not the patient, simulates reason, thus performing the work of representation. While this may nominally account for the ease with which the Papin sisters' insanity went unrecognized, the real impact of Lacan's theory lay in its ability to model the complicated interaction of conscious will, unconscious desire, and social conditioning that produced the murders as a deadly play of representation.

Lacan's theory of paranoia hinges on the notion that paranoiac crime is motivated by an unconscious drive for self-punishment whose misrecognition by the subject results in its eruption, on a social level, as a murderous aggression toward a person who serves as the subject's ego-image. The paranoiac criminal thus "punishes" the wrong person. But this ego-image is not the only instance of representation at work in paranoia, since, as Lacan writes, on every level the unconscious drives bear the imprint of social relations, thus representing their effects in trace form. Even the aggressive drive itself is similarly referential, subject to "social tensions" in both its formation and its expression, insofar as the very will to commit violence is itself the result of a social negotiation. As Lacan writes:

> The intentional content that translates [the aggressive drive] into consciousness cannot manifest itself without a compromise with the social exigencies integrated by the subject, that is, without a camouflage of motives which is precisely the delirium in its entirety.
>
> But even this drive is itself imprinted with a social relativity: it always has the intentionality of a crime; almost constantly that of vengeance; often the sense of a punishment, that is, a sanction issued from social ideas; and often, finally, it identifies itself as the act achieved by morality, having the carriage of an atonement (self-punishment).[47]

Such a play of camouflage and simulacra certainly obfuscates the problem of using paranoia to understand better the relationship between a political subject and the social and material conditions of her life. By mapping psychosis as a structure rather than as a linear relationship of cause and effect, however, Lacan suggests that even if the ultimate causality of motive could not be located, determined, or represented definitively, the interaction of unconscious desire and social relativity could be witnessed in their distortions and imprints on each other. Lacan suggests, in fact, that the real effects of social relations on the subject—so readily misrecognized, in the case of the Papin sisters, as direct class oppression—become recognizable as motives for the crime only insofar as they become visible as motifs. Indeed his title, "Motifs du crime paranoaïque," suggests that, in this sequel to his earlier article on paranoiac style, the French term *motifs* can signify both causal motives and stylistic motifs. That is, Lacan's study of motive stresses how the structure of psychosis involves a simultaneous interpretation and representation of lived reality; within this structure, social and material conditions are manifest not merely as the facts that a subject represents to herself, but also as the determining forces that the unconscious must represent to the consciousness.

Christopher Lane has argued that this psychotic structure—which is not political in itself, since the people involved are unaware of its meaning—may be politicized insofar as its motifs, its exhibitionism, provide a reminder of "the fragile supports on which subjectivity is so reliant, and the way each precarious identification fosters an illusion of psychical stability."[48] To limit the political meaning of psychosis, however, to a subversion of subjectivity alone would require, once again, the separation of the social from the psychological which Lacan, like Crevel after him, strove to eradicate. The "fragile supports" rendered apparent by an understanding of psychotic structure include the social as well as the subjective, or, more accurately, the syntax of reality itself as lived experience in the world. Paranoia's "coherent structure of immediate noumenal apprehension of oneself and the world" is thus, in the words of Dalí, corrosive to reality insofar as it shows lived experience, the phenomenal relation of oneself and the world, to be similarly structured as a mutually distorting interplay of unconscious, conscious, and social forces. Crevel suggests the political utility of this structure in his "Notes toward a Psycho-dialectic." The dialectical nature of Lacan's theory, he argues, can account for the deformations, difficulties, and ambivalence through which an object becomes a subject, and, by extension, through which a subaltern crowd can become a proletariat with a fully developed class consciousness.

The Surrealist Intervention

I call this surrealist understanding of political and psychological reality "noir" because the noir genres studied by the surrealists throughout the movement's history, and with increasing rigor during the 1930s, represented what I argue is a paranoiac response to contemporary historical and political events. Participants as well as observers in a period of developing historical emergency, the surrealists were acutely aware of the danger of remaining unconscious protagonists in the historical drama of the 1930s. For the surrealists writing at the time of the Papin affair, the gothic fiction of writers such as Walpole, Radcliffe, and Sade, the poetry of the symbolists, and the dystopian universe of serial novels and crime films dramatized the movement's own contemporary historical predicament.

As Maurice Heine argues in an essay on the *roman noir* published in *Minotaure* in 1934, noir fictions render a stark contrast between the indifference and lack of awareness of those who take them literally and the analytical power available to those who are attentive to their atmosphere and structure. As Heine writes, commenting on what he calls the "European public's general infatuation with the novel of terror for an entire half century," from the late eighteenth through the mid-nineteenth centuries:

> This [infatuation] is especially remarkable in France, where convulsive changes of political regime had left no apparent influence on the taste of male, and especially female, readers. One might thus wonder what contributed most toward maintaining such spiritual tendencies: the bloody events of a restless era, or an intense repression of the resulting reaction. Let it suffice here to denounce this black cloak of indifference that shrouds acts, works, and souls. For the last are, at this point, so permeated by it that exceptional pathological cases seem to result: the adventures of the necrophilic Sergeant Bertrand, which took place in 1847–48, show a reality more vertiginous than any fictional horror.[49]

Heine rejects the possibility that noir fictions represent historical reality mimetically; the profound interest of noir forms, he claims, lies instead in their structural characteristics: their transposition of marvelous and terrifying elements into contemporary settings, and their ability to provoke "a shiver of terror, no longer by the *mise-en-scène* of supernatural beings, but by the evocation of the invisible forces its distraught characters obey."[50] Staging rather than perpetuating the "black cloak of indifference" to the historical reality of violence, such structural qualities provide material for analysis and critique for which the texts of noir fictions are only the pretext.

This phenomenological means for depicting "the real" itself is best described in an earlier essay by Heine, in which he claims that "the truth only returns through the synthesis of style: art's veracity lies in the stylization of a fetish.[51] The traumatic knowledge of an otherwise disavowed reality—whether the motive for a brutal murder, or the true threat of fascism, or the nature of historical causality more broadly—could be represented only through its disavowal. Whereas the characters in noir fiction struggle in vain to make sense of the forces to which their actions are subject, the stylistic universe of the noir aesthetic itself makes possible the analysis it denies its characters. Through this analytical access, the noir aesthetic becomes theory, itself a speculative means for investigating the structure of reality—exterior to the aesthetic form itself—that made action possible.

To the extent that the presence of the political in *Minotaure* is similarly deferred or exoteric, I contend that this deferral represents an abstraction, rather than a dissolution or failure, of surrealism's political project. The group's resumption of psychoanalytical and formal experimentation in 1933 actually represents a serious investigation into the constitutive elements of political praxis: motive, causality, and the role of signification in political representation. In much the same way, historical noir and gothic forms rarely seem overtly progressive or avant-garde in their politics. In fact, their proliferation of stylistic motifs (from uncanny landscapes and hauntings to the play of light and shadow upon "mean streets") often seems to emphasize explicitly conservative fears: the threat of family dissolution, of sexual and racial corruption, and of political usurpation. And yet even if the terror and "systematized confusion" of noir fictions use such fears to reinforce the existing order or political structure, their exhibitionism nevertheless provides a means for witnessing the otherwise unrepresentable sources of this terror. Indeed, what seems progressive about noir and gothic fictions is precisely their configuration of political, psychological, and historical questions as a problem of representation, or, more accurately, as a problem of style.

As Heine suggests in his article in *Minotaure*, the formal architecture of noir fictions dramatizes the unconscious irruption of an indeterminate but powerful evil into the realm of everyday life. What the evil actually is remains mysterious, yet its traumatic power suggests that, like the "moral illness" Crevel discusses, this evil comprises the simultaneously political and psychological nature of causality itself. It harbors the inadmissible knowledge that violence, crime, and social dissolution are not merely external, alien forces but internal, all too familiar ones as well. Could not the standard noir plot twist be described as the uncanny realization that an evil "out there," against which the protagonists so gallantly attempt to safeguard themselves, is suddenly revealed to have been in their midst all along?

In the historical context of the 1930s, the paranoiac theory Lacan and Crevel develop offered itself as an interpretive structure whose analysis of stylistic motifs functioned as theory, insofar as these motifs bore the imprint, however distorted, of the dialectical interplay of unconscious desire and social pressures. The possibility that the most abjectly alien acts of terror were themselves already both interpretations and representations of lived reality suggested a method for interpreting the historical present. For the surrealists such acts were legible as motifs not only within the narrative framework of gothic fiction but within the contemporary world as well. These motifs took the form of material elements—uncanny objects, architectural forms, media images, and urban spaces—whose significance was disavowed by the historical figures who inhabited them. Similarly, it was surrealism's efforts to account structurally for otherwise invisible, unconscious forces determining the course of history—just as it had once been the group's original claim to "photograph" the unconscious through automatic writing—that lent its noir period a political use-value.

The role of such objective motifs becomes clear in the understated "Homage to the Papin Sisters," a drawing by Paul Nougé and René Magritte published in a 1934 special issue of the Belgian journal *Documents 34* titled "The Surrealist Intervention" (figure 6.2). The image depicts a solitary housemaid, dressed formally in a black dress and shoes with a white apron, drawing a broom across the floor. The figure's posture is erect, her head titled downward as if she is lost in thought. The simple, naturalistic drawing style of the image seems to promise immediate legibility, as does its hand-drawn legend, "Hommage aux soeurs Papin." Yet whereas the Papin affair's domestic setting and class markers are firmly in place, the image's lone, sweeping housekeeper bears neither a physical nor an allegorical resemblance to the Papin sisters, her face betraying neither a reserve nor a madness that might signify whether the scene occurs after or before a murder. Despite its momentary illegibility, though, the image, and the curious expression of the housekeeper,

take on a sudden surplus of meaning in relation to the jug in the background of the drawing. The jug, out of place within the image's portrait of cleanliness and domestic order, seems to belong not on the floor but instead in the litany of household torture devices used in the Papin affair: a pewter jug, kitchen knives, a hammer, and the sisters' bare hands.

The object in the drawing by Nougé and Magritte unsettles its order and "innocence" in a way that no more legitimates the crimes than Éluard and Péret's press review does; what it achieves instead is the effect of transforming the housekeeper's curious expression from an unconscious absorption to a knowing trace of a smile. Whatever stage of awareness her expression suggests, the presence of the jug in the margin of the image performs both an interpretation and a

Fig. 6.2. René Magritte and Paul Nougé, "Homage to the Papin Sisters," *Documents 34* (1934). © 2008 Artists Rights Society (ARS), New York/SABAM, Brussels. © 2008 C. Herscovici, Brussels/Artists Rights Society (ARS), New York.

representation of the Papin sisters' violence as a latent possibility within all kinds of do-mestic labor relations. The means for violence are at hand, the drawing suggests, whether we know it or not. That is, once the object reorders the meaning of the image in relation to its "homage" to the Papins, the drawing's paranoiac depiction of the non-neutrality of innocent spaces becomes all the more immanent.

During the course of the group's relationship with *Minotaure*, the surrealists shifted their efforts from theorizing the validity of revolutionary violence to finding strategies for deriv-ing paranoiac knowledge. The surrealists, in other words, strove to create an atmosphere that did not so much constitute "revolution" as it was conducive to the knowledge repre-sented obliquely in Nougé and Magritte's drawing: the means—moral as well as ma-terial—are at hand.[52] By calling surrealism's period of political and epistemological reassessment both a noir period and a period of negation, I have argued, first, that the group's poetic and political aims in 1933 were not limited to revealing irrational forces at work within exterior reality. Rather, the surrealists studied how such forces were organized as coherent structures of motive, causality, and perception in a way that revealed their con-tiguity with existing structures of political and ideological logic. Second, I maintain that this noir period enabled rather than performed the group's political work. The theoretical experiments of this era provided the basis for a new "morality of revolt" that advocated a massive collective restructuring of society on diverse fronts—from mental institutions to literature to family structure to political parties—instead of the merely destructive violence of Aragon's "Red Front." It is my contention that surrealism's provisional negation of po-litical and formal investigation during its noir period in fact permitted the aggressive po-litical actions of the group's active antifascist militancy and worldwide dissemination, from 1934 ("L'Intervention surrealiste") to the group's final attempts, in the name of an al-lied antifascist campaign, to reunite with the Communist Party in 1934 and 1935, and, af-terwards, to form "Contre-Attaque" with Georges Bataille in 1936.

What has often been considered the fatal error of surrealism was its belief in the pos-sibility for a synthesis between "intransigent" conceptual practices and active political en-gagement—that is, its persistence in fomenting its own version of proletarian revolution instead of devoting itself fully to the more pressing international need to stifle the fascist menace at all costs. The significance of the Papin affair to the surrealist group was that it suggested the terrifying degree to which France's susceptibility to fascist sympathies was already present at the very heart of French bourgeois ideology. This susceptibility became all the more apparent later that year in the Nozière affair, in which efforts to protect the French public against the moral threat posed by an eighteen-year-old murderer revealed a vast patriarchal conspiracy designed to uphold values of thrift, sexual purity, and the sanctity of the family that would characterize French public campaigns during the *drôle de guerre* (the "Phony War" of September 1939–May 1940) and, in particular, during the Vichy regime.

Part Two: Violette Nozière and the Alchemical Rewriting of Rape

> I turned silences and nights into words. What was unutterable,
> I wrote down.
>
> Arthur Rimbaud, "The Alchemy of the Word" (1873)

On August 28, 1933, eighteen-year-old Violette Nozière was arrested for the poisoning murder of her father, which had taken place the previous week. Her mother—the crime's only witness—was still recovering from the dose she received at the same time. At the moment of her capture Violette had eluded police for nearly a week; she had done this, it seemed, without ever trying to hide, instead frequenting nightclubs and jazz bars in Montmartre and Montparnasse, and staying with an assortment of acquaintances and lovers. In her absence the "Affaire de la rue Madagascar" had developed in the daily newspapers from a back page crime incident into a full-scale front page story, as the "double life" led by the increasingly guilty-looking parricide became more clear.

By day a high school student at the Lycée Fénélon, by night Violette was a denizen of the sordid Latin Quarter cafés and nightclubs where, according to the press, bourgeois students mixed with—and often became—prostitutes and criminals. Violette was reportedly an occasional prostitute herself and, according to speculation, syphilitic. Moreover, as cash from her parents' house and her father's 165,000 franc savings were found to be missing, providing a possible motive for the crime, the unwholesome moral fabric of the as yet uncaptured Violette seemed to prove her guilty beyond dispute. The portrait of the murderer that took shape was that of a profligate youth rather than a hardened killer. A contemporary popular song, "L'Ignoble Empoisonneuse, ou, le Crime de la Rue de Madagascar," laments:

> As a looker she was precocious
> Her provocative smile
> At age thirteen—how atrocious
> She gave away fallacious kisses
> Next it was Montmartre, Montparnasse
> The smoke, the heady wines
> The fancy of every man who passes
> The upkeep of a sad monsieur
> And then, her vision of what little money
> Her mom and dad possessed.[53]

Hinting at an almost congenital sexual proclivity, such songs (which became somewhat of a cottage industry for their author, Jules Hubert) focused on the terrible affront Violette's crime posed to the French family. What could parents do to satisfy such brutal off-spring? Would they stop at nothing in assuaging their desire and greed? The possibility that Violette not only poisoned her parents but lusted after their money as well suggested that her covetousness and precocious sexuality presented a great threat to the family as a national institution. Not only was Violette's lifestyle corrosive to so-called family values, but also her moral degeneracy, which led to an actual assault on her family, seemed to be symptomatic of a new generation of spoiled and intransigent youth who had no memory of the hardships of the Great War.

Though shared by the mainstream and sensationalist press alike, such excoriations of Violette as a toxic and degenerate force—a "demon of sexuality" with "poison in her blood" —were not limited to the bourgeois press.[54] Even the communist daily *Humanité* attacked the "decadence" of the young fugitive; an article published under the headline "Violette Nozière, Who Poisoned Her Parents, Has Not Been Found," claims:

> A habituée of the Latin Quarter cafés, this child of honest workers, who bled themselves dry to have her educated at the Lycée Fénélon, rapidly lost all moral sense in this special underworld formed by pimps and young bourgeois fast-livers who mainly throng the es-tablishments of the quartier des Écoles. . . . She no longer tolerated the mediocre life of those who raised her. She's taken up the habit of dancing. She wants money. And perhaps someone is there behind her who pushes her to take it. A grim image of decadence, she is above all the product of a regime of exploitation where money is in the hand of para-sites who drag the Violette Nozières of the world through their rottenness in order to make them into prostitutes and criminals.[55]

Throughout the Nozière affair, *Humanité* would continue to politicize Violette's abandon-ment of the working-class situation of her father, a unionized worker for the railroads, as the result of her corruption and apprenticeship at the hands of degenerate bourgeois "par-asites." The communist paper even continued to insist on the existence of an accomplice, whose identity Violette must have been shielding. The suggestion was clear: as "toxic" as she may have been, Violette could not possibly have acted alone.

Yet it was Violette's own statements on the thirty-first of August that catapulted the af-fair into national prominence. Explaining the motives behind her murderous act, Violette told police that her true object in poisoning her father was to end the years of sexual abuse she had endured. Although she administered poison to both her parents, she asserted:

> I did not wish to end my mother's life. I did not exercise any violence against her. I did not go after her at all. I only wanted to annihilate her powers of intervention. The proof is that I made her take only three packets of prepared powder, whereas I administered six of them to my father.

The latter, for example, I wished to kill. I had had enough. No matter what the cost, this situation needed to end. Just imagine! For six years I have been forced, with threats to back it up, to give in to all his wishes. At the age of twelve I was subjected to odious acts of violence on his part. And since then . . . there have been continual scenes because he threatened me with worse reprisals if he were to learn that I had a boyfriend, and he threatened me with death if I ever revealed this awful situation to my mother.[56]

In the wake of her mother's public expression of outrage against her daughter's "shameful" inculpation of her late father, Violette's accusation was roundly received with disbelief, dismissal, and contempt, causing more than one news journal to memorialize the "Nozière affair" as a double parricide: not only was Violette remorseless about her initial crime, but she added to it as well the assault on her father's memory.[57] Even though Violette's admitted responsibility in killing her father lay beyond dispute, the ire of Mme Nozière, who soon filed a civil suit against her daughter, confirmed the press's reaction to the sexual abuse charge as a secondary act of violence on Violette's part. This in turn only multiplied speculation about why this young girl committed such a hateful deed. Hysteric, femme fatale, or pathogen, Violette Nozière became at once an object of wild speculation and a spectacle of public contempt. Her motives, her sanity, and her underworld acquaintances became regular editorial topics in countless daily and weekly magazines. Few were willing to admit fully the straightforward but "too horrible" explanation offered by Violette herself; the resulting debates and queries made the Nozière affair one of the most widely publicized Parisian scandals of 1933.

In response to the hostile and sensationalistic media climate that surrounded this "double parricide," seventeen members of the surrealist group published a small book, titled *Violette Nozières*, at the end of 1933.[58] The book was printed in Brussels at a publishing house founded by the Belgian surrealist E. L. T. Mesens, Éditions Nicolas Flamel. As the allusion to the medieval alchemist Flamel suggests, the book's imprint bespeaks a perverse relationship to the pseudoscientific language of poison, toxins, and money that characterized much of the media coverage of the Nozière affair. As a literary imprint, Mesens's surrealist press cited Flamel as a secondary allusion to Rimbaud's "alchemy of the word," which championed the ability of poetry to articulate "the inexpressible." On the cultural front, though, the book's press, like its poetic and artistic content, extolled the power of language to exceed the literary and thus "take revenge on all things," to use Breton's words, as well as to transform the unspeakable and give it form.[59] Whereas the mainstream media invoked pathogens and chemicals to portray Violette as a symptom of degeneracy, the surrealists invoked alchemy to portray her as an agent of transformation. Far from being simply a departure into the occult, therefore, the book's allusion to alchemy functioned as an extended metaphor for the surrealist group's manifold efforts

VIOLETTE
NOZIÈRES

EDITIONS NICOLAS FLAMEL
55, rue de Courtrai, 55 - Bruxelles
Dépositaire à Paris : JOSÉ CORTI - 6, rue de Clichy

Fig. 6.3. Man Ray, cover photograph for *Violette Nozières* (1933). Image courtesy of the Ryerson and Burnham Libraries, the Art Institute of Chicago. © 2008 Man Ray Trust/Artists Rights Society (ARS), New York/ADAGP, Paris.

throughout the 1920s and 1930s to reconcile psychoanalytic science and poetic experimentation with Marxist political action.

Unlike many other surrealist responses to public or political issues, however, the book bears little resemblance to a political tract. *Violette Nozières* is a collection containing eight poems and eight drawings, with an unattributed cover photograph by Man Ray. In his introduction to the 1991 reprint edition of the book, José Pierre refers to the book as a "bouquet" presented by the surrealists in Violette's name. While this image may conceptualize the collective nature of anthologies and resonate with the bouquet of violets at the center of Man Ray's cover photograph (figure 6.3), its allusion to the real bouquet of roses presented by Breton and his friends to Germaine Berton in 1923 risks suggesting that the Nozière book was little more than a gesture. On the contrary, the book's artistic format forms the basis of the surrealist intervention into the sphere of public discussion of the crime; yet this "intervention" represented something other than a form of direct political action. As in the case of the Papin murders earlier that year, the surrealist response to the Nozière affair was analytical rather than rhetorical or propagandistic. That is, rather than claiming to transform surrealist art into surrealist action, the book translates the Nozière case from a singular act into the explosion of textual motifs and ulterior motives it soon became.

The Nozière affair did not center on psychosis, as in the case of Christine and Léa Papin; what the surrealists focused on instead was the unconscious structure of motive betrayed by the behavior of the police, the press, and the legal system, which insisted on obscuring Violette's own fully acknowledged motives. Without arguing for Violette's innocence—or, for that matter, her guilt—the surrealist book asserts the legitimacy of her homicidal action. It views her parricide as a liberation from an economy of rape already intimated by the word *viol* (rape) embedded in the name "Violette"; it also demonstrates that the case really hinged on the state's support of the repressive values of petit-bourgeois family life. Indeed, one of the implicit questions of the surrealist book was whether Violette's father, Jean-Baptiste Nozière, could be considered a member of the working class, or whether his position as a railroad conductor for the SNCF (Société nationale des chemins de fer français) qualified him as a national bureaucrat.

But the Nozière affair represented another phenomenon as well: in opposition to Violette's treatment as a femme fatale and a hysteric by the press, the surrealist pamphlet approached her act as if it were a form of writing rather than simply a form of violence. The surrealist discourse around Violette Nozière was not so much constitutive of this writing as it was its mediation. The book documents how the surrealists reordered the facts of the affair to subvert the terms and judgments of the public response to this sensationalized crime. Through its attack on the medical-legal and media response to the case, the book presents the Nozière affair as the field of contestation through which two distinct phenomena became visible: first, the murder itself as the site of Violette's coming-into-being as a subject; and second, the machinations of the French state as the repressive, proto-fascist culture it was, the surrealists argued, already becoming.

Violette Nozières was quickly censored and thus failed to reach even a modest reading public. Still, the book plays a central role in the surrealist political thinking of the early 1930s, representing an expansion of the group's field of political inquiry to include sexual violence as well as class struggle. By rendering this violence legible as a collection of highly referential texts and images, this surrealist intervention had two significant effects. First, the book set the scene for understanding Violette's parricide as a radical act of autobiographical revision, a gesture of erasure in the face of sexual abuse, and not merely a symptomatically violent repetition of violent trauma. In spite of Breton's and Aragon's well-known interest in hysteria as "the greatest poetic invention of the nineteenth century," Violette's crime represented something other than a hysterical or psychotic outburst for the surrealists who published their work in the book. The Nozière murder, and Violette's equally scandalous nocturnal habits, instead performed as a spectacle the return of patriarchy's repressed, in the form of the alarming consensus condemning Violette as a toxic woman, a *détraquée*. Furthermore, the surrealist book uses the Nozière case to view French public and intellectual culture in the midst of its widespread efforts to exercise repression—both in the political sense of enforced restraint and in the psychoanalytical sense of unconscious disavowal—by means of the public responses to her case. What was being repressed, the surrealists implied, was France's susceptibility to fascism—a susceptibility that lay within the very sanctity and institutionalization of patriarchal "family values" which the Nozière case brought to national attention. Indeed, the surrealist attention to the Nozière case depicted these values as direct agents of persecution, suffusing everyday French life within an ideological pattern of possession and control that vilified freedom as a perversion.

As *Humanité*'s coverage of the case suggests, the sociological context of the affair was so heavily speculated about by the press that it was not up to the surrealists alone to draw out the ideological consequences of an otherwise inert domestic crime. The myriad magazines and newspapers may have differed widely in their interpretations of Violette's motives for poisoning her parents; yet with her accusation of sexual abuse as its focal point, the confluence of stories about Violette's character, personal history, and nocturnal habits forged a startling consensus in the media as to her moral—and possibly mental and physical—dissolution. Violette was rendered so indistinguishable from her underworld lifestyle that her accusation seemed only one of the machinations of her deadly allure.

Indeed, Hubert's song "L'Ignoble Empoisonneuse" goes so far as to suggest that any history of sexual abuse in Violette's life could be attributed to her own powers of seduction—powers that were already in full flower, the song claims, by age thirteen. Similarly, the seedy crime exposé *The Poisoner's Secret*, published as a chapbook several weeks after the murder, opens on a scene in which Violette is found soliciting men in the park; part prostitute, part courtesan, she uses her earnings and "gifts" to support her right-wing boyfriend and feed her dreams of impossible luxury.[60] Whether she is cruising in the park or on the lam in Montparnasse, Violette's uncanny presence as a figure of desire poses the threat of a woman—a daughter—dangerously out of place, pathological, and in need of incarceration. Moreover, the pamphlet insinuates that like the countless lies she concocts to help sustain her "double life" as a student and prostitute, Violette's accusation that "extraordinary things happened in my family which modesty doesn't permit me to tell you" was itself a symptom.[61] Her accusation of incestuous sexual abuse was, in other words, a pathological effect similar to her "mysterious" sexual motivations, if not a downright fabrication.

By stressing the fantastic, delusional, or simply invented nature of her accusation of childhood sexual abuse, the press suggested that Violette exhibited the symptoms of a kind of hysteria. The usefulness of such a depiction lay in the fact that it provided a ready-made narrative of Violette's transgression against the family. As Hélène Cixous and Catherine Clément famously suggest in *The Newly Born Woman*, the role of the hysteric bears a kind of textuality which, in spite of its specificity to its cultural and historical context, inscribes the hysterical woman within a recognizable theatrical narrative. As they explain:

This feminine role, the role of sorceress, of hysteric, is ambiguous, antiestablishment, and conservative at the same time. Antiestablishment because the symptoms—the attacks—revolt and shake up the public, the group, the men, the others to whom they are exhibited. . . . The hysteric unties familiar bonds, introduces disorder into the well-regulated unfolding of everyday life, gives rise to magic in ostensible reason. These roles are *conservative* because every sorceress ends up being destroyed, and nothing is registered of her but mythical traces. Every hysteric ends up inuring others to her symptoms, and the family closes around her again, whether she is curable or incurable.[62]

The surrealists themselves were struck by the textuality of hysterical attacks, having celebrated hysteria as "the greatest poetic invention of the latter nineteenth century."[63] Yet in the Nozière affair it was not the surrealists who touted the poetics of hysteria but the media: since Violette did not suffer a hysterical breakdown in prison but, on the contrary, firmly maintained her poise and stuck to her story, it became instrumental for the press to portray her lifestyle itself, her entire persona, as a series of hysterical performances. Her ostensibly sympathetic diagnosis by *Détective* as the "the prey of lies" served to itemize and yet also control her powers of seduction. Even as the acts of a hysteric, though, her "lies" and performances served as proof that the accusation was itself yet another such symptom.

Curiously, this opinion has been perpetuated, not only by contemporary articles such as those in the left-leaning *Détective* but also by later historical accounts of the affair, such Jean-Marie Fitère's 1975 book *Violette Nozière*, on which Claude Chabrol's 1978 film of the same name was based, and whose account of the case is colored by the fact that Violette rescinded her accusation of rape in 1937 as part of her religious conversion in prison.[64] In turn, Fitère's acceptance of this statement at face value, obviating Violette's original testimony altogether, has spawned a hegemonic version of the affair that has endured, to the extent that much contemporary scholarship on surrealism continues to presume the falsehood of Violette's accusation: for instance, Tyler Stovall's "Paris in the Age of Anxiety," an article from the catalogue to the 1990 "Anxious Visions" exhibition, glosses Violette Nozière as "a nineteen-year-old [sic] Parisian who killed her father for the sake of her inheritance. A disturbed young woman who spent much of her time drinking cocktails in cafés and prostituting herself to give money to her lover, Nozière appeared to the Parisian people as a veritable flapper from hell."[65] Even when Violette's accusations remain unchallenged, numerous scholars tend to focus on the surrealist movement's attention to the young murderer as a figure of alterity, one of a litany of figures rendered provocative or radical by their psychological, racial, or gender difference.[66] Such interpretations overlook, however, the degree to which the surrealist book is dedicated to the Nozière affair as a whole and not to the historical figure of Violette alone.

As in the Papin affair, the surrealists found themselves at odds with the communist press coverage of the crime. Articles in *Humanité* claimed that the bourgeois press was favoring what it called the "incest story" as a screen for what the media increasingly held to be a conspiratorial form of class warfare at the heart of the affair. Recalling that the Latin Quarter students were the grandchildren of the bourgeois battalions who massacred the members of the 1871 Paris Commune, a writer for Humanité claimed that "in order to turn our attention away from this nursery for assassins, the bourgeois press tries to substantiate lewd stories about a family of workers, gathering the pathological ravings of the sorry Violette! How all the journalists, how all the bourgeois, were delighted to get hold of her monstrous accusations." This attention to conspiracy, however, caused Humanité in turn to overlook or discount the mounting evidence in support of Violette's accusation of abuse: a discarded rag used to wipe off M. Noziere's semen, a roll of pornographic drawings concealed in the house. The paper adamantly dismissed the possible status of such objects as evidence. The drawings, it claimed, hardly signified incest, and Violette's knowledge of them might only be a testament to her own "genre" as someone known to root through her parents' possessions; moreover, it noted that Mme Noziere's confidential statements to the police had somehow silenced the question of the rag. Moreover, by insisting that the police and the bourgeois press were covering up the existence of an accomplice, the writers not only discredit Violette's "pathological" accusation but completely empty her of any agency, intelligence, or sanity as well, calling her by turns a "détraquée" manipulated by the pimps and gigolos of a "rotten regime."[67]

In spite of Humanité's charges, though, the bourgeois press did not so much focus on the sexual abuse as a diversion tactic as ascribe alternative motives for the accusation itself. And thus the actual content of the charge, and the violence that caused it, were again suppressed, buried beneath a litany of justifications: whether the product of outright lies, as her mother testified in Détective magazine, claiming that "she was unfamiliar with sincerity"; or the perversion of a mental weakling, "envoûtée" (bewitched) by the underworld, who lived beyond her means; or the hateful victim of a hereditary degeneracy who blamed her parents for the "poison in her blood" and, through a horrible reversal, poisoned them in turn. The most vicious explanation, however, combined such hypotheses with the mother's own accusations, claiming that Violette, in knocking off her parents for their 165,000 franc savings, was striving for a liberation—not from six years of sexual abuse but toward the easy life, free from the fetters of responsibility altogether: "the beach, pajamas, casinos . . . the great free life, Free!" crowed The Poisoner's Secret.[68]

The surrealists, in their careful reassembly of the crime's dominant motifs and objects, eradicate this double-edged characterization of freedom and youth culture alike as degenerate social forces. The poems and drawings published in Violette Nozières dismantle the press's litany of justifications and obfuscations in order to argue that it was incontestably clear that Violette Nozière was raped by her father. In his contribution to the book, Benjamin Péret condenses six years of abuse into a single event; his account, which both invokes Jean-Betrand Nozière's profession as a railroad conductor and describes one of the sites where Violette said the abuse took place, brings the act chillingly into the poem's present. Péret writes:

> Daddy
> Dear Daddy you're hurting me
> she said
> But the daddy who felt the fire of his locomotive
> a little below his navel
> raped
> in the arbor of the garden
> amidst the shovel handles that inspired it
> Violette
> who then returned to study
> between the mechanic of misfortune
> and the mother planning her vengeance
> her homework
> which vaunted the sanctity of the family
> the father's kindness, the mother's sweetness[69]

What proliferates throughout the book's poems and drawings are the objects, statements, and other fragments of reportage which appear in accounts of the case, and yet which became charged with an excess of signification as their status as evidence was denied. The stained rag, for instance, becomes for Péret the "blotted napkin forgotten behind the screen," and for Breton a piece of linen "shining mysteriously." The father's pornographic drawings become, in Breton's poem, "the bedside library I mean the night table." Surrounded by the multiplied evidence of his violence, M. Nozière no longer resides in the symbolic safety of his status as a victim but is continually suspended in accusation. As Breton writes, citing Violette's testimony in a way that transforms her euphemism for sexual abuse into an explicit inculpation, "my father forgets sometimes that I'm his daughter."[70] The surrealist book, however, refuses to forget: not only does it suspend Jean-Baptiste Nozière in a state of perpetual accusation, but also it mobilizes this singular accusation toward a broader inculpation of French domestic politics.

The book's more subtle accomplishment lies in its recognition that it was the "second parricide" of Violette's accusation, even more than the actual murder, that formed the object of so much contention, fear, and contempt in the press—as well as from Violette's mother. Even *Humanité*'s vocabulary of class warfare desperately protected Jean-Baptiste Nozière insofar as he, as a unionized worker, represents the "family of workers" persecuted by the bourgeoisie. Indeed, Péret rewrites the communist conspiracy theory as precisely such a form of protection against the threat that Violette's accusation poses to fathers, that is, to patriarchy itself:

> all those who make their pens urinate on newsprint
> the black corpse-sniffers
> the professional assassins with white cudgels
> all the fathers dressed in red for condemning
> or in black for making us believe they defend
> are all intent upon her, she who is like the first chestnut tree in flower
> the first sign of spring which will sweep away their foul winter
> because they are the fathers
> those who rape
> next to the mothers
> those who defend their memory[71]

If the Nozière affair conceals a conspiracy, Péret argues, it is a conspiracy organized around sexual privilege rather than class; the father's memory and the privilege to rape are both shared and protected by the press and the judiciary system, and are defended through the complicity of figures like Violette's mother. Breton similarly describes this confluence of "interest" and privilege as a more iconographically sexualized desire, indicating how the patriarchal "memory" is not just reactive but proactive as well:

> Everyone's the same whether they pretend to deny it or not
> Before your wingèd sex like a flower from the catacombs
> Students old men corrupt journalists phony revolutionaries priests judges
> Doddering lawyers
> They know all too well that the whole hierarchy ends there[72]

Breton's poem shows this patriarchal conspiracy at work: that is, to the degree that Violette has been made an object of desire and an object of media fantasy, she accuses the economy of gender operating within and beneath relations of class.

It is likewise as an object of media attention that Violette's parricide comes into focus as an act of writing—or, more precisely, as an act of rewriting. Both Breton's poem and the surrealist book as a whole assert that the Violette Nozière who committed the "second parricide" so fearful and disruptive to the pan-cultural consensus about her motives was not the same Violette Nozière who poisoned her parents. The culturally toxic, public Violette is no longer subject to the sexual violence of her family but, as Breton explains, has become a mythological figure, a spectacle, and an object. If the Violette who killed her father remains inscribed within the logic of incest and rape, this latter figure, whose sex has taken wing, is both violent and *volant*—flying and stealing: stealing not only her father's money but his name as well.[73] The possibilities for play upon Violette's name dramatize the surrealist awareness of its fateful symbolism, its inscription of rape into the social fabric of her existence—what René Crevel, writing about Lacan's paranoiac patient "Aimée," called "the mockery of the name, destiny's pun."[74] In rendering this inscription perfectly literal, Violette's accusation that her father did in fact commit rape (*viol*) thus dramatically changes the terms of her father's murder. No longer a mere parricide, the murder achieves a kind of autobiographical revision, making conscious the "rape" within Violette's name as well as altering her *nom de famille*—if not by abolishing the name of the father, then by exterminating the father himself.

Man Ray's cover photograph for the surrealists' book helps to illustrate how this revision works (figure 6.3). The image depicts a broken letter "N" lying on a scattered bouquet of violets. Both a still life and an illuminated letter, it functions as a rebus that writes Violette's name in two distinct symbolic languages, in letters and in flowers. The photograph performs and allegorizes Violette's transmutation into language, an "alchemical" transformation that the surrealists recognize, as I have suggested, as the particular effect of her accusation. In addition to dramatizing the polyvalence of Violette's name, Man Ray's photograph also very clearly illuminates the violence that has shattered the "N" and strewn particles across the composition; the photograph might thus also be considered a portrait of the Nozière affair itself, insofar as this shattered composition invokes the complex narrative of murder and sexual violence that kept the Nozière affair intact and legible as a public spectacle. At the same time, the photograph's composition suggests that the cracked letter "N" itself caused this impact.

But what, precisely, is the nature of this impact? Certainly this is not a picture of revolutionary violence; if the photograph harbors an additional pun, then its homonym between the letter "N" and hatred, *la haine*, implies instead that any "real" violence depicted in the photograph is subject to its status as representation and allegory. To read the photograph as a form of propaganda would, in short, be absurd. Nor, I would argue, is Man Ray's photograph a portrait. The name illuminated in the image is less that of Violette the person than of "Violette Nozière" the phenomenon: the murder, the sensationalized criminal affair, and even the surrealist book. The impact of the photograph thus lies within the possibility of rendering textual, even legible, the violence of the case—the rape, the media voyeurism, the medical-legal judgment, as well as the murder itself. That is, the political project of the surrealist pamphlet lay in its recognition of the possibility for "alchemically" transforming into text and image the inexpressible, immeasurable patterns of real violence that the Nozière case set in motion, patterns which, according to the surrealists, already threatened France in the form of a growing fascist sympathy and a hegemonic structure of consensus willing to protect the state and the family at all costs. In other words, Violette's accusation of incestuous rape, her act of murder, and her resulting vilification by the press and the courts functioned together paranoiacally to accuse French patriarchy itself—Breton's "students old men corrupt journalists phony revolutionaries priests judges / Doddering lawyers"—of a conspiracy to engineer repression.

In order to evaluate the political significance of the surrealist book, it is critical to note that the surrealists' reaction to the Nozière affair is different from their relation to Violette herself as either a body, a subject, or the object of their attention. In the book she remains very much a set of signifiers, never photographed or represented "realistically" like Germaine Berton or the Papin sisters, insofar as her features, appearance, and physicality are not fixed in or by a single image. Rather, as Péret's poem and Man Ray's photograph each dramatize, Violette has become an exploded collection of the objects, images, and texts her "criminal" career have mobilized: her accusations, the rag, the drawing, the parts of her body. This becomes clear, too, in Hans Arp's drawing for the collection, in which the figure represented consists of nothing but an almost liquid mass of exploded forms (figure 6.4). Breton explains this process of transmutation into myth in the book's first lines, as a function of the media spectacle Violette has become:

> All the world's curtains drawn before your eyes
> It's pointless for them
> Before their mirror gasping for breath
> To stretch the jinxed bow of ancestry and posterity
> You no longer resemble anyone living or dead
> Mythological to the tips of your fingernails[75]

As both facial features and organs of perception, Violette's eyes register the recognition of a vicious cycle of "ancestry and posterity" whose continuity she can disrupt by literally severing her blood ties. Yet in the last lines of Breton's poem, the "you" addressed also becomes Violette watched, looked at; the visual logic of the poem shifts to portraying Violette as a spectacle, the world looking at her from beyond its curtains. And it is this Violette, the femme fatale, fugitive, and parricide forged in the aftermath of the crime, who is alchemically transformed into myth by the very incantation that both fascinated and threatened the press, that is, by her accusation that "my father sometimes forgets that I am his daughter." On the one hand, the surrealist book laments the loss of subjectivity occasioned by this transmutation: E. L. T. Mesens, for instance, writes that "there you are mute or nearly so now / in the feeble glimmer of the lanterns / of the judiciary labyrinth."[76] On the other hand, the book clearly recognizes this transformation as the moment of Violette's rise to disruptive, transformative power as both an object and a subject, as both a work of surrealist art and the author of a dramatic form of reinscription.

There is no doubt that for the surrealists, Violette is still very much an object, in the sense that she is the focus of their efforts rather than a participant in them; nevertheless,

Fig. 6.4. Jean Arp, untitled drawing for *Violette Nozières* (1933). Image courtesy of the Ryerson and Burnham Libraries, the Art Institute of Chicago. © 2008 Artists Rights Society (ARS), New York/ VG Bild-Kunst, Bonn.

the arguments made in the Nozière book all involve a realization of the stakes of her actions as a subject and the efforts of the press and psychiatric community to minimize or persecute them. Even the surrealist relation to Violette as an object is complicated by what it means to be considered as a surrealist object; beginning in the early 1930s a major focus of writers such as René Crevel, Salvador Dalí, and Claude Cahun was the investigation of the autonomous political and psychological function of material objects. Considered in their material, aesthetic, and psychoanalytical senses alike, certain objects, like the "motifs" of paranoia studied by Lacan in *Minotaure*, posed a crisis to the contemporary understanding of political subjectivity insofar as their participation in the coming-into-being of a subject was active, capable of determining consciousness and action rather than merely being determined and instrumentalized by it. As Lacan and Crevel suggest in their studies of paranoia, and as Maurice Heine later argues in his study of the *roman noir*, the dialectical interaction between unconscious motive and the historical reality of social conditions could be rendered visible in the stylistic motifs and objects that, by their definition, resisted being assimilated as conscious.

It is toward this "crisis of the object" that Bretonian surrealism oriented itself with increasing rigor in the 1930s as an inquiry into political and individual causality.[77] Indeed, Breton's general introduction to surrealism's activities in the face of the contemporary "malady" of European fascism, "What Is Surrealism?" (1934), centers on the role of the surrealist object:

It is essentially upon the *object* that surrealism's increasingly lucid eyes have remained open in recent years. Only the very close examination of the many recent speculations to which this *object* has publicly given rise (the oneiric object, the object that functions symbolically, the real and virtual object, the mute and moving object, the phantom object, the found object, etc.) can allow one to grasp the full import of surrealism's current temptations.

Breton's taxonomy emphasizes the surrealist group's analytical interest in objects for what he elsewhere explains as their ability to make "the distinction between the subjective and the objective lose its necessity and value."[78]

René Magritte's cover illustration for Breton's essay registers the high stakes of this eradication of the distinction between subjects and objects in a way that resonates strongly with the Nozière case (figure 6.5). In his drawing, titled "The Rape" ("Le Viol"), a woman's face becomes a torso; breasts stand in for eyes, and a pudenda for the mouth. The image reassembles the female body as a visual pun—the female figure, in the sense of its bodily shape, is conflated with the face (la *figure*)—in a way that recalls Crevel's words about "the mockery of the name, destiny's pun." Magritte's image draws its violence from the all too obvious distinction between subjects and objects that Breton wishes to dissolve: it presents the idea that rape imposes a narrative that re-scripts and rewrites the female subject as an inanimate collection of parts. In fact, Angela Carter's analysis of rape as "physical graffiti" seems almost to have Magritte's image in mind: "Somewhere in the fear of rape, is a more than mere physical terror of hurt and humiliation—a fear of psychic disintegration, of an essential dismemberment, a fear of a loss or disruption of the self which is not confined to the victim alone."[79] Violette Nozière's crime suggests, in turn, what Breton might mean by the ability of the surrealist object to make such distinctions lose their necessity and value. Violette, by radically rewriting the graffiti of her own history of sexual abuse, does not so much transform Magritte's monstrous image back into a face as kill its author, her father. In doing so, she participates in the authorship of her own transformation—a transformation into the author of this murderous erasure. In the public eye and in the surrealist book alike, she remains objectified as an exploded and fragmented collection of parts. Through this explosion, however, she comes into being as a subject, explicitly rather than implicitly subjected to the law.

I have been claiming that the Nozière case was also the apparatus through which the surrealists both recognized and articulated their diagnosis of disturbing tendencies in French society, the "malady" of fascism Breton confronts in "What Is Surrealism?" This malady, which became explicit during the pro-fascist riots that erupted in Paris on February 6, 1934, is evoked in *Violette Nozières* as the ideological consequence of the spectacle of female otherness both enjoyed and decried by the press. For the surrealists, the public outrage and excitement over Violette's attack on "the name of the father," the patriarchal law,

ANDRÉ BRETON

QU'EST-CE QUE LE
SURRÉALISME?

magritte

RENÉ HENRIQUEZ, Editeur
Rue d'Edimbourg, 13, BRUXELLES

Fig. 6.5. René Magritte, cover design
("Le Viol") for André Breton, *Qu'est-ce
que le surréalisme?* (1934). Image courtesy
of the Ryerson and Burnham Libraries,
the Art Institute of Chicago. © 2008
C. Herscovici, Brussels/Artists Rights
Society (ARS), New York.

reveals this consensus most egregiously. This, it seems, is the subject of Salvador Dalí's drawing for the collection, titled "Paranoiac Portrait of Violette Naziere (Noziere) / (Nazi, Dinazos, Naziere) / (Nose)" and accompanied by a line from Violette's testimony: "They were both asleep in their bed, and when I left at 11:30, they were snoring quietly" (figure 6.6). The image, a female bust imagined as a Dalíesque collection of objects and malleable parts, likewise emphasizes the figure's nose: stretched away from her face and topped with a fried egg, its weight supported by a wooden crutch. Graphically the image seems little more than an offshoot of his similarly anthropomorphic engravings for *Les Chants de Maldoror*, which would be published in 1934. What is remarkable about the image is its inscription, which "paranoiacally" derives from Violette's *nom de famille* not only the long nose (*nez*) of the drawing but also "Nazi" and "Dinazos"—the German and Belgian fascist parties, respectively.

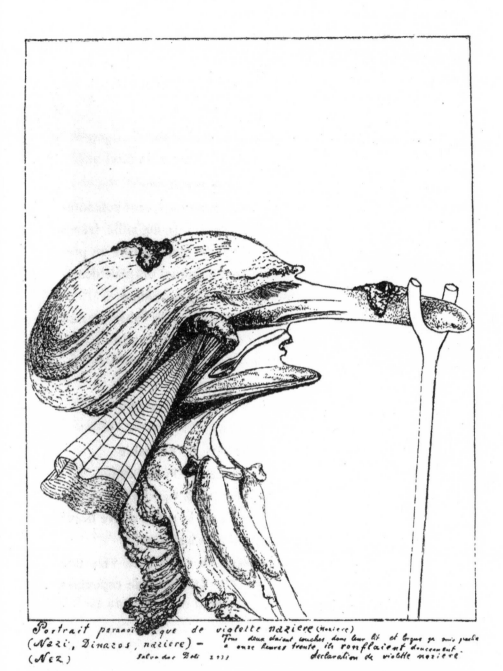

Fig. 6.6. Salvador Dalí, "Paranoiac Portrait of Violette Naziere (Noziere)/(Nazi, Dinazos, naziere)/(Nose)." In *Violette Nozières* (1933). Image courtesy of the Ryerson and Burnham Libraries, the Art Institute of Chicago. © 2008 Salvador Dalí, Gala-Salvador Dalí Foundation/Artists Rights Society (ARS), New York.

This derivation of fascism within both *the nom de famille* and the *nom du père* of French culture and French law, however "paranoiac" in Dalí's drawing, was a deep suspicion consistent with surrealist writing of this time. True antifascism, the surrealists argued, required more than a mobilization against some strange, alien threat. Rather, as the Nozière case fully revealed, it required a fundamental attack on petit-bourgeois values—not just the revolution in class relations to which the surrealists remained committed throughout the 1930s, but, even more fundamentally, a revolution in family values—a revolution, in other words, in gender relations. Like the rewriting of Violette's name, this revolution would require not only violence but also a form of writing and thinking that is at once stealing and flying, a surrealist *libération de l'esprit*.

CHAPTER SEVEN

PERSECUTION MANIA

My memory is encircled with blood. My memory has a belt of corpses!

Aimé Césaire, *Cahier d'un retour au pays natal* (1939)

n his article "Situation of the Writer in 1947," Jean-Paul Sartre advances the withering claim that the surrealists were "victims of the disaster of 1940." The reason for his saying this, he explains, "is that the moment for action had come and that none of them were armed for it. Some killed themselves, others are in exile; those who have returned are exiled among us. They were the proclaimers of catastrophe in the time of the fat cows; in the time of the lean cows they have nothing more to say."[1] By casting the surrealists as victims of history, Sartre achieves the double effect of accusing the surrealist movement of moral weakness in the face of real disaster and of subverting its earlier political activism as little more than a rhetorical pose. Most damning was the notion that the surrealists—and for Sartre, this meant André Breton in particular—did not remain in France to take part in the Resistance. In spite of all their talk of revolution and antifascist mobilization before the war, by 1940 they had fled to America, returning only after the smoke had cleared. Regardless of how inaccurate this accusation might be— since dozens of surrealists in fact remained in Nazi-occupied Europe—Sartre's charge was indicative of the condemnations of the movement's wartime dispersal that a number of intellectuals began voicing after the liberation. Tristan Tzara, who had left the group in 1935 in favor of Stalinism, publicly upbraided the surrealists in 1947 for abandoning the Resistance; even the young poets of the Main à Plume group, the underground surrealist organization founded in Paris during the Occupation, criticized Breton and his peers for their absenteeism.[2]

The charge of political quietism has endured as a lingering ignominy within surrealism's popular and critical legacy, especially since the charge does also seem to characterize the expatriate movement's markedly depoliticized artistic practices in the wartime United States. More focused on hermeticism and collective parlor games than on serving the war effort, surrealism is often said to have escaped Europe only to die as a movement in the United States. Even during the war, American critics dismissed surrealism's claim to political action altogether. In a 1940 essay, "Surrealism: A Dissenting Opinion," the historian Herbert J. Muller writes that "the most charitable course is to agree that the Surrealists are in fact socially irresponsible, and then to drop the whole subject of Revolution. Unhappily, however, charity is now a luxury." The surrealists, Muller argues, "exploit the dark powers that enslave man"; in doing so, they manage to be at once dangerously reactionary, even crypto-fascist, in their conceptual language, and yet utterly ineffectual on the political front.[3]

A similar charge of irresponsibility—albeit based less on collusion than on callousness—comes to us from the memoir of Jimmy Ernst, son of the surrealist painter Max Ernst and his first wife, the German art critic Louise Strauss-Ernst. In his account of the exiled surrealists in New York, Ernst excoriates the group's ostensible lack of concern for the realities of the Holocaust. At a dinner gathering in the Hamptons in the summer of 1944, the younger Ernst shared with his father the news of the deportation of his mother to Auschwitz and her subsequent death in the camp. Ernst writes:

> Max put an arm across my shoulders and we walked in silence. I saw tears in his eyes, and I realized that this was something I had not been able to do, cry. Standing on a dune, we looked down on a group of people sitting in a solemn, almost ritual, circle. "I don't believe it"—he almost whispered it—"they are still playing Breton's inane game of Verité . . . a cadre, a palace guard, playing at 'Surrealist revolution' . . . I'm sorry you saw this today."[4]

In the face of Auschwitz, where Louise Strauss-Ernst had been taken from the Drancy concentration camp in Vichy-controlled Paris, the surrealists played games. Jimmy Ernst, himself an émigré, did not fault Breton and his group for fleeing Europe—a necessary decision, given the stridency of their antifascist politics and their activities as leftist public intellectuals—but became disgusted with their deliberate self-marginalization during a time of world catastrophe. Breton's claim that the surrealists strove "to be objectors in every respect to whatever particular obligation this world attempts to reduce us" might have sounded like a valiant resistance to fascism and Stalinist orthodoxy in 1935.[5] But it now played out as a stubborn and even inhuman refusal to compromise the group's antinationalist, antibourgeois, and anti-Stalinist principles for the sake of fighting Hitler. Why—Ernst's memoir asks—couldn't Breton tear himself away from his surrealist games long enough even to mourn a victim of the Holocaust?

The question of surrealism's political responsibility has tended, both during and since the war, to attach itself to Breton, not only overlooking the fates and actions of other surrealists but ignoring the political refusals of other surrealists in the group as well. Few attacks—or defenses—of the movement's wartime activities have considered it necessary, for instance, to address the women artists and writers of the movement, only further contributing to the overall marginalization of surrealism's female participants. Perhaps such critics have already presumed their status as victims of history. But there is more at stake here than gender bias: it was precisely in the shadow of Hitlerism that women began to assert an active role in the development of surrealist thinking, from Claude Cahun's defense of surrealist poetics in her 1934 polemic Les Paris sont ouverts, to Leonora Carrington's haunting tales of bodily transformation and bodily invasion in the later 1930s. Most significantly, Carrington's largely autobiographical narrative Down Below, published in the New York surrealist magazine VVV in 1944, both encapsulates the movement's antifascist forebodings of the 1930s and confronts the reality of France's capitulation to the Nazis in 1940. Its politics, though, are reluctant rather than militant, and in many ways Carrington's text—which describes the writer's escape through the Pyrenées and subsequent descent into psychosis—seems only to confirm critiques of surrealism's fugitivity. Indeed, whereas Cahun narrowly escaped execution for her Resistance activities on the occupied Channel Island of Jersey, Carrington, like Breton, fled to New York, and was thus never "engaged" in overt resistance.

By the time Sartre published "Situation of the Writer in 1947," Carrington was no longer exiled in the United States but had made Mexico her permanent home. Her absence from occupied France was not rendered visible by a return to liberated Paris. To the extent that she later participated in the 1947 Surrealist Exhibition, it might be said that she did so only as an absence, as an artist whose work already belonged to another place, another order. In a letter to the publisher Henri Parisot written around the time of the French publication of Down Below in 1945, Carrington writes: "I am no longer the Ravishing young girl who passed through Paris, in love—I am an old lady who has lived a lot and I have changed—. . . . Like an old Mole who swims beneath cemeteries I realize that I've always been blind—I seek to understand Death in order to have less fear; I seek to empty the images that have made me blind."[6] Alluding both to Marx's "old mole" of proletarian revolution as well as to her own blindness to the forces of historical change, Carrington's letter enforces a split between her prewar intellectual life in Europe and her postwar career as an "old lady" seeking to understand death.

Yet the composition and publication of Down Below already testifies to Carrington's excentricity from the closed circuit of French intellectual debate in the immediate postwar years. Dictated to the surrealist writer Pierre Mabille and his wife, Jeanne Megnen, who transcribed it, the memoir was published in VVV in 1944, well under the radar of any postwar thinking about the situation of the French writer in 1947. Yet the most significant factor that removed Carrington from any consideration of her wartime political engagement—negative or positive—is that her escape from occupied France through Spain precipitated a mental breakdown that left her incarcerated in a Spanish asylum during the early part of the war. It might be said that Carrington was exempt from Sartrean critique because her "victimization" was literal, and thus invalid as a metaphor for the moral or spiritual failure of surrealism to maintain its commitment to revolutionary principles. Yet even if no one has overtly blamed Carrington for abandoning the Resistance—either in body or in mind—her narrative of this period is remarkable for its own self-accusation, its own assessment of complicity.

Down Below is as much a memoir of self-punishment as it is a narrative of Carrington's wartime descent into madness. This self-punishment is discursive: the text frames her mental breakdown in terms of an understanding of paranoia derived from surrealist and early Lacanian theories of the illness as a delusional system of self-punishment through which the paranoiac subject strikes out at her ego-ideal in misrecognizing her own identificatory desire as a persecution from without. Down Below resists its critical reception as a purely interior journey into madness; it also resists the triumphalism of Marina Warner's claim that Carrington "had truly experienced the dementia Breton and Paul Éluard had only been able to simulate in The Immaculate Conception of 1930, though their impersonation of insanity later won Jacques Lacan's applause."[7] Down Below is as much a work of paranoiac theory as a memoir of Carrington's nervous illness; its paranoia is characterized not only by its unconscious production of symptoms (interpretive delirium, persecution mania) but also by its auto-analysis and its self-conscious ties to surrealist discourse.[8] Indeed, Carrington's narrative of "inner experience" is in dialogue with the writings on paranoia that form a central part of surrealist thinking in the 1930s, and again in the mid-1940s under the aegis of the journal VVV: from the psychotic memoir of Daniel Paul Schreber, which formed the basis of Freud's theory of paranoia, to the surrealist theories of paranoid self-punishment that emerged from writings by Dalí, Lacan, Crevel, Breton, and Ernst, as well as in the visual works of Victor Brauner and Hans Bellmer. At the same time, its internal references to the work of Pierre Mabille, best known for his book The Mirror of the Marvelous (1940), show Carrington in the process of redirecting paranoiac theory toward contemporary surrealist thinking about collective social myths. It is through this intertextuality that Carrington's own delusional responses to and reconstructions of the world crisis under fascism become linked to her interrogation of the surrealist political thinking to which she contributed.

Carrington's writing, to which Breton was especially responsive (dedicating a number of tributes to her work in VVV and elsewhere), reveals much about the exiled movement's political and intellectual practices during the war. Her self-accusatory exploration of psychosis both preempts and anatomizes the demand for intellectual "commitment" levied by postwar critics; its narrative of madness and incarceration addresses such questions of responsibility, agency, and historical causality as more than conscious acts of will. Carrington's memoir thus continues to pursue prewar surrealist questions of causality and motive that looked to the psychoanalytic study of paranoia as a means for diagnosing political as well as criminal persecution. In particular, her account of persecution mania both extends and revises the movement's tendency in the late 1930s to depict political violence through images of persecuted women.

Like *Down Below* itself, my discussion in this chapter interrogates the fate of the surrealist movement's discourses of crime, violence, and intellectual responsibility under the real conditions of fascism and world war. It addresses the paradox of the movement's staunch commitment to antifascism and its equally staunch refusal to abandon its critique of other systems and regimes—whether Stalinism or Western bourgeois culture—for the sake of political expediency. I argue that Carrington's attempt—however self-punishing—to look beyond the politics of immediate action contributes to a body of war-era writing and art that likewise strove to articulate new forms of commitment, collectivity, and knowledge. As Breton writes in 1942, "Not only must the exploitation of man cease, but also the exploitation of man by the so-called 'god' of absurd and exasperating memory."[9] Under global conditions of persecution and dispersal, the surrealist group expanded, rather than focused, its field of inquiry to include the social myths and historical patterns that perpetuate suffering and social order alike.

The Exact Representation of the World

In 1938 Carrington, who had joined the surrealist group in Paris the previous year as a young English art student, took up residence in the village of St. Martin d'Ardèche with her lover, the painter Max Ernst. Ernst had himself temporarily withdrawn from the surrealist group, largely out of loyalty to his friend Paul Éluard, who had been dismissed from the movement for his embrace of Stalinism.[10] Ernst's retirement to the countryside, like Carrington's, has often been portrayed as an idyllic respite from the rigors of antifascist politics, their mutual creativity inspired as much by a fragile denial of reality as by the village's romantic setting. Their work from this period, however, testifies to the imminent catastrophe their fantasy life held temporarily at bay. The majority of Carrington's published stories from this period—"The House of Fear," "The Oval Lady," "The Debutante," "A Man in Love," "Uncle Sam Carrington"—all end abruptly and inconclusively, their protagonists fleeing the scene at the height of the conflict, even occasionally in mid-sentence. Such departures tend to be read as autobiographical, as allegories of Carrington's abandonment of her upper-class British family, or of her and Ernst's mutual abandonment of Parisian surrealism. Yet the stories' lack of resolution seems more threatening than liberatory, populating Carrington's fictional universe with a menagerie of monstrous figures and imbuing it with an unsettling aura of anxiety. Like the zoomorphic figures Carrington and Ernst famously developed as their mythological alter egos—Carrington the wild horse, Ernst the "bird superior" Loplop—the prewar short stories give objective form to fears whose sources, and whose consequences, might otherwise remain beyond comprehension.[11]

The possibility that such scarcely eluded fears might have been grounded in the historical reality of fascism had become a central concern by the time Carrington wrote *Down Below*. Reconstructing the author's escape from France after the Nazi occupation, as well as her subsequent internment in a Spanish mental hospital, *Down Below* nevertheless takes pains at first to maintain an indifference toward the war. Early in the narrative she writes:

> Various events were taking place in the outside world: the collapse of Belgium, the entry of the Germans in France. All of this interested me very little and I had no fear whatsoever within me. The village was thronged with Belgians, and some soldiers who had entered my home accused me of being a spy because someone had been looking for snails at night, with a lantern, near my house. Their threats impressed me very little indeed, for I knew that I was not destined to die.[12]

Yet even as Carrington claims she had no fear within her, her text substitutes for it an objectified fear that exists outside and around her. That is, her disavowed fear of German invasion is replaced by a systematized proliferation of delusional events, prompted by Ernst's internment in first a French, then later a Vichy concentration camp. These events punctuate Carrington's descent into madness: automotive breakdowns, zombified citizens, networks of spies, and systems of hypnotically controlled political influence. Mediated through the deeply personal fact of her separation from Ernst, Carrington's response to the Nazi invasion replaces "internal" fear with external trauma, a correspondence whose recurring pattern structures her delirium of interpretation. Carrington's delusional system takes the form of a growing set of personal symbols and artifacts through which she maps world conflict in terms of her own body and the objects and people immediately surrounding her. The mythic structures of *Down Below* memorialize the traumatic historical forces to which Carrington ostensibly expresses indifference—not only the very real threat of German world domination, but also the atrocities of the Holocaust, the Falangist massacres of the Spanish civil war, and Carrington's own rape by Spanish soldiers.

Carrington begins to develop this system early in the narrative, after Ernst has been detained for the second time. In a series of events that uncannily mirrors France's two defeats—the first in the *drôle de guerre*, the second in the construction of the Vichy regime—Ernst is incarcerated first in 1939 as a "citizen of the German Reich" and again in 1940 after being "denounced by a deaf and dumb fellow who alleged that Max had sent light signals to the enemy."[13] Returning to her house after this second detention, Carrington spends the next day weeping and vomiting, explaining to Pierre Mabille:

> I had realised the injustice of society, I wanted first of all to cleanse myself, then go beyond its brutal ineptitude. My stomach was the seat of that society, but also the place in

which I was united with all the elements of the earth. It was—to resort to your own metaphor—the mirror of the earth, the reflection of which is just as real as the person reflected. That mirror—my stomach—had to be rid of the thick layers of filth (the accepted formulas) in order properly, clearly, and faithfully to reflect the earth; and when I say "the earth," I mean of course all the earths, stars, suns in the sky and on the earth, as well as all the stars, suns, and earths of the microbes' solar system.[14]

More than just an expression of personal grief, Carrington's writing systematizes her self-torture as a "mirror" of the world crisis that Ernst's arrest otherwise overshadows. The allusion to Mabille's work on mirrors, moreover, renders this system explicit: the mirroring performed by Carrington's body refers to a phenomenon of emerging self-consciousness produced by a subject's identification with images that function as exteriorizations of the self. "Soon," as Mabille writes in a 1938 essay in *Minotaure*, "amidst millions of actions, man perceives himself as the essential pivot of all experiences. The muddled sensation of being develops into a clear consciousness when it is translated into representation." While outlining a proto-Lacanian "mirror phase" in the development of selfhood, Mabille's notion of mirroring also takes on an epistemological function: "The senses are turned toward the exterior, toward the exploration of the exterior world."[15] Reciprocally, Carrington's experience of becoming "the mirror of the earth" pathologically inverts her conscious denial of involvement in the exterior world of European politics. Her expressions of grief over Ernst's incarceration form the basis of her delirious method for re-internalizing the trauma of France's defeats, registering her response as a crisis in her inner organs, the "down below" of her digestive system. These delusions form an interpretive system through which Carrington assimilates urgent problems of historical causality and historical agency.

  Down Below reveals its psychoanalytic self-consciousness by recounting how Carrington's friend Catherine "falsely" psychoanalyzes this initial interpretive delirium. Her diagnosis is that Carrington is torturing herself for her "unconscious desire to get rid for the second time of [her] father: Max, whom [she] had to eliminate if [she] wanted to live." Carrington considers this analysis "fragmentary," for not only does it reduce her psychic crisis to a repetition of the Freudian family romance, but also it suggests that the Nazi invasion performed a kind of wish fulfillment. In other words, Carrington's friend is proposing that she is happy to have allowed circumstances to rid her of Max Ernst's paternalistic presence. What this diagnosis ignores, though, is Carrington's disavowed horror of the all too obvious causality behind Ernst's role in her unconscious life—that is, the Nazi invasion itself, which Ernst both represents, as a German, and resists, as an antifascist surrealist. The fear of this invasive threat becomes discernible in Carrington's explanation that her friends' arguments for fleeing France "were distilling into me, hour after hour, a growing fear. For Catherine, the Germans meant rape. I was not afraid of that, I attached no importance to it. What caused panic to rise within me was the thought of automatons, of thoughtless, fleshless beings."[16] It is one such automaton who has arrested Ernst. As Carrington writes, Ernst was led away "under the escort of a gendarme who carried a rifle"—not a German storm trooper, in other words, but a French gendarme mechanically obeying the will of the occupying regime. Thus, although Carrington's self-torture seems to memorialize the grief of this moment, her increasing delirium instead rehearses the trauma of this arrest itself. As she begins her escape by car into Spain, the arrest is repeated in disguised form. When she overhears Catherine say, "The brakes have jammed," Carrington responds: "'Jammed!' I, too, was jammed within, by forces foreign to my conscious will, which were also paralyzing the mechanism of the car. This was the first stage of my identification with the external world. I was the car."[17] This identification of the jammed brakes with Carrington's own state of emotional paralysis fearfully anticipates the body-snatching influence of the Nazis. That is, the fear lurking behind this "jamming"—itself a form of arrest, in the most literal sense—is the projection of the thoughtless automatism she associates with the systematic reproduction of Nazi ideology. This identification with external objects becomes all the more visible, and all the more linked to fantasies of grandeur and persecution, upon Carrington's arrival in Spain.

What is perhaps most remarkable about this complex symptomology is the precision with which Carrington narrates it. As if wary of succumbing to the "wild" analysis of her friend, her interpretive delirium, however pathological, organizes itself systematically. The narrative, structured according to this delirium, is no less systematic. As Jacqueline Chenieux-Gendron has written, Carrington's memoir bears "a quasi-scientific motivation" whose writing functions auto-analytically to decode the shocking phenomena Carrington's protagonist experiences in her conscious and unconscious life.[18] Just as Carrington's earlier stories, with their anthropomorphic horses, hyenas, and birds, reflect the psychic mythmaking explored in Freud's case studies of hysteria and animal phobia, *Down Below* registers the theoretical and analytical function of paranoia. Indeed, Carrington's writing reflects Freud's famous remark that a paranoiac's theories reveal "a striking similarity with our theory," the delirium and mania of the illness bearing a distinct resemblance to the theories developed by psychoanalysis in order to diagnose paranoia. "The paranoiac," Freud writes, "perceives the external world and takes into account any alteration that may happen within it."[19]

As Freud explains in his case study of Daniel Paul Schreber's *Memoirs of My Nervous Illness*, paranoia represents the response to "a world catastrophe," which for Freud signifies a psychic rather than a geopolitical disaster. "The patient," he writes, "has withdrawn from the persons in his environment and from the external world generally the libidinal cathexis which he has hitherto directed on to them. . . . The end of the world is the projection of this internal catastrophe; for his subjective world has come to an end since he has withdrawn his love from it."[20] Yet whereas for Freud this catastrophe refers primarily to a crisis in sexuality, a disguised and inverted representation of a repressed homosexual desire, for Carrington the catastrophe is geopolitical and sexual at the same time. Indeed, her memoir remains faithful to a surrealist understanding of paranoia as what Lacan calls a "coherent structure of immediate noumenal apprehension of oneself and the world," noting the material basis of the illness in social trauma (see chapter 6). Freud's notion that paranoia's interpretive delirium is in fact the beginning of a solution to this "catastrophe" of withdrawal is rendered explicit in Carrington's projection of her biomorphic system of internal strife onto the entire city of Madrid. She writes:

> In the political confusion and the torrid heat, I convinced myself that Madrid was the world's stomach and that I had been chosen for the task of restoring this digestive organ to health. I believed that all the anguish had accumulated in me and would dissolve in the end, and this explained to me the force of my emotions. I believed that I was capable of bearing this dreadful weight and of drawing from it a solution for the world. The dysentery I suffered from later was nothing but the *illness* of Madrid taking shape in my intestinal tract.[21]

In this passage Carrington's earlier notion of mirroring as a dialectical process of identification with the external world fully assumes the megalomaniac properties of paranoia: she posits her own body as both the locus of and cure for Madrid's political illness—namely, its transformation into a fascist state after the Spanish civil war.

At the same time, this projection of her own "internal catastrophe" onto Madrid is doubled by an analogous transference of her psychically overdetermined attachment to Max Ernst onto another man. Both Carrington and her narrative abandon Ernst, replacing him with the more villainous figure of Van Ghent, an employee of her father's company, ICI (the aptly named Imperial Chemicals), who becomes the first of several hostile figures in Carrington's increasingly acute persecution fantasies. In a deliberate act of substitution, she offers Ernst's passport to Van Ghent, who refuses it; Carington's interpretation of this refusal presents what we might call a sublation of her friend Catherine's earlier "wild" analysis, as she writes: "When he refused to take Max's passport, I remember that I replied: 'Ah! I understand, I must kill him myself,' i.e. disconnect myself from Max." In supplanting Ernst as the central figure in Carrington's delusional system, Van Ghent becomes "my father, my enemy, and the enemy of mankind."[22] And thus, as the focus of her persecution fantasies, Van Ghent provides a delusional "solution" to the problem of Madrid's illness; realizing that Van Ghent is the cause of this illness, Carrington reports him to the British embassy in Spain:

> I endeavored to convince [the British consul] that the World War was being waged hypnotically by a group of people—Hitler and Co.—who were represented in Spain by Van Ghent; that to vanquish him it would suffice to understand his hypnotic power; we would

then stop the war and liberate the world, which was "jammed," like me and Catherine's Fiat; that instead of wandering aimlessly in political and economic labyrinths, it was essential to believe in our metaphysical force and divide it among human beings, who would thus be liberated.[23]

Once again Carrington's paranoia articulates her fear of Nazi invasion as the propagation of thoughtless robots, here explained as a system of control by hypnosis made possible by a conspiracy between fascist governments and her father's company, Imperial Chemicals, which Van Ghent represented.

Yet insofar as Carrington's persecution fantasy offers a response to the problem of agency in the face of the monumental historical crisis of the war, the possibility of this mania as an actual solution is brutally interrupted. When Carrington is raped by Spanish soldiers—an incident she suppresses in the VVV version of the memoir but renders explicit in the 1987 revision[24]—this violence is especially disastrous because it not only realizes Catherine's earlier fear of Nazi invasion as a fear of rape but realizes Carrington's fear of "hypnotic" influence as well: the fascist soldiers in Spain did not even have to be German in order to become rapists. From this moment on Carrington's delusions become increasingly acute, prompting her visit to the British embassy and subsequently her institutionalization in Santander. Yet rather than destroying Carrington's paranoiac system, these violent irruptions of "reality" into her life become absorbed as part of her systematized delusional universe in the asylum.

On her awakening after a long blackout, Carrington's paranoia achieves an apotheosis through which her symbolic schemas undergo a process of condensation. Her treatments at the asylum are represented as the most horrific forms of torture, her injections of the drug Cardiazol staged as traumatic repetitions of her rape in Madrid. The drug produces in her the effects of "absence of motion, fixation, and horrible reality"—a simulation of the very automatism she has most feared; the Cardiazol injection becomes the new trauma to which she now responds, albeit with an expression of horror denied her rape. As she writes, describing the moment of her first injection:

A new era began with the most terrible and blackest day in my whole life. How could I write this when I don't even dare think about it? I am terribly anguished, yet I cannot continue living alone with such a memory. . . . I know that once this has been written down, I shall be delivered. You must know, otherwise I shall be persecuted to the end of my living days. But shall I be able to express with mere words the horror of that day?[25]

The shocking pain of the injection produces a new state of arrest, analogous to hysteria: a neurotic obedience to the law of the asylum.[26] These hysterical interludes mark a simultaneous shift in her attentions toward the physical environment of the asylum itself.

This shift in Carrington's thinking allows her to map out her paranoiac "representation of the world" in ways that forge a synthesis between her individual catastrophe, the crisis of the war, and the asylum. Carrington's interpretive delirium begins at this point to play a centripetal role in structuring her consciousness, as Chénieux-Gendron has written; the "down below" of her digestive organs is now projected outward as the name for a pavilion in the hospital that symbolizes the depths of suffering from which must recover. As Carrington explains:

> I believed that I was being put through purifying tortures so that I might attain Absolute Knowledge, at which point I could live Down Below. The pavilion with this name was for me the Earth, the Real World, Paradise, Eden, Jerusalem. Don Luis and Don Mariano were God and His Son. I thought they were Jewish; I thought that I, a Celtic and Saxon Aryan, was undergoing my sufferings to avenge the Jews for the persecutions they were being subjected to. Later, with full lucidity, I would go Down Below, as the third person of the Trinity.[27]

This cosmological, mythical system recalls Daniel Paul Schreber's similarly elaborate theories of cosmic influence, which he relates in his 1903 memoir. Indeed, if we compare the diagrams published in the two memoirs, we can see that each image represents the asylum's physical landscape as the concrete form of the authors' paranoiac systems. Schreber's diagram of Dr. Fleischig's Nerve Clinic at the University of Leipzig, reprinted in his *Memoirs of My Nervous Illness*, appears to be a highly rationalized floor plan of the asylum (figure 7.1). As Schreber writes, it includes "such details as are necessary for my purposes." The clinic, which seems in the rendition to stretch indefinitely off the page to the left, is divided into a male and a female wing; this is consistent with Schreber's notions that he was himself on occasion miraculously transformed from a man into a woman. It is also consistent with the other ordering principles of his delusional system, from its hierarchical religious schemes to its notion that Dr. Fleischig's job was to divide souls, as the doctor himself was divided, into "lower," middle, and "superior" forms. The context for Schreber's inclusion of the drawing in the *Memoirs* is his effort to sort out his recollections of the early months of his confinement: he wishes to distinguish "mere dream images from experiences in a waking state, that is to say to be certain how far all that I had experienced was in fact historical reality."[28] Schreber's document does not so much help him recover a lost sense of certainty, however, as impose a simulacrum of certainty, representing uncertainty only residually, as a little dotted line that extends outward from the male wing. Schreber's map documents the order his persecutions obey in a way that calls to mind at once his subjection to the tyranny of his illness, as well as to the authority of Fleischig's institution.

Carrington's more intricate drawing of the Santander hospital likewise presents both

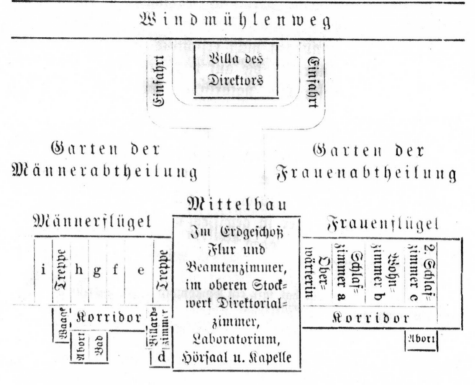

Fig. 7.1. Daniel Paul Schreber, map of Dr. Fleischig's Nerve Clinic. In *Denkwürdigkeiten eines Nervenkranken* (*Memoirs of My Nervous Illness*) (1903).

a map of suffering and an imposition of certainty (figure 7.2). Unlike Schreber's diagram, though, Carrington's map expands its purview from the regimented structure of a single building to the broader geography of the Santander compound. Carrington's map, while reminiscent of Schreber's diagram and other such works of outsider art, represents a later phase in her thinking in which every aspect of her delusional system has become overdetermined. That is, the infinitely complicated universe of Carrington's "representation of the world" evokes the tortured incarnations of the catastrophe through which her illness and her physical body alike had passed.

It is through this complexity and overdetermination that the map proposes a solution, however delusional, to Carrington's world catastrophe. Representing the "Sun Room," a separate building on the asylum grounds, the symbolic representation of "Down Below" as a sunlike orb suggests the possibility of a redemptive final point. Carrington writes: "There, rid of all my familiar objects, which belonged to a murky and emotional past and would have darkened my labors, alone and naked, with my bed sheet and the sun—the

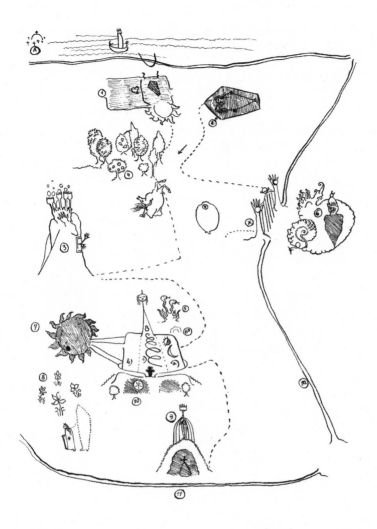

A.—A desert scene, Covagonda cemetery
B.—High wall surrounding the garden
X.—Gate of the garden
1.—Villa Covagonda
2.—Radiography
3—Villa Pilar
4—Apple trees and view of Casa Blanca and the valley
5.—"Africa".
6.—Villa Amachu
6B—Arbor

7.—"Down Below"
8.—Kitchen garden
9.—Bower and cave
10.—Don Mariano's "place"
11.—"Outside World" Street
a.—My room at "Down Below," the eclipse and the limbos
b.—The lair
c.—The library
      Wide "Down Below" alley

Fig. 7.2. Leonora Carrington, map of Santander, from "Down Below," VVV 4 (1944). Image courtesy of the Pennsylvania State University Special Collections Library. © 2008 Leonora Carrington/Artists Rights Society (ARS), New York.

sheet united to my body in a dance which concreted the abstraction of the figures—I found it essential to solve the problem of my Ego in relation to the Sun."[29] Here again, though, the map and its systematic set of "problems" and solutions impose an explanation upon her illness; Carrington's "solution" requires purging her familiar objects, just as her eventual "cure" toward the narrative's close requires eliminating all her delusional systems, which lose their mystical significance. The story, likewise, has been celebrated as Carrington's cure, her path of return from madness. The disoccultation of her magical systems is tragic, though, rather than triumphant, representing a disenchantment of the world she has painfully reconstructed, as well as a new obedience to "accepted formulas." Like her short stories, *Down Below* ends abruptly and inconclusively with Carrington's departure before the consequences of her disenchantment can be fully explored.

In the years to follow, beginning with the composition of the memoir itself in 1943, Carrington would return to the hermetic systems she devised in order to explore the significance of paranoiac thinking as something more than just delusion. As she explains at the moment of her first injection with Cardiazol, for instance, the demands of paranoiac expression—and the sharing of memory—become part of the "cure" never possible to fulfill at the Santander institution but only in the story's telling. It is in the form of exploration and analysis, to which her memoir is dedicated, that Carrington's experiences of persecution can work toward the restoration of health. As the fruit of her epistemological project in reliving the horror of her wartime experiences, this "health" is no longer simply personal but collective, mapped out on the plane of humanism itself. Whereas her own memoir is "but an embryo of knowledge," Carrington expresses "the necessity that others be with me that we may feed each other with our knowledge and thus constitute the Whole."[30]

Carrington, as I have suggested, structured *Down Below* in relation to surrealism's investigations into paranoia. As René Crevel argued in his 1933 "Notes toward a Psychodialetic," paranoia is an illness whose study demands the reconciliation of historical materialism with psychoanalysis, owing to its social as well as psychic development, as I discussed in the preceding chapter. Paranoia was thus politically valuable for the way its auto-punitive structure systematically accuses the very ideological forces and "accepted formulas" that Carrington attempts to purge from her system in the opening pages of *Down Below*. For Crevel, as for Carrington, these accepted formulas, this "thick layer of filth," represented the full force of bourgeois social conditioning on which the spread of fascism throughout Europe was predicated. In this light, the cure for paranoia did not simply mean a reduction of the illness's symptoms (interpretive delirium, megalomania, persecution mania) but, more significantly, required a recognition of the subject's self-punishing drive as having a social genesis.

Recalling Crevel's affirmation of "the healing power of moral illness, shock, and organic illness," Carrington's autobiographical case study engenders a form of self-accusation that maintains surrealism's earlier assault on forms of complicity with totalizing forms of power: colonialism, bourgeois capitalism, and especially fascism. Her persecution mania accuses, but cannot fully expunge, the hypnotic forces of complicity into which she finds herself immersed, even against her will: the capitulation of Spain and France to fascism; the "empire" of capitalism and respectability represented by her father's company, Imperial Chemicals; and, perhaps most broadly, the hypnotic seduction of passivity and escape as an alibi against individual responsibility, whether political, ethical, or mental. Carrington's narrative, in other words, cannot fully reconcile itself with a belief in the healing power of paranoiac illness in the face of the metastasis of fascism into an overwhelming world crisis. In this sense Carrington's entire text places the surrealist discourse of paranoia "under arrest": it too is jammed up, subject to the same accusations of complicity and social conditioning that constituted its value as a critical tool.

The House of Fear

Carrington's Down Below represents both the culmination and the revision of the discourse on persecution that characterized the surrealist group's artistic response to fascism in the late 1930s. Much as Carrington's physical suffering becomes a paranoiac mirror of geopolitical catastrophe, a significant body of prewar surrealist work depicts tortured bodies and persecuted women as a means for theorizing the biomechanics of fascist power. Carrington's expression of panic at "the thought of automatons, of thoughtless, fleshless beings" is anticipated in the Romanian surrealist Victor Brauner's Monsieur K. paintings; depicting a bloated, Ubuesque gentleman in serial guises, the paintings satirize Monsieur K. as a physical embodiment of power whose threat seems to lie in his capacity for replication.

In The Strange Case of Monsieur K. (figure 7.3), which dates from 1933, a painting owned by Breton and reproduced, in part, in the Belgian surrealist journal Documents 34, the titular figure appears in thirty-six separate panels, his massive body figured to represent a series of geopolitical bodies and ideological state apparatuses: Mr. K. appears in bourgeois formal dress, military regalia, clerical vestments, nude, and in combinations thereof; he also appears as a topographical landmass, a fortified city, and a weapons stockpile. In addition, half the panels depict Monsieur K. in a series of sexual poses with a virtually shapeless female figure; four of these final panels have been blacked out, as if censored or unrepresentable, recalling the episodic structure of a pornographic text such as Sade's 120 Days of Sodom. Yet the painting's seriality illustrates more the reproducibility of power itself than the systematic intensification of its effects; it satirizes with particular urgency the nearly seamless continuity between bourgeois masculinity, military order, clerical au-

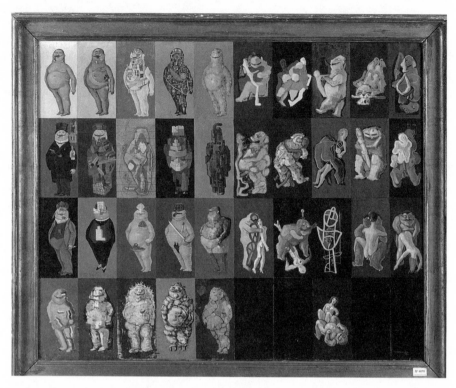

Fig. 7.3. Victor Brauner, *L'Étrange cas de Monsieur K.* (1933). Image courtesy of the Musée d'Art Moderne, Saint-Étienne Métropole. Photograph by Yves Bresson. © 2008 Artists Rights Society (ARS), New York/ADAGP, Paris.

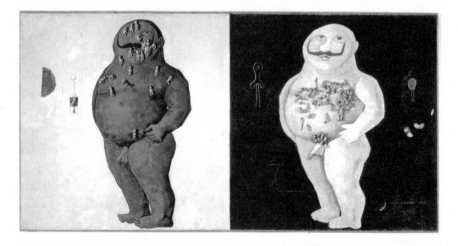

Fig. 7.4. Victor Brauner, *Force de concentration de Monsieur K.* (1934). Oil, plastic dolls, artificial plant pieces, and metal wire on canvas, on paper. Photo: Philippe Migeat. Musee National d'Art Moderne, Centre Georges Pompidou, Paris, France. Photo Credit: CNAC/MNAM/Dist. Réunion des Musées Nationaux/Art Resource, N.Y. © 2008 Artists Rights Society (ARS), New York/ADAGP, Paris.

thority, and nationalist fervor. The reproducibility of such a hegemonic bloc—and its dehumanizing results—is further dramatized in Brauner's 1934 diptych *Monsieur K's Power of Concentration* (figure 7.4). The twin panels of this slightly later work transfer the seriality of the former painting onto the plastic baby dolls and wooden dowels concentrated near Mr. K's head, chest, and genitals. Here the reproduction of Mr. K's power is rendered corporeal, just as the depiction of power itself is rendered bodily in the earlier painting: the serializing and dehumanizing effects of this reproduction are played out through the biomechanical reproduction of anonymous plastic dolls, his ideological as well as physical offspring.

Brauner, along with André Masson, would continue to portray excesses of power satirically, producing scabrous images of Hitler (Brauner) and the pact between Franco, Poincaré, and Hitler (Masson) throughout the 1930s and early 1940s. Yet the majority of surrealist art of this period is notable for its tendency to couch its politics within depictions of victimhood rather than portrayals of fascist aggression, its visual art notorious for its fixation on what Mary Ann Caws has called its "ladies shot and painted."[31] Drawing on the group's theories of paranoia as well as on its continued exploration of sadism, the surrealists increasingly framed their investigations into political persecution biomorphically, articulating their diagnosis of fascism in corporeal terms. Yet whereas in 1933 the group stressed the extent to which bourgeois masculinity and morality provided a screen for the real threat of fascist influence, by the later part of the decade—and throughout the war years—they increasingly pursued the idea that Hitler, Franco, and Mussolini were but the manifest embodiments of a broader fascizing tendency in Western culture.

Accordingly, in spite of its unflagging antifascism, the surrealist group refused to limit its political attention to a single target, scorning the French Popular Front for its "criminal" neutrality toward the Spanish civil war, and refusing to support the growing nationalism in French leftist politics. The radical left was all the more suspect. The fate of Leon Trotsky, expelled from the Communist Party in 1929 and denied asylum in France, became a symptom of the purgative inclinations of Stalinism and the French Republic alike; as the surrealist declaration "The Truth about the Moscow Trials" (1936) maintained, "we have no illusions that Stalin and his acolytes, who have entered into a pact with the capitalist states, are doing everything in their power to fragment [the revolutionary elements in Spain, Italy, and Germany]."[32] Even the surrealists' own political activism fell victim to suspicions of collusion: *Counter-Attack*, the collaborative antifascist venture launched in October 1935 by Bataille, Breton, Heine, Cahun, and others, promised a more "virile" form of political activism than the more socially conservative Popular Front, but foundered in May 1936 as a result of the group's discomfort with Bataille's ideas about appropriating the political tools of fascism. Such a multiplication of persecution mania within the surrealists' political field finds its expression, I contend, in the group's artistic and theoretical attention to the mechanics of implication.

In 1933 the surrealist group's interest in persecuted female criminals such as the Papin sisters and Violette Nozières (see chapter 6) targeted the decomposition of the women's bodies as an effect of their media presence and subjection to legal and medical scrutiny. In the later 1930s, though, such persecuted figures tend to lose their historical specificity, becoming deindividuated as dolls, mannequins, or faceless victims. There have been a number of scholarly explanations for this tendency, from the psychoanalytic to the psycho-political: surrealist works attack the female body, some critics maintain, as the punitive response to a perceived threat against male dominance, a misogynistic projection of social or political anxiety framed as a masochistic fear of castration. Especially in the wake of the fascist victory in Spain, the surrealists increasingly depicted fascism as a bodily threat, but also as a threat that could be represented in bodily terms. As Robin Greeley has noted:

> Fascism's deadly recoding of human desire into the public sphere . . . forced a reevaluation of the [surrealist] movement's efforts to mediate how "representation" might be brought together with "sexuality" and "politics." The gendered body proved crucial time and again for this reappraisal as that site where the violence and confusion of private sexuality became the mode for addressing the chaos (ideological or physical) of the world at large.[33]

Not solely an object and target of the group's desiring gaze, the gendered body, and the female body in particular, became an allegory for subjectivity under threat. But this subjectivity was a formation to be scrutinized and dismantled rather than defended against the evils of fascism; the bodily threat fascism posed was its imposition of an integrity and consistency that tended to equate smooth bodies with ideologically regulated subjects. At stake in the surrealists' reduction of women's bodies to dolls and toys was thus not simply the loss of subjectivity such transformations represented but the encounter with fascistic power they staged as an artistic problem. This encounter, structured according to surrealist theories of paranoia and self-punishment, formed part of the group's self-critique of its complicity with forms of evil it did not yet comprehend.

Most immediately, this self-critique took the form of an interrogation of the movement's own political ties, especially to other left-wing, antifascist organizations whose willingness to compromise with Stalin and the bourgeoisie the surrealists found problematic. As Steven Harris has argued, the movement's political intransigence in the mid-1930s, marked by Crevel's suicide in 1935 as well as by the group's criticisms of the French Popular Front, led its adherents to the ironic situation whereby they could speak only from the place of modern art, other venues being closed to them.[34] More militant left-leaning surrealists such as René Char, Tristan Tzara, Roger Caillois, and Jules Monnerot interpreted the movement's activities after the dissolution of Counter-Attack, epitomized by the highbrow International Surrealist Exhibition of 1938, as a retreat into "pure art," and broke with the group.[35] Throughout this period the surrealists increasingly turned their attention toward what Breton and his critics alike referred to as "postrevolutionary concerns," issues of intellectual, economic, and psychological freedom that remained imperative for the surrealists, however untimely or ill suited to political pragmatism. As Breton explains in "The Political Position of Surrealism" (1935), "what is designated by the word fatherland, or the word justice, or the word duty has become foreign to us. A gaping wound opens before our eyes; we are witnesses of the fact that great evil continues to be perpetuated, and our first task is merely to measure our participation in it. To be objectors in every respect to whatever particular obligation this world attempts to reduce us."[36]

Centering on the problem of "participation" that Breton describes, a large body of surrealist writing and art from this period frames this problem through the visual economy of spectatorial complicity. Surrealist work of the immediate prewar period refuses to guarantee the "objection" Breton advocates, instead configuring its spectatorial relations in terms of obligation, and of an encounter with the "gaping wound" of moral crisis that Breton describes. In such works a spectator's identification hovers ambiguously between the suffering of a victim and the sadism of a persecutor. Such identifications, as Hal Foster has noted, risk reproducing "misogynistic effects that may overwhelm any liberatory intentions."[37] Yet in many surrealist works of the late 1930s, even such so-called liberatory intentions function through complicity and self-accusation, structured according to paranoia's auto-punitive drive.[38] Staging paranoia's reflexive play of delusional identifications as an artistic problem, I argue, offered the surrealists a critical system for diagnosing the social forces that threatened to replicate themselves in the age of fascism. In a way that seemed scandalously to turn its back on the immediate concerns of the Popular Front, the surrealists privileged so-called postrevolutionary questions of social organization and collective beliefs as a corrective to the ideological patterns that tacitly reproduced oppression.

Salvador Dalí's "Non-Euclidean Psychology of a Photograph," published in Minotaure in 1935, most succinctly illuminates surrealism's "paranoiac" strategy of overlooking an obvious threat in order to highlight broader, more latent evils. In the essay, Dalí examines a photograph (figure 7.5) of two expressionless women standing in a doorway, an image rendered sinister by the barely visible face of a man lurking in the doorway's shadows. In response to the image Dalí writes: "Do not believe, dear reader, that I draw your attention to this striking photograph because of its obvious pathetic and disconcerting quality, which arises quite naturally from the climate of criminality surrounding these three psychological beings, fixed in a personal, persevering, and Euclidean pose." Urging his readers to suspend their focus on the three "rapacious and persistent" faces, and especially that of the shadowy man in the doorway, Dalí directs our attention instead to a threadless spool (une bobine sans fil) at the bottom left-hand corner of the image. It is here, Dalí ex-

Fig. 7.5. Anonymous, untitled photograph reprinted in Salvador Dalí, "Analyse non-euclidienne d'une photographie," *Minotaure* 7 (1935). Image courtesy of the Pennsylvania State University Special Collections Library.

plains, that the photograph's true threat lies: the spool, viewed paranoiacally, displaces the sinister affect of the three shadowy figures. "Completely naked, completely pale, completely peeled [*pêlée*], immensely unconscious, clean, solitary, tiny, cosmic, non-Euclidean," the spool invokes threat as a victim, rather than as an agent, of violence.[39] In Dalí's descriptive language, that is, the spool takes on the properties of a corpse: peeled, nude, pale, and abandoned in the street, the spool becomes both an index of the photograph's threat and a reminder of the violence that the photograph does not ostensibly depict. Dalí's point is not to draw our sympathy toward the victimization of the abandoned spool, however, but to recognize it as the photograph's *punctum*, the symptom of the ideological continuities we bring to bear on the scene as soon as we focus on the sinister figures in the doorway.[40] As Dalí explains in the essay, the empty spool dislodges the fixed metaphysical categories of Newtonian, Kantian, and Euclidean time and space which he considers bankrupt; these categories of observation and judgment function to keep the photograph's threat at bay, held in place within the fixed stares of the three human figures. In Dalí's paranoid-critical reading, however, the shadow of evil is no longer comfortably represented in sinister looks but resides in the "Euclidean" categories themselves. In response, Dalí urges his readers to recognize the power of objects like the abandoned spool, "of such insignificance as the ones whose solicitations we surrealists have, first and foremost, learned to listen to, solicitations revealed to us by dreams as characterizing our age, our life, with the utmost violence."[41] As Dalí suggests, the "insignificancies" that threaten real life—represented by and through objects like the empty spool—could be made visible through a paranoiac engagement with their ambiguous status as both stand-ins for victimized subjects and symptoms of a more systematic persecution.

Dalí's theoretical framework takes on more graphic form in Hans Bellmer's notorious doll photographs, which stage persecution mania as a perverse economy of desire, complicity, and threat that takes place between the spectator and the photographs. Whereas the plastic dolls in Brauner's *Monsieur K.'s Power of Concentration* establish the painting's critique of fascist ideological reproduction through a collapse of physical distance between Mr. K. and his manifold offspring, Bellmer's dolls collapse the ordering logic of bodies and dolls altogether. In particular, his second doll series, produced between 1935 and 1938, is arresting for its capacity at once to invoke the anatomical specificity of a woman's body and yet to eradicate its bodily integrity. Composed during the period of Bellmer's expatriation from Germany in France, Bellmer's dolls offer a striking meditation on the psychodynamics of fascism, as numerous critics and art historians have attested; yet the doll photographs, however harrowing, offer neither attacks on, nor paeans to, fascist politics in any explicit sense. Rather, as in Carrington's memoir, the idea of thoughtless, fleshless being becomes a danger for the viewing subject, and not just for the bodies represented in the image. Certainly, as Sue Taylor has pointed out, the second photographic series is staged in a way that emphasizes the doll's environment, in exterior and interior scenes that "present a clandestine and malevolent world."[42] Yet this naturalized environment of persecution provides the conditions for the photographs' configuration of the doll as the victim of an unfolding scene of unknown, or unknowable, violence in which the spectator is trapped as a voyeuristic participant. Like Dalí's "non-Euclidean" analysis, Bellmer's doll images invoke the specter of worldly violence, only to redirect their viewers toward broader, more latent concerns—in Bellmer's case, an examination of the fascizing tendencies already at work in our most intimate experiences of intersubjective desire.

In a photograph from the second doll series, first published in *Minotaure* in 1935 (figure 7.6), a man lurks ominously behind a tree in the background of the image as if spying on the denuded doll posed in the foreground. The man's face and hands are concealed, so his affect—and his intentions—remain illegible. Consisting of two pairs of legs and two pelvises joined at the middle by a ball joint, the doll is posed in an oddly naturalistic contrapposto beside a tree, herself partially concealed from the man in the background. Since

Fig. 7.6. Hans Bellmer, "The Doll" (1935), from *Les Jeux de la Poupée*, plate 6. Hand-colored black and white photograph. Image courtesy of the Ryerson and Burnham Libraries, the Art Institute of Chicago. © 2008 Artists Rights Society (ARS), New York/ADAGP, Paris.

the doll too lacks hands, a face, or a torso to indicate her intentions, her casual pose charges the relationship between the two figures with an unsettling indeterminacy. Introducing narrative possibilities that the faceless bodies refuse to resolve, the photograph instead multiplies the forms of persecution to which it subjects the doll, both hypothetically and actually. As in Dalí's analysis of the photograph in *Minotaure*, the overt threat posed by the looming male figure finds its more pervasive complement elsewhere in the image. Despite whatever immanent danger might be looming within the photographic drama, we are already witness to the more fundamental torture to which the doll's composite body has, through its very composition, been subjected. The fact that Bellmer's doll could be broken down and recomposed becomes the object of our spectatorial gaze.[43]

In the 1935 photograph the discarded bit of clothing serves as the index of this torture of bodily logic, since the shapeless article offers little suggestion about how such a monstrously composite figure might successfully be clothed, or how, for that matter, a body consisting only of lower extremities might dress or undress itself. Bellmer's abuse of the female body as a natural and self-evident anatomical form stages itself as a spectacle whose "reality," in Bellmer's terms, comes into being through the spectator's complicity with—literally, her self-recognition in—the tortured composition of the doll. As Bellmer writes in a 1938 companion essay to the photographs, the doll is "emotionally charged yet nevertheless suspected of being simply imagined and thus fictive reality," at once material and bodily—not to mention gendered and sexualized—yet ambiguous with regard to its relationship to the real.[44] Indeed, the images in Bellmer's second doll series, to which he referred as "poetic stimulators," established their sense of reality in terms of a paranoiac relationship with the spectator. Bellmer writes:

> In order for such a doll . . . to receive hard and fast proof of its own existence during its encounters with the external world, it is also necessary that this world—the tree, the steps, the chair (which one suspects of being mere perceptions)—reveals what the I within them has accumulated of the YOU. In short, an amalgam must ensue from objective reality, an amalgam of a far higher reality because it is simultaneously subjective and objective.[45]

This encounter with the emotionally charged yet still "thoughtless, fleshless beings" of Bellmer's doll photographs stages its accumulation of "I" and "YOU," of spectator and object, persecutor and victim, under the aegis of the doll's anatomical perversion. As "poetic stimulators," the tortured dolls become stand-ins for spectatorial identification, and not simply as representations of Bellmer's own dark psychology on display as perversity: the doll is at once the victim and the index of the spectator's own investment of subjectivity in the "objective" image. The discomfort of Bellmer's image thus lies in its refusal to locate the agency of violence or torture in a determinate figure: it is not simply "fascism," nor the man in the photograph, nor even the artist who threatens the doll, but also you, the viewer.

Similarly ambiguous, half-human figures populate "The Oval Lady," Carrington's darkly comic tale of spectatorial participation in the abuse and reproduction of power. In the story, first published in the journal *Cahiers GLM* in October 1938, Carrington's narrator finds her double in the figure of Lucretia, a cloistered, ten-foot-tall child-woman who has the ability to transform herself into a horse. Lucretia's favorite toy is an ambiguously animate rocking horse named Tartar, who serves both as Lucretia's agent of transformation and as the surrogate victim of Lucretia's punishment. Dancing madly around in the snow with Tartar, as well as with her pet magpie, Matilda, Lucretia becomes increasingly horse-like until she is caught in the act of transformation by her nurse. As a penalty for her defiance of propriety for "playing at horses," Lucretia's father burns the toy horse. The story concludes with the narrator's efforts to block out Tartar's cries of pain: "I stopped my ears with my fingers, for the most frightful neighing sounded from above, as if an animal were suffering extreme torture."[46] Carrington's narrator, a tacit witness, does not intervene but instead registers the horror of the punishment in her very effort to ignore it.

Certainly the father's persecution of Lucretia's toy horse can be read biographically as an allegory of Carrington's well-documented antipathy toward her patrician family, and especially toward her father's ability to meddle in her life away from home, as reflected in the role of Imperial Chemicals in Down Below. As in much of Carrington's work, the horse and the bird stand in for Carrington and Max Ernst, who each produced numerous paintings and texts devoted to their totemistic alter egos. Yet without neglecting this autobiographical gesture, it is important to note that Carrington's writings and paintings of the late 1930s reveal her to be an attentive reader of the other surrealists, as well as of the movement's steadfast, if unorthodox, Freudianism. In spite of Carrington's frequent portrayal as an ingénue during these years, her work testifies to the scientific logic of Freud's case studies, as well as to the group's theoretical attention to the psychodynamics of power. In "The Oval Lady," as in Down Below, power—however domesticated it may seem—becomes horrific at the point where its effects are downplayed rather than sensationalized, reproduced in and by the stories' protagonists rather than singled out as abhorrent. Lucretia's stern father may be the principal antagonist of "The Oval Lady," but the story also outlines a ritual of complicity within which even the narrator becomes a participant. Lucretia herself is punished only by proxy. Instead, the screaming toy becomes the symptom—both the victim and the index—of the ritual's true violence, whose undisclosed torture finds its reflection in Lucretia's own collection of damaged and dismantled toys, as well as in the rasping voice of her pet bird, Matilda, whose tongue she split ten years previously. Lucretia's horse-play has, in the past, been something of a regular event: she has been caught and punished for the seventh time. The nurse, too, forms part of this economy, in her method of disciplining Lucretia with a bit and bridle. Both characters replicate, albeit in miniature, the disciplinary cruelty epitomized by the father's destruction of the toy horse.

Carrington's tale, and its expression of horror toward forms of cruelty that manifest themselves by proxy, synthesize the paranoiac structure of persecution mania explored in the work of Bellmer, Dalí, and other prewar surrealists. Most directly, "The Oval Lady" might be read as a fictionalized response to the penultimate section of Mad Love (1937), André Breton's meditation on having been "in the presence of an evil sufficiently definite for us to decide to uncover its origins."[47] Like Carrington, Breton represents this evil in miniature, recounting not the looming shadow of fascism but the subtle capacity for transmission both writers attribute to domestic and geopolitical violence alike. The episode recounts the "shock of discord" that erupts between Breton and his lover, Jacqueline Lamba, as they pass by a mysterious house while walking on the beach outside Lorient, in Brittany. In recounting the quarrel, Breton recalls "the singular irritation provoked in me by a bustly flock of seagulls squawking against a last ridge of foam. I even started throwing stones at them."[48] Such outbursts only exacerbate his equally uncharacteristic sense of estrangement and coldness toward his lover.

Breton's minor acts of cruelty, he discovers, reproduce in miniature the more harrowing acts of violence that had recently taken place at the mysterious house in whose presence the "shock of discord" first manifested itself. As Breton explains, it was in that same house in 1934 that Michel Henriot, the son of the local attorney general, had murdered his wife of seven months, Georgette Delglave, with a hunting rifle. Georgette's letters to her sister, which were read aloud at the trial, testify to severe domestic abuse during the couple's brief marriage. As Breton notes: "Showing no illusion about the fate awaiting her, she asked for help without managing to have anyone worry about her at all. A lovely testimony in honor of the bourgeois family."[49] Whereas his remark about the bourgeois family professes his critical distance from the repressive ignorance of Georgette's family toward her plight, the argument on the beach in Lorient confronts Breton with his own susceptibility to committing cruelty by proxy. Breton is more alarmed, however, by the fact that Michel Henriot was known to shoot seabirds for pleasure; "and I saw myself," he writes, "a few hours earlier putting these same birds to flight by throwing stones at them. The fact is that for the first time, and in that place, their behavior had been disagreeable to me."[50] Breton's meditation on the "presence of evil" at the Henriot house is striking for the note of self-recrimination it fosters in Breton himself. The incident suggests a hint of despair within Breton's otherwise ecstatic text, an acknowledgment that surrealism's interest in the suggestive power of objects—and in forms of causality that elude human will—did not guarantee liberation.

Carrington, in "The Oval Lady," exacerbates the implicit horror of Breton's anecdote: dramatizing the perpetuation of domestic violence through its expression on toys and animals, she voices Breton's shock at recognizing his tacit complicity with the cruelty and murder of the Henriot case. In Mad Love, Breton urges the need to dismantle the "learned machinations" through which the influence of discord, cruelty, and evil reproduce themselves; as he writes, by way of conclusion, of his lovers' quarrel: "Everything happens as if . . . one were the victim of a learned machination on the part of powers which remain, until things change, highly obscure. If we want to avoid this machination's involving . . . a lasting unrest in love or at least a grave doubt about its continuing, we are faced with the necessity of *undoing* it."⁵¹ In the years that followed, Breton, Carrington, and the exiled surrealists would increasingly dedicate themselves to fathoming such "highly obscure" forces, and to undoing the learned patterns of behavior that naturalize them.

By the time of *Down Below*, Carrington's own approach to countering what she considered the "hypnotic influence" of fascist evil—and the evacuation of agency this influence suggested—had taken on the structured form of paranoiac illness. In place of Breton's tacit self-reproach for his complicity in the domestic violences of the Henriot case, Carrington's memoir construes the reproduction of evil as a forgone conclusion: France has capitulated to the Nazis; Spain has succumbed to fascism; disaster has, in other words, already struck. What remains, though, is the structure of persecution mania itself, which, approached as a coherent structure of perception, acknowledges the otherwise disavowed avenues of complicity and ideological reproduction taking place within the very fabric of human relations. In place of appeals to individual responsibility, Carrington, along with the exiled surrealists, committed herself to undoing such forms of collusion, at the expense of immediate political effectiveness. During the war years the surrealists increasingly focused their attention on forms of social organization, ritual, and social myths that had been destroyed or had become occluded in the contemporary political climate, turning to hermeticism and the study of myth in an effort to dismantle the "learned machinations" that perpetuate violence.

Black Bile, Black Humor

In the 1940 essay "Surrealism: A Dissenting Opinion," Herbert J. Muller ponders Dalí's ideas about the political application of critical paranoia: "May not one succeed in systematizing confusion and so assist the total discrediting of the world of reality?" The answer, Muller responds, "is yes. I should say, however, that it were better to drop the question. The physical world can be expected to survive discrediting, and in the world of man's making, such a performance now seems a little pointless—Hitler needs no assistance."⁵² Muller's critique of surrealism here is twofold. At a point in the war where American cultural critics were still observing the European conflict from afar, Muller's sense of the "world of reality" to be discredited differed enormously from Dalí's: for Muller, what was currently under siege was the "man-made" fabric of European social relations rent apart by fascism, its humanist claims demolished by Hitler's genocidal politics of hatred. The surrealists, though, implicated reality as the set of "learned machinations" that resulted in the West's complicity, conscious or unconscious, with the rise and militarization of fascism. This notion was later expressed most succinctly by Aimé Césaire in his *Discourse on*

Colonialism, in his famous statement that "without his being aware of it," the "very distinguished, very humanistic, very Christian bourgeois of the twentieth century . . . has a Hitler inside him."[53] For Muller, though, such claims on the part of artists and writers could only result in a glaring theoretical and ideological inconsistency. Indeed, Muller's second charge against the surrealists was that the group's predilection for "paranoia and Black Bile" formed a dangerous kinship with Hitler, in spite of the group's adamant antifascism. Muller writes:

> Although the Surrealists pride themselves on fighting against "all forms of reaction," insist upon a "transformation of the world" in the name of liberty, they are actually in the line of the most profoundly reactionary movement of the day, and chiefly exploit the dark powers that enslave man. They hate Hitler, and Hitler despises them. I believe that the feeling is sincere all around. But I suspect that the feeling owes something to an unconscious or unwilling recognition of kinship: each senses in the other the full implications of their creed—the absurd, grotesque, awful logical extreme.[54]

Granting that the surrealists recognized the full implications of Nazism, Muller argues that this awareness has nonetheless lessened rather than heightened the group's political effectiveness: it only renders their interest in "dark powers" suspect and their political claims absurd. Rather than trying to "discredit reality," Muller argues, the surrealists should "forget their sweeping claims and negations and stick to the immediate business of criticism, appraising the representations of their super-reality simply as works of art." Art has no business making political demands, Muller implies, since to do so amounts to little more than wish fulfillment: indeed, he cites the surrealists' interest in medieval hermeticism and magic to prove how ineffectual their methods are. For as Muller argues, "magic is simply the hope of achieving ends without a realistic consideration of means."[55]

The surrealists did—as Carrington's paranoiac cosmologies in *Down Below* confirm—dedicate themselves to the study of magic, hermeticism, and myth during the war years; but this study was less concerned with the political immediacy of means than with an ethical commitment to ends. Political responsibility—which differed fundamentally from political *commitment*—did not reside solely in the hands of individuals but rested in political and social structures that collectivized men and women as social bodies. "Taking no notice of the accusations of mysticism that are sure to be brought against me," Breton writes in the "Prolegomena to a Third Manifesto of Surrealism or Not" in 1942, "[I] think it would not be a bad idea, as a start, to convince man that he is not necessarily the king of creation that he prides himself on being."[56] The study of magic and myth to which the movement turned, as did other contemporary intellectuals in dialogue with surrealism—such as Georges Bataille, Roger Caillois, Michel Leiris, and Césaire—was based on the supposedly "postrevolutionary" recognition that it was ordering systems of knowledge and praxis, rather than isolated villains and heroes, that determined the perpetuation of violence and barbarism. As Breton states in an interview published in *View* in 1941:

> Conquerors and conquered appear to me headed for the same abyss if they do not instruct themselves before it is too late in the process which set them one against the other: in the course of such a process, the exhaustion of the economic causes of the conflict will but emphasize, in effect, the common misery of our contemporaries, which in the last analysis is doubtless of an ideological order: it is rationalism, a *closed rationalism* which is killing the world; physical violence is unconsciously accepted, justified as the issue of mental passivity.[57]

In opposition to Muller's notion that the recourse to magic and the occult represented a morally irresponsible fantasy of effects without causes, the wartime surrealists instead urged a historical reconsideration of discredited or obscure forms of knowledge that might offer, in Pierre Mabille's words, "a new orientation of being, a new way to feel and hope."[58]

Carrington's own occultation of political agency in *Down Below* voices the despair of a surrealist artist and writer—and thus a believer in the power of ideological critique and psychoanalytic politics—in the face of the overwhelming force of historical trauma. How could it ever be possible to fight an enemy like fascism, once its forces have conquered Belgium, taken root in Spain and Italy, and infiltrated France? At the same time, though, Carrington's commitment to writing out this despair, and the interpretive delirium that rehearses it, maintains her faith in using writing and drawing to complicate any definitive understanding of what is "real." Later in her life Carrington would insist on the curative value of her mythic systems themselves as the sacred origins of new patterns of behavior and new social arrangements. Even in the composition of *Down Below*, she suggests that the antidote for trauma and fear is not a servile attachment to realism and certainty but instead a commitment to doubt, dark humor, and myth. Yet at the same time, *Down Below* anatomizes fear and despair in ways that resist its own efforts at recovery. The world reflected in *Down Below* remains in a state of utter catastrophe, an insistent reminder of implication and failure. That is, Carrington's text memorializes the fact that the Second World War brought not the end of the world but something more disturbing: a historical disaster that brought about a deep and unresolved crisis of faith in the potential for resistance.

Breton, in his book *Arcanum 17*, written in Quebec toward the war's end, and thus after the publication of *Down Below*, responds to the news of the liberation of Paris with a warning that extends Carrington's crisis in consciousness into the postwar historical moment: the end of the Second World War was not necessarily the end of fascism. We must not, he urges, confuse liberation with liberty, or the remission of an illness with the onset of health. "Recovery," in both Breton's and Carrington's accounts, refers not to the simple relieving of symptoms but to "a constant renewal of energy." As Breton writes, "Liberty is not, like liberation, a struggle against sickness, it is health." That is, whereas liberation is a negative concept, defined as an opposition to "an actual and sharply defined plundering that must be stopped," the concept of liberty reflects "an unconditional view of what *denominates* a human being and it alone gives an appreciable meaning to human growth."[59]

For Carrington, likewise, the abolition of her paranoiac fantasies at Santander represents yet another defeat, at once an abandonment of the delusional systems she has labored to construct and a capitulation to the normalizing treatments she is forced to undergo. As I have suggested, it is in the telling of the story itself—and the quest for discovery toward which she uses it—that Carrington's broader project takes shape as an investigation into alternative practices of social organization and knowledge production that had been lost, destroyed, or discredited. A similar project animates the work of a broader corpus of war-era writing that includes George Bataille's *Inner Experience*, Michel Leiris's *Manhood*, Aimé Césaire's *Notebook for a Return to the Native Land*, and Breton's own *Arcanum 17*, which likewise dwell on the significance of collective social myths that exceed the authority of individual human agency. The possibility that writing itself could offer a form of political historical engagement that superseded this authority became a central concern for the postwar surrealists; the final chapter takes up this question in addressing the debates about "engaged literature" that centered on surrealist writing in postwar France.

CHAPTER EIGHT

THE TRANSATLANTIC MYSTERIES OF PARIS: SURREALISM AND THE SÉRIE NOIRE

To animate the flagging conversation, someone posed the eminently original question: "Why do we write?"

To which I, who do not write, responded:

—Because something stronger than oneself pushes you to it, a need to protest, to denounce a certain state of things, I imagine.

Marcel Duhamel, *Raconte pas ta vie!* (1972)

Compiled during the dark years of Europe's consumption by fascist forces (*les années noires*), André Breton's *Anthology of Black Humor* was suppressed by the Vichy regime. The book represented the culmination of Breton's theoretical work in the years since the surrealists' definitive break with communism, shadowing the movement's aggressive antifascist militancy with a seemingly apolitical attention to the conceptual universe of gothic and symbolist literature. Neither funny nor especially comic in the generic sense, black humor (l'humour noir) describes the quality of indifference with which certain writers portray acts of injustice, destruction, and evil in their works. This indifference, Breton suggests, is social as well as aesthetic or analytical; it yields a means of perception undistorted by morality or law, and it thus offers, too, a form of intellectual commerce Breton describes as "the mysterious exchange of humorous pleasure between individuals."[1] This pleasure was not necessarily joyful. Indeed in both its prewar and postwar historical contexts, black humor paraded a degree of stylistic and moral recklessness—a *jouissance*—at odds with an era of serious political commitment; yet this exchange of humorous pleasure paradoxically gave voice to unconscious political desires, including forms of anger and unrest otherwise inadmissible to intellectual discourse.

In a later critique of Breton's book, the situationist writer Raoul Vaneigem acknowledged the logic of its censorship during the Vichy regime. Vaneigem writes, "The texts assembled by Breton in his anthology, and thus made available to all, were undoubtedly of a highly explosive nature, and the Vichy government was quite right to ban the book."[2] Breton's *Anthologie de l'humour noir* contains selections from the works of several dozen "explosive" authors, among them Swift, Sade, De Quincey, Poe, Baudelaire, Lautréamont, Rimbaud, Allais, Jarry, and Kafka. France's period of occupation by and capitulation to Nazi forces was, presumably, no time for disseminating such texts, whose celebrations of cruelty and evil clashed with the Vichy government's carefully controlled ideological program of "work, family, and fatherland."[3]

When the volume was eventually published in 1945, in the aftermath of the war, its coinage of a conceptual term derived from the gothic novel (le roman noir) lent an immediate legibility to the violent, paranoiac universe of the texts in ways that extended far beyond the anthology itself. The haunted world of decayed mansions and invisible menace invoked by Breton's reference to the historical gothic could just as easily describe the exploded state of Europe in the immediate postwar era. Indeed, Breton's humour noir would be directly invoked by the French critics who developed the notion of film noir to describe the rash of American crime films that became popular in Paris shortly thereafter, largely for their ability to evoke the haunted atmosphere of the postwar city.[4]

In what follows I address the literary reception of Breton's surrealist notion of black humor as a strategy for interrogating the status of political writing and of political violence alike in the postwar world. Whereas many artists and writers of the postwar surrealist group turned their attention toward ethnography and hermeticism in their investigation of alternative social myths, many of the critics, intellectuals, and popular writers who responded to surrealism centered their attention on the poetics of black humor. For Breton—and, as we will see, for other figures of the postwar era who might also be considered "black humorists," principally Chester Himes, Marcel Duhamel, and Léo Malet—the concept was far from an aesthetic or literary-historical category alone. Rather, black humor formed a significant part of postwar French intellectual discourse surrounding the question of writing as a political and ethical practice. Although this public discourse was initiated primarily by existentialist writers such as Jean-Paul Sartre, Simone de Beauvoir, Maurice Merleau-Ponty, and Albert Camus, it focused much of its polemical energy on the surrealist movement's political legacy. The writers and thinkers implicated in this discourse included not only the current and former surrealists who found their way into later editions of the Anthology of Black Humor—Salvador Dalí, Benjamin Péret, Jacques Prévert, Gisèle Prassinos, and Leonora Carrington appeared in Breton's revised edition of the book in 1950—but also more popular writers who directed the surrealist project toward the study of film and the writing of crime fiction. Though less well known as surrealists, a surprising number of popular postwar writers and intellectuals had participated in the movement, from Raymond Queneau and Francis Ponge to Prévert, Gaston Bachelard, and Léo Malet.

This chapter traces the continuities between the surrealist notion of black humor and the formation of the Série Noire, the crime fiction series at Gallimard developed after the war by the translator and editor Marcel Duhamel, himself a former surrealist. The discussion focuses in particular on one of the most significant events in the history of Duhamel's Série Noire: the publication in 1958 of the first "original" novel commissioned specifically for the series, a crime thriller by the expatriate African American novelist

Chester Himes, titled *La Reine des pommes* (or *The Five-Cornered Square*).[5] Independently of any formal affiliation with the movement, Himes's foray into crime fiction achieves what might be called a vernacular surrealism, one that registers the effects of his commerce with Duhamel, insofar as Duhamel established a large part of the material and formal conditions of Himes's transformation into a crime writer.[6] This vernacular surrealism is one of the legacies of the movement's interest in crime, significant less for its popularity than for its implicit response to intellectual conditions in France after the Second World War.

Duhamel's series had formerly issued translations of previously published works of American and British hard-boiled fiction; its publication of Himes's first crime thriller as an original novel in the series thus represented a shift in the genealogy of French popular fiction. Whereas authors such as Léo Malet and Boris Vian, two of the most popular writers of French crime fiction in the 1940s and 1950s, adapted the tropes and atmosphere of American hard-boiled crime fiction in revitalizing the French *roman noir*, Himes's commission to write such "French" novels was founded on his dislocation from both contemporary French fiction and Himes's own naturalistic "social protest" novels of the 1940s.[7] Himes's early fiction, published before his move to France in the 1950s, had struggled to represent clearly the psychic residue of the color line in the United States. His later crime fiction, written and composed in France, instead suspended access to political reality, subjecting any claim to political immediacy within what Kevin Bell has called "the aphasic and suspenseful compulsions of thought, desire, and question that . . . cut art loose from any idea of its fixed comprehensibility."[8] Himes's first novel, the neo-naturalist *If He Hollers, Let Him Go* (1945), remained faithful to Richard Wright's early mandate for African American writers to achieve "an angle of vision" that "can show . . . all the forces of modern society in process"; what Wright called "perspective" denoted "that fixed point in intellectual space where a writer stands to view the struggles, hopes, and sufferings of his people."[9] Yet Himes's career as a crime novelist was founded on the very collapse of any such "fixed point in intellectual space." His first crime novel for the Série Noire, *La Reine des pommes*, exploits its disintegration into absurdity and misprision.

In *La Reine des pommes*, Himes breaks with the instrumental use of language that characterized both Wright's and, in France, Jean-Paul Sartre's notions of "engaged writing." In its place he develops a violently comic fictional universe to which he later referred in terms of absurdity. Extending linguistic slippage and excess to the level of narrative itself, Himes's crime writing flies doubly in the face of social realism and existentialism by embracing absurdity as both a social condition and a narrative apparatus. At the same time, Himes always stressed that this humor was not a formal invention but something borrowed. That is, what he called "absurdity" was, in the lived experience of black Americans in Harlem, also emphatically real. Like Wright, Himes considered African American vernacular culture (blues, jazz, folk humor) to be subversively comic forms, what the existentialist antihero of Wright's novel *The Outsider* (1953) calls "the scornful gesture of men turned ecstatic in their state of rejection; it was the musical language of the satisfiedly amoral, the boastings of the contentedly lawless, the recreations of the innocently criminal."[10] Yet whereas the expatriate Wright of the 1950s would reject this "language" for its refusal, or inability, to engage in political action—that is, to *be* political—Himes embraces it as a protest against what he perceived to be the limits of a writer's claim to literary action. Rather than offering a language of racial authenticity to be judged on the basis of its political effectiveness, Himes's recourse to black vernacular forms redresses political literature's presumption of linguistic authenticity.

As writing composed and published in France, Himes's novels for the Série Noire took part in an ongoing French public discourse surrounding the status of writing as a form of political and historical engagement. In its abandonment of protest fiction's epistemological and ethical certainty, Himes's writing for the Série Noire reveals a comic affectation consistent with the surrealist notion of *l'humour noir*, itself a critical intervention into the field of political writing that was hostile to literary and political naturalism. Indeed what Himes's crime writing shares with surrealist thinking of the post–World War II period is its affected indifference to truth and justice, its sympathy with the shared spirit of writers who expunge the expected characteristics of aesthetic or moral value. This helps to explain what Himes meant when he claimed that although he had "no literary relationship with what is called the Surrealist school," and that he "didn't become acquainted with that term until the fifties," nevertheless "it just so happens that in the lives of black people, there are so many absurd situations, made that way by racism, that black life could sometimes be described as surrealistic. The best expression of surrealism by black people, themselves, is probably achieved by blues musicians."[11]

It has been argued that Himes's Harlem novels gained such immediate popularity in France because their sensationalistic details about U.S. race relations and African American urban life offered an appealing spectacle for a French intellectual culture already fascinated by blackness. Any such charge of commodification is inevitably double-sided, however, implying that the very absurdity of Himes's Harlem crime fiction demonstrates the extent to which his earlier political commitment had already been lost in translation.[12] I would argue instead that Himes's transformation into a "French" writer is characterized not by what his fiction loses in translation but by what it gains: namely, an involvement in French, and particularly surrealist, thinking about modes of writing that frustrate instrumentality through their irretrievable lapses and excesses of meaning. What postwar French thought gained, in turn, was a transatlantic arbiter of conflict within literary and political expression, a body of fiction that violently reimagines what Brent Edwards refers to as the *décalage*, or translation gap, already implicit within the history of diasporic modernism in Paris.[13] As the fruit of this French transformation, Himes's recourse to black humor bears a double conceptual framework: first, it represents Himes's revision of his early political tactics as a writer of what he called "social protest fiction"; and second, in doing so, it extends both the critical and the geographical range of postwar surrealism.

The publication of *La Reine des pommes* in 1958 as an original French novel represents an incarnation of surrealist *humour noir* insofar as it establishes a continuity between surrealist thinking about language, violence, and revolt, and hard-boiled fiction's stylized abstraction of political and racial experience in the United States. Taking part in a refusal of social realism's presumption of clear vision and a stoic subject, to which Breton's *Anthology* likewise alludes, Himes's novels seek access to the political and the real only by means of the "dissonant, discordant, always jarring" affect of the noir aesthetic.[14] Duhamel, who translated Himes's *If He Hollers, Let Him Go* in 1947 (as *S'il braille, lâche-le*), already considered Himes's fiction to be part of the interpretive framework of the crime series to which he later invited him to contribute.[15] At the same time, as self-consciously "French" writing composed in dialogue with Wright's own "French" novels written and published in Paris, Himes's crime fiction participates in the broad field of contemporary French debate over engaged writing and the ethics of political violence, which surrounded the reception of Breton's *Anthology of Black Humor*, and which continued to gather force through the 1950s and 1960s.

Les Fleurs du Mal / les fleurs de Malet / les fleurs Duhamel

> One last word
> Is a bird flying black
> And the devil always at the Y in the road
> Where the lonely house with the Z of its green shutters
> Constitutes the X of the human problem.
>
> Léo Malet, "Roman-Policier" (1941)

The *Anthology of Black Humor* was intended as a kind of coping mechanism for France's political situation in the late 1930s. Its most significant contribution to postwar thought was its dramatic, albeit implicit, juxtaposition of gothic and sadistic imagery against the tableau of the European crisis under Hitler. For Breton, the anthology's "noir" character signified a genealogical return to poetic works that seemed to celebrate violence while somehow articulating latent or sublimated political drives. Such a project was salutary, Breton claimed, because its simultaneous invocation of humor and horror corresponded to the necessarily split subject of contemporary existence. On the one hand, its jokes represented a narcissistic preservation of the subject through an appeal to the pleasure prin-

ciple. In language reminiscent of his earliest surrealist manifesto (1924), Breton invokes
a "shared concern with atmospheric conditions, so to speak, in which the mysterious exchange of humorous pleasure between individuals can occur—an exchange to which,
over the past century and a half, a rising price has been attached, which today makes it the
basis of the only intellectual commerce that can be considered high luxury."[16] On the
other hand, this awareness of the luxury of humorous pleasure represents black humor's
"objective" recognition of the real conditions of life, an awareness made all the more acute
by its utter divorce from sentimentality or moralization. Refusing to adhere to a code of
immediate political use-value or, for that matter, to champion a politics of subversion,
Breton's black humor in its very latency sought an alternative mode of reaction to the contemporary world.

Critics of the surrealist movement, however, were deeply suspicious of the way this notion of detachment seemed a tacit justification of Breton's exile in the United States during the war, as well as a trivialization of the violence from which western Europe had
recently emerged. Breton's *Anthology of Black Humor*, in providing this detachment with
both a literary genealogy and a theoretical justification, became one of the key targets in
a general backlash against the surrealist movement. In "Situation of the Writer in 1947,"
Jean-Paul Sartre attacks the movement for its paradoxical amalgamation of quietism and
the "permanent practice of violence."[17] Still more vituperative was the former surrealist
Raymond Queneau, who writes in a 1945 review of the *Anthology*:

> Black humor rebels, says Breton. Among other things, against the bourgeois world. It
> gives an outrageous picture of it, which has a powerful dissociative value. But this outra-
> geous painting is only fully carried out by Nazism, which makes happen in the real the
> bad pleasantries of a Sade or a Kafka. . . . Thus, the struggle against Nazism, itself, did
> not happen on the plane of this black humor. It was accomplished through submachine
> guns and ten-ton bombs.[18]

With the luxury of hindsight, Queneau could condemn l'humour noir as a concept that,
much like the more material fact of Breton's exile in the United States during the war,
played no direct role in Hitler's eventual defeat. In *The Rebel* (1951), Albert Camus identifies
surrealism's entire project as a dead end: "Surrealism, the gospel of chaos, found itself
compelled, from its very inception, to create an order."[19] The problem, according to the
movement's existentialist critics, was not that surrealism embraced violence, but that this
violence represented the blind alley into which the logical development of its "gospel of
chaos" inevitably led. It was acceptable to Camus's own theory of revolt that surrealism
"chose as its hero Violette Nozière or the anonymous common-law criminal, affirming in
this way, in the face of crime, the innocence of man." But this affirmation of individual innocence, he argues, went too far:

[Surrealism] was also rash enough to say—and this is the statement that André Breton must have regretted ever since 1933—that the simplest surrealist act consisted in going out into the street, revolver in hand, and shooting at random into the crowd. Whoever refuses to recognize any other determining factor apart from the individual and his desires, any priority other than that of the unconscious, actually succeeds in rebelling simultaneously against society and against reason.[20]

With his reference to Hitler's appointment as German chancellor in 1933, Camus chides Bretonian surrealism for what he considers its narcissism and lack of "commitment." Yet his own essay does not stray all that far from surrealism's project, a recognition shared by Breton, who never attacked Camus with the vehemence he unleashed on his other critics. Indeed, in its serial denunciation of its precursors in the fields of literary and historical rebellion—among them Sade, Rimbaud, Baudelaire, and Lautréamont—The Rebel seems to configure itself as a kind of counter-anthology to Breton's Anthology of Black Humor. Such epitaphs for surrealism stressed what Roland Barthes more broadly identified as the impossibility for any writing to be lastingly revolutionary.[21] By the war's end the movement had, as Maurice Blanchot wrote in 1949, become historical.

Yet as Blanchot asserts, while there may no longer have been a viable surrealist school after the war (at least in France), "a state of mind survives. No one belongs to this movement anymore, and everyone feels he could have been part of it." Has surrealism vanished, he asks? "It is no longer here or there: it is everywhere. It is a ghost, a brilliant obsession. In its turn, as an earned metamorphosis, it has become surreal."[22] Breton himself, in a 1951 interview, lamented the fragmentation of the surrealist endeavor in the contemporary intellectual climate, yet he admired its widespread dissemination. "The main thing," Breton explained, "is for Surrealism to express itself regularly, and globally. Its incursions in different domains would thus be much more perceptible. We are arbitrarily reduced to fragmenting our viewpoint, to parceling it out piece by piece, as the opportunities arise."[23] One of these opportunities, never fully recognized by Breton, was the contribution made to the dissemination of surrealism by former surrealists such as Léo Malet and Marcel Duhamel, two of the most significant figures in popular French literature after the war.

Malet, who joined the surrealist movement in 1931 as a young anarchist agitator and cabaret singer, would become best known for his cycle of fifteen detective novels, The New Mysteries of Paris, which he published between 1954 and 1959. A close friend of the Sade expert Maurice Heine, Malet devoted his prewar work, like his later mystery novels, to the poetics of urban spectacle and the literature dedicated to it: the feuilleton novel, crime films, faits-divers, and the writings of the symbolists. He remained in Paris during the Occupation, working with the underground surrealist group La Main à Plume until he was arrested in May 1940 for subversive activities.[24] After a period of internment in French and German prison camps, Malet returned to Paris and continued to write poems and articles for the Main à Plume group, with a renewed interest in the poetics of criminality; his 1943 poem "Le Frère de Lacenaire" (Lacenaire's Brother), dedicated to Heine's memory, describes its addressee as "wak[ing] up / to place the *feuilleton* novel in the reality of flesh and bone."[25]

By this time, too, Malet had himself likewise woken up to the appeal of writing detective fiction; after his internment he began to write American-style detective novels for the Minuit series under various pseudonyms until 1942, when he published *120, rue de la Gare* under his own name. Like "Le Frère de Lacenaire," Malet's crime novel is in many ways dedicated to Maurice Heine, its title and plot laden with references to Sade, as well as to a number of other surrealists. The commercial success of his crime writing drew him further and further away from the practicing surrealists both during and after the war; Malet seems to have ended his formal ties with the group in 1949, most likely after the exclusion of his friends Roberto Matta and Victor Brauner for their own "fragmentation" of surrealist practices.[26] Even so, his novels maintained their investment in a surrealist intellectual genealogy, and Malet continued to reflect on surrealist practices throughout his career, composing new "surrealist" poems as late as 1983.[27] Malet's *New Mysteries of Paris* received the Grand Prix de l'Humour Noir in 1958, an award that testifies both to Malet's continued pursuit of a popular surrealism and to the popular legacy of Breton's own theories of black humor.

Marcel Duhamel's prominence in the postwar literary milieu was less visible than Malet's. Yet as a translator and founding editor of the Série Noire, he played a role that was all the more significant to the persistence of surrealism as a "state of mind" throughout the 1950s and beyond.[28] Duhamel, who had owned the house at 54, rue du Château, in which the group developed its games of exquisite corpse, had, in 1945, launched a series of hard-boiled crime novels at the prestigious Gallimard press. Although Duhamel was fast friends with a number of young surrealists (Jacques and Pierre Prévert, Max Morise) who had broken angrily with Breton in 1929, Duhamel himself quietly left the group in 1928, selling his house to Georges Sadoul and André Thirion. During the 1930s, Duhamel participated in the October group, a workers' theater organization affiliated with the leftist Fédération du Théâtre Ouvrier Français. Dedicated to proletarian and antifascist politics, the group's members included Lou Tchimoukov, Sylvia Bataille, Guy Decomble, and the former surrealists Marcel Jean, Jacques Prévert, and Morise, with scripts composed by Prévert or adapted by Duhamel himself.[29] In 1935 the group became the ensemble cast for Jean Renoir's film *The Crime of M. Lange*, written in collaboration with Prévert, whose plot centers on a publishing house for American-style popular fiction. The group disbanded in 1936, greatly disillusioned with Stalinism and the French Communist Party's nationalist turn in France—a position the group shared with the surrealists. In 1944 the publisher Gaston Gallimard hired Duhamel to direct a new collection of detective fiction in the American hard-boiled style. Duhamel was already a translator of W. R. Burnett, Raoul

Whitfield, and Ernest Hemingway—and, by the late 1940s, of John Steinbeck, Erskine Caldwell, and Richard Wright, as well as Himes's *If He Hollers*—and his editorial choices for the Série Noire were similarly American in origin and style. The majority of titles in the series were either direct translations of American hard-boiled fiction—Hammett, James Cain, Raymond Chandler, Horace McCoy, Whitfield—or the work of European authors influenced by this type of genre fiction, such as Peter Cheney in England and Albert Simonin in France.[30]

In addition to his role as the founding editor of the Série Noire, Duhamel was also known for his translations of Richard Wright's *Black Boy*, which appeared in early issues of Sartre and Beauvoir's leading postwar intellectual journal *Les Temps Modernes*, in the same issues as Sartre's critical assault on surrealism. All the same, Duhamel, who never renounced his affiliation with the surrealist movement, professed his intellectual ties to surrealism in his preface to the seminal 1955 study of film noir, Raymond Borde and Étienne Chaumeton's *Panorama du film noir américain*. In this brief preface the former surrealist defines the terms "roman noir" and "film noir" as "pleonasms" for which "the latent presence of the idea of death, far from appearing symptomatic of a morbid state, seems on the contrary to be eminently sane and suitable for engendering skepticism, and thus humor, and thus a certain optimism."[31] Explicitly attributing this sensibility to his period of engagement with the surrealists in the mid-1920s, he cites the Bretonian practice of entering and leaving film screenings at will as a key to his understanding of the hard-boiled crime genre. Indeed, Duhamel locates this humorous practice of narrative disruption at the origin of both the Série Noire and film noir alike. As James Naremore has written, this synthetic and disruptive practice allowed the surrealists to use cinema "as an instrument for the destruction of bourgeois art and the desublimation of everyday life."[32] Breton, in a 1951 article on film, explains that during this period, what the surrealists valued most about the cinema, "to the point of taking no interest in anything else, was its *power to disorient*."[33] What Duhamel and Breton each describe is an atmosphere— whether "magnetic," "marvelous," or "comic"—consistent with the concept of l'humoir noir; indeed, Breton's notion of black humor as the mortal enemy of sentimentality is here extended to a literal disruption of commercial cinema's sentimentalized atmospheres and narrative structures.

Breton, in fact, places Duhamel firmly within the development of surrealist humor as a form of structural disruption, referring to the meetings held at Duhamel's house as "the veritable alembic of humor, in the Surrealist sense of the word."[34] As he explains:

Never had Surrealism shown such an organic unity, nor known greater effervescence than during that time, when our evening meetings were most often held in the old house (since demolished) at 54 Rue du Château. It was there, in the heart of a neighborhood unforgettably depicted by Huysmans in *Les Soeurs Vatard*, that Marcel Duhamel, long before he thought of launching the "*série noire*" and the "*série blême*," lodged his friends Prévert and Tanguy. Péret and Queneau also enjoyed long stays in that house, at his expense. Absolute nonconformism, total irreverence, and the most wonderful humor held sway there. In a corner papered with movie posters—vampish looks and drawn pistols—stood a small but always well-stocked bar. There were seven or eight cats, upon whom they lavished attention. And frogs behind green-tinted glass. I know of no easier gestation than the one that later gave birth to Prévert's "Attempt to Describe a Dinner of Heads in Paris-France," of Péret's *Je ne mange pas de ce pain-là* [I'll Have None of It], or Queneau's *Exercises in Style*. That was the veritable alembic of humor, in the Surrealist sense of the word.[35]

Breton is doing more here than inserting some of the most significant postwar literary successes into a surrealist genealogy—claiming Prévert's runaway success with *Paroles* and Duhamel's crime series as part of surrealism's trajectory. For at the same time, Breton is attributing his own notion of surrealist humor, and by extension of his *humour noir*, to this distillation or "alembic" that was the house at 54, rue du Château. For Breton, the irreverence he attributes to this physical environment describes precisely the combination of populism and "absolute nonconformism" that Duhamel would ascribe to the Série Noire.

Indeed, the "noir" writing collected and fostered by Duhamel bore a distinctive ideological stamp. As he describes in the promotional blurb for the series, "the lover of enigmas à la Sherlock Holmes won't often get anything out of it. Nor will the systematic optimist." For Duhamel, the Série Noire did more than reject the formal structure of the classic detective mystery; it envisioned an entirely different moral universe that eradicated the comforts of justice. He continues: "Immorality, generally admitted into this genre of work uniquely as a foil for conventional morality, is just as much a part [of the Série Noire] as the fine sentiments, indeed, as much as morality, period. The spirit is rarely conformist."[36] Yet the shadowy presence of immorality was hardly the Série Noire's only distinction. In a 1966 magazine article celebrating the series' thousandth title, Gilles Deleuze noted that this distance from the classic mystery novel is not only aesthetic or moral but epistemological as well. Abandoning the detective story's Oedipal search for truth, the stories supplant any such "metaphysical or scientific" quests with an economic system of retribution based instead on the exchange of falsehood for falsehood, error for error.[37] There is no metaphysical certainty, no definitive object, to compensate for the proliferation of falsehoods: the hyperbolic economy of exchange is, in Deleuze's words, "a process of restitution that permits a society, at the limits of cynicism, to conceal that which it wishes to conceal, to show that which it wishes to show, to deny evidence and to proclaim the unrealistic." Deleuze lauds those novels in Duhamel's series whose formal elements embrace this representation of society "in the fullest power of its falsehood." Only here do the stories offer any access to a world whose ostensible reality was always a product of the "unity of the grotesque and the terrifying."[38]

Though formally a pastiche of "false Faulkners, false Steinbecks, false Caldwells," the Série Noire represents for Deleuze a synthesis best achieved through parody, and thus he concludes that

> the great books of the Série Noire are those in which the real finds a parody specific to it, so that this parody shows us, in turn, directions within the real that we would never have found alone. The great parodic books take on very different forms: *Miss Shumway jette un sort* [Miss Shumway Waves a Wand] by Chase; *Fantasia chez les ploucs* [The Diamond Bikini] by Williams, and the Negro novels of Himes, which always have extraordinary moments. Parody is the category that surpasses the real and the imaginary.[39]

As postwar French translations (or imitations) of American prose styles and depression-era social concerns, the early novels of the Série Noire already seem to verge on self-parody, as their often newly minted French slang attests. Deleuze's notion of parody refers less to the novels' play on the conventions of the detective story form, however, than to their parodic relation to "the real" itself. He suggests that the novels presuppose the artificiality and even "falsehood" of lived reality, supplanting mimetic representation with the projection of simulacra. We might imagine here a form of caricature whose deliberate misrepresentation articulates unforeseen connections: to use Duhamel's more conversational terms, the Série Noire's "reflection of society" is a reflection only insofar as it is a reflection of excesses.[40]

Black Humor and White-Hot Rage

Chester Himes's Harlem crime thrillers, and *La Reine des pommes* in particular, take this parodic ambition to precisely the baroque excesses at which Deleuze hints. Yet in doing so, the novels end up embracing this parody in a very different way, with a complex combination of political anger and a vernacular ear that resonates more with the cultural project of surrealism than with Deleuze's "copy without an original." *La Reine des pommes* likewise has little to do with the "classic" English and French mysteries of the prewar era. Written in English as *The Five-Cornered Square* in 1957, the novel was translated by Minnie Danzas for its original French publication in March 1958 as *La Reine des pommes*—Danzas's French for the "sucker" named in the English version, the square so square as to have a fifth corner. Like the title, or titles, themselves, the stylistic universe of Himes's detective novel embraces the cacophony of exaggerations, jokes, and divergent stories that people use to describe their lived experience. Himes doubly indulges the social and interpretive excesses on which the classic detective story necessarily forecloses: first, by embracing the hard-boiled vernacular of depression-era crime fiction, and second, by amplifying the dismembered babble of vernacular urban life. Rather than committing to the "clear vision" of engaged literature, Himes's "Parisian" novel of Harlem violence wagers on linguistic excess: for Himes, les paris sont ouverts—literally, the bets (les paris) are open; it's anyone's guess.

For it wasn't until Himes became a Paris expatriate that his career as a detective writer opened up. The "surrealism" of Himes's crime fiction for the Série Noire emerged through the specific conditions under which he wrote his first detective novel; it also becomes visible in the way his novel can be read in response to the contemporary debates between the existentialists (with whom Wright had allied himself in the late 1940s) and the "ghosts" of surrealism over the problem of literature's political engagement.[41] For Himes, the question of a surrealist affinity or a surrealist method did not hinge on his cultural access to French ideas or his contact with the actual movement. Rather, for him, hard-boiled crime fiction already exceeded, even exploited, the limits of literary naturalism in ways that resonated with surrealist ideas about representation. Like Duhamel, Himes was an aficionado of the curt American style of writing of the 1920s and 1930s—writing that, in Himes's words, "tells it like it is." This truthfulness went beyond the positivist limitations of mere naturalism: Himes later explained that, having cut his teeth on Dashiell Hammett, he would read William Faulkner's Sanctuary "to sustain my outrageousness and give me courage," since Faulkner's fiction was "the most absurd ever written."[42] It is a similarly outrageous mixture of anarchic violence and bluntly depicted unreason that Himes creates in La Reine des pommes. Yet he adamantly distinguishes between absurdity, a set of conditions that could be depicted realistically by an autonomous viewing subject, and the "sense" of this absurdity, a form of thinking in which there is, as Kevin Bell has suggested, "something that takes possession of [the subject] from a distance, transfiguring his being, splintering him from an organized unit of coherence and autonomy into a highly volatilized swarm of disjointed affects, impressions, sensations, memories and constructs."[43]

Indeed, whereas there may still be detectives in La Reine des pommes, there is no "private eye," no structuring Oedipus character whose narrative presence functions as the novel's lens of perception, however flawed or implicated within its cycles of retribution. Instead, the novel is stricken a priori with an epidemic of blindness, both literal and metaphorical, whose manifestations sabotage the possibility of clear vision or metaphysical insight. The novel's characters and the Harlem they inhabit are plagued by the irrationality of rage or fear, the obliviousness of naïveté or infatuation, or the more strategic sleights of hand of hoaxes and scams. In a scene that anticipates Deleuze's notion of error, Himes's two detectives are themselves infected by this blindness. The scene begins as Coffin Ed and Grave

Digger burst into a warehouse in which the gang they are pursuing has taken refuge. Only moments earlier, Jackson, the "five-cornered square" himself, has arrived, also in pursuit of the gang. The detectives' entrance incites an outburst of violence that at first unfolds as straightforward action-thriller narration until the novel's female protagonist cries out a warning:

> Imabelle saw the poised knife and screamed, "Look out, Daddy!"
>
> Her scream was so piercing that everyone except the two detectives ducked involuntarily. It even scratched the case-hardened nerves of Grave Digger. His finger tightened spasmodically on the hair trigger of his pistol and the explosion of the shot in the small room deafened everyone.[44]

With this spasmodic pull of the trigger, the hard-boiled, tersely narrated situation (already complicated by the sheer number of names, characters, and blows) unravels into a veritable ballet of violence:

> Gus had ducked into the line of fire and the .38 bullet penetrated his skull back of the left ear and came out over the right eye. As he fell dying, Gus made one more grab at Jackson, but Jackson leaped aside like a shying horse, and Jodie grappled with him. . . .
>
> Taking advantage of the commotion, Hank snatched up a glass of acid sitting on the desk. The acid had been used to demonstrate the purity of the gold ore, and Hank saw his chance to throw it into Coffin Ed's eyes.
>
> Imabelle saw him and screamed again, "Look out!"
>
> Everybody ducked again. Jackson and Jodie butted heads accidentally. By dodging, Slim came between Coffin and Hank just as Hank threw the acid and Coffin Ed shot. Some of the acid splashed on Slim's ear and neck; the rest splashed into Coffin Ed's face. Coffin Ed's shot went wild and shattered the desk-lamp.
>
> Slim jumped backward so violently he slammed into the wall.
>
> Hank dropped behind the desk a fraction of a second before Coffin Ed, blinded with the burning acid and a white-hot rage, emptied his pistol, spraying the top of the desk and the wall behind it with .38 slugs.
>
> One of the bullets hit a hidden light-switch and plunged the room into darkness.
>
> "Easy does it," Grave Digger shouted in warning, and backed toward the door to cut off escape.
>
> Coffin Ed didn't know the lights were out. He was a tough man. He had to be a tough man to be a colored detective in Harlem. He closed his eyes against the burning pain, but he was so consumed with rage that he began clubbing right and left in the dark with the butt of his pistol.

He didn't know it was Grave Digger who backed into him. He just felt somebody within reach and he clubbed Grave Digger over the head with such savage fury that he knocked him unconscious. Grave Digger crumpled to the floor at the same instant that Coffin Ed was asking in the dark, "Where are you, Digger? Where are you, man?"[45]

What may be most arresting about this scene is, in the end, how ridiculous it becomes—in spite, or precisely because, of its explosion of violence. The scene, if not exactly a parody of its own subject-verb-object sentence construction, nevertheless degenerates from the relatively straightforward entanglements of its first series of blows into a deadly comedy of errors in which everybody is literally plunged into darkness. Gus's eye is shot out of its socket, the lights are extinguished, Coffin Ed is blinded by acid, his partner is knocked unconscious, and Jackson, afterward, scrambles away in a scarcely more conscious panic. Moreover, Imabelle's cries to "look out" only contribute to the scene's vaudevillian frenzy, their dreadful irony amplifying the ocular nature of its anti-Oedipal descent into chaos.

The synesthesia of Imabelle's scream, its conflation of sound with optics, is consistent with her similarly rhetorical function in the novel as a figure of misattributed causality. Both the novel's English title—For Love of Imabelle—and the cast of male characters lusting after her configure Imabelle as the cause of the novel's violence. As Himes writes, for the love of Imabelle, Jackson was "solid ready to cut throats, crack skulls, dodge police, steal hearses, drink muddy water, live in a hollow log, and take any rape-fiend chance to be once more in the arms of her high-yellow heart."[46] As Manthia Diawara has suggested, what this passage describes is not "love" but the condensed expression of a form of black rage that permeates Himes's noir universe. "By black rage," Diawara writes, "I mean a set of violent and uncontrollable relations in black communities induced by a sense of frustration, confinement, and white racism. This rage often takes the form of an eroticized violence by men against women and homosexuals, a savage explosion on the part of some characters against others whom they seek to control, and a perverse mimicry of the status quo."[47] In Imabelle's case, the eroticized violence is exercised metaphorically, in the way her desirability is configured both as the cause of violent expression and as an expression of rage in its own right. However beautiful she may be as an object of desire, this desire always takes on the insistence of fetishism.

When we first meet Imabelle in the novel's opening scene, a con game engineered against Jackson, her lover, we learn that "she was a cushion-lipped, hot-bodied, banana-skin chick with the speckled-brown eyes of a teaser and the high-arched, ball-bearing hips of a natural-born amante. Jackson was as crazy about her as a moose for doe."[48] Even as Himes seems in the previously discussed scene to endorse the "shrill" agency of Imabelle's scream as a mere irony—or duplicity—within her character, the text also reveals the extent to which her embodiment of causality is fictional. As even this passage suggests, Imabelle is little more than a collection of parts, images, and part-objects of desire, a quasi-surrealist "exquisite corpse." She is configured in the text as a kind of counterfeit, however sympathetic, whose falsehood is unseen by the novel's characters but patently visible to readers. Moreover, Himes's use of this blindness in the service of a materialist critique—the rage against social, racial, and economic conditions described by Diawara—explicitly connects this "falsehood" to commodity fetishism through the poetic links between the numerous scams, counterfeits, and trunks of fool's gold with which Imabelle is continually involved. It is this second "blindness" of economic and sexual desire that contributes to the kind of chaos Imabelle's scream of "Look out, daddy" announces. Moreover, this blindness toward the commodity—to which Himes adds the gendered, erotic, and racial allure of the "golden" and "banana-skinned" Imabelle—suggests a critique of the political blindness Himes finds in contemporary America. The chaos of Himes's parodic crime universe is thus a function not just of blinding rage but of misrecognized desire as well, its falsehoods even more deeply embedded in the unconscious than any momentary effect of "white-hot rage."

Far from a merely formal conceit, Himes's sense of absurdity thus pertains specifically to the conditions of black life in America, through which African Americans become interpolated into racist relations independently of their will, and in spite of their recognition. What Himes calls "absurdity" should therefore not be conflated with surrealism proper, nor is it synonymous with what he refers to as his own dark humor—which is a whole lot funnier. This absurdity is the dominant motif of the second volume of Himes's autobiography, which opens with an allusion to Camus's own recourse to the absurd:

> Albert Camus once said that racism is absurd. Racism introduces absurdity into the human condition. Not only does racism express the absurdity of the racists, but it generates absurdity in the victims. And the absurdity of the victims intensifies the absurdity of the racists, ad infinitum. If one lives in a country where racism is held valid and practiced in all ways of life, eventually, no matter whether one is a racist or a victim, one comes to feel the absurdity of life.[49]

This absurdity suggests, etymologically speaking, a kind of deafness (surdité), through which white people and black people fail to make sense of each other; far from describing the dark humor of the detective novels, it denotes a set of conditions that are emphatically real, encompassing even the conditions of Himes's own writing. Consistent with Camus's discussion of absurdity in both The Rebel and The Myth of Sisyphus (translated into English in 1952 and 1955, respectively), this set of conditions can be described as the confrontation between the irrationality of the world and "the wild longing for clarity whose call echoes in the human heart."[50] These are the conditions whose effects on the conscious individual are the "confrontations" Himes's early novels strive to represent, and whose cycles of repetition and reproduction he struggles to destroy.

This absurdity has the frightening tendency, however, to absorb even the fictional works that try to represent it and engage with it politically. As Himes explains, discussing his 1953 novel The End of a Primitive: "It had not been my intention to write about absurdity. I had intended to write about the deadly venom of racial prejudice which kills both racists and their victims. I had not intended to write about absurdity because the book was about me and I had not known at the time that I was absurd."[51] While Camus writes that absurdity necessitates revolt as "one of the only coherent philosophical positions," Himes shows how this revolt risks being co-opted by the very conditions of absurdity against which it rebels.[52] It is not coherent at all, but a mise-en-abyme that threatens both to absorb and to split the individual subject into countless fragments. In his detective novels Himes thus abandons any such "coherent" philosophical position, seeking instead a "handle" on absurdity itself as a way of describing how racism operates in the American imaginary. It is here, in questioning the ability of writing either to channel or to represent the "deadly venom" of racism and rage alike, that Himes reveals his distance from writers such as Wright, Camus, and Sartre.

The Idea of Violence

Himes's diagnosis, which, in his autobiography, he applies to his own writing, finds its expression as early as 1945, in If He Hollers, Let Him Go. In a conversation about Richard Wright's Native Son, Himes's protagonist, Bob Jones, angrily defends Wright's Bigger Thomas against a group of detractors. Bigger, he argues, has value as a literary device for manifesting the effects of racism; yet he suggests that Wright's creation is nevertheless powerless to change the conditions he so forcefully represents. Himes writes:

"Native Son turned my stomach," Arline said. "It just proved what the white Southerner has always said about us; that our men are rapists and murderers."

"Well, I will agree that the selection of Bigger Thomas to prove the point of Negro oppression was an unfortunate choice," Leighton said.

"What do you think, Mr. Jones?" Cleo asked.

I said, "Well, you couldn't pick a better person than Bigger Thomas to prove the point. But after you prove it, then what? Most white people I know are quite proud of having made Negroes into Bigger Thomases."[53]

The structure of this conversation seems to reiterate Jones's doubts (about the "then what?"), since both Arline, who is black, and Leighton, who is white, express concern over what it is that Bigger Thomas proves. Arline is sickened by the idea that Wright has "proved" a racial stereotype; Leighton seems to suggest that Wright could have "selected" a better, less "unfortunate" one, thus subtly accusing Wright of a rhetorical error in proving his point. Yet in suggesting that Wright's proof is rhetorical, Leighton ultimately denies that anything has been proved at all. Indeed, Jones's remark implies that the proof of the "point of Negro oppression" is in fact the same thing as Arline's proof about "what the white Southerner has always said about us": he sees racism operating as a form of interpolation through which an African American is nominated as something alien, nauseating to himself or herself. In spite of his insight, Jones finds himself locked in a narrative in which he risks at any moment being interpolated as a Bigger Thomas himself. Plagued by murderous rage throughout the novel, Jones participates in a sexualized game of hateful racial performance with a white female co-worker. Until the novel's ending, where Jones is falsely accused of rape and thus framed as precisely the Bigger Thomas–like stereotype Arline fears, Jones's first-person narration deals with the absurdity of his conflicts by mitigating his anger and fear with laughter and jokes. Here, though, the humor is described in, rather than performed by, the text. Jones's bitter laughter in *If He Hollers, Let Him Go*, as well as the jokes and dozens bandied about by his politically ineffective gang of black co-workers, function as palliatives against actual violence—whether criminal or political—in a way that Himes's novel reveals to be painfully dissatisfying. Consistent with Wright's dismissal of vernacular culture as quietist and self-deluding, the humor in *If He Hollers* (unlike the dark humor in *La Reine des pommes*) is certainly not very funny. Insofar as it is mobilized in the service of an oppressive social order, it only becomes further entangled in the absurdity it voices.

Himes's realization that his own social protest novels were themselves entangled in this equilibrium of falsehoods coincides with his abandonment of this form of writing. As he explains in *My Life of Absurdity*, his turn to a genre in which violence is neither the stuff of tragedy nor perpetually looming as the burden of an ironic fate was itself a protest against the protest novel. Himes writes: "I wanted to break through the barrier that labeled me as a 'protest writer.' I knew the life of an American black needed another image than just the victim of racism."[54] The violence with which Himes populates his detective fiction thus represents a twofold adjustment: first, its multiplication of falsehood within a Harlem teeming with crime and deception gives free rein to the exploration of the "unconscious" desires of Himes's previous novels, which are given no opportunity to distinguish between different kinds of violence. For Bob Jones, any black-on-white violence, regardless of its political motive, would be criminalized. Second, Himes's crime fiction abandons his earlier frustration with the ideological circuit of absurdity and instead embraces it to the extent that these conditions, though oppressive, nevertheless constitute the imaginative fabric of African American life and vernacular culture. Certainly in *La Reine des pommes* Himes embraces the jokes, dozens, and witticisms he implicitly condemns in *If He Hollers*. This double adjustment constitutes Himes's rejection of both Wright's and Sartre's notions of engaged writing in favor of an indulgently disengaged dark humor; removing the responsibility for "real" political action from its presumed place immediately manifest within the text, this humor leaves the question of violent rebellion to simmer in the imagination.

Rather than trying to make his own writing powerful enough to end racism, or, as Himes suggests more cynically, aspiring to the position of bourgeois political analyst Wright had attained in France, Himes remarks instead:

> Shooting people in the head generates power. This is what I think black writers should write about. I remember Sartre made a statement which was recorded in the French press (I never had any use for Sartre since) that in writing his play *The Respectful Prostitute* he recognized the fact that a black man could not assault a white man in America. That's one of the reasons I began writing the detective stories. I wanted to introduce the idea of violence. After all, Americans live by violence, and violence achieves—regardless of what anyone says, regardless of the distaste of the white community—its own ends.[55]

The play to which Himes refers, Sartre's "farce" about the Scottsboro case, addresses what Wright, in his 1948 preface to the American translation of *La Putain respectueuse*, refers to as "America's White Problem." Sartre's play, Wright argues, adopts a "jocular, almost flippant tone" in order to portray the "moral comedy of the white American character."[56] Reprising the theme of false accusations of rape that dominates the early work of Wright and Himes alike, Sartre's play dramatizes the respect for authority that seems to have influenced the accusations leveled by Victoria Price and Ruby Bates against the nine Scottsboro Boys in 1931.

Sartre's farce claims to represent "logically" and "rigorously" the truth of "white America's ambiguous morality where things racial are concerned." This logic and rigor is, however, directed almost exclusively toward the oppressor, since Sartre neglects to name the sacrificial "Negro" around whom the play revolves, or to make this character anything other than a tragic victim of this "moral comedy."[57] Still, the play might be read as Sartre's attempt to replicate his analysis of Wright's *Native Son* in "What Is Literature?," in which he praises Wright for his ability to address a "split public." Read by oppressed and oppressor alike, *Native Son* succeeded as a protest novel by "furnishing the oppressor with his image, both inner and outer, being conscious with and for the oppressed of the oppression, contributing to the formation of a constructive and revolutionary ideology."[58] In other words, Sartre attempts to counter the absurdity of racism with a kind of double speech, replacing deafness with a logical, rational comedy that would, in turn, yield a revolutionary clarity of vision. Only in the play's affect—its impact on "the oppressor"—is there any recourse to violence; yet even this ideological violence remains subject to the "clarity" and sharpness of the comedy itself. Himes's writing, by contrast, strives to introduce the idea of violence more concretely, indulging that which remains off-limits to Sartre's tragic "Negro." At the same time, it refuses to substitute itself for real political insurrection. Instead it turns a blind eye to the clear-sighted search for political truth in writing, instigating a vicious, and viciously comic, multiplication of crime, that is, of political error.

Les Paris Sont Ouverts

> Now I was a French writer and the United States of America could kiss
> my ass.
>
> Chester Himes, *My Life of Absurdity* (1972)

While Himes identified the rule by violence as American, his crime writing for the Série Noire, which depicts and entertains this violence, occupied a cultural position that was not only recognizable to French readers but also, I have suggested, immersed in French debates over the nature of engaged literature. Describing the black humor of his detective novels, Himes writes:

> I was writing some strange shit. Some time before, I didn't know when, my mind had rejected all reality as I had known it and I had begun to see the world as a cesspool of buffoonery. Even the violence was funny. A man gets his throat cut. He shakes his head to say you missed me and it falls off. Damn reality, I thought. All of reality was absurd, contradictory, violent and hurting. It was funny really. If I could just get the handle to joke. And I had got the handle, by some miracle.[59]

Deleuze suggests that such a "handle" designates the parodic structure that shows the social universe "in the fullest power of its falsehood."[60] At the same time, this handle also shares a conceptual and genealogical connection to the surrealist notion of *humour noir,* itself an attempt to get a "handle" on its own traumatic set of historical circumstances. In each case the necessary critical distance derives from a strict enforcement of the distinction between even the most overtly "political" writing and actual action.

Indeed, as both Himes and Breton maintain, to evaluate writing—whether the vocation, the writerly "instrument," or the text itself—as a substitute for armed rebellion would be absurd. Even in its most "active" form, surrealist writing was committed to a much different kind of ideological warfare than either social realism or existentialism: it envisioned a broad rejection of social and moral constraints which, despite the group's efforts to combat fascism throughout the 1930s, could not possibly measure up to global military power. Like Himes, Breton argued that writing provided the means for exploring and understanding the forces—good and evil, and often painful and unconscious—that structure lived experience. But it was no substitute for political violence, for actual rebellion. Instead, as the surrealist photographer and writer Claude Cahun writes in her 1934 polemic *Les Paris sont ouverts* (The Bets Are Open), the strength of poetic language lies in its resistance to the cognitive certainty presumed by propaganda and protest writing alike: it "keeps its secret" even as it paradoxically "hands over its secret [*livre son secret*]."[61] This latter idea is expressed through a pun on *livre* (book) that both demonstrates and parodies the openness of meaning Cahun ascribes to language.

Distinguishing a poem's manifest content from its "latent" content, Cahun argues that language is as much an agent of conflict as it is of connection and communication: "Whereas science is oriented toward direct knowledge of the universe, and philosophy toward an indirect knowledge of the universe, poetry intervenes here, there, and everywhere, provoking short circuits within this coming into human awareness—these 'magic' shortcuts of which sexual love and extreme suffering also hold the 'secret.'"[62] These short circuits both produce and protect the latent, unconscious, and intransigent elements of imagination and desire that for Cahun, and for the surrealist writing she supports, are the critical forces for true liberation because they keep "the bets open."

While Himes's crime novels share an affinity, as well as a counter-existentialist stance, with Breton's concept of black humor, it was through Marcel Duhamel's pulp fiction incarnation of surrealist practice that this shared critical position became explicit. The "handle" on reality that induced Himes to laugh refers, I am suggesting, to the conceptual machinery offered by Duhamel in the guise of instructions for writing genre fiction for the Série Noire. The moment is recorded in both Himes's autobiography and in Duhamel's 1970 preface to the French translation of *Blind Man With a Pistol*.[63] I cite Himes's slightly later version:

Marcel chuckled and took me by the arm and steered me into a corner of the waiting room. Probably scared of someone overhearing him, I thought.

"Get an idea," Marcel said. "Start with action, somebody does something—a man reaches out a hand and opens a door, light shines in his eyes, a body lies on the floor, he turns, looks up and down the hall. . . . Action always in detail. Make pictures. Like motion pictures. Always the scenes are visible. No stream of consciousness at all. We don't give a damn who's thinking what—only what they're doing. Always doing something. From one scene to another. Don't worry about it making sense. That's for the end. Give me 200 typed pages."[64]

The conspiratorial tone of Duhamel's "assignment" is misleading insofar as it implies that Himes's turn to crime fiction was the product of editorial influence. In his autobiography Himes recalls his suspicion that this moment might have been a confidence trick to seduce him into political complacency: "I got news for you, I thought. I had started out to write a detective story when I wrote that novel [*If He Hollers*, in 1945], but I couldn't name the white man who was guilty because all white men were guilty."[65] What this air of suspicion and conspiracy confirms, however, is the uncanny extent to which Himes and Duhamel were already in accord: not only was Himes completely familiar with the noir form, but Duhamel was himself intimately familiar with Himes's writing as well.

Rather than recording a moment of direct cultural transmission, this scene articulates a shared set of ideas about writing: resistant to the narrative and cognitive certainty of naturalism, this writing is consistent with the critical aims of postwar surrealism. As I have argued, Duhamel's absorption of surrealist principles into the editorial framework of the Série Noire achieved an extension of surrealism into the public sphere; this "public" surrealism carried on the group's rejection of linearity and narrative "streams of consciousness" in favor of a pastiche of images, scenes, and fragments whose combination could, as Deleuze writes, "shows us . . . directions within the real which we would never have found alone."[66] Yet while both Duhamel and Breton imagined such a pastiche in terms of film—Duhamel couching his "instructions" to Himes in filmic terms, Breton invoking the films of Sennett and Chaplin in his introduction to the *Anthology of Black Humor*—this pastiche, for Himes, is primarily verbal, a function of the conflicting ways in which people respond to the same event.

Himes spoke about his version of Duhamel's "public" surrealism in a 1970 interview. Describing his method for constructing "comic" scenes, Himes illustrates what he meant when he claimed not to have invented his own *humour noir* but to have borrowed the dark humor of the ghetto, grafting together its fragments into a kind of vernacular collage:

> My way of creating a scene is to describe enough things in order to make an entire picture. Take for an example the scene from *La Reine des pommes*, where Jackson is driving away in his stolen hearse, with the boy in the coffin, and so on. All those details make the scene complete. You know, if you get a police report about an incident, and get all the statements from the witnesses, you tend to get a rather jumbled and confused picture. In a way, that's another form of reality. I think that's the kind of reality that you find in Harlem. You not only have the actual reality of the incident, but also the individual realities of each person who tries to remember it. Probably the nature of life in Harlem is such that the eyewitness accounts of any given event will be conflicting. I try to present things in such a way that the reader can understand this phenomenon.[67]

This method, rather than subsuming its political anger and desire within a singular narrative consciousness, a single "private eye," instead multiplies the inconsistencies of vernacular speech and the confusing vicissitudes of American absurdity. Much like Walter Benjamin's notion of how surrealist photography achieves a "salutary estrangement between man and his surroundings," Himes's absurdist universe blinds the "private" eye in order to give instead "free play to the politically educated eye, under whose gaze all intimacies are sacrificed to the illumination of detail."[68]

What Himes refers to as his own version of surrealism, a vernacular surrealism allied with the blues, thus has less to do with the formal descriptions of surrealist practices found in Breton's manifestoes than with the political legacy of the group in the postwar public domain. This legacy, especially in its infiltration within the "philosophy" of Duhamel's Série Noire, lingered as an insistence on the conflicts and even falsehoods of language, the resistance of writing and its motives to an immediate political use-value. This is not to suggest that Himes thought writing could have no voice in the world of politics; rather—to cite Grave Digger's words in *Cotton Comes to Harlem* (1965)—this voice speaks "in a language never heard," a language perpetually misdirected, exaggerated, and broken into bits.[69] Like Cahun's ideas about surrealist poetry, Himes's black humor contradicts the existentialist faith in African American vernacular forms as means of expression alone, suggesting instead that they "guard their secrets" in order that their political anger, their unconscious, subterranean cachet of revolutionary knowledge and desire, remain open. So too, I contend, does there remain an openness within surrealist discourse more broadly; no longer limited to the active movement, this discourse was distributed throughout postwar intellectual life, and throughout the world, as an intransigent form of political expression as much attuned to the "mysterious exchange of humorous pleasure" as to the objective recognition of social injustice.

CONCLUSION: ANTIHUMANISM AND TERROR

In the inaugural issue of the postwar surrealist magazine *Le Surréalisme, Même* (1956), the young surrealist writer Alain Joubert printed a brief anecdote in the "Notes" section. The anecdote, titled "So Be It" ("Ainsi soit-il"), provides a darkly humorous commentary on France's postwar colonial situation, as well as on the politics of the surrealists and their fellow leftist intellectuals. Joubert begins:

> In the equatorial jungle lives a tribe of Indians, the Aucas, who have always refused any relationship with whites, so as to avoid the civilizing gangrene.
>
> Last January, however, a small team of missionaries decided to go teach the Gospel to these last representatives of the Paleolithic era. A group of five pure-hearted Americans, in whose midst could be distinguished a rugby player and a former paratrooper, thought they could successfully approach the Aucas by offering them gifts of the "little-aluminum-kettle-filled-with-brightly-colored-buttons" kind.
>
> This was to miscalculate how little affection the Indians bore toward whites in general and, it seems, toward "God's messengers" in particular. No sooner had they completed their settlement near the village, which lay on a branch of the Curaray River, than the evangelists found themselves in the presence of a group of Aucas who, with the help of a few deftly thrown spears, soon managed to give the forest back its initial purity.
>
> I would say, as far as I'm concerned, that I can only agree with this definitive way of ridding oneself of such undesirable visitors.[1]

Written during the early years of the Algerian war for independence—and just weeks before the Soviet invasion of Hungary—Joubert's anecdote of preemptive anticolonial violence humorously reflects on the surrealist movement's nearly forty years of discussion about political violence and the "civilizing gangrene" of Western imperialism. The story itself is historically accurate, as are the Aucas themselves; yet both Joubert's title, "So Be It," and even the French valences of the name "Aucas"—a homonym for "OK" as well as for the open-ended causality of *au cas* (in the event that)—overdetermine the anecdote's appeal to the naturalness of "giv[ing] the forest back its initial purity." The "purity" here, in other words, designates not an irredeemable state of virgin primitivism but a state of equilibrium that can be exchanged, preserved, or taken away.

Joubert's report bears scrutiny because its microcosm of anticolonial violence self-consciously condenses the argument of Aimé Césaire's 1955 *Discourse on Colonialism*, an essay very much at the forefront of the surrealist imagination in the 1950s. Joubert's anecdote appropriates a real news item to illustrate Césaire's famous insistence that colonial relations not only impose the very notion of "the primitive" on so-called primitive societies but also, in doing so, disrupt the "harmonious and viable economies adapted to the indigenous population."[2] André Breton likewise appeals to Césaire's *Discourse* in a speech reprinted in the opening pages of the same issue of *Le Surréalisme, Même*. Breton's speech, "For the Defense of Liberty," was delivered in April 1956 to an organization of leftist intellectuals mobilizing against France's military suppression of colonial uprisings in Algeria, as well as against de Gaulle's incarceration of left-wing French reporters who printed dissenting views. Breton explicitly invokes Césaire's diatribe against colonialism as an obliteration of indigenous culture, closing with a number of citations from Césaire's text, whose distribution he calls a "spiritual weapon par excellence."[3]

But what is a spiritual weapon? And to what extent does Breton's notion of a spiritual weapon imply the kind of violence Joubert's article reports? Joubert's "So Be It" condones anticolonial violence in a way that neither Césaire nor Breton makes explicit in their more overtly political speeches.[4] The question of whether or not Joubert's Aucas Indians reduce the subtleties of anticolonial political theory to a kind of terrorism or even ethnic cleansing is a question his anecdote defiantly poses. Indeed, to claim the innocence of the Aucas would be to misread the story entirely: the assassination of the missionaries is a rejection of the very position of "innocence"—in the sense of both "primitives" and "dupes"—that the Aucas are trying to avoid. Joubert thus articulates the problem of violence at stake in such theories of insurrectional politics in portraying anticolonial violence as something more than just a "spiritual weapon." But what happens when the revolutionary group is no longer a small tribe of Amazonian natives but the colonized peoples of Algeria, a group of militants, or a former revolutionary state such as the Soviet Union? This was a question that would become one of the most pivotal in postwar French and francophone intellectual debate, not only with regard to the politics of surrealism, but with regard as well to the nature of anticolonial struggle, and even revolution itself more broadly. As I have argued throughout this book, the surrealists' rhetorical and analytical recourse to criminality persistently raised this question, becoming an object of contention on which such political and moral debates centered.

The ties between surrealism's politics and the problem of terrorist violence briefly became a public issue once more in 2001, in the wake of the September 11 attacks. Recalling the surrealist movement's anticolonial and anti-Western rhetoric, which had been especially visible during the 1920s and 1930s, the prominent French curator Jean Clair excoriated the movement for its resemblance to al-Qaeda. In a newspaper editorial published in December 2001, Clair juxtaposed the destruction of the World Trade Center with Louis Aragon's 1925 rant against the "white buildings" of New York City, suggesting a causal (rather than merely analogical) relationship between fundamentalist terrorism and the interwar European avant-garde. In making this juxtaposition, Clair contends that "the surrealist ideology never stopped hoping for the death of an America it saw as materialist and sterile, and for the triumph of an Orient that served as the repository for the values of the mind."[5] More than simply a historical coincidence, Clair argues, surrealism's anti-Western and pro-"Oriental" ideology helped "prepare the minds" of European civilization—yet prepared them not for revolution but for an antihumanism complicit with the forms of totalitarianism and state terror that would follow, from Stalinist purges to the Holocaust.

Clair's polemic was an attack on avant-garde rhetoric, though, rather than a critique of the surrealist movement's actual political thinking, as represented in the many tracts, pamphlets, and speeches the surrealists produced throughout the movement's history. Indeed, Clair's own charge of surrealism's complicity in 9/11—a rhetorical gesture par excellence—is a reaction, he claims, against the ideological stakes of surrealism's own intensified rhetoric, whose insults and violent polemics "are no different from those found in the fiery attacks of the fascist leagues or, on the other side of the political spectrum, those soon to be addressed to the 'mad dogs' in the Moscow trials. They signal an era."[6] Violent rhetoric produces violent action, Clair maintains; and because surrealism spoke, and because its rhetoric thus served as the conduit between its artistic practices and the political sphere, surrealist appeals to violence and to the dissolution of Western humanistic ideals cannot safely be viewed as autonomous artistic utterances. In "seeking to conflate *vita contemplativa* and *vita politica*," Clair argues, the movement's members become as subject to judgment and condemnation as any member of a political party.[7]

Clair's argument against the totalitarian and terrorist consequences of avant-garde rhetoric is hardly a recent invention; it recalls the situation in which French intellectuals found themselves after World War II, as they struggled to forge a political platform in the wake of National Socialism, Stalinism, and the increasing conservatism of de Gaulle's France during the cold war. Clair's polemic in fact rehearses the anxieties of a large body of French writing published in the late 1940s and early 1950s; these studies likewise attacked the "totalizing" and terrorist tendencies in communism, in Marxism, and even in Hegelian philosophy—ideological and philosophical systems that had significantly oriented avant-garde practices between the wars, and most heroically during the Resistance.

Among the most significant of such works are Maurice Merleau-Ponty's 1947 book *Humanism and Terror* and Albert Camus's 1951 book *The Rebel*, each of which uses the lesson of the prewar Moscow trials as an occasion to interrogate the opposition between liberal values and the political tactics of violence, propaganda, and terror used to implement them. Camus, in particular, attacks "revolutionary" movements—whether communism, fascism, or surrealism—for becoming murderous, in principle, precisely at the moment when their commitment to action makes their rhetoric transparent and "demands the suspension of freedom." At this point, Camus writes, "terror, on a grand or small scale, makes its appearance to consummate the revolution."[8] Like Clair, many postwar French intellectuals were anxious about the tendency for the utopian promises of insurrectional movements to become conflated with, or even implicated in, the mechanics of state terror. As recent world events had revealed, these forms of terror were not the work of isolated madmen but, according to Camus, the "logical conclusion of inordinate technical and philosophical ambitions."[9]

The surrealist movement's political thinking of the 1950s offers a useful platform for addressing such concerns because it confronted, as I have argued in this book, the ethical and epistemological stakes of contemplating violence as a political weapon. Surrealist thinking of the 1950s shared with existentialism and anticolonialism a theoretical project that strove to assimilate the spiritual or intellectual liberation promised by prewar avant-gardism with the practical liberation of insurrectional politics. Yet it sought to do this in ways that avoided the formalism, and thus the systematic violence, of "totalitarian" ideological platforms, whether communist, fascist, or even humanist. The surrealist movement's heterogeneous theoretical tendencies derived from the intensity of its commitment to intellectual and political liberation. At stake in so many of the group's internal and external disagreements, as I have claimed in this book, was the matter of distinguishing collective order from institutionalized control, discipline from totalization, and justifiable revolutionary violence—whether rhetorical or physical—from murderous crime.

The movement's postwar debates with existentialist intellectuals like Sartre and Camus were especially sensitive to the urgency, yet also the ambiguity, of such distinctions. In light of these debates, surrealism's discourses on crime and criminography work against the "logical conclusions" of political parties and platforms, instead functioning within the broader, antihumanist framework of leftist theory. In place of a rigid ideological program or a distinctive set of artistic and political practices, the surrealists of the 1950s developed a collective strategy for thinking about political responsibility that short-circuited the "barbarous" rigidity of terror.

The title of the glossy new surrealist magazine that appeared in 1956, *Le Surréalisme, Même*, articulates the movement's peculiar cultural and political situation during the mid-1950s. It thus also offers a fitting reflection on the place of the movement in contemporary intellectual history, since the magazine was especially attentive to its own historicity. For one thing, the title's self-reflexivity (Surrealism Itself) alludes to recent speculations about the movement's datedness, which claimed that surrealism had become institutionalized and solipsistic. At the same time, the title's allusion to Marcel Duchamp's similarly reflexive *Large Glass* from 1923, *La Mariée mise à nu par ses célibataires, même* (The Bride Stripped Naked by Her Bachelors, Even), advertised not only that Duchamp's works would feature heavily in the magazine but that his theories of reflection and reflexivity were significant to 1950s surrealism as well. Duchamp's notion that a work of art comes into being through the aporia of judgment and interpretation that takes place between the art object and its spectators—the notion that "it's the SPECTATORS who make paintings"[10]—would serve as surrealism's answer to existentialist phenomenology.

The editorial preface to *Le Surréalisme, Même*, in response to its question, "A new surrealist journal! Why?," set out to dissuade the movement's adherents and critics alike from falling into the trap of thinking that surrealism was merely about itself, a style or a school of thought. As the preface states, the magazine sought "to forestall that current confusion brought about, for unprepared minds, by the increasing profusion of ventures whose aim is artificially to reproduce the climate of surrealism with the intention of promoting, both towards and against it, strangeness for the sake of strangeness, humour for humour's sake, or any other solution just as aberrant as that of art for art's sake."[11] Even as the rise of popular surrealisms in film, in detective fiction, in art, and in advertising disseminated the movement's formal—and occasionally its epistemological—pursuits, the new magazine sought to frustrate the cultural assimilation of surrealism as an aesthetic. Surrealism, the magazine claimed, was an organized collective whose intellectual practices were grounded in the political and the social. The title of the movement's latest magazine may have suggested self-reflection, but its attentions were directed outward.

The means for preventing or forestalling any "confusion" about the movement's priorities was for the group to remind itself, and especially its more recent members, of the conditions that had determined surrealism's political turn during the 1920s. As Breton's speech for the "Defense of Liberty" meeting makes explicit, the movement's political engagement in the mid-1920s was a direct response to France's military suppression of Abd el-Krim's anticolonial insurgency in the Rif section of Morocco. In a postwar era scarred not only by the horrors of fascism but also by Stalinist invasions and France's own mobilization against Algerian and Vietnamese independence, Breton's reminder about the 1920s locates the impetus for surrealist politics within its support for decolonization. In other words, the Communist Party affiliation that had promised, for several years in the late 1920s, to provide a concrete means for political intervention had been only a temporary means, rather than the goal or cause, of surrealism's political commitment. The movement's subsequent years of debate with and ultimate rejection of orthodox communism had clouded this earlier commitment to decolonization. Ever since the early 1930s, and increasingly after the Moscow trials of 1936 and 1937, the surrealists had excoriated Stalinism as a form of state terror not just complicit with capitalism and fascism but co-extensive with their imperial aims: to be anticolonial meant rejecting party communism, as Aimé Césaire likewise did in 1956.[12]

As the young surrealist writer Nora Mitrani put it more broadly, under such conditions the true murderers were no longer individual criminals but the systematic organizations that committed violence under the aegis of principles, laws, or the state. Mitrani writes: "The collective massacres of these last few years have proved only too well that the crime of passion had ceased to be a solitary and magnificent mystery but instead organized itself, crumbled into office files, into racial laws, faded into concepts of the Good and the Honorable."[13] Mitrani's ironic appeal to the mystery and romance of old-fashioned crimes of passion is not a real expression of nostalgia, of course, but an accusation of the facility with which acts of state terror or even genocide conceal their criminality behind the abstractions of administration and humanistic principles. The organizations Mitrani and the surrealists reviled, in other words, gave terror and murder an alibi.

Oscillating between Trotskyite and neo-anarchist political affiliation throughout the 1950s, surrealism's postwar project was oriented toward defending political and intellectual freedom against the military and ideological state apparatuses that worked to suppress it. Thus, although it recalled the anticolonialism of the 1920s in its political imperative, by the mid-1950s surrealism's project was not defined in the same terms as its prewar incarnations; rather than seeking to incite revolutionary thought or action through their works, the surrealists instead committed themselves to defending and extending such thought and action as it happened. As in the example of the Aucas—but also in Algeria, Vietnam, and elsewhere—uprisings were taking place. The immediate task of surrealism was to defend these uprisings against the external and internal forces that threatened their liberatory potential: against the military powers that strove to crush them, but also against the tendency toward dogmatism that could pervert revolutionary violence into terror.

Two essays by Benjamin Péret dramatize this adjustment. The first, a hopeful essay published in the first issue of Le Surréalisme, Même, "Is This the Dawn" ("Est-ce l'aube"), praises the Algerian insurgency alongside proletarian uprisings against communist rule in Poznan and in East Berlin, as well as student demonstrations in Prague and Budapest, as evidence that "we are witnessing the first attempts of the international proletariat to seize back the direction of its struggles, in rejecting the dead weight of traditional organizations."[14] A second essay, published a few months later in the second issue of the magazine, chronicles the violent suppression of the Hungarian revolution by Russian troops in November 1956 as the deadly final phase in the evolution of Stalinism, which, from its beginnings, "sought nothing other than to profit from the possibilities granted by the new revolutionary order."[15] Péret's essays, written after years of travel between Spain, France,

Mexico, and Brazil as a militant Trotskyite, are by far the most adamant surrealist writings in their criminalization of the Soviet Union and the French republic as terrorist states. Yet Péret nevertheless shared with the other 1950s surrealists, as well as with contemporary anticolonial theorists such as Sartre and Fanon, the notion that colonial and imperial power was responsible for the revolts their oppression provoked. Anticolonial violence, in other words, was justifiable as a form of self-defense; and the military suppression of such revolts by the powers that instigated them became, in turn, a kind of double crime.[16]

Given their hostility toward the systematic violence, whether explicit or implicit, of state apparatuses, the surrealists would seem to be in concert with the numerous attacks on Stalinism that proliferated after the war, especially after the publication of Arthur Koestler's novel *Darkness at Noon* (*Le Zéro et l'infini*), which appeared in French in 1945. Yet whereas the surrealists would share the left's contempt for, or at least discouragement with, the fate of Bolshevism under Stalin, they were skeptical of the way other French intellectuals modeled their broader critiques of revolution and insurgency after the Soviet example. Koestler's fictionalized account of the Moscow trials notably cites them as the culminating moment at which, he writes, "revolutionary theory had frozen to a dogmatic cult, with a simplified, easily graspable catechism, and with No. 1 [i.e., Stalin] as the high priest celebrating the mass."[17] For Koestler's protagonist, Rubashov, the experiences of imprisonment and examination put on trial Rubashov's own complicity with the "dogmatic cult" of Stalinism he had recently been serving as well as the "revolutionary theory" itself. What comes flooding back to Rubashov during his sleep-deprived days of interrogation is the question that would be posed by many French intellectuals in the years after the war: At what point did the revolution's historical logic of necessity stifle and overwhelm the lives of the human subjects it was designed to liberate?

As Rubashov muses, the object of revolution may be the abolition of suffering, but the removal of suffering has turned out to be possible only at the price of an enormous increase in suffering. "Was such an operation justified?" Rubashov asks, to which he responds: "Obviously it was, if one spoke in the abstract of 'mankind'; but, applied to 'man' in the singular . . . , the real human being of bone and flesh and blood and skin, the principle led to absurdity."[18] Rubashov's conundrum—and especially his appeal to the basic humanism that his party activities had so long repressed—is the starting point of Maurice Merleau-Ponty's 1947 study of Koestler's implications, *Humanism and Terror*. For Merleau-Ponty, the problem exceeds merely the absurd contradiction between the abolition of suffering in theory and the increase of suffering in practice, to comprise the paradoxes of revolutionary movements more broadly.

Merleau-Ponty's titular allusion to the French Terror of 1793 suggests that the question of revolutionary policy, and the question of a revolution's future, is intrinsic to the relationship of radical thought to what he calls "the ambiguity of history." Since, Merleau-Ponty writes, we are not spectators of a closed history but in fact actors in an open history, "our *praxis* introduces the element of construction rather than knowledge as an ingredient of the world, making the world not simply an object of contemplation but something to be transformed."[19] Because there can be no absolute knowledge of historical ends, political action is based only on probabilistic calculation. That is, the justification for any revolutionary end is based on a historical wager that renders every revolution a matter of force and violence. For Merleau-Ponty this is a broader problem than that of Stalinism; the Terror of History itself, which frames violence as part of any historical decision, demands that we seek a new humanism in order to preserve the possibility of real revolution. He defines this new humanism as a "harmony with ourselves and others, in a word, truth, not only in *a priori* reflection and solitary thought but through the experience of concrete situations and in a living dialogue with others apart from which internal evidence cannot validate its universal right." This radically contingent form of dialogic social reorganization forms the core of Merleau-Ponty's understanding of existentialism, the conception of the human world as an open or unfinished system that posits "the experience of the other person as an alter ego."[20]

Albert Camus, in *The Rebel*, published four years later in 1951, extends Merleau-Ponty's problematic even further. In a way that would soon provoke the disapproval of the surrealists, Camus isolates revolt as a Cartesian and Kantian principle of humanism through which the archetypal rebel—for Camus, a "slave" who says "no" to the master—risks his life "for the sake of a common good which he considers more important than his own destiny. . . . He acts, therefore, in the name of certain values which are still indeterminate but which he feels are common to himself and to all men."[21] The critical difference between Merleau-Ponty's existentialist humanism and Camus's "man in revolt" lies in each author's conception of the forces that pervert the historical wager of "revolt" and transform it into a form of terror that exterminates the very values it stood for. Whereas Merleau-Ponty strives to rescue revolutionary Marxism from terror by stressing how it advocates a dialectical process of knowledge and praxis, Camus implicates virtually the entire genealogy of revolutionary thought in France as bearing the seeds of terror within its own logic. Indeed, *The Rebel* pathologizes not only Marx but also Nietzsche, Hegel, Sade, Baudelaire, Lautréamont, and the surrealists. Unlike Jean Clair, though, Camus does not so much denounce these figures as the causes of totalitarianism as demonstrate how they succumb to the same dynamic of corruption that transforms idealism into terror. This dynamic describes any form of thought that subjects man, as Camus writes, to a formal principle:

Historical thought was to deliver man from subjection to a divinity; but this liberation demanded of him the most absolute subjection to historical evolution. Then man takes refuge in the concept of the permanence of the party in the same way that he formerly prostrated himself before the altar. That is why the era which dares to claim that it is the most rebellious that has ever existed only offers a choice of various types of conformity. The real passion of the twentieth century is servitude.[22]

The real passion of the twentieth century was not, in other words, the suppression or re-pression of freedom but the servitude and conformity of so-called revolutionaries. What disturbed the surrealists most about Camus's formulation was the tendency for his ab-straction of terror to conflate the revolutionary and the terrorist, and in doing so, to place the onus of historical responsibility on the oppressed, on Camus's "slave" who says no.

To its credit, The Rebel seeks to isolate a form of revolt that does not become an im-moderate mechanism of violence and murder; in opposition to "revolution in the name of power and of history," Camus proposes a new rebellion "in the name of moderation and of life."[23] Breton, however, considered such an attempt to introduce a revolt "emptied of its impassioned content" to be a logical contradiction. As he writes in a response to Ca-mus's book, "Can revolt be both itself and mastery, the perfect domination of itself, at the same time?"[24] Breton criticizes Camus's overall logic for presuming a constant and ir-revocable historical progression of revolutionary thought from "revolt" to terror. That is, not only did Camus abstract "revolt" from the recourse to violence that rendered it possi-ble in the first place, but also Camus's reading of historical figures such as Marx, Hegel, Lautréamont, and the surrealists presupposed the conclusions of servitude and complic-ity he wished to derive from them in advance. Camus did not allow the possibility for truly revolutionary thought to disrupt its own tendency toward dogmatism.

Benjamin Péret redresses Camus's blindness in his contribution to a collection of sur-realist responses to The Rebel; philosophical influences, like violence, are not themselves dogmatic but are only made so by their proscriptive use. In language that resonates strongly with 1950s surrealism's theories of intellectual and artistic practice, Péret writes: "The instrument is neutral; it's only the use one makes of it that bestows dignity or indignity. A pen can just as well serve to write a poem as a police report."[25] It is still the responsibility of the revolutionary to resist the canonization of concepts, and to short-cir-cuit the administrative formalism that leads to ideological and genocidal forms of terror. The fate of Marxian thought demonstrates the imperative for this resistance; as Péret writes: "Marx is a principal element in the revolutionary and socialist thought of the past century. What matters is submitting him to the critique to which he submitted his prede-cessors and contemporaries, in order that the living elements of them all . . . might find their place in a theory better adapted to the necessities of our time." Péret does not deny, in other words, that there is a link between Marxist thought and Stalinism; but this link is analogous to "the meat and the fly that spoils it; [to] liberty and the gendarme; [to] the revolution and the counterrevolution."[26] The historical revision Péret describes requires something more, however, than a simple process of bargain and compromise enacted according to humanist principles; instead, the work of surrealist theory involved submitting knowledge to the challenge of thinking that came, in Breton's words, "from elsewhere."

For the surrealists, the responsibility to resist the perversion of revolutionary theory into terror did not demand a return either to Merleau-Ponty's existentialist intersubjectivity or to Camus's "moderation and life" as necessary forms of humanist mediation. Rather it demanded an abandonment of humanism altogether. "I formally contest," writes Gérard Legrand in the pages of *Le Surréalisme, Même,*

> that surrealism is a humanism (or a "sur-humanism") at all. I would say that liberty can think itself and even conceptualize itself without taking into account *the human,* that hybrid of medieval Thomism, post-Renaissance skepticism (Montaigne), and the "open" morals of university skepticism. Surrealism is not a philosophy: it is the crossroads, the meeting place of several philosophies that have significance only in mutually completing themselves before the flaming hearth of poetry. But if it has been able to coincide, under precise conditions, with contemporary humanisms for the defense of interests and values belonging to "the mind," this is not because man was the bearer of these values; in my opinion it is for these values, and for the mind itself.[27]

As Legrand's essay suggests, surrealism posited its own form of mediation—indeed, the group's very reason for existence might be described as its desire to organize the relationship between political revolution and art in a way that would short-circuit the orthodoxies Merleau-Ponty and Camus describe.

Such an organization, however, demanded a redefinition not only of the relationship between political thought and aesthetics—a relationship the surrealists configured as a dialectic—but also of the nature of poetry and art themselves as something other than a means for human expression. In place of a traditional understanding of art as representation, the surrealists posited the role of art within political thought as being constituted within and by the dialectic of interpretation that takes place between the object and its spectators. The appeal of Marcel Duchamp's formulation that "it's the SPECTATORS who make paintings" to the 1950s surrealists lay in its simply worded yet radically suggestive elimination of the classical notion of art's intrinsic communicative faculty. Poetry and art came into existence through their encounter with an audience; reciprocally, the forms of intersubjectivity promoted by the existentialists were mediated, in turn, by the nonhuman objects and texts whose resistance to immediate comprehension provoked interpretation and critique. This resistance, rather than the liberal practices of debate and compromise alone, was fundamental to the work of thinking, and to the work of liberation.

Surrealism came into being as a movement that operated within the field of possibility created at the points of encounter between ideologies, ordering systems, and ways of knowing. In its responses to contemporary intellectual and political problems, the movement drew from—but also revised—its understanding of Marxism, psychoanalysis, and German Romanticism, but also of scientific positivism, mysticism, ethnography, alchemy, and even error. As members of a group who were as much witnesses at the "crossroads" of philosophies, art objects, and values as they were participants in their coming into being, the surrealists subjected their own thinking, too, to a rigorous dynamic of disruption and openness. The result, as I have argued in this book, is that the movement constituted at once a social practice and an epistemological break: it represented a displacement of subjectivity and individualism in favor of collective intellectual practices attuned as much to the demands of words, objects, and philosophies as to the "common good."

In refusing the mantle of humanism, surrealism opened itself to the discomfiting possibility that its work would be overshadowed by the allure of terrorist action or of political expediency. Yet as the group's long-standing fascination with crime reveals, the movement was dedicated less to destroying all laws than to thwarting the tendency for experimental thought to become law. The surrealist experiment, then, might be understood as the attempt to mobilize art to "suppress the exploitation of man by man" by causing an insurrection within thought. Herein lies surrealism's essential contribution to twentieth-century thought: not, as Jean Clair claimed, in "preparing the mind" for the atrocities of terrorism and the Holocaust, but in preparing the mind to defend itself against the forms of ideological closure that ensure the continuation of such atrocities.

NOTES

Introduction

1 Louis Aragon, "Idées," *La Révolution Surréaliste* 3 (1925): 30. Translations are my own where no other translator is credited.

2 Whereas intellectual historians such as Tony Judt have tended to disavow the place of surrealism in European intellectual history, more recent studies assert the intimate ties between surrealism and experimental philosophy during the interwar and postwar periods. See Michel Surya, *La Révolution rêvée: pour une histoire des écrivains et des intellectuels révolutionnaires, 1944–1956* (Paris: Fayard, 2004); Bruce Baugh, *French Hegel: From Surrealism to Postmodernism* (New York: Routledge, 2003); and Suzanne Guerlac, *Literary Polemics: Bataille, Sartre, Valéry, Breton* (Stanford: Stanford University Press, 1997). On the role of surrealism in French psychoanalysis, see especially Elisabeth Roudinesco, *Jacque Lacan & Co.: A History of Psychoanalysis in France, 1925–1985* (Chicago: University of Chicago Press, 1990). On the relations of surrealism with *négritude*, see Michael Richardson and Krzysztof Fijalkowski, *Refusal of the Shadow* (New York: Verso, 1996), and Robin D. G. Kelley, *Freedom Dreams: The Black Radical Imagination* (Boston: Beacon Press, 2002). See also Wole Soyinka, *Myth, Literature, and the African World* (Cambridge: Cambridge University Press, 1976).

3 Breton's language from the opening page of the *Second Manifesto of Surrealism* (1929), "une crise de conscience," is highly condensed, signifying both "an attack of conscience" as well as "crisis in consciousness." André Breton, *Oeuvres complètes*, ed. Marguerite Bonnet et al., vol. 1 (Paris: Gallimard, 1988), 781.

4 See, for instance, Gérard Durozoi, *History of the Surrealist Movement* (Chicago: University of Chicago Press, 2002); Katharine Conley, *The Automatic Woman* (Lincoln: University of Nebraska Press, 1996); Richardson and Fijalkowski, *Refusal of the Shadow*; Mary Ann Caws, *Surrealism: Themes and Movements* (London: Phaidon, 2004); Martica Sawin, *Surrealism in Exile and the Beginning of the New York School* (Cambridge: MIT Press, 1995); and Alyce Mahon, *Surrealism and the Politics of Eros, 1938–1968* (London: Thames and Hudson, 2005).

5 Jacqueline Chénieux-Gendron, *Surrealism*, trans. Vivian Folkenflik (New York: Columbia University Press, 1990), 12.

6 Maurice Blanchot, *The Infinite Conversation*, trans. Susan Hanson (Minneapolis: University of Minnesota Press, 1993), 9, 437.

7 Georges Bataille, "Surrealism and How It Differs from Existentialism," in *The Absence of Myth: Writings on Surrealism*, trans. Michael Richardson (London: Verso, 1994), 59.

8 Georges Bataille, "On the Subject of Slumbers," ibid., 51.

9 André Breton, *Second Manifesto of Surrealism*, in *Manifestoes of Surrealism*, trans. Richard Seaver and Helen Lane (Ann Arbor: University of Michigan Press, 1969), 125.

10 See Jean-Paul Sartre, "Situation of the Writer in 1947," in *"What Is Literature?" and Other Essays*, ed. Stephen Ungar (Cambridge: Harvard University Press, 1988), esp. 157.

11 Breton, *Second Manifesto*, 126.

12 Theodor Adorno, *Aesthetic Theory*, trans. Robert Hullot-Kentor (Minneapolis: University of Minnesota Press, 1997), 5.

13 Robin Walz, *Pulp Surrealism: Insolent Popular Culture in Early Twentieth-Century Paris* (Berkeley: University of California Press, 2000), 145, 3.

14 On the role of aestheticized violence in surrealist thinking, see Amy Lyford, "The Aesthetics of Dismemberment: Surrealism and the Musée du Val-de-Grâce in 1917," *Cultural Critique* 46 (Autumn

2000): 45–79, which discusses the French military's aestheticization of wartime violence at the military medical museum at Val-de-Grâce, where Breton and Aragon trained during the war.

15 See Dominique Kalifa, L'Encre et le sang: récits de crimes et société à la Belle Époque (Paris: Fayard, 1995), 10.

16 Philippe Soupault, "L'Ombre de l'ombre," La Révolution Surréaliste 1 (1924): 24–25.

17 Recent scholarly works that share this methodology include Steven Harris, Surrealist Art and Thought in the 1930s: Art, Politics, and the Psyche (Cambridge: Cambridge University Press, 2004); Johanna Malt, Obscure Objects of Desire: Surrealism, Fetishism, and Politics (Oxford: Oxford University Press, 2004); and David Bate, Photography and Surrealism: Sexuality, Colonialism, and Social Dissent (London: I. B. Tauris, 2004).

18 Renée Riese Hubert gives a historical overview of the group's interest in criminal figures throughout the 1920s and 1930s in "Images du criminel et du héros surréalistes," Mélusine 1 (1979): 187–97. Laurie Monahan has written about André Masson and violence in the 1930s, for instance, in "Masson: The Face of Violence," Art in America 88.7 (July 2000): 76–79, 121–22.

19 Among the best recent studies are Elza Adamowicz, Surrealist Collage in Text and Image: Dissecting the Exquisite Corpse (Cambridge: Cambridge University Press, 1998), and Alexander Waintrub's doctoral dissertation, "Crimes of Passion: Surrealism, Allegory, and the Dismembered Body" (UCLA, 1996).

20 See, most generally, Maria Tatar, Lustmord: Sexual Murder in Weimar Germany (Princeton: Princeton University Press, 1995); Joel Black, The Aesthetics of Murder: A Study in Romantic Literature and Contemporary Culture (Baltimore: Johns Hopkins University Press, 1991); and Mark Seltzer, Serial Killers: Death and Life in America's Wound Culture (New York: Routledge, 1999).

21 See, for instance, Xavière Gauthier, Surréalisme et sexualité (Paris: Gallimard, 1971); Mary Ann Caws, "Ladies Shot and Painted: Female Embodiment in Surrealist Art," in The Female Body in Western Culture, ed. Susan Suleiman (Cambridge: Harvard University Press, 1986), 262–87; and Whitney Chadwick, Women Artists and the Surrealist Movement (Boston: Little, Brown, 1985).

22 See esp. Robin Adèle Greeley, Surrealism and the Spanish Civil War (New Haven: Yale University Press, 2006), and Sidra Stich, ed., Anxious Visions: Surrealist Art (New York: Abbeville Press, 1990). For one of the most provocative studies of Bataille's conceptual ties with surrealism, see Carolyn Dean, The Self and Its Pleasures: Bataille, Lacan, and the History of the Decentered Subject (Ithaca: Cornell University Press, 1992).

23 See Hal Foster, Compulsive Beauty (Cambridge: MIT Press, 1993), xvii; and Rosalind Krauss, The Originality of the Avant-Garde and Other Modernist Myths (Cambridge: MIT Press, 1985), 118.

24 See especially Krauss, The Originality of the Avant-Garde and The Optical Unconscious (Cambridge: MIT Press, 1993). See also Denis Hollier, Against Architecture: The Writings of Georges Bataille, trans. Betsy Wing (Cambridge: MIT Press, 1989).

25 See Margaret Cohen, Profane Illumination: Walter Benjamin and the Paris of Surrealist Revolution (Berkeley: University of California Press, 1993), as well as Michel Löwy, L'Étoile du matin: surréalisme et marxisme (Paris: Syllepse, 2000), and Révolte et melancolie: le romantisme à contre-courant de la modernité (Paris: Payot, 1992); Krauss, The Optical Unconscious and The Originality of the Avant-Garde; and Foster, Compulsive Beauty.

26 Walter Benjamin, "Little History of Photography" (1931), trans. Edmund Jephcott and Kingsley Shorter, in Selected Writings, vol. 2, 1927–1934, ed. Michael W. Jennings et al. (Cambridge: Harvard University Press, 1999), 527.

27 On surrealist militancy, see Harris, Surrealist Art and Thought in the 1930s; Carole Raynaud Paligot, Parcours politique des surréalists, 1919–1969 (Paris: CNRS, 1995); Mahon, Surrealism and the Politics of Eros; and Helena Lewis, The Politics of Surrealism (New York: Paragon House, 1988).

28 Walter Benjamin, "Surrealism: The Last Snapshot of the European Intelligentsia" (1929), trans. Edmund Jephcott, in Selected Writings, vol. 2, 208.

29 Maurice Blanchot, "Reflections on Surrealism," in *The Work of Fire* (1949), trans. Charlotte Mandell (Stanford: Stanford University Press, 1995), 89.

30 André Breton, "What Is Surrealism?" (1934), in *What Is Surrealism? Selected Writings*, ed. Franklin Rosemont (New York: Pathfinder Press, 1978), 115–16.

31 Ibid., 116.

32 Ibid., 117.

33 Paul Éluard to Salvador Dalí (1933), in Éluard, *Lettres à Gala, 1924–1948* (Paris: Gallimard, 1984), 202–3.

1. Locked Room, Bloody Chamber

1 Raoul Vaneigem (pseud. J. Dupuis), *A Cavalier History of Surrealism*, trans. Donald Nicholson-Smith (Edinburgh: AK Press, 1999), 35.

2 The term is Breton's. See André Breton, *Conversations: The Autobiography of Surrealism*, trans. Mark Polizzotti (New York: Marlowe and Company, 1993), 112.

3 André Breton, "Max Ernst" (1921) in *The Lost Steps*, trans. Mark Polizzotti (Lincoln: University of Nebraska Press, 1996), 60.

4 André Breton, *Manifesto of Surrealism*, in *Manifestoes of Surrealism*, trans. Richard Seaver and Helen Lane (Ann Arbor: University of Michigan Press, 1969), 7.

5 Ibid., 7 (original italics removed).

6 Ibid.

7 In addition to Ernst in *Au Rendezvous des amis*, other surrealists cited Dostoyevsky, most notably René Crevel, who describes a recent film version of *Crime and Punishment* in his review of Marcel Arland's *Terres étrangères* (1924) and in his response to an inquiry on "Les Lettres, la pensée moderne et le cinéma" (1925). See the dossier reprinted in Crevel, *Détours* (Paris: Pauvert, 1985), 141–42 and 160–62.

8 Louis Aragon, "Une Vague de rêves," *Commerce* 2 (Autumn 1924), rpt. in *Chroniques, 1918–1932*, ed. Bernard Leuilliot (Paris: Stock, 1998), 191. Translation adapted from Adam Cornford's electronically published translation (http://www.durationpress.com/authors/aragon/wave.html). Page numbers refer to the French text.

9 Ibid.

10 Breton, *Manifesto*, 8.

11 Ibid.

12 Fyodor Dostoyevsky, *Crime and Punishment* (1866), trans. David McDuff (London: Penguin, 1991), 37–38.

13 Breton, *Manifesto*, 10.

14 Ibid.

15 Breton, "Max Ernst," 60.

16 Breton, *Manifesto*, 23.

17 Walter Benjamin, "The Paris of the Second Empire in Baudelaire" (1938), trans. Harry Zohn, in *Selected Writings*, vol. 4 (1938–1940), ed. Michael W. Jennings et al. (Cambridge: Cambridge University Press, 2003), 27.

18 Breton, "Max Ernst," 60.

19 Ibid.

20 In her 1981 essay on surrealism's photographic conditions, Rosalind Krauss cites the photograph's ability to frame, crop, and select among the "inchoate sprawl of the real" as the principal condition of possibility for the surrealist movement. That is, photography's "natural" presentation of reality as codified made possible surrealism's experience of understanding and manipulating reality as

representation. By highlighting the imaginative role of photography in surrealist production, Krauss argues for a semiological coherence at the core of surrealist aesthetics. Though I remain critical of Krauss's efforts to find an organic definition for surrealism that surpasses the movement's self-understanding, her essay has dramatically expanded the conditions of possibility for the study of surrealism. See Rosalind E. Krauss, "The Photographic Conditions of Surrealism," in The Originality of the Avant-Garde and Other Modernist Myths (Cambridge: MIT Press, 1985), esp. 118.

21 See also Breton's "encyclopedia" definition of surrealism in the Manifesto, which states that surrealism "tends to ruin once and for all other psychic mechanisms and to substitute itself for them in solving all the principle problems of life" (26).

22 Philippe Weil, "Au Clair de la lune," Littérature, n.s. 3 (May 1922): 3–4.

23 Ibid., 4.

24 "L'Inconnu," Littérature, n.s. 3 (May 1922): 2.

25 Philippe Soupault, À la dérive (Paris: J. Ferenczi et Fils, 1923), 77–105. I am grateful to Myriam Boucharenc's thorough study of Soupault's writings, L'Échec et son double: Philippe Soupault romancier (Paris: Honoré Champion, 1997), 236–37, in which she mentions "Au Claire de la lune" as an instance of Soupault's interest in "secret texts."

26 Philippe Soupault, "Raymond Roussel," Littérature, n.s. 2 (April 1922): 16–19, 18.

27 Raymond Roussel, "La Vue" (1897), cited ibid., 2, 18.

28 Pierre MacOrlan, "Photographie: éléments de fantastique social," Le Crapouillot (January 1929): 3.

29 Ibid., 3–4.

30 Ibid., 4.

31 Soupault, "Raymond Roussel," 17. The ironic formalism in Soupault's "Au Clair de la lune" mirrors the false naturalism of Roussel's Impressions of Africa, whose method of composition Weil's title seems to invoke. As Soupault most likely could not have known, the very line "au clair de la lune" forms a central part of Roussel's secret method of composition, which he revealed in his posthumous text, How I Wrote Certain of My Books. See Raymond Roussel, How I Wrote Certain of My Books, ed. and trans. Trevor Winkfield (Boston: Exact Change, 1995), 12–13.

32 Michel Foucault, "Speaking and Seeing in Raymond Roussel," in Aesthetics, Method, and Epistemology: Essential Works of Michel Foucault, 1954–1984, vol. 2, ed. James D. Faubion (New York: New Press, 1998), 25.

33 Soupault, "Raymond Roussel," 16.

34 Ibid. As Roussel's posthumous writings reveal, his "impressions" of Africa were also derived from plays on words, suggesting that the principal referent in Rousselian signification was not "Africa" but language itself; see note 31. See also Elizabeth Ezra, "Raymond Roussel and the Structure of Stereotype," in The Colonial Unconscious: Race and Culture in Interwar France (Ithaca: Cornell University Press, 2000), 47–74.

35 Pierre Bayard, Who Killed Roger Ackroyd? The Mystery behind the Agatha Christie Mystery, trans. Carol Cosman (New York: Norton, 2000), 25.

36 Ibid., 144.

37 Soupault would later assassinate the detective, too, in his 1926 novella La Mort de Nick Carter. See chapter 4.

38 See Alphonse Bertillon, La Photographie judiciaire (Paris: Gauthier-Villars, 1890).

39 Walter Benjamin, "The Paris of the Second Empire in Baudelaire," 27.

40 Ibid.

41 For a summary of the Fantômas plots, see Robin Walz, Pulp Surrealism: Insolent Popular Culture in Early Twentieth-Century France (Berkeley: University of California Press, 2000). See also Daniel Gercke, "On the Eve of Distraction: Gaumont's Fantômas," Sites 1.1 (Spring 1997): 157–69.

42 In 1928 Magritte wrote his own Fantômas plot in which Inspector Juve ties up a sleeping Fantômas, only to discover, before his very eyes, that the Fantômas who awakens is no longer tied up. Juve

then resolves to pursue the criminal by entering his dreams. See René Magritte, "Note sur Fantômas," *Distances* 2 (March 1928), reprinted in *Écrits complets*, ed. André Blavier (Paris: Flammarion, 1979), 48–49.

43 Dalia Judovitz, *Unpacking Duchamp* (Berkeley: University of California Press, 1995), 107.

44 Soupault, "Raymond Roussel," 17.

45 As Éluard explains in a 1919 article for *Littérature*, even Leroux's more puerile mysteries were valuable to the proto-surrealist Dada poets for their delightful solipsism: "Mystery resembles mystery, with neither a need for mirrors nor for memory. It is made up of all the heart's childishness. The science of details." Paul Éluard, "Gaston Leroux est l'auteur du fauteil hanté," *Littérature*, n.s. 9 (November 1919): 32.

46 Gaston Leroux, *The Mystery of the Yellow Room* (New York: Brentano's, 1908), 11.

47 For an illuminating discussion of Leroux's novel and the visual logic of deduction, see Andrea Goulet, *Optiques: The Science of the Eye and the Birth of Modern French Fiction* (Philadelphia: University of Pennsylvania Press, 2006), esp. 136–52.

48 As Leroux's narrator describes it, "The words ["The presbytery has lost nothing of its charm, nor the garden its brightness"] had hardly left the lips of Rouletabille than I saw Robert Darzac quail. Pale as he was, he became paler. His eyes were fixed on the young man in terror." Gaston Leroux, *The Mystery of the Yellow Room*, 46.

49 Walter Benjamin, "Surrealism: The Last Snapshot of the European Intelligentsia," trans. Edmund Jephcott, in *Selected Writings*, vol. 2 (1927–1934), ed. Michael W. Jennings et al. (Cambridge: Harvard University Press, 1999), 210.

50 Maxime Alexandre, *Mémoires d'un surréaliste* (Paris: La Jeune Parque, 1968), 105.

51 André Breton, "Max Ernst," 61.

52 Maurice Blanchot, *The Infinite Conversation*, trans. Susan Hanson (Minneapolis: University of Minnesota Press, 1993), 409.

53 Breton, *Manifesto of Surrealism*, 45.

54 G. K. Chesterton, "The Blue Cross" (1911), in *The Complete Father Brown* (New York: Dodd, Mead & Co., 1982), 6–7.

55 Breton, *Manifesto of Surrealism*, 45.

56 Walter Benjamin, "Little History of Photography" (1931), in *Selected Writings*, vol. 2, 1927–1934, 507–30, 527.

57 Philippe Soupault, *A la dérive* (Paris: J. Ferenczi et fils, 1923), 88.

2. On Murder, Considered as One of the Surrealist Arts

1 Lautréamont (Isodore Ducasse), *Maldoror and the Complete Works of the Comte de Lautrémont*, trans. Alexis Lykiard (Cambridge: Exact Change, 1994), canto 6, esp. 193.

2 Man Ray's early reading of *Les Chants de Maldoror* around 1914 (possibly in the pages of *The Egoist*) predates its similar "discovery" by André Breton, Louis Aragon, and Philippe Soupault in the immediate aftermath of the First World War.

3 For discussions of Man Ray's image, see Renée Riese Hubert, *Surrealism and the Book* (Berkeley: University of California Press, 1988), 192; and Elsa Adamowicz, *Surrealist Collage in Text and Image: Dissecting the Exquisite Corpse* (Cambridge: Cambridge University Press, 1998), 67.

4 See Louis Aragon, "Une Vague de rêves," *Commerce* 2 (Autumn 1924), rpt. in *Chroniques, 1918–1932*, ed. Bernard Leuilliot (Paris: Stock, 1998), 193.

5 *Le Petit Parisien*, 28–29 February and 1–6, 11, and 18 March 1920. *Le Figaro* also printed a *fait-divers* on 28 February 1920, titled "Une Enfant coupée en morceaux."

6 *Le Petit Parisien*, 28 February 1920.

7 Henri Desiré Landru was arrested in 1919 on suspicion of his involvement in the disappearance of ten women and a boy; the case became a great mystery since little evidence was ever found. Landru

was not convicted until 25 February 1922. Proto-surrealist responses to the case include Jacques Baron, "L'Affaire Landru," *Aventure* 2 (December 1921): 8; and Philippe Soupault and André Breton's encounter with Landru's lawyer shortly after Landru's execution: "Entrevue avec Maître de Moro-Giafferi," *Littérature*, n.s. 1 (March 1922): 23–24. For a detailed historiography of the Landru case, see Robin Walz, *Pulp Surrealism: Insolent Popular Culture in Early Twentieth-Century Paris* (Berkeley: University of California Press, 2000).

8 Benjamin Péret, "Assassiner," *Littérature* 15 (July–August 1920), rpt. in *Œuvres complètes*, vol. 7 (Paris: José Corti, 1995), 13. Cardinal Amette was the archbishop of Paris from 1908 until his death in late August 1920, shortly after Péret published his essay. Gustave de Lamarzelle was a member of the French Senate, a right-wing royalist who published a book on anarchism in 1919, *L'Anarchie dans le monde moderne.*

9 See Walz, *Pulp Surrealism*, 76–113.

10 Péret, "Assassiner," 13.

11 Thomas De Quincey, "On Murder, Considered as One of the Fine Arts," in *The Collected Writings of Thomas De Quincey*, ed. David Masson, vol. 13 (1890; rpt. New York: AMS Press, 1968), 13.

12 Ibid., 20.

13 Péret, "Assassiner," 13.

14 André Breton, *Anthology of Black Humor* (1939), trans. Mark Polizzotti (San Francisco: City Lights Press, 1997), 53.

15 Ibid., 55.

16 See Maria Tatar, *Lustmord: Sexual Murder in Weimar Germany* (Princeton: Princeton University Press, 1995).

17 Such a metaphorical relationship to the sociological fact of murder finds its more gleeful expression, for instance, in Jean Cocteau's 1932 essay "Des Beaux-Arts considerés comme un assassinat." in *Essai de critique indirect* (Paris: B. Grasset, 1932).

18 Raymond Meunier, "Criminalité cubéo-dadaïste," *Liberté*, 16 February 1922.

19 Péret, "Assassiner," 13.

20 See *Littérature* 18 (March 1921): 1–7, where representatives of the Dada group rate a long alphabetized list of famous names on a scale of −25 (lowest) to +20 (highest), with 0 signifying "absolute indifference."

21 Charles Baudelaire translated numerous works by De Quincey, including "On Murder, Considered as One of the Fine Arts" (*De l'assassinat, considéré comme un des beaux-arts*) and *Confessions of an English Opium-Eater*, which formed the larger part of Baudelaire's *Paradis artificiels*. Alfred Jarry, a reader of Baudelaire's translations, adapted the "On Murder" essays for part of *Jours et nuits* as well as for a short play.

22 Péret, "Assassiner," 13.

23 See, for instance, Carole Renaud-Paligot, *Parcours politique des surréalistes, 1919–1969* (Paris, CNRS, 1995).

24 For the canonical account of this evening (6 July 1923), see Michel Sanouillet, *Dada à Paris* (Paris: Flammarion, 1969), 380–87.

25 Aragon, "Une Vague de rêves," 195.

26 Susan Rubin Suleiman, *Subversive Intent: Gender, Politics, and the Avant-Garde* (Cambridge: Harvard University Press, 1990), 82.

27 André Breton, "The Mediums Enter," in *The Lost Steps*, trans. Mark Polizzotti (Lincoln: University of Nebraska Press, 1996), 90.

28 In a letter to Tristan Tzara from the summer of 1923, Crevel writes: "Were you in Paris when I had the honor to send Breton a letter of rupture. I did not hold it against him personally but against Desnos, with whom he reckons he has a sense of solidarity and whose insulting and stupid politics brought my disgust to a head one evening when I went to rue Fontaine [Breton's studio]." Letter rpt. in René Crevel, *Mon Corps et moi* (Paris: Pauvert, 1974), 185.

29 René Crevel, "Which Way?" *The Little Review* (Autumn 1923–Winter 1924): 31.

30 This one exception is the short piece titled "La Négresse aux bas blancs" (The Negress with White Stockings), which was transcribed from the séances and published in *Littérature*.

31 Breton, "The Mediums Enter," 92–93.

32 See André Breton, "Words without Wrinkles," in *The Lost Steps*, 100–102.

33 Breton, "The Mediums Enter," 95.

34 André Breton, "L'Entrée des médiums" (from MS version), in *Œuvres complètes*, ed. Marguerite Bonnet et al., 3 vols. (Paris: Gallimard, 1988), vol. 1, 1303.

35 The oft-cited term derives from Lautréamont; see Lautréamont, *Maldoror*, 36.

36 See Marguerite Bonnet, *André Breton: naissance de l'aventure surréaliste* (Paris: José Corti, 1988), 263–64.

37 Simone Breton to Denise Lévy, 25 September 1922, in Simone Breton, *Lettres à Denise Lévy*, ed. Georgiana Colvile (Paris: Éditions Joelle Losfeld, 2005), 106–7. Selections from this letter are cited in Bonnet, *André Breton*, 263–64.

38 Simone Breton's letter continues to recount Crevel's uncharacteristically violent mediumistic performances, replicating both their syntax and their associative logic: "Another day it was: 'The Axe, I said, the Axe'—an old man brandishes it. The woman will be naked; she is, naturally, an adulteress, etc. Another day he crushes the eyes of all the women under his heels, or else presses them into their brains with his two thumbs, etc. On yet another day: 'I have discovered my cook's secrets,' in a sarcastic tone; she is the heroine of an obscene and criminal scene that took place in the Bois de Vincennes, with a soldier from the 13e as its hero, and into which Mount Blanc finds itself mixed, at the foot of which someone had dug a 4,810 meter ditch *with his nails*—a formidable and extremely poetic imbroglio, always dramatic and exorbitant. And on the last occasion: 'The Princess of Lamballe's dresses are being sold at auction—but they're not selling her hats. . . . She's put all 15,000 hats on her head, atop the iron spade that is now her body. This woman, two meters tall, is as far from thick as your little finger. And she is naked. The human skin is never naked. For who has ever stripped down so far as to show the iron spade beneath? It has to do with her *odd body!*' Imagine these stories, told in the darkness—at times almost screamed, and at other times trailing off, never to finish." Breton, *Lettres à Denise Lévy*, 107.

39 Lautréamont, *Maldoror*, 114–15.

40 Ibid., 115.

41 Bonnet, *André Breton*, 143.

42 Ibid., 145–46.

43 André Breton, "Les Chants de Maldoror," in *Les Pas perdus*, in *Œuvres complètes*, 1:235.

44 René Crevel, review of Breton, *Les Pas perdus*, rpt. in *Mon Corps et Moi* (1926; rpt., Paris: Pauvert, 1974), 191.

45 Ibid., 192.

46 René Crevel, "Après Dada," *Les Nouvelles Littéraires* 69, 9 February 1924, rpt. in *Babylone* (1927; rpt., Paris: Pauvert, 1986), 242.

47 Marcel Arland, "Sur un nouveau mal de siècle," *La Nouvelle Revue Française* 128 (1924): 156.

48 Crevel, "Après Dada," 243.

49 Ibid.

50 See Elizabeth Ezra, *The Colonial Unconscious: Race and Culture in Interwar France* (Ithaca: Cornell University Press, 2000), 75–96.

51 See Michel Carassou, "Mal de vivre, mal du siècle," in René Crevel, *Détours* (1925; rpt., Paris: Pauvert, 1985), 10–11; see also Carassou's biography, *René Crevel* (Paris: Fayard, 1989).

52 Crevel, *Détours*, 40.

53 René Crevel, "Deux Livres de Jean Paulhan," *L'Université de Paris* 240 (March 1922), rpt. in *Babylone*, 234–35.

54 Crevel, "Après Dada," 243.

55 Crevel, *Détours*, 73–74.

3. Germaine Berton and the Ethics of Assassination

1 René Crevel, review of "Les Pas perdus," in *Mon Corps et moi* (Paris: Pauvert, 1974), 191.

2 Tristan Tzara, cited by Louis Aragon in the epigraph to *Anicet, ou le panorama, roman* (Paris: Nouvelle Revue Française,, 1921). Aragon paraphrases Tzara's "Dada Manifesto 1918"; see Tristan Tzara, *7 Dada Manifestos and Lampisteries*, trans. Barbara Wright (London: Calder, 1977), 9.

3 Crevel, "Which Way?" *The Little Review* (Autumn–Winter 1923–24): 29.

4 See Marguerite Bonnet, *André Breton: naissance de l'aventure surréaliste* (Paris: José Corti, 1988), 62–63. See also Louis Aragon, *The Libertine*, trans. Jo Levy (London: John Calder, 1987).

5 Crevel, "Which Way?" 31.

6 On Marius Plateau and the *camelots du roy*, see Paul Cohen, "Heroes and Dilettantes: The *Action Française, Le Sillon*, and the Generation of 1905–14," *French Historical Studies* 15.4 (Autumn 1988): 673–87.

7 Louis Aragon, "A Man," *The Little Review* (Autumn–Winter 1923–24): 18–22, 21.

8 Louis Aragon, "Il m'est impossible . . . ," *Littérature*, n.s. 9 (February–March 1923), rpt. in *Chroniques, 1918–1932*, ed. Bernard Leuilliot (Paris: Stock, 1998), 136.

9 Aragon, "A Man," 21.

10 Ibid., 18.

11 Ibid., 21.

12 Ibid., 22.

13 Louis Aragon to Denise Lévy, in *Lettres à Denise*, ed. Pierre Daix (Paris: Maurice Nadeau, 1994), 25–26.

14 Ibid.

15 This intention was cited in numerous reports; significantly, Germaine Berton committed suicide on July 6, 1942, six days after Léon Daudet's death on June 30. The *New York Times* reported: "Germaine Berton, 34 [sic] years old, who in 1923 shot and killed Marius Plateau, former director of the Royalist Action Française, died Saturday in a Paris hospital from an overdose of drugs. The French press reported it a suicide. Mlle Berton had testified at her trial that she had mistaken M. Plateau for his associate, Léon Daudet. M. Daudet died last Wednesday at Saint-Rémy-en-Provence." "Germaine Berton a Suicide," *New York Times*, 7 July 1942, 5.

16 *Le Libertaire*, 4 December 1923, 1.

17 *Le Libertaire*, 21 September 1923, 1.

18 In his memoirs Maxime Alexandre maintains the possibility that Léon Daudet's reactionary interpretation of Philippe's death was true: "There are two versions of the end of the young Daudet. According to the first, he shot himself with a revolver in a taxi, at the moment when he passed in front of the cell window of Germaine Berton, with whom he was in love. He took the taxi while leaving the Anarchist bookstore, managed by someone named Le Flaouter. According to the other version, that of Léon Daudet, which still remains as realistic today as the first, it was all about a police crime, Le Flaouter having been in fact a police informant." Maxime Alexandre, *Mémoires d'un surréaliste* (Paris: La Jeune Parque, 1968), 60.

19 See Georges Claretie, "L'Acquittement de Germaine Berton," *Le Figaro*, 25 December 1923, 1; and Louis Martin-Chauffier, "'Tu peux tuer cet homme avec tranquilité,'" *Le Figaro*, 28 December 1923, 1.

20 Henri Vonoven, "Le Triomphe de la violence," *Le Figaro*, 25 December 1923, 1.

21 Alexandre, *Mémoires d'un surréaliste*, 62.

22 Carolyn J. Dean, *The Self and Its Pleasures: Bataille, Lacan, and the History of the Decentered Subject* (Ithaca: Cornell University Press, 1992), 209; see also 212–13 and 249.

23 See David Bate, *Photography and Surrealism: Sexuality, Colonialism and Social Dissent* (London: I. B. Tauris, 2004), 46–53.

24 Aragon, "Il m'est impossible," 136.

25 *Le Libertaire*, 26 January 1923, 1.

26 "Lettre à Georges Vidal," 2 or 3 December 1923, in *Tractes surréalistes et déclarations collectives*, ed. José Pierre, vol. 2, 1940–1969 (Paris: Terrain Vague, 1982), 438.

27 Daniel Cottom, "Purity," *Critical Inquiry* 16.1 (1989): 175.

28 "Avant de s'expliquer aux Assises Germaine Berton satisfait aux curiosités du Juge," *Le Libertaire*, 9 March 1923, 1.

29 "Autour du Jury," *Le Figaro*, 31 December 1923, 3.

30 See Bonnet, *André Breton*, 270–71, fn. 55; for the full complement of Simone's letters to Lévy, see Simone Breton, *Lettres à Denise Lévy*, ed. Georgiana Colvile (Paris: Éditions Joelle Losfeld, 2005), esp. 165–66.

31 Breton, *Lettres à Denise Lévy*, 166.

32 "Le Procès Germaine Berton commencera demain," *Paris-Soir*, 18 December 1923, 1. André Breton kept a copy of Berton's mug shot in his personal papers throughout his life; the photograph was part of the auction of Breton's possessions in 2003.

33 Hauteclaire, "Aux Femmes," *Le Libertaire*, 26 January 1923, 1.

34 On hysterical women in surrealism, see Susan Rubin Suleiman, *Subversive Intent: Gender, Politics, and the Avant-Garde* (Cambridge: Harvard University Press, 1990), 88–118.

35 Germaine Berton, testimony of 24 January 1923, *Le Libertaire*, 26 January 1923, 1.

36 Louis Aragon, "Germaine Berton," *La Révolution Surréaliste* 1 (December 1924): 12.

37 According to the ledger of the Surrealist Research Bureau, the montage was to supplement the subscription bulletin of *La Révolution Surréaliste*, which described the contributors to the journal. See Paule Thévenin, *Bureau de Recherches Surréalistes: cahier de la permanence, Octobre 1924–Avril 1925*, Archives du surréalisme, vol. 1. (Paris: Gallimard, 1988), 18–19.

38 Robert Desnos, "Le Cimitière de la 'Semillante,'" in *Nouvelles Hébrides et autres textes, 1922–1930*, ed. Marie-Claire Dumas (Paris: Gallimard, 1978), 103. On this image in relation to other surrealist group portraits, see Amy Lyford, "The Aesthetics of Dismemberment: Surrealism and the Musée du Val-de-Grâce in 1917," *Cultural Critique* 46 (Autumn 2000): 45–79, esp. 59–64.

39 Bate, *Photography and Surrealism*, 48–49.

40 *La Révolution Surréaliste* 1 (December 1924): 17; see also Charles Baudelaire, *Artificial Paradises*, trans. Stacy Diamond (New York: Citadel, 1996), 29.

41 Baudelaire, *Artificial Paradises*, 30.

42 Aragon, "Germaine Berton," 12.

4. Dime Novel Politics

1 André Négis, "Enquête," *Les Cahiers du Sud* 64 (January 1925): 78.

2 André Breton, "Légitime Défense," trans. as "Legitimate Defence," in *What Is Surrealism? Selected Writings*, ed. Franklin Rosemont (New York: Pathfinder Press, 1978), 39.

3 Ibid., 31.

4 Éluard collected articles written about and by members of the surrealist group; a number of his scrapbooks are housed in the Bibliothèque Littéraire Jacques Doucet in Paris. Also, in 1925 and 1926, the surrealist and *Clarté* groups organized committees for surveying the literary landscape. One committee read works by the group itself; another was in charge of archives; and a third, which included Péret and Éluard, was in charge of current events. See Marguerite Bonnet, ed., *Vers l'action politique: de la Révolution d'abord et toujours! (Juillet 1925) au projet de la Guerre Civile (Avril 1926)*, vol. 2 of *Archives du Surréalisme* (Paris: Gallimard, 1988), 127–29.

5 Marguerite Bonnet, ed., *Adhérer au Parti Communiste? Septembre–Décembre 1926*, vol. 3 of *Archives du Surrealisme* (Paris: Gallimard, 1992), 63.

6 Ibid., 57–58.

7 Soupault's severance from the group was not absolute; he reviewed Desnsos's *Liberté ou l'amour!* in 1927 and Crevel's *Mort difficile* in 1928, praising the surrealist texts in glowing language despite having been excluded from the movement. Moreover, as Myriam Boucharenc has argued, Soupault's 1929 novel *Les Derniers Nuits de Paris* can be read as a response—not altogether unfavorable—to Breton's 1928 novel *Nadja*. See Myriam Boucharenc, *L'Échec et son double: Philippe Soupault romancier* (Paris: Honoré Champion, 1997), 51. On surrealism's abandonment of avant-garde poetry for politics, see Jean Cassou, "Propos sur le surréalisme," *La Nouvelle Revue Française* 24 (January 1925): 30–34.

8 Louis Aragon, "'900': Revue fasciste," *Clarté* (October–November–December 1926),. rpt. in *Chroniques, 1918–1932*, ed. Bernard Leuilliot (Paris: Stock, 1998), 278. See also Clara Moressa, "Quand les surréalistes décidèrent de faire adhérer Soupault au parti fasciste," in *Présence de Philippe Soupault*, ed. Myriam Boucharenc and Claude Leroy (Caen: Presses Universitaires de Caen, 1999), 156–72.

9 Aragon, "'900': Revue fasciste," 277–79.

10 Soupault cited in Bonnet, *Archives du surréalisme*, 3:56.

11 Philippe Soupault, "The Death of Nick Carter," trans. Maive Sage, *transition* 7 (October 1927): 64.

12 Ibid., 67.

13 Ibid., 74.

14 On the pen name of "Nicholas Carter," see Régis Messac, *Le Détective Novel et l'influence de la pensée scientifique* (Paris: Honoré Champion, 1929), esp. the chapter titled "The Deaths of Nick Carter," Book 6, chapter 3.

15 See, for instance, Philippe Soupault, "L'Explorateur au long nez," *La Révolution Surréaliste* 4 (July 1925): 8.

16 See "Les Appels de l'Orient," a special issue of *Les Cahiers du Mois* 9–10 (February–March 1925). See also Marguerite Bonnet, "L'Orient et le surréalisme: mythe et réel," *Revue de Littérature Comparée* 544 (October–December 1980): 411–29, esp. 418–19.

17 *The Revolution First and Always*, *L'Humanité*, 21 September 1925, in *Surrealism against the Current: Tracts and Declarations*, ed. and trans. Michael Richardson and Krzysztof Fijalkowski (London: Pluto Press, 2001), 96.

18 "Lettre ouverte à Monsieur Paul Claudel, ambassadeur de France au Japon," 1 July 1925, rpt. in *Tractes surréalistes et declarations collectives*, ed. José Pierre, vol. 1 (Paris: CNRS, 1980), 49–50. Text is available in English in Maurice Nadeau, *The History of Surrealism* (New York: Collier Books, 1965), 238–39.

19 Pierre Drieu La Rochelle, "La Véritable Erreur des surréalistes," *La Nouvelle Revue Française* 25 (August 1925): 168.

20 Ibid., 169.

21 Ibid.

22 For Aragon's response, see *Nouvelle Revue Française* 26, 1 September 1925, rpt. in Aragon, *Chroniques*, 242–44.

23 Georges Auriol, "The Occident," trans. Elliot Paul, *transition* 2 (May 1927): 153–59, esp. 153–54.

24 Ibid., 154.

25 Massimo Bontempelli, "Justification," *900: Cahiers d'Italie et d'Europe* 1 (1926): 12.

26 Auriol, "The Occident," 157–58.

27 Philippe Soupault, "Vanité de l'Europe," *Les Cahiers du Mois* 9–10 (February–March 1935): 65.

28 Ibid., 67.

29 Philippe Soupault, *Le Coeur d'or* (Paris: Grasset, 1927), 146.

30 Reusing this passage in a 1926 travel narrative about Lisbon, Soupault recounts how he flees the Hotel Europe—worthy of its name because it is full of Europeans—into the streets of Lisbon, where he "loses himself in those streets that are like the rivers of dreams." Philippe Soupault, *Carte Postale* (Toulouse: Éditions des Cahiers Libres, 1926), 20–21.

31 Matthew Josephson, *Life among the Surrealists: A Memoir* (New York: Holt, Rinehart, and Winston,

1962), 121. For an unattributed photograph that appears to depict Soupault in blackface, see Petrine Archer-Straw, *Negrophilia: Avant-Garde Paris and Black Culture in the 1920s* (London: Thames and Hudson, 2000), 87.

32 "Lettre ouverte à Monsieur Paul Claudel," 50.

33 Marcel Fourrier, letter to the editor, *Europe* 53 (15 May 1927): 67.

34 Marcel Martinet, "Contre le courant," *Europe* 41 (15 May 1926): 98–99.

35 Ibid., 99–100.

36 Pierre Naville, *Le Temps du surréel*, vol. 1 (Paris: Éditions Galillé, 1977), 299.

37 Naville, "La Révolution et les intellectuels," cited ibid., 300.

38 See, for instance, Helena Lewis, *The Politics of Surrealism* (New York: Paragon House, 1990); Carole Paligot, *Parcours politique des surréalistes, 1919–1969* (Paris: CNRS, 1995); and Steven Harris, *Surrealist Art and Thought in the 1930s: Art, Politics, and the Psyche* (Cambridge: Cambridge University Press, 2004). See also my essay "That Obscure Object of Revolt: Heraclitus, Surrealism's Lightning-Conductor," *Symploke* 8.1–2 (Spring 2000): 180–204.

39 Jean Bernier, "Projet de modification de la définition de la révolution arrêtée par le groupe l'année dernière," in *Adhérer au parti communiste?* 107–8.

40 Friedrich Engels, *Anti-Dühring*, cited ibid., 108.

41 *Vers l'action politique*, 2, 60.

42 Philippe Soupault, *Le Nègre* (Paris: Gallimard, 1997), 14. Except where otherwise noted, all translations from this source are by Randall Cherry, to whom I am greatly indebted for access to his unpublished translation. Page references are to the French text.

43 Ibid., 28.

44 As Marek Kohn writes, Manning's sanitized press autobiography "My Life as the Dope King of London" was published in *World's Pictorial News* in February 1926, soon after Manning's release from prison in November 1925. See Marek Kohn, *Dope Girls: The Birth of the British Drug Underground* (London: Granta, 1992), 150–65, esp. 158. Thanks to Randall Cherry for bringing this text to my attention.

45 Georges Ribemont-Dessaignes, "*Le Nègre*, par Philippe Soupault," *Les Feuilles Libres* (December 1927–January 1928): 69.

46 Ibid.

47 Soupault, *Le Nègre*, 22.

48 Soupault's general discussion of "negro" characteristics reprints a brief exercise in automatic writing first published in *La Révolution Surréaliste* 4 in early 1925, titled "L'Explorateur au long nez" (The Long-Nosed Explorer).

49 See Kohn, *Dope Girls*, 150–65, esp. 158.

50 Soupault, *Le Nègre*, 24–25.

51 Ibid., 28 (my translation).

52 Ibid., 39. For the headlines, see Kohn, *Dope Girls*, 158–60.

53 Soupault, *Le Nègre*, 30.

54 See, for instance, Soupault's essays "Guillaume Apollinaire," *La Revue européenne* 35 (January 1926); "Isodore Ducasse, Comte de Lautréamont," *La Revue européenne* 39 (May 1926); and "À la recherche de Rimbaud," *La Revue nouvelle* 27 (February 1927), rpt. in *Littérature et le reste, 1919–1931*, ed. Lydie Lachenal (Paris: Gallimard, 2006), 238–48; 249–73; 278–83. See also also Boucharenc, *L'Échec et son double*, 141–60; and Claude Leroy, "Sous le signe d'Arthur Rimbaud," *Europe* 769 (May 1993): 61–69.

55 See Soupault, "À la recherche de Rimbaud," 280.

56 Soupault, *Le Nègre*, 36.

57 Ibid., 88.

58 Ibid., 75.

59 Ibid., 81.

60 Ibid., 87.

61 Ibid., 86.

62 Ibid., 107.

63 Ibid., 108.

64 Ibid.

65 Ibid., 120–21.

66 Ibid.

67 Ribemont-Dessaignes, "Le Nègre, par Philippe Soupault," 71.

68 Soupault, Le Nègre, 108.

69 Victor Crastre, "Europe," La Révolution Surréaliste 6 (1 March 1926): 28.

70 Paul Éluard, "De l'usage des guerriers morts," La Révolution Surréaliste 6 (March 1926): 29.

71 Benjamin Péret, "Life of Foch the Murderer," in Death to the Pigs and Other Writings, trans. Rachel Stella et al. (Lincoln: University of Nebraska Press, 1988), 34–35. Péret's poem begins: From a pool of liquid dung one day a bubble rose / and burst / From the smell the father could tell / He'll be a famous killer."

72 Éluard, "De l'usage des guerriers morts," 6, 29.

73 Hal Foster, Compulsive Beauty (Cambridge: MIT Press, 1993), 152.

74 André Breton, Second Manifesto of Surrealism, in Manifestoes of Surrealism, trans. Richard Seaver and Helen R. Lane (Ann Arbor: University of Michigan Press, 1969), 179.

75 Ibid. For the original French, see Breton, Œuvres Complètes, vol. 1, ed. Marguerite Bonnet (Paris: Gallimard, 1988), 822.

76 Maurice Blanchot, The Infinite Conversation, trans. Susan Hanson (Minneapolis: University of Minnesota Press, 1993), 409.

77 André Breton, "The Exquisite Corpse: Its Exaltation," in Surrealism and Painting, trans. Simon Watson Taylor (New York: Harper and Row, 1972), 289.

78 Catherine Vasseur, "L'Image sans mémoire: à propos du cadavre exquis," Cahiers du Musée Nationale d'Art Moderne 55 (Spring 1996): 72.

79 Alexander Waintrub, "Crimes of Passion: Surrealism, Allegory, and the Dismembered Body" (Ph.D. diss., UCLA, 1996), 46.

80 Breton, Légitime Défense, 31.

81 Ibid., 39, fn. 6.

82 Ibid., 38.

83 The "Jack L'Éventreur" section of the article has been republished as "Les Crimes Sadiques: Jack L'Éventreur," in Robert Desnos, ed. Marie-Claire Dumas (Paris: Éditions de l'Herne, 1987), 246–63. The Vacher section has never been republished.

84 Ibid., 246.

85 In a 1925 review in Journal Littéraire (4 April) Desnos chided the makers of the film Waxwork for their poor portrayal of the Ripper, who, as "a modern demigod, deserved better." Rpt. in Robert Desnos, Les Rayons et les ombres: cinéma, ed. Marie-Claire Dumas (Paris: Gallimard, 1992), 63–64. In longer works, such as La Liberté ou l'amour (Paris: Aux Éditions Sagittaire, 1927), Desnos invokes Jack the Ripper more methodically as a phantom haunting modern history.

86 Robert Desnos, film review for Journal Littéraire, 18 April 1925, rpt. in Les Rayons et les ombres, 67.

87 Ibid.

88 Robert Desnos, "La Morale du cinéma" (1923),in Œuvres, ed. Marie-Claire Dumas (Paris: Gallimard, 1999), 187.

89 Robert Desnos, "André Breton ou face à l'infini" (1924), ibid., 234.

90 Robert Desnos, "Le Sens révolutionnaire du surréalisme," Clarté 78 (November 1925): 338.

91 See Robert Desnos, "Le Troisième Manifeste du surréalisme" (1930), in Œuvres, 484–87.

92 On the notion of a mediatized popular surrealism, see Katharine Conley, "Le Surréalisme médiatisé de Robert Desnos," in Desnos pour l'an 2000: Colloque de Cérisy-la-Salle, ed. Katharine Conley and

Marie-Claire Dumas (Paris: Gallimard, 2000), 13–24. See also Robert Desnos, "Imagerie moderne," *Documents* 7 (December 1929), rpt. in Œuvres, 459–61.

93 Desnos, *Troisième Manifeste du surréalisme*, 487.

94 See especially Robert Desnos, "La Morale du cinéma" (1923), "Le Rayon mortel" (1924), "Les Rêves de la nuit transportés sur l'écran" (1927), and "La Morale et le cinéma" (1928), all rpt. in *Les Rayons et les ombres*, 32–34; 43–44, 80–82; 137–38.

95 See Alina Clej, *A Genealogy of the Modern Self: Thomas De Quincey and the Intoxication of Writing* (Stanford: Stanford University Press, 1995), 181–82.

96 Desnos, "Jack L'Éventreur," 257.

97 As Marie-Claire Dumas has shown, Desnos's article draws heavily from Alexandre Lacassagne's 1899 study *Vacher L'Éventreur et les crimes sadiques*, borrowing much of the book's narrative reconstruction of the murder sprees. See Marie-Claire Dumas, "La Guillotine sans couperet," in *Poétiques de Robert Desnos*, ed. Laurent Flieder (Fontenay-aux-Roses: ENS Éditions, 1995). Lacassagne introduces the term "epic" to describe the Vacher murders; Desnos instead applies the term to Jack the Ripper. See Alexandre Lacassagne, *Vacher L'Éventreur et les crimes sadiques* (Paris: Masson et Cie., 1899), 12.

98 Desnos, "Jack L'Éventreur," 249.

99 Ibid., 255. Lacassagne writes, "The postmortem mutilations were committed with a sharpened knife by someone accustomed to cutting up, or watching someone cut up, animals, but there is no reason to assume he was familiar with human anatomy" (*Vacher L'Éventreur et les crimes sadiques*, 264).

100 Dr. Pierre Dofessez to Eugène Merle, editor of *Paris Matinal*, 13 February 1928 (on letterhead postcard reading Docteur Pierre Dofessez, 6, rue de Lille, Toucoing), Fonds Jacques Doucet, Paris.

101 Desnos, "Jack L'Éventreur," 251.

102 For a discussion of Marcel Duchamp's relation to a De Quinceyan (and Kantian) aesthetics of murder, see Jean-Michel Rabaté, "Étant donné: 1° l'art 2° le crime: Duchamp criminel de l'avant-garde," *Interfaces* 14, "Les Avant-Gardes" (June 1998): 113–30.

103 Desnos, "Jack L'Éventreur," 246.

104 Ibid., 251.

105 Ibid., 247.

106 Ibid., 258.

107 Ibid., 261.

108 See Louis Aragon, "Corps, âme et biens," *Le Surréalisme au service de la Révolution* 1 (July 1930): 13.

109 See Conley, "Le Surréalisme médiatisé de Robert Desnos," 24.

110 Manuscript letter to Eugène Merle from R. Margil (?), 6 February 1928, Fonds Jacques Doucet, Paris.

111 Dumas, "La Guillotine sans couperet," 75.

112 Aragon, "Corps, âme, et biens," 15.

113 Katharine Conley, *Robert Desnos and the Marvelous in Everyday Life* (Lincoln: University of Nebraska Press, 2004), 61.

5. X Marks the Spot

1 *X Marks the Spot: Chicago Gang Wars in Pictures* (Chicago: The Spot Publishing Company, 1930), 1.

2 Ibid.

3 Georges Bataille, "Revue des publications: 'X Marks the Spot,'" *Documents* 2.7 (1930): 437–38.

4 Georges Bataille, "The Castrated Lion," in *The Absence of Myth: Writings on Surrealism*, trans. Michael Richardson (London: Verso, 1994), 29.

5 The term is Marcel Martinet's, from his essay "Contre le courant," *Europe* 41 (15 May 1926): 99–100.

6 On surrealism's struggles with the shifting program of the Communist International, see Steven Harris, *Surrealist Art and Thought in the 1930s: Art, Politics, and the Psyche* (Cambridge: Cambridge University Press, 2004), esp. 49–136. See also Carole Reynaud Paligot, *Parcours politique des surréalistes, 1919–1969* (Paris: CNRS, 1995).

7 André Breton, *Manifestoes of Surrealism*, trans. Richard Seaver and Helen R. Lane (Ann Arbor: University of Michigan Press, 1969), 126.

8 Ibid., 126–27.

9 Ibid., 186.

10 See the meeting notes for the surrealist gathering on 23 January 1923 in *Archives du surréalisme*, vol. 1, *Bureau de recherches surréalistes: cahier de la permanence, Octobre 1924–April 1925*, ed. Paule Thévenin (Paris: Gallimard, 1988), 114.

11 Jean Paulhan, "The Marquis de Sade and His Accomplice," in *Justine, Philosophy in the Bedroom, and Other Writings*, ed. and trans. Richard Seaver and Austryn Wainhouse (New York: Grove Press, 1965), 6.

12 Marcel Hénaff, "Preface to the English Edition," in *Sade: The Invention of the Libertine Body*, trans. Xavier Callahan (Minneapolis: University of Minnesota Press, 1999), xii. For a history of Sade's reception in France, see Carolyn Dean, *The Self and Its Pleasures: Bataille, Lacan, and the History of the Decentered Subject* (Ithaca: Cornell University Press, 1992), 127–69.

13 Maurice Heine published Sade's *Dialogue entre un prêtre et un moribond* and *Historiettes, contes et fabliaux* in 1926, *Les Infortunes de la virtu* in 1930, and *Les 120 Jours de Sodom* in 1931. On the surrealist Sade, see esp. Neil Cox, "Critique of Pure Desire, or, When the Surrealists Were Right," in *Surrealism: Desire Unbound*, ed. Jennifer Mundy (Princeton: Princeton University Press, 2001), 245–73. See also Simon Baker, "The Unacceptable Face of the French Revolution," *Object* 2 (1999): 5–27; Dean, *The Self and Its Pleasures*; and Cox, "La Mort posthume: Maurice Heine and the Poetics of Decay," *Art History* 23.3 (September 2000): 417–49.

14 The Surrealist Group, *The Revolution First and Always*, in *Surrealism against the Current: Tracts and Declarations*, ed. and trans. Michael Richardson and Krzysztof Fijalkowski (London: Pluto Press, 2001), 95–97.

15 Ibid., 95.

16 Angela Carter, *The Sadean Woman and the Ideology of Pornography* (New York: Pantheon, 1978), 11.

17 Paul Éluard, "D. A. F. de Sade, écrivain fantastique et révolutionnaire," *La Révolution Surréaliste* 8 (1 December 1926): 8–9.

18 See Paul Éluard, "L'Intelligence Révolutionnaire: Le Marquis de Sade (1740–1814)," *Clarté* (1927), reprinted in *Œuvres Complètes*, vol. 2, ed. Lucien Scheler et al. (Paris: Gallimard, 1968), 809–12.

19 See Harris, *Surrealist Art and Thought in the 1930s*, esp. 55–83.

20 Breton, *Second Manifesto*, 151.

21 André Masson, "Tyrranie du temps," *La Révolution Surréaliste* 6 (1926): 29.

22 Georges Bataille, "The Use-Value of D. A. F. de Sade (An Open Letter to My Current Comrades)," in *Visions of Excess: Selected Writings, 1927–1939*, trans. Allan Stoekl (Minneapolis: University of Minnesota Press, 1985), 92. Bataille's article was composed around 1929–30 but remained unpublished during his lifetime.

23 *L'Âge d'or* program, 19; my translation. A facsimile of the program was included in *L'Âge d'Or: Correspondance Luis Buñuel–Charles de Noiailles*, special issue of *Les Cahiers du Musée National d'Art Moderne* (1993). Also translated as "Manifesto of the Surrealists concerning *L'Âge d'or*" (1930), in *The Shadow and Its Shadow: Surrealist Writings on the Cinema*, 3rd ed., trans. Paul Hammond (San Francisco: City Lights, 2000), 182–89.

24 *L'Âge d'or* program, 19.

25 "Manifesto of the Surrealists concerning *L'Âge d'or*," 185.

26 On the Saint-Pol-Roux banquet and its role in surrealism's political development, see Raymond

Spiteri and Donald LaCoss, "Introduction: Revolution by Night," in Surrealism, Politics, and Culture, ed. Spiteri and LaCoss (Burlington, Vt.: Ashgate, 2003), 1–10.

27 André Breton, Nadja, trans. Richard Howard (New York: Grove Press, 1960), 141.

28 Cited by Paul Abély in the report reprinted in the Second Manifesto, in Breton, Manifestoes of Surrealism, 120.

29 Breton, Nadja, 143.

30 Cited in Breton, Manifestoes of Surrealism, 120.

31 Cited Ibid., 122–23.

32 Breton, Nadja, 139.

33 Breton, Manifestoes of Surrealism, 125.

34 Ibid., 126.

35 Georges Bataille, "Eye," Documents 4 (September 1929), rpt. in Visions of Excess, 19.

36 Ibid.

37 Ibid.

38 Georges Bataille, "The Lugubrious Game," Documents 7 (December 1929), rpt. in Visions of Excess, 29.

39 Ibid., 27.

40 Ibid.

41 Ibid., 28.

42 Ibid.

43 Bataille, "The Use-Value of D. A. F. de Sade," 101.

44 Carter, The Sadean Woman and the Ideology of Pornography, 4.

45 Mary Drach McInnes, "Taboo and Transgression: The Subversive Aesthetics of Georges Bataille and Documents" (Ph.D. diss., Boston University, 1994), 231–81.

46 Georges Sadoul, "Bonne Année! Bonne Santé!" La Révolution Surréaliste 12 (December 1929): 45.

47 Ibid., 47.

48 Ibid., 45.

49 Ibid., 47.

50 David Walker, Outrage and Insight: Modern French Writers and the "Fait Divers" (Oxford: Berg, 1995), 38.

51 Louis Aragon, "Introduction à 1930," La Révolution Surréaliste 12 (December 1929): 64.

52 Ibid.

53 L'Âge d'or program, 19.

54 Pamphlet rpt. in L'Âge d'Or: Correspondance Luis Buñuel–Charles de Noiailles, 115–16.

55 L'Âge d'or program, 18–19.

56 Jean Frois-Wittmann to André Breton, cited in L'Âge d'Or: Correspondance Luis Buñuel–Charles de Noiailles, 119.

57 Maurice Nadeau, The History of Surrealism (1944), trans. Richard Howard (New York: Collier, 1965), 175.

58 Salvador Dalí, "L'Âne pourri," Surréalisme au Service de la Révolution 1 (1930), trans. as "The Rotting Donkey" by Yvonne Shafir in Oui: The Paranoid-Critical Revolution, ed. Robert Descharnes (Boston: Exact Change, 1998), 119.

59 Marcel Fourrier, "Police, haut les mains!" La Révolution Surréaliste 12 (1929): 40.

60 Ibid., 38.

61 Dalí, "The Rotting Donkey," 117.

62 Ibid., 116.

63 Ibid., 116–17.

64 On Aragon's and Sadoul's participation in the Kharkov conference, see especially Harris, Surrealist Art and Thought in the 1930s, 57–69; Helena Lewis, The Politics of Surrealism (New York: Paragon

House, 1990), 97–107; and André Thirion, *Revolutionaries without Revolution* (New York: Macmillan, 1975), 266–95.

65 Louis Aragon, "Front Rouge," trans. "Red Front," in Nadeau, *The History of Surrealism*, 287–88; see also e. e. cummings's translation in *Complete Poems, 1904–1962*, ed. George J. Firmage (New York: Liveright, 1994), 881–97.

66 Aragon, "Red Front," 286–87.

67 Ibid., 289 (translation adapted).

68 Ibid., 293.

69 André Breton, "Misère de la poésie," trans. "The Poverty of Poetry," in *What Is Surrealism? Selected Writings*, ed. Franklin Rosemont (New York: Pathfinder Press, 1978), 76.

70 Ibid., 77.

71 Ibid., 78.

72 Steven Harris makes this point, in a slightly different context, in *Surrealist Art and Thought in the 1930s*, 95–96.

73 See René Ménil, introduction (1978) to *Légitime Défense*, in *Refusal of the Shadow: Surrealism and the Caribbean*, ed. and trans. Michael Richardson and Krzysztof Fijalkowski (London: Verso, 1996), 37.

74 "Légitime Défense: *Declaration*" (1932), ibid., 43.

75 Ibid., 42.

76 Ibid., 41.

77 André Breton, "Legitimate Defense," in *What Is Surrealism?*, 32.

78 Ibid.

79 "Légitime Défense: *Declaration*," 41.

80 Ibid.

81 See Elisabeth Roudinesco, *La Bataille de cent ans: une histoire de la psychanalyse en France*, vol. 2 (Paris: Fayard, 1986), 56; trans. Jeffrey Mehlman as *Jacques Lacan & Co.: A History of Psychoanalysis in France, 1925–1985* (Chicago: University of Chicago Press, 1990).

82 Jules Monnerot, "Note Bearing on the Coloured French Bourgeoisie," in *Refusal of the Shadow*, 46.

83 Étienne Léro, "Civilization," ibid., 54.

84 Paul Éluard, "La Vérité sur les colonies," in Adam Jolles, "'Visitez l'exposition anti-coloniale!' Nouveaux éléments sur l'exposition protestaire de 1931: Paul Éluard, *La Vérité sur les colonies*; Aragon, *La Vérité sur les colonies: Une salle d'exposition anti-impérialiste*," *Pleine Marge* 35 (June 2002): 106–27, 117–19. Translation by Adam Jolles.

85 Ibid., 117–19.

86 Jules Monnerot, "Notes Bearing on the Colored French Bourgeoisie," in *Refusal of the Shadow*, 43.

87 Étienne Léro, "Poverty of a Poetry," ibid., 58.

88 Jules Monnerot, untitled poem, in *Légitime Défense* (1932), reprint ed. (Paris: Jean-Michel Place, 1979), 19.

89 Jules Monnerot, "On Certain Common Characteristics of the Civilized Mentality," *Le Surréalisme au Service de la Révolution* 5 (1933), trans. in *Refusal of the Shadow*, 59.

90 Ibid., 61.

91 Ibid., 63–64.

92 Ibid., 64.

6. Surrealism Noir

1 On Crevel's suicide and its immediate political circumstances, see Gérard Durozoi, *Histoire du mouvement surréaliste* (Paris: Hazan, 1997), 296–300. On the events of 6 February 1934, see Dudley An-

drew and Steven Ungar, *Popular Front Paris and the Poetics of Culture* (Cambridge: Harvard University Press, 2005).

2 André Breton to Paul Éluard, 11 March 1933, cited in Carole Reynaud Paligot, *Parcours politique des surréalistes, 1919–1969* (Paris: CNRS, 1995), 95.

3 See Steven Harris, *Surrealist Art and Thought in the 1930s: Art, Politics, and the Psyche* (Cambridge: Cambridge University Press, 2004), 55–83. On Breton and the AEAR, see also Durozoi, *Histoire du mouvement surréaliste;* André Thirion, *Revolutionaries without Revolution,* trans. Joachim Neugroschel (New York: Macmillan, 1975); Mark Polizzotti, *Revolution of the Mind: The Life of André Breton* (London: Bloomsbury, 1995); and Paligot, *Parcours politique des surréalistes.*

4 Éluard considered issue 3–4 representative of the surrealists' "success" in the journal; see Paul Éluard, *Lettres à Gala, 1924–1948,* ed. Pierre Dreyfus (Paris: Gallimard, 1984), 220.

5 Paul Éluard to Salvador Dalí, February–March 1933, ibid., 202–3.

6 The term "exasperated" is Éluard's; see ibid.

7 See Harris, *Surrealist Art and Thought in the 1930s,* 105.

8 Durozoi, *Histoire du mouvement surréaliste,* 244.

9 For a recent history of the Stavisky affair, see Paul F. Jankowski, *Stavisky: A Confidence Man in the Republic of Virtue* (Ithaca: Cornell University Press, 2002).

10 See Louis Martin-Chauffier, "Le Poison dans le sang," *Vu* (6 September 1933): 1385–86.

11 *Détective* 244 (9 February 1993): cover. For other readings of the double portrait, see Christine Coffman, *Insane Passions: Lesbianism and Psychosis in Literature and Film* (Middletown, Conn.: Wesleyan University Press, 2006), 66–71; Christopher Lane, "The Delirium of Interpretation: Writing the Papin Affair," *differences* 5.2 (1993): 24.

12 See Rachel Edwards and Keith Reader, *The Papin Sisters* (Oxford: Oxford University Press, 2001), 3.

13 André Breton, preface for Max Ernst's 1921 exhibition catalogue, in *Œuvres complètes,* ed. Marguerite Bonnet et al., 3 vols. (Paris: Gallimard, 1988), 1:246. See also Dawn Ades, *Photomontage* (London: Thames and Hudson, 1986), 115.

14 Harris, *Surrealist Art and Thought in the 1930s,* 124.

15 Jacques Lacan, "Le Problème du style et la conception psychiatrique des formes paranoïaques de l'expérience," *Minotaure* 1 (1933): 69.

16 Ibid. Lacan's article immediately follows Salvador Dalí's well-known "Interprétation paranoïaque-critique de l'image obsédante 'Angelus' de Millet."

17 See Paulette Houdoyer, *Le Diable dans le peau: l'affaire des soeurs Papin* (Paris: Juliard, 1966). Two crime scene photographs are reprinted in Francis Dupré, *La "Solution" du passage à l'acte: le double crime des soeurs Papin* (Toulouse: Erès, 1984).

18 *Détective* 244 (9 February 1933): cover, 3, 7.

19 Janet Flanner, *Paris Was Yesterday, 1925–1937,* ed. Irving Drutman (New York: Harcourt, Brace, Jovanovich, 1972), 98–99.

20 Ibid., 98.

21 *L'Humanité,* 5 February 1933, 3.

22 As Edwards and Reader point out, *L'Humanité*'s trial reports were surprisingly attentive to the conditions of gender oppression in play during the sisters' employment as housemaids. Edwards and Reader, *The Papin Sisters,* 16.

23 On the sisters' incomprehension, see Lane, "The Delirium of Interpretation."

24 Paul Éluard and Benjamin Péret, "Revue de la presse," *SASDLR* 5 (May 1933): 28.

25 Louis Aragon, untitled article, *Littérature,* n.s. 9 (February–March 1923): 15.

26 René Crevel, "Notes en vue d'une psycho-dialectique," *SASDLR* 5 (May 1933): 52. For the full text in English, see Mary Ann Caws, ed., *Surrealism* (London: Phaidon, 2004), 265–67. Page numbers cited here refer to the original text in *SASDLR.*

27 Statement of the Soviet directors at Kharkov, cited in Paligot, *Parcours politique des surréalistes*, 80. See also Elisabeth Roudinesco, *La Bataille de cent ans: une histoire de la psychanalyse en France*, vol. 2 (Paris: Fayard, 1994), 56.

28 Crevel, "Notes toward a Psycho-dialectic," 48.

29 See Jacques Lacan, *De la Psychose paranoïaque dans ses rapports avec la personnalité* (1932; rpt., Paris: Éditions du Seuil, 1975).

30 Roudinesco, *La Bataille de cent ans*, 45.

31 For evidence of the early influence on Lacan of surrealist practices (themselves based on French and Freudian psychiatric theories), see J. Lévy-Valensi, P. Migault, and J. Lacan, "Écrits 'inspirées': schizographie," reprinted in Lacan, *De la Psychose*, 365–82.

32 Crevel, "Notes toward a Psycho-dialectic," 51–52.

33 On the history of the concept of self-punishment in French psychiatry, see Carolyn Dean, *The Self and Its Pleasures: Bataille, Lacan, and the History of the Decentered Subject* (Ithaca: Cornell University Press, 1992), 36–42.

34 Crevel, "Notes toward a Psycho-dialectic," 50.

35 Ibid.

36 Lautréamont, *Les Chants de Maldoror*, chant 6; see *Maldoror*, trans. Alexis Lykiard (Cambridge: Exact Change, 1994), 193.

37 Crevel, "Notes toward a Psycho-dialectic," 51.

38 Crevel, "Notes toward a Psycho-dialectic," 51, 52.

39 See the articles by Jérôme and Jean Tharaud from *Paris-Soir*, 30 September–8 October 1933, rpt. *Littoral* 9 (June 1983): 132–46. Also Maurice Coriem, "A-t-on comdamné deux folles?" an article serialized in *Police* throughout November 1933; and Coriem, "Histoire d'un drame passionnel: 'Le Crime des soeurs Papin,'" *Scandale* 5 (December 1933): 233–36.

40 Article 64 of the 1810 Penal Code, repealed in 1994, reads, "There is neither crime nor misdemeanor when the accused was in a demented state at the time of the action, or when he was driven by a force which he could not resist." See André Breton, "La Médecine mentale devant le Surréalisme," in *Œuvres complètes*, 2: 322–25.

41 Jacques Lacan, "Le Problème du style," *Minotaure* 1 (1933): 68.

42 For a compelling critique of Lacan's early writings on paranoia, especially in their assumptions about lesbianism and homosexuality as "inherently morbid," see Coffman, *Insane Passions*, esp. 54–60.

43 See the sources cited in note 39.

44 Jacques Lacan, "Motifs du crime paranoïaque: le crime des soeurs Papin," *Minotaure* 3–4 (1933): 26. On the history of the sisters' misdiagnosis, see Coffman, *Insane Passions*, 36–43.

45 Lacan, "Motifs du crime paranoïaque," 25–26.

46 Lacan, "Le Problème du style," 69.

47 Lacan, "Motifs du crime paranoïaque," 26.

48 Lane, "The Delirium of Interpretation," 31.

49 Maurice Heine, "Promenade à travers le roman noir," *Minotaure* 5 (1934): 1.

50 Ibid., 3.

51 Maurice Heine, "Testimonial to Picasso," *Documents* (1930): 175–76.

52 On Breton's "gothic Marxism," see Margaret Cohen, *Profane Illumination: Walter Benjamin and the Paris of Surrealist Revolution* (Berkeley: University of California Press, 1993), esp. 111–27.

53 Jules Hubert, "L'Ignoble Empoisonneuse, ou, le Crime de la Rue de Madagascar" (Paris: Chaffange et Cie., n.d.).

54 See, for instance, the Parisian weekly *Vu* for the weeks of 6 and 13 September 1933; the magazine published articles with titles such as "Le Poison dans le sang," by Louis Martin-Chauffier, and "Le Démon de la sexualité," by Magnus Hirschfeld. The weekly press review *Lu dans la Presse Universelle* 36 (8

September 1933) excerpts numerous similar articles, such as the newspaper *Lumière*'s lament, "Triste Jeunesse!"

55 *Humanité*, 26 August 1933, 1.

56 J. Pidault and M.-I. Sicard, *L'Affaire Nozières: crime ou châtiment?* (Paris: Enquêtes et Documents, 1 September 1933), 33.

57 See *Vu*, 11 September 1933, under the headline "Violette Nozières, la double parricide." The previous week, the magazine printed the article "D'où vient cette haine?" (Where Does This Hatred Come From?), in which the author writes that her father's sexual abuse lies "at the origin of her hatred"; rpt. *Lu dans la Presse Universelle* 36 (8 September 1933): 7. Yet without actually dismissing this accusation, the article later claims that the "real" reason for Violette's hatred was not this abuse but some hereditary disease (syphilis or sexual precocity) for which she wished to punish her father, "an eye for an eye, a tooth for a tooth."

58 The book contains poems by André Breton, René Char, Paul Éluard, Maurice Henry, E. L. T. Mesens, César Moro, Benjamin Péret, and Guy Rosey, as well as illustrations by Hans Arp, Victor Brauner, Salvador Dalí, Max Ernst, Alberto Giacometti, Marcel Jean, René Magritte, and Yves Tanguy. *Violette Nozières*, rpt., ed. José Pierre (Paris: Éditions Terrain Vague, 1991).

59 See André Breton, *Second Manifesto* (1929), in *Manifestoes of Surrealism*, trans. Richard Seaver and Helen Lane (Ann Arbor: University of Michigan Press, 1969), 174.

60 Jacques Niger, *Le Secret de l'empoisonneuse; le crime de Violette Nozières. Son arrestation. Ses complices(?)* (Paris, 1933).

61 Ibid., 28.

62 Hélène Cixous and Catherine Clément, *The Newly Born Woman*, trans. Betsy Wing (Minneapolis: University of Minnesota Press, 1986), 5.

63 Louis Aragon and André Breton, "La Cinquantenaire de l'hystérie," *La Révolution Surréaliste* 11 (15 March 1928): 22, 20.

64 Jean-Marie Fitère, *Violette Nozière* (Paris: Presses de la Cité, 1975).

65 Tyler Stovall, "Paris in the Age of Anxiety, 1919–1939," in *Anxious Visions: Surrealist Art*, ed. Sidra Stich (New York: Abbeville Press, 1990), 216. Sarah Maza, in a book in progress on the Nozière case, is more convincing; as her research in the court documents suggests, Violette did indeed have syphilis, yet her father was not infected; this would be the strongest argument against her accusation of her father.

66 See, for instance, Harris, *Surrealist Art and Thought in the 1930s*, 202; and Jean Clair, *Du Surréalisme considéré dans ses rapports au totalitarianisme et aux tables tournantes* (Paris: Mille et Une Nuits, 2004), 202. Laurie Monahan's approach is more subtle; she argues that the surrealists appropriated, yet in many ways unwittingly replicated, Violette's portrayal in the popular press as a dangerous femme fatale. See Laurie Monahan, "Crimes against Nature: Violette Nozières, Surrealism, and Mass Culture," *Collapse* 4 (1999): 72–105.

67 See esp. *L'Humanité*, 31 August 1933, 1; 10 September 1933, 3; 11 September 1933, 3; 14 September 1933, 3; and 17 September 1933, 3.

68 Niger, *Le Secret de l'empoisonneuse*, 9.

69 Benjamin Péret, "Elle était belle comme un nénuphar sur un tas de charbon," in *Violette Nozières*, 39–40.

70 For Peret, see ibid., 42; André Breton, "Tous les rideaux du monde," ibid., 18.

71 Péret, "Elle était belle," 42–43.

72 Breton, "Tous les rideaux du monde," 22.

73 See Cixous and Clément, *The Newly Born Woman*, 96: "To fly/steal is woman's gesture, to steal into language to make it fly. . . . It's not just luck if the word "voler" volleys between the "vol" of theft and the "vol" of flight, pleasuring in each and routing the sense police."

74 Crevel, "Notes en vue d'une psycho-dialectique," 50.

75 Breton, "Tous les rideaux du monde," 17.

76 E. L. T. Mesens, "On ne conduit pas sa fille comme un train," in *Violette Nozières*, 35.

77 On the political significance of surrealist objects in the, see esp. Harris, *Surrealist Art and Thought in the 1930s*.

78 André Breton, "Qu'est-ce que le surréalisme?" (1934), in *Œuvres complètes*, ed. Marguerite Bonnet et al., 3 vols. (Paris: Gallimard, 1988), 2:258. Translation adapted from *What Is Surrealism: Selected Writings*, ed. Franklin Rosemont (New York: Pathfinder, 1978), 138.

79 Angela Carter, *The Sadean Woman and the Ideology of Pornography* (New York: Pantheon, 1978), 6.

7. Persecution Mania

1 Jean-Paul Sartre, "Situation of the Writer in 1947," in *"What Is Literature?" and Other Essays*, ed. Stephen Ungar (Cambridge: Harvard University Press, 1988), 164.

2 On wartime surrealism, see esp. Martica Sawin, *Surrealism in Exile and the Beginning of the New York School* (Cambridge: MIT Press, 1995); Alyce Mahon, *Surrealism and the Politics of Eros, 1938–1968* (London: Thames and Hudson, 2005); and Michel Fauré, *Histoire du surréalisme sous l'Occupation* (Paris: La Table Ronde, 1982). For Tzara's postwar radio lectures attacking surrealism, see Tristan Tzara, *Œuvres complètes*, vol. 5 (Paris: Flammarion, 1982).

3 Muller's essay (along with an essay by Kenneth Burke) served as the afterword for the 1940 *New Directions* anthology dedicated to surrealism. Herbert J. Muller, "Surrealism: A Dissenting Opinion," *New Directions* 40 (1940): 549.

4 Jimmy Ernst, *My Not-So-Still Life* (New York: St. Martin's, 1984), 251.

5 See André Breton, "The Political Position of Surrealism," in *Manifestoes of Surrealism*, trans. Richard Seaver and Helen R. Lane (Ann Arbor: University of Michigan Press, 1969), 216.

6 Leonora Carrington to Henri Parisot, reprinted in *En Bas* (Paris: Eric Losfeld, 1973), 7–8.

7 Marina Warner, introduction to *The House of Fear: Notes from Down Below* (New York: Dutton, 1988), 16.

8 Katharine Conley describes the discursive self-consciousness in her discussion of the textual apparatus of *Down Below*'s journal form: "The narrative's structure and metanarrational components . . . highlight the role of language itself—in the story's statement of intent, in its unfolding, and in its resolution." Katharine Conley, *Automatic Woman: The Representation of Woman in Surrealism* (Lincoln: University of Nebraska Press, 1996), 67.

9 André Breton, "Prolegomena for a Third Surrealist Manifesto or Not" (1942), in *Manifestoes of Surrealism*, 285.

10 On Éluard's break with the group, see esp. Francis Carmody, "Éluard's Rupture with Surrealism," *PMLA* 76.4 (September 1961): 436–46.

11 On Ernst's personal mythology, see esp. Werner Spies, *Loplop: The Artist in the Third Person* (New York: Braziller, 1983); and Samantha Kavky, "Authorship and Identity in Max Ernst's Loplop," *Art History* 28.3 (2005): 357–85. On Carrington's, see esp. Whitney Chadwick, "Leonora Carrington: Evolution of a Feminist Consciousness," *Woman's Art Journal* 7.1 (Spring–Summer 1986): 37–42; and Susan Aberth, *Leonora Carrington: Surrealism, Alchemy, and Art* (Burlington: Lund Humphries, 2004).

12 Leonora Carrington, "Down Below," in *The House of Fear: Notes from Down Below* (New York: Dutton, 1988), 165.

13 Max Ernst, "Biographical Notes: Tissue of Truth, Tissue of Lies," in *Max Ernst: A Retrospective*, ed. Werner Spies (New York: Prestel, 1991), 319.

14 Leonora Carrington, "Down Below," *VVV* 4 (1944): 70. In the 1988 revised version of the text, Carrington has expurgated the reference to Mabille's work on mirrors.

15 Pierre Mabille, "Miroirs," *Minotaure* 11 (Spring 1938): 14–15.

16 Carrington, "Down Below" (*VVV*), 71. In the French version of the text, published by Henri Parisot in 1945, Carrington uses the term "zombies." In the revised English version she has altered the term to "robots."

17 Carrington, "Down Below" (*House of Fear*), 167.

18 Jacqueline Chénieux-Gendron, *Le Surréalisme et le roman* (Paris: L'Âge d'Homme, 1983), 200–201.

19 Sigmund Freud, "Psychoanalytic Notes upon an Autobiographical Account of a Case of Paranoia (Dementia Paranoides)" (1911), in *Three Case Studies* (New York: Collier, 1963), 178.

20 Ibid., 173.

21 Carrington, "Down Below" (*House of Fear*), 170–71.

22 Ibid., 171.

23 Ibid., 173.

24 In the *VVV* version of "Down Below," Carrington's protagonist seems to manage to fight off a single rapist (72); in the later version she is attacked by a group of Requeté officers, who rape her and abandon her in the street, where she is later picked up by police (*House of Fear*, 171).

25 Carrington, "Down Below" (*VVV*), 81.

26 On the clinical use of Cardiazol as an anti-schizophrenia drug during the 1930s, see Niall Mc-Crae, "'A Violent Thunderstorm': Cardiazol Treatment in British Mental Hospitals," *History of Psychiatry* 3.17 (2006): 67–90.

27 Carrington, "Down Below" (*House of Fear*), 195.

28 Daniel Paul Schreber, *Memoirs of My Nervous Illness* (1903), trans. Ida MacAlphine and Richard A. Hunter (Cambridge: Harvard University Press, 1988), 82–83.

29 Carrington, "Down Below" (*VVV*), 81.

30 Carrington, "Down Below" (*House of Fear*), 163–64.

31 See Mary Ann Caws, "Ladies Shot and Painted: Female Embodiment in Surrealist Art," in *The Female Body in Western Culture: Contemporary Perspectives*, ed. Susan Suleiman (Cambridge: Harvard University Press, 1987), 262–87. For a valuable analysis of Dalí's Hitler paintings and the artist's ensuing conflict with the surrealist movement, see esp. Robin Adèle Greeley, *Surrealism and the Spanish Civil War* (New Haven: Yale University Press, 2006), 51–90.

32 "Declaration: 'The Truth about the Moscow Trials'" (1936), in *Surrealism against the Current: Tracts and Declarations*, ed. and trans. Michael Richardson and Krzysztof Fijalkowski (London: Pluto, 2001), 117–18.

33 Greeley, *Surrealism and the Spanish Civil War*, 6.

34 Steven Harris, *Surrealist Art and Thought in the 1930s: Art, Politics, and the Psyche* (Cambridge: Cambridge University Press, 2004), 146.

35 Ibid., 152.

36 Breton, "Political Position of Surrealism," 216.

37 Hal Foster, *Compulsive Beauty* (Cambridge: MIT Press, 1993), 122.

38 The writings of Gilbert Lély and Léo Malet, both friends of the Sade expert Maurice Heine, are notable for their poetic staging of criminal voyeurism, as are the collage-novels of Max Ernst and Georges Hugnet. See esp. Gilbert Lély, *Je ne veux pas qu'on tue cette femme* (Paris: Éditions Surréalistes, 1936). See also Léo Malet, *J'arbre comme cadavre* (Paris: Les Feuillets de "Sagesse," 1937); *Hurle à la vie* (Paris: Éditions Surréalistes, 1940); and *Le Frère de Lacenaire* (Paris: Les Pages Libres de la "Main à Plume," 1943). See also Georges Hugnet, *Le Septième Face du dé* (Paris: Éditions Jeanne Bucher, 1936); and Max Ernst, *Une Semaine de bonté* (Paris: Éditions Jeanne Bucher, 1934).

39 Salvador Dalí, "Psychologie non-euclidienne d'une photographie," *Minotaure* 7 (1935); trans. by Haim Finkelstein as "Non-Euclidean Psychology of a Photograph," in *The Collected Writings of Salvador Dalí* (Cambridge: Cambridge University Press, 1998), 302.

40 For a brief but illuminating discussion of Dalí's essay in comparison to Roland Barthes's *Cam-*

era Lucida, see Ian Walker, *City Gorged with Dreams: Surrealism and Documentary Photography in Interwar Paris* (Manchester: Manchester University Press, 2002), 18–23.

41 Dali, "Non-Euclidean Psychology," 306.

42 Sue Taylor, *Hans Bellmer: The Anatomy of Anxiety* (Cambridge: MIT Press, 2000), 74.

43 On the linguistic nature of Bellmer's dolls, see esp. Malcolm Green, introduction to *The Doll* (London: Atlas Press, 2005), 7–30.

44 Hans Bellmer, "The Ball-Joint," trans. Malcolm Green, ibid., 59.

45 Ibid., 59–60.

46 Leonora Carrington, "The Oval Lady," in *The House of Fear*, 43.

47 André Breton, *Mad Love*, trans. Mary Ann Caws (Lincoln: University of Nebraska Press, 1987), 100.

48 Ibid., 102.

49 Ibid., 108. Georgette Delglave also kept a journal, which describes Michel's regular death threats and the life insurance policy he bought to profit from her death. For a contemporary account of the Henriot case, see René Allendy, *Le Crime et les Perversions Instinctives*, special issue of *Le Crapouillot* (May 1938): esp. 35–38. Allendy, a practicing psychoanalyst, had been René Crevel's analyst, and also treated Antonin Artaud.

50 Breton, *Mad Love*, 109.

51 Ibid., 111.

52 Herbert J. Muller, "Surrealism: A Dissenting Opinion," *New Directions* 40 (1940): 548.

53 Aimé Césaire, *Discourse on Colonialism* (1955), trans. Joan Pinkham (New York: Monthly Review Press, 2000), 6.

54 Muller, "Surrealism: A Dissenting Opinion," 549.

55 Ibid., 548, 550.

56 Breton, "Prolegomena to a Third Manifesto of Surrealism or Not," 291.

57 Interview with André Breton, *View* 1.7–8 (October–November 1941): 2.

58 Pierre Mabille, letter (May 1941), *View* 1.7–8 (October–November 1941): 5

59 André Breton, *Arcanum 17*, trans. Zack Rogow (Los Angeles: Sun and Moon, 1994), 94.

8. The Transatlantic Mysteries of Paris

1 André Breton, *Anthology of Black Humor* (1945), trans. Mark Polizzotti (San Francisco: City Lights Press, 1997), xiii.

2 Raoul Vaneigem (as J.-F. Dupuis), *A Cavalier History of Surrealism*, trans. Donald Nicholson-Smith (Edinburgh: AK Press, 1999), 122.

3 On the publication history of Breton's anthology and the conditions of its censorship, see André Breton, *Œuvres complètes*, vol. 2, ed. Marguerite Bonnet et al. (Paris: Gallimard, 1992), 1745–70.

4 See James Naremore, *More Than Night: Film Noir in Its Contexts* (Berkeley: University of California Press, 1998), 16. See also Marc Vernet, "Film Noir on the Edge of Doom," in *Shades of Noir*, ed. Joan Copjec (London: Verso, 1993), 1–31, esp. 4–6. For a selection of contemporary surrealist writings on cinema, see Paul Hammond, ed. and trans., *The Shadow and Its Shadow: Surrealist Writings on the Cinema* (San Francisco: City Lights, 2000).

5 *La Reine des pommes*, literally "The Queen of Apples," is a slang approximation of Himes's original title, *The Five-Cornered Square*. Though written for the Série noire, *The Five-Cornered Square* first appeared in English as *For Love of Imabelle* (late 1957) and is now available as *A Rage in Harlem*.

6 On the efforts to popularize surrealism during the immediate pre–World War II years, see Katharine Conley, *Robert Desnos, Surrealism, and the Marvelous in Everyday Life* (Lincoln: University of Nebraska Press, 2003). On postwar surrealism, see esp. Carole Raynaud Paligot, *Parcours politique des sur-*

réalistes, 1919–1969 (Paris: CNRS, 1995); Alyce Mahon, *Surrealism and the Politics of Eros, 1938–1968* (London: Thames and Hudson, 2005); and Michel Surya, *La Révolution rêvée: pour une histoire des écrivains et des intellectuels révolutionnaires, 1944–1956* (Paris: Fayard, 2004).

7 See esp. Claire Gorrara, "Cultural Intersections: The American Detective Novel and the Early French 'Roman Noir,'" *Modern Language Review* 98,3 (July 2003): 590–601; and *The Roman Noir in Postwar French Culture* (Oxford: Oxford University Press, 2003).

8 Kevin Bell, "Assuming the Position: Fugitivity and Futurity in the Work of Chester Himes," *Modern Fiction Studies* 51.4 (2005): 858.

9 Richard Wright, "Blueprint for Negro Writing," *New Challenge*, (Fall 1937), rpt. in *The Portable Harlem Renaissance Reader*, ed. David Levering Lewis (New York: Penguin, 1994), 201.

10 Richard Wright, *The Outsider* (New York: Harper & Brothers, 1953), 129.

11 Michel Fabre and Robert E. Skinner, eds., *Conversations with Chester Himes* (Jackson: University Press of Mississippi, 1995), 140. Himes is responding to critical assessments of his work as "surrealist." See Stephen Milliken, *Chester Himes: A Critical Appraisal* (Columbia: University of Missouri Press, 1976), 5.

12 See, for instance, Stephanie Brown, "Black Comme Moi: Boris Vian and the African American Voice of Translation," *Mosaic* 36.1 (March 2003): 51–68; and Christopher M. Jones, *Boris Vian Transatlantic: Sources, Myths, and Dreams* (New York: Peter Lang, 1998). See also Robert P. Smith, "Chester Himes in France and the Legacy of the Roman Policier," *CLA Journal* 25.1 (September 1981): 18–27, esp. 18–20; cf. Sean McCann's more subtle argument in *Gumshoe America: Hard-Boiled Crime Fiction and the Rise and Fall of New Deal Liberalism* (Durham: Duke University Press, 2000), 251–305. Also see Michael Denning, "Topographies of Violence: Chester Himes' Harlem Domestic Novels," *Critical Texts* 5.1 (1988): 10–18.

13 Brent Hayes Edwards, *The Practice of Diaspora: Literature, Translation, and the Rise of Black Internationalism* (Cambridge: Harvard University Press, 2003), 13–15.

14 Bell, "Assuming the Position," 852.

15 Marcel Duhamel, *Raconte pas ta vie!* (Paris: Mercure de France, 1972), 589.

16 Breton, *Anthology of Black Humor*, xiii.

17 See Jean-Paul Sartre, "Situation of the Writer in 1947," trans. Bernard Frechtman, in *What Is Literature?*, ed. Steven Ungar (Cambridge: Harvard University Press, 1988), 141–238, esp. 158.

18 Raymond Queneau, "L'Humour Noir," *Front National* (16 June 1945), cited in Breton, *Œuvres complètes*, 2:1750.

19 Albert Camus, *The Rebel: An Essay on Man in Revolt* (1951), trans. Anthony Bower (New York: Vintage, 1956), 92.

20 Ibid., 93.

21 Roland Barthes, *Writing Degree Zero* (1953), trans. Annette Lavers and Colin Smith (New York: Hill and Wang, 1968), 75.

22 Maurice Blanchot, "Reflections on Surrealism," in *The Work of Fire* (1949), trans. Charlotte Mandell (Stanford: Stanford University Press, 1995), 85.

23 André Breton, *Conversations: The Autobiography of Surrealism*, trans. Mark Polizzotti (New York: Marlowe and Company, 1993), 247.

24 On Malet and the Main à Plume group, see Michel Fauré, *Histoire du surréalisme sous l'Occupation* (Paris: La Table Ronde, 1982), esp. 43–54 and 366–69.

25 Léo Malet, "Le Frère de Lacenaire" (1943), in *Poèmes surréalistes* (Paris: Éditions de la Butte aux Cailles, 1983), 111.

26 For Malet's brief explanation of his "rupture" with the surrealists, see Léo Malet, *La Vache enragée* (Paris: Hoëbeke, 1998), 185. On the exclusions of Matta and Brauner, see Paligot, *Parcours politique des surréalistes*, 147–51.

27 See Malet, *Poèmes surréalistes*, 139–46. On Malet's detective fiction and its ties to surrealism, see esp. Michelle Emanuel, *From Surrealism to Less-Exquisite Cadavers: Léo Malet and the Evolution of the French Ro-*

man Noir (Amsterdam: Rodopi, 2006); see also Claire Gorrara, "Malheurs et Ténèbres: Narratives of Social Disorder in Léo Malet's *120, rue de la Gare*," *French Cultural Studies* 12 (2001): 271–83.

28 On Duhamel's polite refusal to consider Malet's novels for the Série Noire, see Malet, *La Vache enragée*, 185–86.

29 On Duhamel and the October group, see Michel Fauré, *Le Groupe Octobre* (Paris: Christian Bourgeois, 1977).

30 For a bibliography of the series, see Claude Mesplède, *Les Années "Série Noire,"* 2nd ed., 5 vols. (Amiens: Enorage, 1992).

31 Marcel Duhamel, preface to *Panorama du film noir américain*, ed. Raymond Borde and Émile Chaumenton (Paris: Éditions du Minuit, 1955), vii.

32 Naremore, *More Than Night*, 18.

33 André Breton, "As in a Wood," *L'Âge du Cinéma* 4–5 (August–November 1951), rpt. in Hammond, *The Shadow and Its Shadow*, 73.

34 Breton, *Conversations*, 112.

35 Ibid.

36 Marcel Duhamel, promotional introduction to the Série Noire, rpt. in Robert Girard and Pierre Ditalian, *L'Argot de la Série Noire* (Paris: Joseph K., 1996).

37 Gilles Deleuze, "Philosophie de la Série Noire," *Arts et Loisirs* 18 (26 January 1966): 12–13. For a published English translation, see "The Philosophy of Crime Novels," in *Desert Islands and Other Texts: 1953–1974*, ed. David Lapoujade, trans. Mike Taormina (Cambridge: Semiotext(e), 2003), 81–85.

38 Deleuze, "Philosophie de la Série Noire," 12.

39 Ibid., 13.

40 Duhamel refers to the "paraliterature" of the Série Noire as "a reflection of society. It reflects its excesses; it only gives a certain image, but it's an image of society all the same. If society evolves, the Série Noire will evolve." Luc Geslin and Georges Rieben, "Interview du mois: Marcel Duhamel," *Mystère-Magazine* (July 1972): 125. Compare René Micha's article for Sartre and Beauvoir's *Temps Modernes*, which describes Himes's novels as "very good mirrors: carnival mirrors deforming all things in the direction of truth." René Micha, "Les Paroissiens de Chester Himes," *Les Temps Modernes* 225 (February 1965): 1523.

41 On the popularity of the *roman noir* among the existentialists, see esp. Gorrara, "Cultural Intersections."

42 Chester Himes, *My Life of Absurdity: The Autobiography of Chester Himes*, vol. 2 (New York: Thunder's Mouth Press, 1972), 106.

43 Bell, "Assuming the Position," 858.

44 Chester Himes, *A Rage in Harlem* (1957; rpt., New York: Vintage, 1991), 69.

45 Ibid.

46 Ibid., 96.

47 Manthia Diawara, "Noir by *Noirs*: Toward a New Realism in Black Cinema," in Copjec, *Shades of Noir*, 266.

48 Himes, *A Rage in Harlem*, 6.

49 Himes, *My Life of Absurdity*, 1.

50 Albert Camus, *The Myth of Sisyphus* (1955), trans. Justin O'Brien (New York: Vintage, 1991), 21.

51 Himes, *My Life of Absurdity*, 1.

52 Camus, *The Myth of Sisyphus*, 54.

53 Chester Himes, *If He Hollers, Let Him Go* (1945; rpt., New York: Thunder's Mouth Press, 1986), 88.

54 Himes, *My Life of Absurdity*, 36.

55 Fabre and Skinner, *Conversations with Chester Himes*, 170.

56 Richard Wright, "Introductory Note to *The Respectful Prostitute*," *Art and Action* (1948; rpt., New York: Krauss Reprint Corp., 1967), 14.

57 Ibid., 15.

58 Sartre, *What Is Literature?*, 195–96.

59 Himes, *My Life of Absurdity*, 126.

60 Deleuze, "Philosophie de la Série Noire," 12.

61 Claude Cahun, *Les Paris sont ouverts* (Paris: José Corti, 1934), rpt. in *Écrits*, ed. François Leperlier (Paris: Jean-Michel Place, 2002), 519.

62 Ibid., 532. Cahun's phrase "magic shortcuts" (*raccourcis magiques*) is a pun on *raccourci*, denoting both a shortcut and a pithy turn of phrase.

63 Duhamel reprints the preface in his memoirs. Duhamel, *Raconte pas ta vie!*, 589–91.

64 Himes, *My Life of Absurdity*, 102.

65 Ibid.

66 Deleuze, "Philosophie de la Série Noire," 13.

67 Fabre and Skinner, *Conversations with Chester Himes*, 92.

68 Walter Benjamin, "Little History of Photography" (1931), in *Selected Writings*, vol. 2, 1927–1934, ed. Michael W. Jennings (Cambridge: Harvard University Press, 1999), 519.

69 Chester Himes, *Cotton Comes to Harlem* (1965; rpt., New York: Vintage, 1988), 33–34.

Conclusion

1 Alain Joubert, "Ainsi soit-il," *Le Surréalisme, Même* 1 (3rd trimester 1956): 152–53.

2 Aimé Césaire, *Discourse on Colonialism* (1955), trans. Joan Pinkham (New York: Monthly Review Press, 1972), 43.

3 André Breton, "Discours au meeting 'Pour la Défense de la Liberté,' Salle des Horticulteurs, le 20 avril 1956," *Le Surréalisme, Même* 1 (1956), rpt. in *Perspective cavalière*, ed. Marguerite Bonnet (Paris: Gallimard, 1970), 126. See also Jean Schuster, "Open Letter to Aimé Césaire," *Le Surréalisme, Même* 1 (1956): 146–47.

4 A more direct interrogation of anticolonial violence became a focus of Frantz Fanon's *The Wretched of the Earth*, published in 1961, at the height of the Algerian war.

5 Jean Clair, *Du surréalisme considéré dans ses rapports au totalitarianism et aux tables tournantes* (Paris: Mille et une nuits, 2003), 118.

6 Ibid., 124–25.

7 Ibid., 195, 65.

8 Albert Camus, *The Rebel: An Essay on Man in Revolt*, trans. Anthony Bower (New York: Knopf, 1954), 77. See also Jules Monnerot, *Sociologie du communisme* (1949), in English, *The Sociology and Psychology of Communism* (Boston: Beacon Press, 1953), which compares communism to Islam and medieval Christianity, insofar as its converts "were able to attack in the name of the true Faith the very societies which had brought the Faith to them" (15). Péret considered Monnerot's book to be an unacknowledged source for *The Rebel*.

9 Camus, *The Rebel*, 177.

10 Marcel Duchamp, cited in Jean Schuster, "Conclusions," *Le Surréalisme, Même* 3 (Autumn 1957): 85.

11 "Note for *Le Surréalisme, Même*," *Le Surréalisme, Même* 1 (1956), in *Surrealism against the Current: Tracts and Declarations*, ed. and trans. Michael Richardson and Krzysztof Fijalkowski (London: Pluto Press, 2001), 51.

12 See Aimé Césaire, *Lettre à Maurice Thorez* (Paris: Présence Africaine, 1956).

13 Nora Mitrani, "De l'objectivité des lois," *Le Soleil Noir* 2, "Le temps des assassins" (June 1952), rpt. in *Rose au coeur violet* (Paris: Terrain Vague, 1988), 49.

14 Benjamin Péret, "Est-ce l'aube," *Le Surréalisme, Même* 1 (1956): 156.

15 Benjamin Péret, "Calendrier accusateur," *Le Surréalisme, Même* 2 (1957): 59.

16 See Benjamin Péret, "Assez de tortures," *Le Surréalisme, Même* 3 (Autumn 1957), rpt. in *Œvres complètes*, vol. 5 (Paris: José Corti, 1989), 305: "Every colonial power is thus responsible for the revolts its oppression provokes and for the inevitable violences they include, without which such revolts are admissible in spite of themselves."

17 Arthur Koestler, *Darkness at Noon* (1941), trans. Daphne Hardy (New York: Time Inc., 1962), 143.

18 Ibid., 206.

19 Maurice Merleau-Ponty, *Humanism and Terror: An Essay on the Communist Problem*, trans. John O'Neill (Boston: Beacon Press, 1969), 92.

20 Ibid., 187.

21 Camus, *The Rebel*, 21.

22 Ibid., 203–4. As Debarati Sanyal argues, the novelty of *The Rebel* lies in its "treatment of terror as a formal principle that could be deployed in the distinct fields of philosophy, politics, and aesthetics." Debarati Sanyal, "Broken Engagements," *Yale French Studies* 98 (2000): 32.

23 Camus, *The Rebel*, 272.

24 André Breton, "Dialogue avec Aimé Patri à propops de 'l'Homme révolté' d'Albert Camus," in *Œvres complètes*, vol. 3, ed. Marguerite Bonnet (Paris: Gallimard, 1999), 1054.

25 Benjamin Péret, "Le Revolté du dimanche" (1952), rpt. in *Œuvres complètes*, vol. 7 (Paris: José Corti, 1995), 180.

26 Ibid., 178.

27 Gérard Legrand, "Le Surréalisme est-il une philosophie?" *Le Surréalisme, Même* 1 (1956): 144.

BIBLIOGRAPHY

Aberth, Susan. *Leonora Carrington: Surrealism, Alchemy, and Art.* Burlington: Lund Humphries, 2004.

Action (1920–22). Paris: Jean-Michel Place, 1999.

Adamowicz, Elza. *Surrealist Collage in Text and Image: Dissecting the Exquisite Corpse.* Cambridge: Cambridge University Press, 1998.

Ades, Dawn. *Photomontage.* London: Thames and Hudson, 1986.

Adorno, Theodor. *Aesthetic Theory.* Trans. Robert Hullot-Kentor. Minneapolis: University of Minnesota Press, 1997.

L'Âge d'or: correspondance Luis Buñuel–Charles de Noiailles. Special issue of *Les Cahiers du Musée National d'Art Moderne* (1993).

Alexandre, Maxime. *Mémoires d'un surréaliste.* Paris: La Jeune Parque, 1968.

Allain, Marcel, and Pierre Souvestre. *Fantômas.* Introduction by John Ashbery. New York: Morrow, 1986.

Allendy, René. *Le Crime et les perversions instinctives.* Special issue of *Le Crapouillot* (May 1938).

Alquié, Ferdinand. *The Philosophy of Surrealism.* Ann Arbor: University of Michigan Press, 1965.

Andrew, Dudley, and Steven Ungar. *Popular Front Paris and the Poetics of Culture.* Cambridge: Harvard University Press, 2005.

Aragon, Louis. *The Adventures of Telemachus.* Trans. Renée Riese Hubert and Judd David Hubert. Lincoln: University of Nebraska Press, 1988.

———. *Anicet, ou le Panorama, roman.* Paris: Nouvelle Revue Française, 1921.

———. *Chroniques, 1918–1932.* Ed. Bernard Leuilliot. Paris: Stock, 1998.

———. *Lettres à Denise.* Ed. Pierre Daix. Paris: Maurice Nadeau, 1994.

———. *The Libertine.* Trans. Jo Levy. London: John Calder, 1987.

———. "A Man." *The Little Review* (Autumn–Winter 1923–24): 18–22.

———. *Paris Peasant.* Trans. Simon Watson Taylor. Boston: Exact Change, 1994.

———. *Projet d'histoire littéraire.* Paris: Mercure de France, 1994.

———. *Treatise on Style.* Trans. Alyson Waters. Lincoln: University of Nebraska Press, 1991.

———. "A Wave of Dreams." Trans. Adam Cornford. Electronic Publication. http://www.durationpress .com/authors/aragon/wave.html.

Archer-Straw, Petrine. *Negrophilia: Avant-Garde Paris and Black Culture in the 1920s.* London: Thames and Hudson, 2000.

Arland, Marcel. "Sur un nouveau mal de siècle." *La Nouvelle Revue Française* 128 (1924): 149–58.

Auriol, Georges. "The Occident." Trans. Elliot Paul. *transition* 2 (May 1927): 153–59.

Bandier, Norbert. *Sociologie du surréalisme.* Paris: La Dispute, 1999.

Barthes, Roland. *Writing Degree Zero.* 1953. Trans. Annette Lavers and Colin Smith. New York: Hill and Wang, 1968.

Bataille, Georges. *The Absence of Myth: Writings on Surrealism.* Trans. Michael Richardson. New York: Verso, 1994.

——. *Choix de Lettres: 1917–1962.* Ed. Michel Surya. Les Cahiers de la NRF. Paris: Gallimard, 1997.

——. *Visions of Excess: Selected Writings, 1927–1939.* Trans. Allan Stoekl. Minneapolis: University of Minnesota Press, 1985.

Bate, David. *Photography and Surrealism: Sexuality, Colonialism, and Social Dissent.* London: I. B. Tauris, 2004.

Baudelaire, Charles. *Artificial Paradises.* Trans. Stacy Diamond. New York: Citadel, 1996.

Baugh, Bruce. *French Hegel: From Surrealism to Postmodernism.* New York: Routledge, 2003.

Bayard, Pierre. *Who Killed Roger Ackroyd? The Mystery behind the Agatha Christie Mystery.* Trans. Carol Cosman. New York: Norton, 2000.

Beaujour, Michel. *Terreur et rhétorique: Breton, Bataille, Leiris, Paulhan, Barthes & Cie autour du surréalisme.* Paris: J. M. Place, 1999.

Bell, Kevin. "Assuming the Position: Fugitivity and Futurity in the Work of Chester Himes." *Modern Fiction Studies* 51.4 (2005): 846–72.

Bellmer, Hans. *The Doll.* Trans. Malcolm Green. London: Atlas Press, 2005.

Benjamin, Walter. *Selected Writings.* 4 vols. Ed. Michael W. Jennings et al. Cambridge: Harvard University Press, 1999.

Black, Joel. *The Aesthetics of Murder: A Study in Romantic Literature and Contemporary Culture.* Baltimore: Johns Hopkins University Press, 1991.

Blanchot, Maurice. *The Infinite Conversation.* Trans. Susan Hanson. Minneapolis: University of Minnesota Press, 1993.

——. *Lautréamont et Sade.* Paris: Éditions de Minuit, 1949.

——. *The Space of Literature.* Lincoln: University of Nebraska Press, 1982.

——. *The Work of Fire.* 1949. Trans. Charlotte Mandell. Stanford: Stanford University Press, 1995.

Bonaparte, Marie. *The Life and Works of Edgar Allan Poe: A Psycho-analytic Interpretation.* 1933. Trans. John Rodker. London: Imago Publishing, 1949.

Bonnet, Marguerite, ed. *Adhérer au Parti Communiste? Septembre–Décembre 1926.* Vol. 3 of *Archives du Surréalisme.* Paris: Gallimard, 1992.

——, ed. *L'Affaire Barrès.* Paris: José Corti, 1987.

——. *André Breton: Naissance de l'aventure surréaliste.* Paris: José Corti, 1975.

——. "L'Orient et le surréalisme: mythe et réel." *Revue de Littérature Comparée* 544 (October–December 1980): 411–29.

——, ed. *Vers l'action politique: de la Révolution d'abord et toujours! (Juillet 1925) au projet de la Guerre Civile (Avril 1926).* Vol. 2 of *Archives du Surréalisme.* Paris: Gallimard, 1988.

Bontempelli, Massimo. "Justification." *900: Cahiers d'Italie et d'Europe* 1 (1926): 12.

Borde, Raymond, and Étienne Chaumenton. *Panorama du film noir américain.* Paris: Éditions du minuit, 1955.

Boucharenc, Myriam. *L'Échec et son double: Philippe Soupault romancier.* Paris: Honoré Champion, 1997.

Boucharenc, Myriam, and Claude Leroy, eds. *Présence de Philippe Soupault.* Caen: Presses Universitaires de Caen, 1999.

Breton, André. *Anthology of Black Humor.* 1939. Trans. Mark Polizzotti. San Francisco: City Lights, 1997.

——. *Arcanum 17*. Trans. Zack Rogow. Los Angeles: Sun and Moon, 1994.

——. *Communicating Vessels*. Trans. Mary Ann Caws. Lincoln: University of Nebraska Press, 1990.

——. *Conversations: The Autobiography of Surrealism*. Trans. Mark Polizzotti. New York: Marlowe and Company, 1993.

——. *The Lost Steps*. Trans. Mark Polizzotti. Lincoln: University of Nebraska Press, 1997.

——. *Mad Love*. Trans. Mary Ann Caws. Lincoln: University of Nebraska Press, 1987.

——. *Manifestoes of Surrealism*. Trans. Richard Seaver and Helen R. Lane. Ann Arbor: University of Michigan Press, 1969.

—— *Nadja*. Trans. Richard Howard. New York: Grove Press, 1960.

——. *Œuvres complètes*. Ed. Marguerite Bonnet et al. 3 vols. Paris: Gallimard, 1988.

——. *Perspective cavalière*. Ed. Marguerite Bonnet. Paris: Gallimard, 1970.

——. *Qu'est-ce que le surréalisme?* Paris: R. Henriquez, 1934.

——. *Surrealism and Painting*. Trans. Simon Watson Taylor. New York: Harper and Row, 1972.

——, ed. *This Quarter: Surrealist Number (September 1932)*. New York: Arno Press, 1969.

——. *What Is Surrealism? Selected Writings*. Ed. Franklin Rosemont. New York: Pathfinder Press, 1978.

Breton, André, and Paul Éluard. *Dictionnaire abrégé du surréalisme*. Paris: Galerie Beaux-Arts, 1938.

——. *The Immaculate Conception*. 1st English ed. London: Atlas, 1990.

——. *Violette Nozières: poèmes, dessins, correspondance, documents*. Paris: Terrain Vague, 1991.

Breton, André, and André Parinaud. *Conversations: The Autobiography of Surrealism*. New York: Paragon House, 1993.

Breton, André, et al. *André Breton: la beauté convulsive: Musée National d'Art Moderne, Centre Georges Pompidou*. Paris: Éditions du Centre Pompidou, 1991.

Breton, Simone. *Lettres à Denise Lévy*. Ed. Georgiana Colvile. Paris: Éditions Joelle Losfeld, 2005.

Bridel, Yves. *Miroirs du surréalisme: essai sur la réception du surréalisme en France et en Suisse française (1916–1939)*. Lausanne: L'Âge d'homme, 1988.

Brown, Stephanie. "Black Comme Moi: Boris Vian and the African American Voice of Translation." *Mosaic* 36.1 (March 2003): 51–68.

Cahun, Claude. *Écrits*. Ed. François Leperlier. Paris: Jean-Michel Place, 2002.

——. *Les Paris sont ouverts*. Paris: José Corti, 1934.

Caillois, Roger. *Le Roman policier: ou, comment l'intelligence se retire du monde pour se consacrer à ses jeux et comment la société introduit ses problèmes dans ceux-ci*. Buenos Aires: Éditions des lettres françaises: SUR, 1941.

Camfield, William A., et al. *Max Ernst: Dada and the Dawn of Surrealism*. Munich: Prestel, 1993.

Camus, Albert. *The Myth of Sisyphus*. Trans. Justin O'Brien. New York: Vintage, 1991.

——. *The Rebel: An Essay on Man in Revolt*. Trans. Anthony Bower. New York: Vintage, 1956.

Carassou, Michel. *René Crevel*. Paris: Fayard, 1989.

Carmody, Francis. "Éluard's Rupture with Surrealism." *PMLA* 76. 4 (September 1961): 436–46.

Carrington, Leonora. *En bas*. Paris: Eric Losfeld, 1973.

——. *The House of Fear: Notes from Down Below*. New York: Dutton, 1988.

——. *La Maison de la Peur*. Paris: H. Parisot, 1938.

Carter, Angela. *The Bloody Chamber*. London: Penguin, 1979.

——. *The Sadean Woman and the Ideology of Pornography.* New York: Pantheon, 1978.

Cassayre, Sylvie. *Poétique de l'espace et imaginaire dans l'œuvre de Phillippe Soupault.* Paris: Lettres modernes, 1997.

Caws, Mary Ann. "Ladies Shot and Painted: Female Embodiment in Surrealist Art." In *The Female Body in Western Culture: Contemporary Perspectives.* Ed. Susan Suleiman. Cambridge: Harvard University Press, 1986. 262–87.

——, ed. *Surrealism: Themes and Movements.* London: Phaidon, 2004.

——. *The Surrealist Look: An Erotics of Encounter.* Cambridge: MIT Press, 1997.

Caws, Mary Ann, Rudolf E. Kuenzli, and Gloria Gwen Raaberg, eds. *Surrealism and Women.* Cambridge: MIT Press, 1991.

Césaire, Aimé. *Discourse on Colonialism.* 1955. Trans. Joan Pinkham. New York: Monthly Review Press, 1972.

——. *Lettre à Maurice Thorez.* Paris: Présence Africaine, 1956.

Chadwick, Whitney. "Leonora Carrington: Evolution of a Feminist Consciousness." *Woman's Art Journal* 7.1 (Spring–Summer 1986): 37–42.

——. *Women Artists and the Surrealist Movement.* Boston: Little, Brown, 1985.

Chénieux-Gendron, Jacqueline. *Surrealism.* Trans. Vivian Folkenflik. New York: Columbia University Press, 1990.

——. *Le Surréalisme et le roman, 1922–1950.* Lausanne: Âge d'homme, 1983.

Chénieux-Gendron, Jacqueline, and Myriam Bloedé. *Patiences et silences de Philippe Soupault.* Paris: L'Harmattan, 2000.

Chénieux-Gendron, Jacqueline, and Timothy Mathews. *Violence, théorie, surréalisme.* Paris: Lachenal & Ritter, 1994.

Chénieux-Gendron, Jacqueline, Marie Claire Dumas, et al. *Jeux surréalistes et humour noir.* Paris: Lachenal & Ritter, 1993.

Chesterton, G. K. "The Blue Cross." 1911. In *The Complete Father Brown.* New York: Dodd, Mead & Co., 1982. 3–23.

Cixous, Hélène, and Catherine Clément. *The Newly Born Woman.* Trans. Betsy Wing. Minneapolis: University of Minnesota Press, 1986.

Clair, Jean. *Du Surréalisme considéré dans ses rapports au totalitarianisme et aux tables tournantes.* Paris: Mille et Une Nuits, 2004.

Clébert, Jean-Paul. *Dictionnaire du surréalisme.* Paris: Seuil, 1996.

Clej, Alina. *A Genealogy of the Modern Self: Thomas De Quincey and the Intoxication of Writing.* Stanford: Stanford University Press, 1995.

Coffman, Christine. *Insane Passions: Lesbianism and Psychosis in Literature and Film.* Middletown: Wesleyan University Press, 2006.

Cohen, Margaret. *Profane Illumination: Walter Benjamin and the Paris of Surrealist Revolution.* Berkeley: University of California Press, 1993.

Cohen, Paul. "Heroes and Dilettantes: The Action Française, Le Sillon, and the Generation of 1905–14." *French Historical Studies* 15.4 (Autumn 1988): 673–87.

Conley, Katharine. *Automatic Woman: The Representation of Woman in Surrealism.* Lincoln: University of Nebraska Press, 1996.

——. *Robert Desnos and the Marvelous in Everyday Life.* Lincoln: University of Nebraska Press, 2004.

——. "Le Surréalisme médiatisé de Robert Desnos." In *Desnos pour l'an 2000: Colloque de Cérisy-La-Salle.* Ed. Katharine Conley and Marie-Claire Dumas. Paris: Gallimard, 2000. 13–24.

Copjek, Joan, ed. *Shades of Noir.* London: Verso, 1993.

Coriem, Maurice. "Histoire d'un drame passionnel: 'Le Crime des Soeurs Papin.'" *Scandale* 5 (December 1933): 233–36.

Cottom, Daniel. *Abyss of Reason: Cultural Movements, Revelations, and Betrayals.* New York: Oxford University Press, 1991.

Courtot, Claude. *Introduction à la lecture de Benjamin Péret.* Paris: Le Terrain Vague, 1965.

Cox, Neil. "La Mort posthume: Maurice Heine and the Poetics of Decay." *Art History* 23.3 (September 2000): 417–49.

Crevel, René. *Babylon: A Novel.* San Francisco: North Point Press, 1985.

——. *Babylone.* 1927. Paris: Pauvert, 1986.

——. *Détours.* 1925. Paris: Pauvert, 1985.

——. *Êtes-vous fous?* Paris: Gallimard, 1929.

——. *L'Esprit contre la raison, et autres écrits surréalistes.* Paris: Pauvert, 1986.

——. *Mon Corps et moi.* 1926. Paris: Pauvert, 1974.

——. *La Mort difficile.* Paris: Pauvert, 1974.

——. "Notes toward a Psycho-dialectic." Trans. Jonathan P. Eburne. In *Surrealism: Themes and Movements.* Ed. Mary Ann Caws. London: Phaidon, 2004; 265–67.

——. *Les Pieds dans le plat.* Paris: Éditions du Sagittaire, 1933.

——. *Putting My Foot in It.* Normal, Okla.: Dalkey Archive Press, 1992.

——. *Le Roman cassé et derniers écrits.* Paris: Pauvert, 1989.

——. "Which Way?" *The Little Review* (Autumn 1923–Winter 1924): 29–34.

cummings, e. e. *Complete Poems, 1904–1962.* Ed. George J. Firmage. New York: Liveright, 1994.

Daix, Pierre. *La Vie quotidienne des surréalistes, 1917–1932.* Paris: Hachette, 1993.

Dalí, Salvador. *The Collected Writings of Salvador Dalí.* Ed. Haim N. Finkelstein. Cambridge: Cambridge University Press, 1998.

——. *Oui: The Paranoid-Critical Revolution.* Trans. Yvonne Shafir. Boston: Exact Change, 1998.

Dalí, Salvador, et al. *Salvador Dalí: The Early Years.* London: Thames and Hudson, 1994.

Dean, Carolyn J. *The Self and Its Pleasures: Bataille, Lacan, and the History of the Decentered Subject.* Ithaca: Cornell University Press, 1992.

Deleuze, Gilles. "Philosophie de la Série Noire." *Arts et Loisirs* 18 (1966): 12–13.

——. "The Philosophy of Crime Novels." In *Desert Islands and Other Texts: 1953–1974.* Ed. David Lapoujade. Trans. Mike Taormina. Cambridge: Semiotext(e), 2003. 81–85.

Denning, Michael. "Topographies of Violence: Chester Himes' Harlem Domestic Novels." *Critical Texts* 5.1 (1988): 10–18.

De Quincey, Thomas. "On Murder, Considered as One of the Fine Arts." In *The Collected Writings of Thomas De Quincey.* Ed. David Masson. Vol. 13. 1890. New York: AMS Press, 1968. 70–124.

Desnos, Robert. *Deuil pour Deuil.* Paris: Aux Éditions du Sagittaire, 1924.

——. *Jack l'Éventreur.* Paris: Allia, 1997.

——. *La Liberté ou l'amour!* Paris: Aux Éditions du Sagittaire, 1927.

——. *Liberty or Love!* London: Atlas, 1993.

——. *Mourning for Mourning.* London: Atlas Press, 1992.

——. *Nouvelles Hébrides et autres textes, 1922–1930.* Ed. Marie Claire Dumas. Paris: Gallimard, 1978.

——. *Œuvres.* Ed. Marie-Claire Dumas. Paris: Gallimard, 1999.

——. *Les Rayons et les ombres: cinéma.* Ed. Marie-Claire Dumas. Paris: Gallimard, 1992.

Diawara, Manthia. "Noir by Noirs: Toward a New Realism in Black Cinema." In *Shades of Noir*. Ed. Joan Copjec. London: Verso, 1993. 261–278.

Documents (1929–30). 2 vols. Ed. Denis Hollier. Paris: Jean-Michel Place, 1991.

Documents 34. "L'intervention Surréaliste." June 1934. Brussels: Didier Devillez, 1998.

Dostoyevsky, Fyodor. *Crime and Punishment.* Trans. David McDuff. London: Penguin, 1991.

Drieu La Rochelle, Pierre. "La Véritable Erreur des surréalistes." *Nouvelle Revue Française* 25 (August 1925): 166–71.

Duhamel, Marcel. "Préface." In *Panorama du film noir américain*. Ed. Raymond Borde and Emile Chaumenton. Paris: Éditions du Minuit, 1955. vii–x.

——. Promotional introduction to the Série Noire. In Robert Girard and Pierre Ditalian. *L'Argot de la Série Noire.* Paris: Joseph K., 1996.

——. *Raconte pas ta vie!* Paris: Mercure de France, 1972.

Dumas, Marie Claire. "La Guillotine sans couperet." In *Poétiques de Robert Desnos*. Ed. Laurent Flieder. Fontenay-aux-Roses: ENS Editions, 1995. 65–81.

——. *Robert Desnos: ou, l'exploration des limites.* Paris: Klincksieck, 1980.

Dupré, Francis. *La "Solution" du passage à l'acte: le double crime des soeurs Papin.* Toulouse: Erès, 1984.

Durozoi, Gérard. *Histoire du mouvement surréaliste.* Paris: Hazan, 1997.

——. *History of the Surrealist Movement.* Trans. Alison Anderson. Chicago: University of Chicago Press, 2002.

Eburne, Jonathan P. "That Obscure Object of Revolt: Heraclitus, Surrealism's Lightning-Conductor." *Symploke* 8.1–2 (2000): 180–204.

Edwards, Brent Hayes. *The Practice of Diaspora: Literature, Translation, and the Rise of Black Internationalism.* Cambridge: Harvard University Press, 2003.

Edwards, Rachel, and Keith Reader. *The Papin Sisters.* Oxford: Oxford University Press, 2001.

Éluard, Paul. *Œuvres complètes,* Vol. 2. Ed. Lucien Scheler et al. Paris: Gallimard, 1968.

Éluard, Paul, and Pierre Dreyfus. *Lettres à Gala, 1924–1948.* Paris: Gallimard, 1984.

Emanuel, Michelle. *From Surrealism to Less-Exquisite Cadavers: Léo Malet and the Evolution of the French Roman Noir.* Amsterdam: Rodopi, 2006.

Ernst, Jimmy. *My Not-So-Still Life.* New York: St. Martin's, 1984.

Ernst, Max. "Biographical Notes: Tissue of Truth, Tissue of Lies." In *Max Ernst: A Retrospective*. Ed. Werner Spies. New York: Prestel, 1991. 281–340.

——. *Une Semaine de bonté.* 1934. New York: Dover, 1976.

Eugène, Marcel. "Sur l'enquête des 'Cahiers du Mois': les appels de l'Orient," *Clarté* 75 (1925): 13–14.

Ezra, Elizabeth. *The Colonial Unconscious: Race and Culture in Interwar France.* Ithaca: Cornell University Press, 2000.

Fabre, Michel, and Robert E. Skinner, eds. *Conversations with Chester Himes.* Jackson: University Press of Mississippi, 1995.

——. *From Harlem to Paris: Black American Writers in France, 1840–1980*. Urbana: University of Illinois Press, 1991.

Fauré, Michel. *Le Groupe Octobre*. Paris: Christian Bourgeois, 1977.

——. *Histoire du surréalisme sous l'Occupation*. Paris: La Table Ronde, 1982.

Flanner, Janet. *Paris Was Yesterday, 1925–1937*. Ed. Irving Drutman. New York: Harcourt, Brace, Jovanovich, 1972.

Foster, Hal. *Compulsive Beauty*. Cambridge: MIT Press, 1993.

Foucault, Michel. *Essential Works of Foucault, 1954–1984*. Vol. 2. *Aesthetics, Method, and Epistemology*. Ed. James D. Faubion. New York: New Press, 1998.

——. *I, Pierre Rivière, having slaughtered my mother, my sister, and my brother . . . : A Case of Parricide in the 19th Century*. Trans. Frank Jellinek. New York: Pantheon, 1975.

Freud, Sigmund. *The Interpretation of Dreams*. Trans. James Strachey. New York: Avon, 1965.

——. *Three Case Studies*. New York: Collier, 1963.

——. "The Uncanny." 1919. In *The Complete Psychological Works of Sigmund Freud*. Vol. 17. Trans. and ed. James Strachey. London: Hogarth Press, 1953–73. 234–35.

Gauthier, Xavière. *Surréalisme et sexualité*. Paris: Gallimard, 1971.

Gercke, Daniel. "On the Eve of Distraction: Gaumont's *Fantômas*." *Sites* 1.1 (Spring 1997): 157–69.

Gershman, Herbert S. *The Surrealist Revolution in France*. Ann Arbor: University of Michigan Press, 1969.

Geslin, Luc, and Georges Rieben. "Interview du mois: Marcel Duhamel." *Mystère-Magazine* (1972): 125–27.

Gibson, Ian. *The Shameful Life of Salvador Dalí*. London: Faber and Faber, 1997.

Gilman, Sander L. "'Who Kills Whores?' 'I Do,' Says Jack: Race and Gender in Victorian London." In *Death and Representation*. Ed. Sarah Webster Goodwin and Elisabeth Bronfen. Baltimore: Johns Hopkins University Press, 1993. 263–84.

Girard, Robert, and Pierre Ditalian. *L'Argot de la Série Noire*. Paris: Joseph K., 1996.

Gorrara, Claire. "Cultural Intersections: The American Detective Novel and the Early French 'Roman Noir.'" *Modern Language Review* 98.3 (July 2003): 590–601.

——. "Malheurs et ténèbres: Narratives of Social Disorder in Léo Malet's 120, rue de la Gare." *French Cultural Studies* 12 (2001): 271–83.

——. *The Roman Noir in Post-war French Culture*. Oxford: Oxford University Press, 2003.

Goulet, Andrea. *Optiques: The Science of the Eye and the Birth of Modern French Fiction*. Philadelphia: University of Pennsylvania Press, 2006.

Greeley, Robin Adèle. *Surrealism and the Spanish Civil War*. New Haven: Yale University Press, 2006.

Green, Malcolm. Introduction. In Hans Bellmer. *The Doll*. London: Atlas Press, 2005. 7–30.

Gubar, Susan. "Representing Pornography: Feminism, Criticism, and Depictions of Female Violation." *Critical Inquiry* 13 (1987): 712–41.

Guerlac, Suzanne. *Literary Polemics: Bataille, Sartre, Valéry, Breton*. Stanford: Stanford University Press, 1997.

Guiol-Benassaya, Elyette. *La Presse face au surréalisme de 1925 à 1938*. Paris: CNRS, 1982.

Hammond, Paul, ed. and trans. *The Shadow and Its Shadow: Surrealist Writings on the Cinema*. San Francisco: City Lights Books, 2000.

Harris, Steven. *Surrealist Art and Thought in the 1930s: Art, Politics, and the Psyche.* Cambridge: Cambridge University Press, 2004.

Heine, Maurice. "Promenade à travers le roman noir." *Minotaure* 5 (1934): 1–3.

Hénaff, Marcel. *Sade: The Invention of the Libertine Body.* Trans. Xavier Callahan. Minneapolis: University of Minnesota Press, 1999.

Himes, Chester. *If He Hollers, Let Him Go.* 1945. New York: Thunder's Mouth Press, 1986.

——. *My Life of Absurdity: The Autobiography of Chester Himes.* Vol. 2. New York: Thunder's Mouth Press, 1972.

——. *A Rage in Harlem.* 1958. New York: Vintage, 1991.

——. *La Reine des Pommes.* Trans. Minnie Danzas. Série Noire. Paris: Gallimard, 1958.

Hollier, Denis. *Against Architecture: The Writings of Georges Bataille.* Trans. Betsy Wing. Cambridge: MIT Press, 1989.

Houdoyer, Paulette. *Le Diable dans le peau: l'affaire des soeurs Papin.* Paris: Juliard, 1966.

Hubert, Jules. *L'Ignoble Empoisonneuse, ou, le crime de la rue de Madagascar.* Paris: Chaffange et Cie, n.d. [ca. 1934].

Hubert, Renée Riese. "Images du criminel et du héros surréalistes." *Mélusine* 1 (1979): 187–97.

——. *Surrealism and the Book.* Berkeley: University of California Press, 1988.

Hugnet, Georges. *Pleins et déliés: souvenirs et témoignages, 1926–1972.* La Chapelle-sur-Loire: G. Authier, 1972.

——. *Le Septième Face du dé.* Paris: Éditions Jeanne Bucher, 1936.

Hulak, Fabienne, and Marguerite Bonnet. *Folie et psychanalyse dans l'expérience Surréaliste.* Nice: Z'éditions, 1992.

Institut Catholique de Paris. *Philippe Soupault: l'ombre frissonnante.* Paris: Jean-Michel Place, 2000.

Jaguer, Édouard. *Les Mystères de la chambre noire: le surréalisme et la photographie.* Paris: Flammarion, 1982.

Jankowski, Paul F. *Stavisky: A Confidence Man in the Republic of Virtue.* Ithaca: Cornell University Press, 2002.

Jean, Marcel. *The Autobiography of Surrealism.* New York: Viking Press, 1980.

Jolles, Adam. "'Visitez l'exposition anti-coloniale!' nouveaux éléments sur l'exposition protestaire de 1931: Paul Éluard, *La Vérité sur les colonies;* Aragon, *La Vérité sur les colonies: une salle d'exposition anti-impérialiste.*" *Pleine Marge* 35 (June 2002): 106–27.

Jones, Christopher M. *Boris Vian Transatlantic: Sources, Myths, and Dreams.* New York: Peter Lang, 1998.

Josephson, Matthew. *Life among the Surrealists: A Memoir.* New York: Holt, Rinehart, and Winston, 1962.

Judovitz, Dalia. *Unpacking Duchamp.* Berkeley: University of California Press, 1995.

Kalifa, Dominique. *L'Encre et le sang: récits de crimes et société à la Belle Époque.* Paris: Fayard, 1995.

Kavky, Samantha. "Authorship and Identity in Max Ernst's Loplop." *Art History* 28.3 (2005): 357–85.

Kelley, Robin D. G. *Freedom Dreams: The Black Radical Imagination.* Boston: Beacon Press, 2002.

Koestler, Arthur. *Darkness at Noon.* 1941. Trans. Daphne Hardy. New York: Time Inc., 1962.

Kohn, Marek. *Dope Girls: The Birth of the British Drug Underground.* London: Granta, 1992.

Krauss, Rosalind E. *The Optical Unconscious.* Cambridge: MIT Press, 1993.

——. *The Originality of the Avant-Garde and Other Modernist Myths.* Cambridge: MIT Press, 1985.

Krauss, Rosalind E., et al. *L'Amour Fou: Photography and Surrealism.* New York: Abbeville Press, 1985.

Lacan, Jacques. *De la Psychose paranoïaque dans ses rapports avec la personnalité.* 1932. Paris: Éditions du Seuil, 1975.

——. "Motifs du crime paranoïaque: le crime des soeurs Papin." *Minotaure* 3–4 (1933): 25–28.

——. "Le Problème du style et la conception psychiatrique des formes paranoïaques de l'expérience." *Minotaure* 1 (1933): 68–69.

Lacassagne, Alexandre. *Vacher l'Éventreur et les crimes sadiques.* Paris: Masson et Cie, 1899.

Lane, Christopher. "The Delirium of Interpretation: Writing the Papin Affair." *differences* 5.2 (1993): 24–61.

Laplanche, Jean, and Pontalis, J.-B. *The Language of Psycho-analysis.* New York, Norton, 1973.

Lautréamont (Isodore Ducasse). *Maldoror and the Complete Works of the Comte De Lautréamont.* Trans. Alexis Lykiard. Cambridge: Exact Change, 1994.

Lautréamont (Isodore Ducasse), et al. *Œuvres complètes.* Paris: GLM, 1938.

Légitime Défense. 1932. Paris: Jean-Michel Place, 1979.

Lély, Gilbert. *Je ne veux pas qu'on tue cette femme.* Paris: Éditions Surréalistes, 1936.

Leroux, Gaston. *The Mystery of the Yellow Room.* New York: Brentano's, 1908.

Lewis, Helena. *The Politics of Surrealism.* New York: Paragon House, 1990.

Littérature (1919–1924). 2 vols. Paris: Jean-Michel Place, 1978.

Löwy, Michel. *L'Étoile du matin: surréalisme et marxisme.* Paris: Syllepse, 2000.

——. *Révolte et mélancolie: le romantisme à contre-courant de la modernité.* Paris: Payot, 1992.

Lyford, Amy. "The Aesthetics of Dismemberment: Surrealism and the Musée du Val-de-Grâce in 1917." *Cultural Critique* 46 (Autumn 2000): 45–79.

MacOrlan, Pierre. "Photographie: éléments de fantastique social." *Le Crapouillot* (January 1929): 3–6.

Magritte, René, and André Blavier. *Écrits complets.* Paris: Flammarion, 1979.

Magritte, René, et al. *René Magritte: catalogue raisonné.* New York: Philip Wilson, 1992.

Mahon, Alyce. *Surrealism and the Politics of Eros, 1938–1968.* London: Thames and Hudson, 2005.

Malet, Léo. *Nestor Burma.* 4 Vols. Ed. Nadia Dhoukar. Paris: Robert Laffont, 2006.

——. *Poèmes surréalistes.* Paris: Éditions de la Butte aux Cailles, 1983.

——. *La Vache enragée.* Paris: Hoëbeke, 1998.

Malt, Johanna. *Obscure Objects of Desire: Surrealism, Fetishism, and Politics.* Oxford: Oxford University Press, 2004.

Martin-Chauffier, Louis. "Le Poison dans le sang." *Vu* (6 September 1933): 1385–86.

Martinet, Marcel. "Contre le courant." *Europe* 41 (15 May 1926).

McCann, Sean. *Gumshoe America: Hard-Boiled Crime Fiction and the Rise and Fall of New Deal Liberalism.* Durham: Duke University Press, 2000.

McCrae, Niall. "'A violent thunderstorm': Cardiazol Treatment in British Mental Hospitals." *History of Psychiatry* 3.17 (2006): 67–90.

McDonagh, Josephine. *De Quincey's Disciplines.* Oxford: Clarendon Press, 1994.

McInnes, Mary Drach. "Taboo and Transgression: The Subversive Aesthetics of Georges Bataille and *Documents.*" Ph.D. dissertation, Boston University, 1994.

Merleau-Ponty, Maurice. *Humanism and Terror: An Essay on the Communist Problem.* Trans. John O'Neill. Boston: Beacon Press, 1969.

Mesplède, Claude. *Les Années "Série Noire" 2e édition*. 5 vols. Amiens: Enorage, 1992.

Messac, Régis. *Le Détective Novel et l'influence de la pensée scientifique*. Paris: Honoré Champion, 1929.

Meunier, Raymond. "Criminalité cubéo-dadaïste." *Liberté*, 16 February 1922.

Micha, René. "Les Paroissiens de Chester Himes." *Les Temps Modernes* 225 (1965): 1506–23.

Milliken, Stephen. *Chester Himes: A Critical Appraisal*. Columbia: University of Missouri Press, 1976.

Minotaure (1933–39). 3 vols. Geneva: Skira, 1983.

Mitrani, Nora. *Rose au coeur violet*. Paris: Terrain Vague, 1988.

Monahan, Laurie. "Crimes against Nature: Violette Nozières, Surrealism and Mass Culture." *Collapse* 4 (Spring 1999): 72–105.

——. "Masson: The Face of Violence." *Art in America* 88.7 (July 2000): 76–79, 121–122.

Monnerot, Jules. *La Poésie moderne et le sacré*. Paris: Gallimard, 1945.

——. *The Sociology and Psychology of Communism*. Boston: Beacon Press, 1953.

Muller, Herbert J. "Surrealism: A Dissenting Opinion." *New Directions* 40 (1940): 548–62.

Mundy, Jennifer, et al. *Surrealism: Desire Unbound*. Princeton: Princeton University Press, 2001.

Museum of Modern Art, New York, and Alfred Hamilton Barr. *Fantastic Art, Dada, Surrealism*. New York: Museum of Modern Art, 1936.

Nadeau, Maurice. *The History of Surrealism*. New York: Collier Books, 1965.

Naremore, James. *More than Night: Film Noir in Its Contexts*. Berkeley: University of California Press, 1998.

Naville, Pierre. *Le Temps du surréel*. Paris: Éditions Galilée, 1977.

Négis, André. "Enquête." *Cahiers du Sud* 64 (January 1925): 78.

Niger, Jacques. *Le Secret de l'empoisonneuse; le crime de Violette Nozières. Son arrestation. Ses complices(?)*. Paris, 1933.

Nougé, Paul. *L'Histoire de ne pas rire*. Brussels: Les Lèvres Nues, 1956.

Paligot, Carole Reynaud. "L'Éthique libertaire du surrealisme." In *Littérature et anarchie*. Ed. Alain Pessin. Toulouse: Presse Universitaire de Mirail, 1998. 491–500.

——. *Parcours politique des surréalistes, 1919–1969*. Paris: CNRS, 1995.

Parry, Eugenia. *Crime Album Stories, Paris, 1886–1902*. New York: Scalo, 2000.

Paulhan, Jean. "The Marquis de Sade and His Accomplice." In *Justine, Philosophy in the Bedroom, and Other Writings*. Ed. and trans. Richard Seaver and Austryn Wainhouse. New York: Grove Press, 1965.

Péret, Benjamin. *Death to the Pigs and Other Writings*. Trans. Rachel Stella. Lincoln: University of Nebraska Press, 1988.

——. *Œuvres complètes*. 7 vols. Paris: Losfeld, José Corti, 1969.

Pidault, J., and M.-I. Sicard. *L'Affaire Nozières: crime ou châtiment?* Paris: Enquêtes et Documents, 1 September 1933.

Pierre, José, ed. *Tracts surréalistes et déclarations collectives*. Vol. 1. 1922–1939. Paris: Terrain Vague, 1980.

——, ed. *Tracts surréalistes et déclarations collectives*. Vol. 2. 1940–1969. Paris: Terrain Vague, 1982.

Polizzotti, Mark. *Revolution of the Mind: The Life of André Breton*. 1st ed. New York: Farrar Straus and Giroux, 1995.

Poe, Edgar Allan. *Edgar Allan Poe: Poetry and Tales*. Ed. Patrick Quinn. New York: Library of America, 1984.

Rabaté, Jean-Michel. "Étant donné: 1° l'art 2° le crime: Duchamp criminel de l'avant-garde." *Interfaces* 14, "Les Avant-gardes" (1998): 113–30.

La Révolution surréaliste (1924–29). Paris: Jean-Michel Place, 1975.

Ribemont-Dessaignes, Georges. *Déjà jadis; ou, du mouvement Dada à l'espace abstrait*. Paris: R. Julliard, 1958.

———. "LE NEGRE, par Philippe Soupault." *Feuilles libres* (December 1927–January 1928): 69–70.

Richardson, Michael, and Krzysztof Fijalkowski, ed. and trans. *Refusal of the Shadow: Surrealism and the Carribean*. New York: Verso, 1996.

———. *Surrealism against the Current: Tracts and Declarations*. London: Pluto Press, 2001.

Rimbaud, Arthur. *Œuvres*. Ed. S. Bernard and A. Guyaux. Paris: Garnier, 1983.

Rosello, Mireille. *L'?Humour noir selon André Breton*. Paris: J. Corti, 1987.

Rosemont, Penelope. *Surrealist Women: An International Anthology*. Austin: University of Texas Press, 1998.

Rosenheim, Shawn, and Stephen Rachman. *The American Face of Edgar Allan Poe*. Baltimore: Johns Hopkins University Press, 1995.

Roudinesco, Elisabeth. *La Bataille de cent ans: une histoire de la psychanalyse en France*. Vol. 2. Paris: Fayard, 1986.

———. *Jacques Lacan*. Trans. Barbara Bray. New York: Columbia University Press, 1997.

———. *Jacques Lacan & Co: A History of Psychoanalysis in France, 1925–1985*. Trans. Jeffrey Mehlman. Chicago: University of Chicago Press, 1990.

Roussel, Raymond. *How I Wrote Certain of My Books*. Ed. and trans. Trevor Winkfield. Boston: Exact Change, 1995.

Sade, D. A. F. de. *Justine, Philosophy in the Bedroom, and Other Writings*. Ed. and trans. Richard Seaver and Austryn Wainhouse. New York: Grove Press, 1965.

———. *The 120 Days of Sodom and Other Writings*. Ed. and trans. Austryn Wainhouse and Richard Seaver. New York: Grove Press, 1966.

Sanouillet, Michel. *Dada à Paris*. Paris: Flammarion, 1969.

Sanyal, Debarati. "Broken Engagements." *Yale French Studies* 98 (2000): 29–49.

Sartre, Jean-Paul. *"What Is Literature?" and Other Essays*. Ed. Stephen Ungar. Cambridge: Harvard University Press, 1988.

Sawin, Martica. *Surrealism in Exile and the Beginning of the New York School*. Cambridge: MIT Press, 1995.

Schreber, Daniel Paul. *Memoirs of my Nervous Illness*. 1903. Trans. Ida MacAlphine and Richard A. Hunter. Cambridge: Harvard University Press, 1988.

Seltzer, Mark. *Serial Killers: Death and Life in America's Wound Culture*. New York: Routledge, 1999.

Smith, Robert P. "Chester Himes in France and the Legacy of the Roman Policier." *CLA Journal* 25.1 (September 1981): 18–27.

Soupault, Philippe. *À la dérive*. Paris: J. Ferenczi et Fils, 1923.

———. *Carte postale*. Toulouse: Éditions des Cahiers Libres, 1926.

———. *Le Coeur d'or*. Paris: Grasset, 1927.

———. "The Death of Nick Carter." Trans. Maive Sage. *transition* 7 (October 1927): 64–74.

———. *Écrits de cinéma*. Ed. Alain Virmaux and Odette Virmaux. [Paris]: Plon, 1979.

———. *Littérature et le reste, 1919–1931*. Ed. Lydie Lachenal. Paris: Gallimard, 2006.

——. *Mémoires de l'oubli.* Vol. 1. 1914–1923. Paris: Lachenal & Ritter, 1981.

——. *Mémoires de l'oubli.* Vol. 2. 1923–1926. Paris: Lachenal & Ritter, 1986.

——. *Mémoires de l'oubli.* Vol. 3.1927–1933. Paris: Lachenal & Ritter, 1997.

——. *Le Nègre.* Paris: Gallimard, 1997.

——. Vanité de l'Europe," *Cahiers du mois* 9–10 (February–March 1935): 64–68.

Soupault, Philippe, and William Carlos Williams. *Last Nights of Paris.* New York: Full Court Press, 1982.

Souvestre, Pierre, and Marcel Allain. *Fantômas.* New York: Morrow, 1986.

Soyinka, Wole. *Myth, Literature, and the African World.* Cambridge: Cambridge University Press, 1976.

Spies, Werner. *Loplop: The Artist in the Third Person.* New York: Braziller, 1983.

——, ed. *Max Ernst: A Retrospective.* New York: Prestel, 1991.

Spiteri, Raymond, and Donald LaCoss, eds. *Surrealism, Politics, and Culture.* Burlington: Ashgate, 2003.

Stich, Sidra. *Anxious Visions: Surrealist Art.* New York: Abbeville Press, 1990.

Suleiman, Susan Rubin. *The Female Body in Western Culture: Contemporary Perspectives.* Cambridge: Harvard University Press, 1986.

——. *Subversive Intent: Gender, Politics, and the Avant-Garde.* Cambridge: Harvard University Press, 1990.

Le Surréalisme au service de la Révolution. New York: Arno Press, 1968.

Le Surréalisme, Même. Paris: Jean-Jacques Pauvert, 1956–59.

Surya, Michel. *La Révolution rêvée: pour une histoire des écrivains et des intellectuels révolutionnaires, 1944–1956.* Paris: Fayard, 2004.

Tatar, Maria. *Lustmord: Sexual Murder in Weimar Germany.* Princeton: Princeton University Press, 1995.

Taylor, Sue. *Hans Bellmer: The Anatomy of Anxiety.* Cambridge: MIT Press, 2000.

Tharaud, Jérôme, and Jean Tharaud. *Paris-Soir,* 30 September–8 October 1933. Reprint, *Littoral* 9 (June 1983).

Thévenin, Paule. *Archives du Surréalisme.* Vol. 1. *Bureau de recherches surréalistes: cahier de la permanence, Octobre 1924–Avril 1925.* Paris: Gallimard, 1988.

Thirion, André. *Revolutionaries without Revolution.* New York: Macmillan, 1975.

Tzara, Tristan. *Œuvres complètes.* Vol. 5. Paris: Flammarion, 1982.

——. *7 Dada Manifestos and Lampisteries.* Trans. Barbara Wright. London: Calder, 1977.

Vaneigem, Raoul [J.-F. Dupuis, pseud.]. *A Cavalier History of Surrealism.* Trans. Donald Nicholson-Smith. Edinburgh: AK Press, 1999.

Variétés, "Le Surréalisme en 1929." Brussels: Éditions Didier Devillez, 1994.

Vasseur, Catherine. "L'Image sans mémoire: à propos du cadavre exquis." *Cahiers du Musée Nationale d'art moderne* 55 (Spring 1996): 71–91.

Vernet, Marc. "Film Noir on the Edge of Doom." In *Shades of Noir.* Ed. Joan Copjec. London: Verso, 1993. 1–31.

View. 1940–47. Ed. Charles-Henri Ford.

Violette Nozières. Brussels: Nicolas Flamel, 1933. Reprint, Brussels: Terrain Vague, 1991.

VVV 1–4. Ed. André Breton and David Hare. 1942–44.

Waintrub, Alexander. "Crimes of Passion: Surrealism, Allegory, and the Dismembered Body." Ph.D. dissertation, University of California, Los Angeles, 1996.

Walker, David H. *Outrage and Insight: Modern French Writers and the "Fait Divers."* Oxford: Berg, 1995.

Walker, Ian. *City Gorged with Dreams: Surrealism and Documentary Photography in Interwar Paris.* Manchester: Manchester University Press, 2002.

Walz, Robin. *Pulp Surrealism: Insolent Popular Culture in Early Twentieth-Century Paris.* Berkeley: University of California Press, 2000.

Weisberger, Edward, and Solomon R. Guggenheim Museum. *Surrealism, Two Private Eyes: The Nesuhi Ertegun and Daniel Filipacchi Collections.* New York: Guggenheim Museum, 1999.

Wright, Richard. "Blueprint for Negro Writing." *New Challenge* (Fall 1937). Reprinted in *The Portable Harlem Renaissance Reader.* Ed. David Levering Lewis. New York: Penguin, 1994. 194–205.

———. "Introductory Note to the Respectful Prostitute." In *Art and Action,* New York: Twice a Year Press, 1948. 16–17. Reprint, New York: Krauss Reprint Corp., 1967.

———. *The Outsider.* New York: Harper and Row, 1953.

X Marks the Spot: Chicago Gang Wars in Pictures. Chicago: Spot Publishing Company, 1930.

Žižek, Slavoj. *Enjoy Your Symptom: Jacques Lacan in Hollywood and Out.* New York: Routledge, 1992.

INDEX

Italic page numbers refer to figures.

L'Action Française, 3, 76, 78, 81, 82–83, 87, 89

Adorno, Theodor, 8

aesthetics: and break with positivism, 21; consequences of, 61; and Desnos, 127, 128, 136; as
judgment, 15, 50, 57, 59; and Lautréamont, 50,
65, 66, 69, 188; of murder, 15, 51, 52–56, 57, 58;
and paranoia theories, 188–89; relationship of
political thought to, 51, 52, 60, 275; and Soupault, 100; surrealist influence on, 4; and surrealist language, 49; of violence, 50–51, 74–75,
80, 90, 130, 278n14

L'Âge d'or (film), 147, 153, 157–58, 160, 166, 169

L'Âge d'or pamphlet, 158, 159

Alexandre, Maxime, 44, 84, 85, 156, 157, 284n18

Algerian war of 1950s, 2, 17, 266, 267, 270, 271

Allain, Marcel, 7, 8

anarchism, 14, 55–56, 60, 67, 75–76, 79–80, 86,
88, 94

anticolonial violence, 2, 113–14, 266–67, 269, 271,
272

antihumanism, 11, 56, 171, 268, 269, 276

Anti-Jewish League, 157, 158

Apollinaire, Guillaume, 91, 117, 120, 144

Aragon, Louis: and aesthetic treatment of murder,
15, 76; al-Qaeda compared to, 268; on avant-
garde, 75–76; and Berton, 78–79, 80, 84–88,
90–91, 94–95; and communism, 14, 16, 156, 157,
165, 173, 174, 184; on Crevel, 62, 74; and Desnos,
136–37; and Drieu La Rochelle, 104–5; exclusion
from surrealist movement, 173; and fascism, 158;
and hysteria, 202; and Lautréamont, 65, 69; on
literary naturalism, 22–23; on the marvelous, 2;
and Marxism, 141, 167; and morality, 60, 74, 76,
78, 80, 85; and nominalism, 146; on police, 157;
and political thought, 97; and revolution, 129,
160, 162–63, 165; on Soupault, 99–100; and Stalinist propaganda, 16, 162, 164–67, 171–74; on
violence, 74–75, 79–80, 143, 162, 173, 184, 185

Aragon, Louis, works of: "Introduction to 1930,"
157, 162; "A Man," 78, 79–80, 86; Paysan de Paris,
99; "Red Front," 14, 143, 160, 162–67, 170, 172,
173–74, 184, 187, 197; "A Wave of Dreams," 22,
52, 61–62, 65, 73

Arland, Marcel, 70

Arp, Hans (Jean), 209, 210

Artaud, Antonin, 97, 129

Association des Écrivains et Artistes Révolutionnaires (AEAR), 174

Auriol, Jean-Georges, 105–6

automatic writing: Crevel's criticism of, 63; development of, 26, 27, 62; and Lautréamont, 65; and
noir surrealism, 174, 175, 195; and paranoia theories, 180; photography compared to, 25, 27; and
Soupault, 103, 287n48; surrealist techniques of,
10, 26, 71

avant-garde: Aragon on, 75–76; and Auriol, 105;
Clair's attack on, 268; and collectivity, 98; Crevel
on, 70, 71, 74, 75; criminalization of, 57–58,
282n17; experimentation of, 63, 74; interest in
crime, 10; in Latin America, 4; and literary naturalism, 22; murder depictions, 57; political role
of, 3, 17, 109, 110; and Soupault, 108; surrealist
movement's role in, 1, 4, 12, 17

Bachelard, Gaston, 245

Baron, Jacques, 19, 30, 61

Barthes, Roland, 250

Bataille, Georges: and critical work, 162; and fascism, 231; and hermeticism, 241; heterology theory of, 172; and noir surrealism, 197; reviews of
surrealist movement, 5–6, 11, 150–51, 153–54,
160; on Sadean materialism, 16, 146, 150, 151,
153–55, 165; and violence, 139, 141, 143, 146,
150, 156, 161; and voyeurism, 151, 154, 155–56

Bataille, Georges, works of: Inner Experience, 243;
"On the Subject of Slumbers," 5–6

Bate, David, 93

Baudelaire, Charles, 59, 91, 93, 101, 144, 273,
282n21

Bayard, Pierre, 36, 38, 42, 44

Beauvoir, Simone de, 4, 245, 252

Bell, Kevin, 246, 255

Bellmer, Hans, 218, 235–37, 236, 238

Benjamin, Walter, 11–12, 14, 26, 34, 37–38, 43, 48,
265

Bernard, Pierre, 99

Bernier, Jean, 99, 112

Bertillon, Alphonse, 36–38

Berton, Germaine: acquittal of, 79, 80, 83, 83, 84,
85, 90; agency of, 82–83, 86, 87, 93–95; Forain's
cartoon of, 84–86, 85, 91; group photograph
with surrealists, 76, 77, 90, 91, 93–95, 285n37;
and mass media, 78, 81–83, 85, 90–91; motives
of, 89; representation of, 209; surrealists' support of, 3, 16, 76, 88, 101, 183, 201

black humor: and Breton, 56, 244–45, 248–49,
251, 252–53, 263, 265; and Himes, 17, 245, 247–
48, 258, 261–62, 264–65

Blanchot, Maurice, 5, 6, 13, 46, 124, 125, 250
Bonnet, Marguerite, 66, 69
Bontempelli, Massimo, 99, 105
Boucharenc, Myriam, 286n7
Brauner, Victor, 218, 229, 230, 231, 235, 251
Breton, André: and Aragon, 163, 166–67, 173–74; Bataille on, 6, 150; and Berton, 88–89, 90, 94, 285n32; and black humor, 56, 244–45, 248–49, 251, 252–53, 263, 265; and Brauner, 229; and capital punishment, 190; and Carrington, 218; and collectivity, 127, 128; on colonialism, 267; and Crevel, 64–66, 67, 69, 282n28; on crime stories, 20–21; and crisis in consciousness, 5, 160, 161, 166, 277n3; and Dada, 46, 61; definition of surrealism, 46, 62–63, 129, 280n21; on De Quincy, 56, 58; on Dostoyevsky, 21–25, 27, 43, 47; Ernst essay of, 25, 26, 32, 46; on evolution of surrealism, 13–15; exile in America, 215, 216, 249; and exquisite corpse game, 124–25, 126; and fascism, 231, 242–43, 244; and Lautréamont, 65, 69; and Marxism, 141; and Nozière affair, 200, 202, 206, 207–8, 209; on Papin sisters, 179; and paranoia theories, 218; on photography, 25–27, 35; and political thought, 97; and Resistance, 215; and revolution, 129, 149, 160, 166, 274; and Rif War, 147; on Sadean materialism, 16; on Soupault, 47–48, 115–16; and surrealist language, 13; on surrealist writing, 262–63; and unconscious, 52, 63
Breton, André, works of: Anthology of Black Humor, 56, 244–45, 248–50, 264; Arcanum 17, 242, 243; "The Exquisite Corpse," 125; "For the Defense of Liberty," 267, 270; The Immaculate Conception, 180, 218; "Introduction to the Discourse on the Paucity of Reality," 18, 104; Légitime Défense, 96, 110, 125–26, 168; Mad Love, 238–40; Manifesto of Surrealism, 18, 21, 24, 25, 26, 42, 46–47, 62, 63, 129, 280n21; "The Mediums Enter," 18, 61, 62, 63–65; "Misère de la poésie," 166; Nadja, 91, 98, 143, 147–49, 286n7; Les Pas perdus, 62, 64, 69, 70; Poisson soluble, 18; "The Political Position of Surrealism," 233; "Prolegomena to a Third Manifesto of Surrealism or Not," 241; Second Manifesto of Surrealism, 6, 124, 125, 128, 142, 143, 145, 146, 148, 149, 160, 161; "What Is Surrealism?," 13–14, 210–11
Breton, Simone, 18, 19, 66–68, 88, 90, 94, 283n38
Buñuel, Luis, 147, 151, 157, 160

Un Cadavre (pamphlet), 128, 141
Cahiers du Mois, 103, 106
Cahiers du Sud, 96, 97
Cahiers GLM, 237
Cahun, Claude, 174, 210, 217, 231, 263, 265
Caillois, Roger, 232, 241
Camus, Albert: and black humor, 245; on racism, 258; on surrealist movement, 249–50, 269; sur-

realist responses to, 17; on terror, 273–74, 275, 302n22
Camus, Albert, works of: The Myth of Sisyphus, 258; The Rebel, 249, 258, 269, 273–74, 302n22
Carassou, Michel, 71
Carrington, Leonora: in asylum, 224–26, 228; and black humor, 245; and bodily transformation, 217; fears of, 219–20, 242; and hermeticism, 242; and paranoia, 17, 218, 222–25, 228–29, 243; psychosis of, 217–18, 220; rape of, 220, 221, 224, 297n24
Carrington, Leonora, works of: "The Debutante," 219; Down Below, 17, 217–18, 219, 220–26, 227, 228–29, 235, 238, 240, 241, 242, 243, 296n8, 297n24; "The House of Fear," 219; "A Man in Love," 219; "The Oval Lady," 219, 237–40; "Uncle Sam Carrington," 219
Carter, Angela, 144, 154, 211
Caws, Mary Ann, 231
Cendrars, Blaise, 115
Césaire, Aimé, 17, 240–41, 243, 267, 271
Char, René, 232
Chénieux-Gendron, Jacqueline, 5, 13, 222, 225
Chesterton, G. K., 47
Chiappe, Jean, 156, 157
Un Chien andalou (film), 151
Christie, Agatha, 36
Cixous, Hélène, 203–4
Clair, Jean, 268, 269, 273, 276
Clarté, 97, 99–101, 103, 109–13, 121–22, 126–27, 129, 285n4
Clément, Catherine, 203–4
Clérambault, Gaétan Gatian de, 148–49, 150
Cocteau, Jean, 282n17
collage, 10, 36, 46, 49
collectivity: and Berton, 93, 94, 95; and Breton, 127, 128; and château myth, 20; and common good, 276; and communism, 122; and contemporary political debates, 4, 98, 270; and Desnos, 91, 127–30; and displacement of subjectivity and individualism, 276; and exclusions from surrealist movement, 99; exquisite corpse game, 98, 122, 123, 124–27; and leftist politics, 16, 97, 110, 112; and participatory thinking, 2, 5; and role of murder, 51
Colonial Exposition of 1931, 160, 167, 169
colonialism: anticolonial violence, 2, 113–14, 266–67, 269, 271, 272; and leftist politics, 109; political struggles against, 12, 17, 113, 149; and Soupault, 103; and surrealist poetry, 4, 170–71; and surrealist writings, 2, 98, 167, 168–70. See also Rif War of 1925
communism: and Aragon, 14, 16, 156, 157, 165, 173, 174, 184; and Desnos, 128, 129; and Freud, 185; and insurrectional agency, 101; and Nozière affair, 204–5; and revolution, 108; and Rif War, 97; and Sade, 145, 146; and Soupault, 99; and state

terror, 109; surrealism's break with, 16–17, 173, 174, 186–87, 244, 270–71; surrealism's relations with, 3, 14, 15, 96, 97, 111–12, 142, 167, 168, 197; and terror, 268

Comte, Auguste, 22

Conley, Katharine, 135, 138, 296n8

Coriem, Maurice, 191

Coryell, John Russell, 102

cosmopolitanism, 97, 100, 103, 112

Cottom, Daniel, 89

Counter-Attack, 231, 232

Crastre, Victor, 99, 121

Crevel, René: and aesthetic treatment of murder, 15; on avant-garde, 70, 71, 74, 75; and Berton, 80, 89; and Breton, 64–66, 67, 69, 282n28; and communism, 174; on Dostoyevsky, 279n7; and Éluard, 61, 62; and paranoia theories, 16, 176, 186, 188–89, 193, 195, 208, 210, 218, 228; and psychoanalysis, 62–64, 70, 72, 187, 188; and revolution, 160; somnambulistic trances of, 52, 61–70, 73, 74, 283n30; suicide of, 173, 232; on violence, 74–75, 79, 88

Crevel, René, works of: "Après Dada," 70; *Détours*, 71–72; *La Mort difficile*, 98, 114, 286n7; "Notes Toward a Psycho-dialectic," 180, 184–90, 193, 228; "Which Way?," 75

crime: art of crime, 8–9; discourses of, 8, 9, 13, 40–41; and gothic literature, 195; and mass media, 7–8, 52–53, 56, 68, 178; public responses to, 13; surrealists' insights from, 1–2, 4, 8, 10–12, 276; violent crime, 1, 2, 4, 6, 8, 10, 11, 13, 15, 55. *See also* crime scenes; murder; murder cases

crime fiction: Breton on, 20–21; and Desnos, 16, 97; dime novels, 16, 98, 101, 102; and Himes, 246–47, 254–55, 260–61, 263, 264; and Malet, 250, 251; and Soupault, 16, 97, 98, 100–104, 106, 108, 112–20, 126; and surrealist movement, 245, 270. *See also* locked room mystery story; Série Noire

The Crime of M. Lange (film), 251

crime scenes: Bertillon method of photography, 36–37, 37; figurative representation of, 38; Mac-Orlan on, 33–34; and Magritte, 40–41; mechanical rationalism of, 20–21; and positivism, 41–42; Weil on, 28–32, 34, 48

Cunard, Nancy, 170

Dada: and aesthetics, 69; and Breton, 46, 61; criminality of, 57–58, 59; and cultural negation, 53–54, 75; and *Littérature*, 28; and morality, 78, 79; ratings of, 59, 282n20; scandals of, 61, 74, 80, 95; and Soupault, 108; surrealism distinguished from, 18, 50–51, 52, 62; surrealism's emergence from, 61, 63, 65, 80, 147; and Tzara, 61, 62, 65, 74; and Weil, 30

Daladier, Édouard, 173, 175

Dalí, Salvador: and black humor, 245; and Éluard, 174; films of, 147, 151, 157–58, 160; and paranoia theories, 16, 143, 160–62, 176, 180, 193, 218, 238, 240; and Sade, 156; and unconscious, 160

Dalí, Salvador, works of: "L'Âne pourri," 161, 180; *Honey is Sweeter Than Blood*, 151, 152; *The Lugubrious Game*, 151, 153; "Non-Euclidean Psychology of a Photograph," 233–35, 234, 236; "Paranoiac Portrait of Violette Naziere," 212, 213, 214

Danzas, Minnie, 254

Daudet, Léon, 76, 81, 82, 89, 284nn15, 18

Daudet, Philippe, 76, 80–82, 83, 86, 88, 93, 95, 284n18

Dean, Carolyn, 11, 86

de Gaulle, Charles, 267, 268

Deleuze, Gilles, 253–54, 255, 262, 264

Delglave, Georgette, 239, 298n49

De Quincey, Thomas: aesthetics of, 59, 130, 136; and Baudelaire, 59, 282n21

De Quincey, Thomas, works of: *Confession of an English Opium-Eater*, 56; "On Murder, Considered as One of the Fine Arts," 15, 52, 54, 55, 56, 60, 79, 90, 130, 131

Desnos, Robert: and Bataille, 151; and collectivity, 91, 127–30; crime stories of, 16, 97; exclusion from surrealist movement, 127; and Jack the Ripper, 127, 129–33, 134, 135–37, 155, 288n85; Malkine's portrait of, 135, 137; and mediumistic abilities, 18, 62–66, 69, 91, 130, 137; in Ray's photograph, 18, 19, 19

Desnos, Robert, works of: *Le Cimitière de la "Semillante"*, 91, 92, 93; *Corps et biens*, 136; *Liberté ou l'amour!*, 99, 286n7, 288n85; "Surrealism's Revolutionary Meaning," 129; "Third Manifesto of Surrealism," 130, 137

Détective magazine, 156–57, 178, 179, 181, 204, 205

Dey, Frederick Van Rensselaer, 102

dialectic materialism, 141, 142–43, 165, 168, 186

Diawara, Manthia, 257

Documents, 11, 139, 151, 154, 155

Documents 34, 196, 196, 229

Dostoyevsky, Fyodor, 20, 21–25, 27, 42, 43, 47, 279n7

dream interpretation, 49, 60, 94, 128, 175

Dreyfus affair, 110

Drieu La Rochelle, Pierre, 104–5

Ducasse, Isodore Lucien. *See* Lautréamont, comte de

Duchamp, Marcel, 41, 58, 64, 132, 135, 270, 275

Duhamel, Marcel: and black humor, 245, 252–53; and exquisite corpse game, 122, 251; and Himes, 246, 248, 255, 263, 264; and Série Noire, 245–47, 251–54, 263–65, 300n40; and shared residences, 20; and surrealist movement, 250, 264

Dumas, Marie-Claire, 136, 289n97

Durozoi, Gérard, 175

Edwards, Brent Hayes, 247

Einstein, Albert, 187–88, 190

Éluard, Paul: and Breton, 174; and Colonial Exposition, 169; and Crevel, 61, 62; and cult of dead, 121; exclusion from surrealist movement, 219; and group portrait with Berton, 93; on Leroux, 42, 281n45; and *Minotaure*, 174, 293n4; newspaper clippings, 285n4; and noir surrealism, 15; on Papin sisters, 182–83, 196; and political thought, 97; on Sade, 145; and Vidal, 88

Éluard, Paul, works of, *The Immaculate Conception*, 180, 218

Engels, Friedrich, 112, 142

Ernst, Jimmy, 216

Ernst, Max: arrest of, 222; Breton on, 25, 26, 32, 46; and Carrington, 219–23, 238; collage-novels of, 297n38; and concentration camps, 220; as exile, 216; and paranoia theories, 218; and superimposed images, 23, 27

Ernst, Max, works of, *Au rendezvous des amis*, 18, 22, 279n7

ethics: Aragon on, 74, 76, 78–79, 88, 95, 184; Arland on, 70; and black humor, 245; Crevel on, 71, 72, 74, 75, 95; and revolutionary desire, 60; and Soupault, 100; within surrealist aesthetics, 15, 57, 60, 62, 69, 86, 88; of terror, 75

ethnography, 245, 276

Europe, 109

existentialism, 4, 245, 249, 255, 259, 269, 270, 273

fait-divers, 2, 9, 53, 72, 181, 198, 250

Fanon, Frantz, 4, 272, 301n4

Fantômas serials, 8, 38–40, 59, 98, 102–3, 128, 130, 136

fascism: and Breton, 231, 242–43, 244; and Carrington, 218, 220, 229, 242; glorification of murder, 14; Nazism, 186, 189, 217, 220, 221, 222, 224, 241, 244; and police, 156, 157, 158; political struggles against, 12, 172, 173, 175, 176, 179, 186, 189, 219; and surrealist art, 231; surrealist rejection of, 99–100, 189, 197, 202–3, 208, 210–12, 214–17, 231, 241, 244

Faulkner, William, 255

Fégy, Camille, 99

Feuillade, Louis, 38, 130

Les Feuilles Libres, 69, 97, 99, 113, 115

Le Figaro, 84, 89–90, 97, 281n5

Fitére, Jean-Marie, 204

Flanner, Janet, 181–82

Forain, Jean-Louis, 84–86, 85, 91

Foster, Hal, 11, 124, 233

Foucault, Michel, 35

Fourrier, Marcel, 99, 109, 110, 161

Fraenkel, Theodore, 69

French Popular Front, 231, 232, 233

Freud, Sigmund: Breton on, 25; and Carrington, 238; and communism, 185; and crime, 2; on culture, 189; and dream-work, 49, 128; and Einstein, 187–88, 190; and paranoia theories, 192, 218,

222–23; and surrealist movement, 4, 12, 142, 168

Frois-Wittmann, Jean, 158, 160, 163

Giacommetti, Alberto, 154–55, 155, 156, 160

gothic literature, 2, 14, 17, 20, 174–75, 194–95, 245

Greeley, Robin, 232

Hammett, Dashiell, 252, 255

Harris, Steven, 180, 232

Hegel, Georg Wilhelm, 4, 142, 166, 268, 273, 274

Heine, Maurice, 144, 147, 194, 195, 210, 231, 250, 251

Hénaff, Marcel, 144

Henriot, Michel, 239

Heraclitus, 142

Himes, Chester, and surrealist black humor, 17, 245, 247–48, 258, 261–62, 264–65

Himes, Chester, works of: *Blind Man with a Pistol*, 263; *Cotton Comes to Harlem*, 265; *The End of a Primitive*, 259; *If He Hollers, Let Him Go*, 246, 248, 252, 259–60, 261, 264; *My Life of Absurdity*, 260; *La Reine des pommes*, 17, 246–47, 248, 254–59, 260, 261, 264, 298n5

Hitler, Adolf, 14, 186, 187, 216, 217, 231, 240, 241, 248, 250

Hollier, Denis, 11

Holocaust, 216, 220

Hubert, Jules, 198, 203

Hughes, Langston, 170

Hugnet, Georges, 297n38

Hugo, Victor, 84

humanism, 2, 273, 275, 276. *See also* antihumanism

L'Humanité, 97, 100, 168, 181–82, 185, 199, 203, 204–5, 206, 293n22

Hungary, Soviet invasion of, 266, 271

hysteria, 64, 91, 200, 202, 203–4, 222, 224

International Surrealist Exhibition of 1938, 233

L'Intransigeant, 97

Jack the Ripper, 68, 98, 127, 129–33, 134, 135–37, 155, 288n85

Janet, Pierre, 25, 148

Jarry, Alfred, 59, 91, 282n21

Jaurès, Jean, 78

Jean, Marcel, 251

Jolas, Eugène, 103

Josephson, Matthew, 108

Joubert, Alain, 266–67

Joyce, James, 105

Judovitz, Dalia, 41–42

Judt, Tony, 277n2

Kalifa, Dominiqe, 9

Kant, Immanuel, 22, 55, 56

Koestler, Arthur, 272

Krauss, Rosalind, 11, 279–80n20
Abd el-Krim, Mohammed Ben, 2–3, 96, 113, 144, 270. *See also* Rif War of 1925

Lacan, Jacques: and conceptual framework of surrealism, 11, 192; on Papin sisters, 182, 183, 184, 191–92; and paranoia theories, 3, 16, 176, 180, 184–86, 188–93, 195, 208, 210, 218, 223
Lacassagne, Alexandre, 289nn97, 99
Lacenaire, Pierre François, 59
Lamarzelle, Gustave de, 53, 54, 282n8
Lamba, Jacqueline, 239
Landru, Henri, 53, 54, 58, 59, 68, 281–82n7
Lane, Christopher, 193
Lautréamont, comte de: and aesthetics, 50, 65, 66, 69, 188; and automatic writing, 25, 65; Camus on, 273, 274; and crime, 2; and morality, 62; as precursor of surrealists, 91, 101, 142; and Soupault, 65, 117, 120; and surrealist language, 49
Lautréamont, comte de, works of, *Les Chants de Maldoror*, 49–50, 52, 65, 67–68, 69, 71, 72–73, 183, 281n2, 2112
leftist politics: antihumanist framework of, 296; and collectivity, 16, 97, 110, 112; and colonialism, 109; and de Gaulle, 267; and Desnos, 138; function of leftist theory, 17; historical causality, 110–11, 124, 165, 194, 218, 221; and nationalism, 231; and popular writing, 16, 98; and revolutionary rhetoric, 11; and Rif War, 3, 96, 103–4, 109; and Sade's critique of morality, 16; and Soupault, 99, 100
Légitime Défense (journal), 167–71
Legrand, Gérard, 275
Leiris, Michel, 35, 147, 151, 241, 243
Lély, Gilbert, 297n38
Lenin, V., 168
Leprieux, Rolande, 52
Léro, Étienne, 167, 169, 170
Leroux, Gaston, 20, 42–47, 281n48, 281n45
Lévy, Denise, 66, 80, 90
Lewis, Matthew, 12
Le Libertaire, 80–82, 82, 86–88, 90, 91, 97
literary naturalism, 15, 20–27, 36, 246, 247, 255, 264
Littérature, 28, 30–32, 50–53, 57, 59, 61–64, 69–70, 87–88, 282n20, 283n30
Little Review, 63, 75, 78, 79
locked room mystery story: and detail, 38; and epistemology, 15, 20, 21, 27, 36, 39–40, 47; and Leroux, 42–47, 281n48; and Magritte, 40–42; mechanical rationalism of, 20–21; and *papillons*, 44–45; and prevention of thought, 36, 38, 42, 44; and psychological causality, 24–25; surrealist ties to, 20; and Tanguy, 38–39; and Weil, 28–32, 34, 38
Lombroso, Cesare, 37

Mabille, Pierre, 217, 218, 220–21, 242
MacOrlan, Pierre, 33–34, 33, 38
Magritte, René, and Fantômas, 40, 280–81n42
Magritte, René, works of: *L'Assassin menacé*, 38, 39–42, 40; cover design for Breton's "What is Surrealism?," 211, 212; "Homage to the Papin Sisters," 196–97, 196
Main à Plume group, 215, 250–51
Malaparte, Curzio, 99
Malet, Léo, 245, 246, 250–51, 297n38
Malkine, Georges, 135, 137
Manning, Edgar, 103, 114, 116, 287n44
Martinet, Marcel, 109–10, 120, 141
Marx, Karl, 142, 166–67, 168, 217, 274
Marxism: Bataille on, 11, 141, 143; Benjamin on, 12; and crime writing, 98; gothic Marxism, 12; and Martinet, 110, 120, 141; and Naville, 111; and Papin sisters, 182; Péret on, 274; and psychoanalysis, 71, 72; revisions of, 103, 168, 276; and revolution, 122, 126, 129; and terror, 268, 273
mass media: aesthetics of, 53, 54; and Berton, 78, 81–83, 85, 90–91; and crime as spectacle, 7–8, 52–53, 56, 68, 178; and Nozière affair, 198, 199, 200, 202, 203, 204, 205, 207, 208, 209, 210; and Papin sisters, 16, 179, 181–82, 191; and police, 160; relationship of surrealism to, 3, 97
Masson, André, 20, 142–46, 151, 156, 160, 231
Massot, Pierre de, 61
Matta, Roberto, 251
Maza, Sarah, 295n65
McInnes, Mary Drach, 154–55
McKay, Claude, 170
Megnen, Jeanne, 217
Ménil, René, 167, 169
Merleau-Ponty, Maurice, 245, 269, 272–73, 275
Mesens, E. L. T., 200, 209
Messac, Régis, 102
Meunier, Raymond, 57–58, 59
Minotaure: and Age of Fear, 175; and Bellmer, 235; and Dalí, 233, 236; and Éluard, 174; and Heine, 194, 195; and Lacan, 180, 190, 191–92, 210; and Mabille, 221; and Papin sisters, 179; and paranoiac knowledge, 197
Miró, Joan, 20
Mitrani, Nora, 271
Monnerot, Jules, 143, 167, 168–72, 232, 301n8
morality: and Aragon, 60, 74, 76, 78, 80, 85; and Bataille, 141; and Berton, 84, 85, 88, 95; and Dada, 78, 79; and definitions of insanity, 190; De Quincey's critique of, 55, 56; and Desnos, 131, 136; and literary moralism, 70; and noir surrealism, 197; and Nozière affair, 197, 198, 199; Péret's critique of, 54, 55–56, 60, 76; Sade's critique of, 16, 62, 145; Sartre on, 215
Morise, Max, 19, 90, 99, 251
Morroco. *See* Rif War of 1925
Moscow trials, 269, 271, 272

motive, and murder cases, 2, 89, 190–93, 201–2
Muller, Herbert J., 216, 240–41, 242
murder: aesthetic treatment of, 15, 51, 52–56, 57, 58, 59–60, 188; changing surrealist responses to, 15; and Crevel's mediumist activity, 62–65, 71; and disinterestedness, 65
murder cases: and motive, 2, 89, 190–93, 201–2; and noir surrealism, 175–76; surrealists' study of, 2, 7, 51, 60. See also Nozière, Violette; Papin sisters, Christine and Léa
"Murderous Humanitarianism," 169–70
Mussolini, Benito, 74, 231
Mysteries of New York (film), 128

Nadeau, Maurice, 160
Naremore, James, 252
Naville, Pierre, 19, 99, 111, 126, 129
Nick Carter Detective Library, 107, 108
900, 99–100, 105, 106
Nougé, Paul, 196–97, 196
noumenon, 22–23, 25, 26, 36, 180, 192, 193
Nouvelle Revue Française, 99, 104, 157
Nozière, Jean-Baptiste, 202, 205, 206
Nozière, Violette: and family values, 198–99, 202, 203, 206–7, 208, 214; motive of, 201–2; and sexual abuse, 176, 199–200, 202, 203, 204, 205, 206–9, 211, 295n57; surrealist assessment of, 16–17, 176, 183, 197, 201–5, 209, 232, 249; and surrealist writings, 3, 200–202, 205–12, 214

L'Œil de la Police, 151, 152, 153, 156, 157
Orientalism, 104–6, 111, 128, 268

Paligot, Carole, 14
Pantaine, Marguerite (Aimée), 188
Papin sisters, Christine and Léa: double portrait of, 176, 177, 178–79, 182, 209; Lacan on, 182, 183, 184, 191–92; motives of, 190–93; surrealists' study of, 3, 16, 176, 179–84, 189, 196, 196, 197, 201, 204, 232
paranoia theories: and Carrington, 17, 218, 222–25, 228–29, 243; and Dalí, 16, 143, 160–62, 176, 180, 193, 218, 238, 240; and fascism, 232, 233, 235, 239; and Lacan, 3, 16, 176, 180, 184–86, 188–93, 195, 208, 210, 218, 223; and Muller, 241; and Papin sisters, 179, 180
Paris Matinal, 127, 128, 130, 131, 135, 136
Parisot, Henri, 217
Paris Soir, 90, 191
Pénisson, Marcel, 53, 54, 55, 56, 67, 68, 80
Péret, Benjamin: and aesthetic treatment of murder, 15, 51–55, 57, 58–60, 67, 73; on anticolonial violence, 272, 302n16; and black humor, 245, 253; and Camus, 274; and Crime of Versailles, 52–54, 58; and criminalization of Soviet Union, 272; critique of morality, 54, 55–56, 60, 76; and mediumistic abilities, 62; and Nozière affair, 205–7, 209;

on Papin sisters, 182–83, 196; and political thought, 97; on Soupault, 99; and Vidal, 88
Péret, Benjamin, works of: "Assassiner," 53–54, 58, 60, 80, 127, 282n8; "Is This the Dawn," 271; "Life of the Murderer Foch," 121, 288n71
Le Petit Parisien, 52, 53, 54
Philosophies, 97, 99, 110
Phony War, 197, 220
photography: Bertillon method of, 36–38, 37; Breton on, 25–27, 35; commercial use of, 22; impact of, 21, 25–26; Soupault on, 32–35, 37; surrealist photography, 38; and theories of representation, 25–27, 32–34, 279–80n20
Picabia, Francis, 18, 57–58
Pierre, José, 201
Pinkerton National Detective Agency, 156
Plateau, Marius, 76, 78, 79, 80, 83, 86, 87, 88, 90, 91, 93, 94, 284n15
Poe, Edgar Allan, 12, 20, 28, 29, 133, 135
The Poisoner's Secret, 203, 205
police, 156–58, 160–63, 165–66, 173, 198
Police magazine, 191
political agency, 16, 86, 93–94, 97–98, 124, 127–28, 143, 215–16
political thought: and anticolonial struggle, 267; Berton's effect on, 90, 95; and black humor, 245, 247; disagreements about, 6, 98, 142; and exclusions from surrealist movement, 97, 99; historical antecedents of, 142; and noir surrealism, 175, 195, 197; and Nozière affair, 202, 209; and Orient-Occident debate, 104–6, 108, 109, 110, 115; and paranoia theory, 179; political responsibility of intellectuals, 17; relationship to aesthetics, 51, 52, 60, 275; and Rif War, 96, 97; and Soupault, 100; and violent crime, 1
political violence, 2–3, 7, 219, 245, 266, 269
Ponge, Francis, 245
positivism: and crime scenes, 41–42; and epistemology, 22, 23, 36; philosophical positivism, 15, 20; and photography, 27; and Roussel, 35, 36; scientific positivism, 20, 21, 27, 276; surrealist ties to, 25
Prassinos, Gisèle, 245
Prevert, Jacques, 20, 122, 245, 251, 253
Prevert, Pierre, 20, 251
Proudhon, Pierre-Jean, 166–67
psychoanalysis: and Crevel, 62–64, 70, 72, 187, 188; impact of, 21; and noir surrealism, 175; and paranoia theories, 180, 184, 186, 222, 228; and prevention of thought, 36; and revolution, 112; and subjectivity, 185; surrealist influence on, 4; surrealist ties to, 20, 65, 69–70, 71, 95, 168, 174, 276

Queneau, Raymond, 151, 245, 249, 253

race relations, 169, 247, 257, 258, 259, 260, 261–62
Radcliffe, Anne, 2, 12, 194

Ray, Man, and Lautréamont, 49, 281n2
Ray, Man, works of: cover photograph for *Violette Nozières*, 201, 201, 208, 209; *The Enigma of Isodore Ducasse*, 49–50, 51; *Waking Dream Séance*, 18, 19, 19
Renoir, Jean, 251
representation, theories of: and Himes, 255; and manifest content, 65–66; and noir surrealism, 175, 195; and Nozière affair, 209; and paranoia theories, 180, 189, 192; and photography, 25–27, 32–34, 279–80n20; and political thought, 275; role of crime in, 1, 56, 57
Resistance, 215, 217, 268
revolution: and anticolonial struggle, 267; and Aragon, 129, 160, 162–63, 165; and Bataille, 153; and Breton, 129, 149, 160, 166, 274; and communism, 108, 112; and Desnos, 128, 137; and Marxism, 122, 126, 129; and Masson, 142–46; and Monnerot, 172; Naville on, 111; and Papin sisters, 181; and political thought, 97, 101; and pure revolt, 14, 88–89, 90, 94, 95; rhetoric of, 11, 16, 111, 112, 121–22; Sartre on, 6; and Soupault, 126; surrealism as revolutionary movement, 4, 5, 13, 109–10, 141; and terror, 183, 269, 271, 273–75
La Révolution Surréaliste: and Éluard, 145; and Fourrier, 161; and group photograph with Berton, 76, 77, 90, 91, 93, 94, 285n37; and leftist politics, 97, 121; and police, 156; and Ray's work, 18, 50; and Soupault, 9
La Revue Européene, 97, 99, 106
Ribemont-Dessaignes, Georges, 115, 119, 120, 121
Rif War of 1925: and Auriol, 105; and communism, 14, 16, 122; and Marxism, 121, 126; and political thought, 97, 109, 122; surrealism's solidarity with, 2–3, 96, 98, 144, 168, 270; and violence, 103–4, 125
Rimbaud, Arthur: and alchemy of the word, 200; and automatic writing, 25; and Breton, 146; and crime, 2; as precursor of surrealists, 91, 101, 142; secret poetry of, 31; and Soupault, 117, 120
roman noir. See gothic literature
Roussel, Raymond, 28, 30, 32–36, 37, 42, 280n31

Sade, D. A. F. de: Camus on, 273; and crime, 2; gothic fiction of, 194; as influence on surrealism, 62, 69, 101, 142–43, 144; and Malet, 251; materialism of, 143, 144, 145, 146, 150, 151, 153–55; and morality, 16, 62, 145; theories of, 16
Sade, D. A. F. de, works of: "Last Will and Testament," 146; *120 Days of Sodom*, 147, 229; *Philosophy in the Boudoir*, 143; "Yet Another Effort, Frenchmen, If You Would Become Republicans," 145
Sadoul, Georges, 20, 156–57, 158, 160, 161, 251
Sanyal, Debarati, 302n22
Sartre, Jean-Paul: and anticolonialism, 272; and black humor, 245; and engaged writing, 246, 259, 261; on racism, 261–62; on surrealism, 4,

6, 150, 215, 252, 269; surrealist responses to, 17
Sartre, Jean-Paul, works of: *La Putain respectueuse*, 261–62; "Situation of the Writer in 1947," 215, 217, 249
Scandale magazine, 191
Schreber, Daniel Paul, 218, 222, 225, 226
Scottsboro case, 169, 170, 261
September 11 attacks, 268
Série Noire: and Duhamel, 245–47, 251–54, 263–65, 300n40; formation of, 17, 245–46; and Himes, 246–47, 255, 262, 263
Sorel, Georges, 150
Soupault, Philippe: and automatic writing, 103, 287n48; Breton on, 47–48, 115–16; and counter-revolutionary literary activities, 97, 99, 100; on crime stories, 20; crime stories of, 16, 97, 98, 100–104, 106, 108, 112–20, 126; and criminography, 9; exclusion from surrealist movement, 97, 99, 100, 109, 112, 113, 114, 120, 126, 129, 286n7; and impersonation, 108; and Lautréamont, 65, 117, 120; and *Littéature*, 31; and locked room mystery story, 36, 280n37; and Orient-Occident debate, 106; on photography, 32–35, 37; and race, 100, 101, 103, 104, 105–6, 108, 113, 114, 115–17, 119–20, 121, 122, 128, 287n48; and revolution, 126; and Rif War, 147; on Roussel, 28, 32–36, 42, 280n31; travel narrative of, 286n30; and unconscious, 63; urban fiction of, 21; as Philippe Weil, 28–32, 34, 38, 48
Soupault, Philippe, works of: *Á la dérive*, 31, 48; *Le Coeur d'or*, 106; "The Death of Nick Carter," 100–103, 105, 108, 114, 280n37; *Les Derniers Nuits de Paris*, 286n7; *Le Nègre*, 98, 100, 101, 103, 108, 113–22; "The Shadow's Shadow," 9
Souvestre, Pierre, 7, 8
Soyinka, Wole, 4
Spengler, Oswald, 103
Stalinism: and Aragon, 16, 162, 164–67, 171–74; and Éluard, 291; political struggles against, 2, 12, 16, 17, 122, 160, 167, 271, 272; purgative inclinations of, 231; and surrealists, 156, 157, 232, 271, 272
Stavisky affair, 175
Stovall, Tyler, 204
Strauss-Ernst, Louise, 216
Sue, Eugène, 2, 67
Suleiman, Susan, 62
Le Surréalisme, Même, 17, 266, 267, 269–70, 271, 275
Le Surréalisme au Service de la Révolution (SASDLR): and Crevel, 184–85; and Dalí, 161; and leftist politics, 174; and Monnerot, 171; and Papin sisters, 176, 177, 178, 179, 182, 184; and Sadoul, 156
Surrealist Exhibition (1947), 217
surrealist language: and Cahun, 263, 301n62; and Desnos, 63, 130, 132, 138; and epistemology, 2; Lautréamont on, 49; as new form of materialism, 12–13, 151; and noir surrealism, 176; and Nozière affair, 200; and violence, 147

surrealist movement: al-Qaeda compared to, 268; backlash against, 249; conceptual framework of, 11; conflicts and contradictions of, 5, 7, 60, 61–62, 95, 98, 104, 141, 142, 147, 160, 173, 174–75, 269; and dissidents, 11; and European public sphere, 4, 277n2; evolution of, 13–15; exclusions from, 97, 98; and exile, 215–16, 218; group photograph with Berton, 76, 77, 90, 91, 93–95, 285n37; heterogeneous nature of, 12, 13, 20, 269; historicity of, 25, 270; intuitive epoch of, 14; legacy of, 215–16, 245, 276; Muller's critique of, 216, 240–41, 242; noir phase, 14, 15, 17, 174–75, 193–97, 244–45; and Nozière affair, 200–201; origins of, 18, 19, 20, 50, 63; and papillons, 44, 45, 45; reasoning phase of, 14; response to violence, 1, 14–15, 17, 67–68, 69, 74–75, 268; as synthesis, 4, 6, 7; as unitary society, 18, 19, 20; women artists and writers of, 217
surrealist poetry: collage-poetry, 49; and colonialism, 4, 170–71; and noir surrealism, 197; and Nozière affair, 201, 205–7, 209
Surrealist Research Bureau, 20, 44, 46, 285n37
surrealist writings: and collectivity, 126; and criminal violence, 7; and critique of ideology, 12; and engaged literature, 243; and Nozières affair, 3, 200–202, 205–12, 214; photographic writing, 33–35, 42; and political thought, 97, 111, 112; and rejection of social and moral constraints, 262–63; and revolution, 122; and spectatorial complicity, 233
symbolists, 52, 174, 175, 195, 250

Tanguy, Yves, 20, 38–39, 39, 122, 253
Tatar, Maria, 56–57
Taylor, Sue, 235
Les Temps Modernes, 252
terror: and anticolonial political theory, 267, 268; Aragon on, 184; Berton on, 89; Camus on, 273–74, 275, 302n22; Crevel on, 75; ethics of, 75; and fascism, 190; French Terror, 272–73; and gothic literature, 194, 195; and noir surrealism, 175, 178, 195; and political thought, 268; and revolution, 183, 269, 271, 273–75; state terror, 109, 268, 269, 271, 272
Tharaud, Jean and Jérôme, 191
Thirion, André, 20, 251
transition, 97, 99, 103, 105, 106
Tropmann, Jean-Baptiste, 68
Trotsky, Leon, 231
"The Truth about the Moscow Trials," 231
Tzara, Tristan: and communism, 174; and Dada, 61, 62, 65, 74; and revolution, 160; and surrealist movement, 215, 232

unconscious: and Carrington, 221, 222; and Crevel, 62, 63, 70, 71–73, 185, 188; and Dalí, 160; and

Desnos, 136; and gothic literature, 195; and noir surrealism, 193–94, 195; and Nozière affair, 201–2; and Papin sisters, 182, 185, 191, 192; and paranoia theories, 184, 186, 188, 189, 192–93, 195; surrealism movement's understanding of, 52, 60, 70, 71, 75, 180; as text-producing mental function, 65
Unik, Pierre, 156, 157

Vacher, Joseph, 68, 127, 130, 131, 289nn97, 99
Les Vampires (film), 128, 130
Vaneigem, Raoul, 19–20, 244
Vasseur, Catherine, 125
vernacular surrealism, 246, 265
Vian, Boris, and crime fiction, 246
Vichy regime, 197, 216, 220, 244–45
Vidal, Georges, 81, 82, 88
Vietnam, 169, 270, 271
View, 242
violence: aestheticization of, 50–51, 74–75, 80, 90, 130, 278n14; anticolonial violence, 2, 113–14, 266–67, 269, 271, 272; Aragon on, 74–75, 79–80, 143, 162, 173, 184, 185; and Bataille, 139, 141, 143, 146, 150, 156, 161; and Berton, 78, 79; and Breton, 148; criminal violence, 4, 6, 8, 10, 11, 13, 55; epistemological violence, 75, 269; and gothic literature, 194, 195; and Himes, 255, 256, 257, 260, 261, 262; and Nozière affair, 200, 202, 205, 206, 208; and Papin sisters, 179, 181, 183–84, 185, 197; political violence, 2–3, 7, 14, 15, 110, 118, 219, 245, 266, 269; surrealist movement's response to, 1, 14–15, 17, 67–68, 69, 74–75, 268
Violette Nozières, 200–202, 201, 205–12, 295n58
Vitrac, Roger, 19, 97, 129, 151
Vu, 294–95n54, 295n57
VVV, 17, 217, 218, 224

Walker, David, 156–57
Walz, Robin, 9
Warner, Marina, 218
Weil, Philippe. See Soupault, Philippe
Whitfield, Raoul, 251–52
Wright, Richard: on black writing, 246; Duhamel's translation of, 252; and engaged writing, 261; and existentialism, 255, 259
Wright, Richard, works of: Black Boy, 252; Native Son, 259, 260, 261; The Outsider, 247

X Marks the Spot (pamphlet), 139, 140, 141, 143, 146, 151, 153, 154, 156

Yoyotte, Pierre, 167, 169

Zola, Émile, 67